Making British Culture

Routledge Studies in Cultural History

Making British Culture

English Readers and the Scottish Enlightenment, 1740–1830

David Allan

Routledge
Taylor & Francis Group
New York   London

First published 2008
by Routledge
270 Madison Ave, New York, NY 10016

Simultaneously published in the UK
by Routledge
2 Park Square, Milton Park, Abingdon, Oxon OX14 4RN

Routledge is an imprint of the Taylor & Francis Group, an informa business

Typeset in Sabon by IBT Global.
Printed and bound in the United States of America on acid-free paper by IBT Global.

Library of Congress Cataloging-in-Publication Data
Allan, David.
    Making British culture : English readers and the Scottish enlightenment, 1740–1830 / by David Allan.
        p. cm. — (Routledge studies in cultural history)
    Includes bibliographical references and index.
    ISBN-13: 978-0-415-96286-5 (hardcover)
    ISBN-10: 0-415-96286-2 (hardcover)
    ISBN-13: 978-0-203-89479-8 (e-book)
    ISBN-10: 0-203-89479-0 (e-book)
    1. Great Britain—Intellectual life—18th century. 2. Scotland—Intellectual life—18th century. 3. Scotland—Intellectual life—18th century—Public opinion. 4. Reading—Great Britain—History—18th century. 5. Public opinion—Great Britain—History—18th century. 6. Enlightenment—Scotland. 7. Historiography—Scotland—History—18th century. I. Title.
    DA485.A527 2008
    941.07'3—dc22
    2007051925

ISBN10: 0-415-96286-2 (hbk)
ISBN10: 0-203-89479-0 (ebk)

ISBN13: 978-0-415-96286-5 (hbk)
ISBN13: 978-0-203-89479-8 (ebk)

Contents

Abbreviations

Alston	Library History Database (by Robin Alston): www.r-alston.co.uk
Altick	Richard D. Altick, *The English Common Reader: A Social History of the Mass Reading Public, 1800–1900* (Chicago, IL, 1957)
AL	Autograph letter
AR	*Annual Register*
AS	Archive Service
Beinecke	Beinecke Rare Book and Manuscript Library, Yale University
BL	British Library
Bodl.	The Bodleian Library, University of Oxford
Chetham's	Chetham's Library, Manchester
CL	Central Library
Comp. Bar.	*The Complete Baronetage, 1603–1800*, (ed.) G.E.C., 5 vols. (Exeter, 1900—1909)
Comp. Peer.	*The Complete Peerage*, (ed.), G.E.C., 12 vols. (London, 1910–1959)
CR	*Critical Review*
CUL	Cambridge University Library
ER	*Edinburgh Review* (1802-)
GM	*Gentleman's Magazine*
HE	*David Hume, History of England*, 6 vols. (Indianapolis, IN 1983)

HP(1) *History of Parliament: House of Common, 1715–1754,* (ed.), Romney Sedgwick (London, 1970)

HP(2) *History of Parliament: House of Commons, 1754–1790,* (ed.), Sir Lewis Namier and John Brooke (London, 1964)

HP(3) *History of Parliament: House of Commons, 1790–1820,* (ed.), R.G. Thorne (London, 1986)

Huntington The Henry E. Huntington Library, San Marino, California

LJ James Boswell, *Life of Samuel Johnson* (Ware, 1999)

LS Local Studies

ML *Monthly Ledger*

MM *Monthly Magazine*

MR *Monthly Review*

ODNB *Oxford Dictionary of National Biography*: www.oxforddnb .com

Pearson Jacqueline Pearson, *Women's Reading in Britain 1750–1835. A Dangerous Recreation* (Cambridge, 1999)

PL Public Library

RO Record Office

Sher Richard B. Sher, *The Enlightenment and the Book: Scottish Authors and Their Publishers in Eighteenth-Century Britain, Ireland and America* (Chicago, IL, and London, 2007)

St Clair William St Clair, *The Reading Nation in the Romantic Period* (Cambridge, 2004)

SUL Stanford University Library

UCLA Charles E. Young Research Library, University of California, Los Angeles

TCM *Town and Country Magazine*

Walpole W.S. Lewis Walpole Library, Farmington, Connecticut

Acknowledgments

It is a great pleasure to be able to thank those friends, colleagues, and institutions whose advice and material assistance not only helped make this book possible in the first place but, in many cases, may also have made it marginally better than it would otherwise have been.

Some rashly agreed to read parts of my work as it was written, whether in the form of draft materials or in the series of discrete essays on related topics through which some of its central ideas and concerns were initially worked out. For favours beyond the call of duty, and probably also that of friendship, I thank for their different contributions Hamish Scott, Mark Spencer, Richard Sher, Marion McClintock, Roger Emerson, Nicholas Phillipson, Rab Houston, Stephen Parks, Henry Petroski, Alastair Mann, Keith Manley, Andrew White, Sheila Hingley, Earle Havens, Ann Blair, Mark Towsey, and Andrew Crosby. Given that they by no means always agreed with what I had written, it is more than usually important to offer the conventional disclaimer that responsibility for what appears hereafter remains entirely my own.

Throughout a laborious and time-consuming search for surviving evidence of the Scottish Enlightenment's impact on contemporary English readers, which at times felt like a frantic hunt for needles in haystacks (without, unfortunately, any guarantee that they actually existed), I grew to appreciate very much the expertise, the patience and—on numerous occasions—the sheer generosity of the overwhelming majority of professional archival staff and librarians both in Britain and in the United States. Such favours as a willingness to open specially at the weekend for a one-off visitor (at Whitby), and vital reproductions freely offered and gratefully received (notably from Tameside Local Studies Library and from Chetham's Library), as well as illuminating telephone discussions before and after visits (involving solicitous archivists aplenty), made the research far smoother, as well as rather more agreeable, than it might otherwise have been.

I am therefore delighted to have this opportunity to express my gratitude to those people—regrettably far too many for individual citation—who assisted me at Bath Central Library; Bedfordshire and Luton Records Service in Bedford; Berkshire Record Office in Reading; Blackburn Central

Library; Bolton Archive and Local Studies Service; Brighton Local Studies Centre; Bristol Record Office; Bristol University Library; the British Library; the John Hay Library at Brown University; the Centre for Buckinghamshire Studies in Aylesbury; Bury Archive Service; the Charles E. Young Research Library at the University of California, Los Angeles; Cambridge University Library; Cambridgeshire County Record Office in Cambridge and Huntingdon; Canterbury Public Library; Carlisle Central Library; Cheltenham Library; Cheshire and Chester Archives and Local Studies Service in Chester; Chetham's Library in Manchester; Cornwall Record Office in Truro; Coventry Public Library; Cumbria Archive Service in Carlisle, Kendal and Whitehaven; Derby Public Library; Dorchester Reference Library; Dorset Record Office in Dorchester; Durham County Record Office in Durham; Durham University Library; East Riding of Yorkshire Archive Office in Beverley; East Sussex Record Office in Lewes; Edinburgh University Library; Essex Record Office in Chelmsford; Exeter Cathedral Library; Gloucestershire Record Office in Gloucester; Hackney Archives Department; Hampshire Record Office in Winchester; the Houghton Library and Widener Library at Harvard University; Hereford City Library; Herefordshire Record Office in Hereford; Hertfordshire Archives and Local Studies in Hertford; the Henry E. Huntington Library in San Marino, California; the Centre for Kentish Studies in Maidstone; Kettering Public Library; Lancashire Record Office in Preston; Lancaster City Library; Lancaster University Library; the Brotherton Library at the University of Leeds; the Record Office for Leicestershire, Leicester and Rutland, in Leicester; Lincolnshire Archives in Lincoln; Liverpool Record Office and Local Studies Service; the Sydney Jones Library at the University of Liverpool; Manchester Central Library; the Morrab Library in Penzance; the National Library of Scotland; Newcastle upon Tyne City Library; the Robinson Library at the University of Newcastle upon Tyne; New York Public Library; Norfolk Record Office in Norwich; Northamptonshire Record Office in Northampton; Northumberland Record Office in North Gosforth; Norwich Millenium Library; Nottingham Central Library; Nottinghamshire Archives in Nottingham; the Pierpont Morgan Library in New York; the Portico Library in Manchester; the Bodleian Library at the University of Oxford; Oxfordshire Record Office in Oxford; Portsmouth Central Library; St Andrews University Library; the Scottish National War Museum; Sheffield Archives; Sheffield City Library; Shropshire Records and Research Centre in Shrewsbury; Somerset Archive and Record Service in Taunton; Staffordshire and Stoke-on-Trent Archive Service in Lichfield and in Stafford; Suffolk Record Office in Bury St Edmunds, Ipswich and Lowestoft; Surrey History Centre in Woking; Tameside Local Studies Library in Stalybridge; the Department of Special Collections at Stanford University; Tyne and Wear Archives in Newcastle upon Tyne; Warwickshire County Record Office in Warwick; West Sussex Record Office in Chichester; West Yorkshire Archive Service in Bradford and Halifax; Whitby

Museum; Wigan Archives Service; Wiltshire and Swindon Record Office in Trowbridge; Worcester Public Library; Worcestershire Library and History Centre and Worcestershire Record Office, both in Worcester; the Beinecke Rare Book and Manuscripts Library, the Divinity Library and the Sterling Memorial Library at Yale University; and, alphabetically last but certainly by no means least, York Reference Library. I am also grateful to many of these institutions for permission to quote from manuscripts and individual printed books now in their care.

Undertaking such a labour-intensive and (as the preceding roll call will have emphasised) widely geographically dispersed project also requires throwing oneself upon the mercy of institutions with the resources that might conceivably help bring one's work to a significantly earlier conclusion. I am therefore much obliged to the School of History at the University of St Andrews which unflinchingly agreed to finance what might well have appeared the strange predilection of a member of the former Department of Scottish History for spending every available day visiting so many of England's local archives and libraries. I am similarly grateful to my colleagues for allowing me research leave at a difficult time.

Other institutions and funding bodies on both sides of the Atlantic also assisted greatly in the completion of this book. Yale University first granted me a Visiting Fellowship at the W.S. Lewis Walpole Library, bringing with it privileged access to a collection affording some extraordinary insights into the literary culture of Georgian England. For helping me to exploit this marvellous opportunity I am grateful to Dr. Maggie Powell and her colleagues in Farmington, Connecticut. I also subsequently received the James M. Osborn Fellowship in English Literature and History at the Beinecke Library, making possible my exploration of what, by the end of my research, I was able to recognise as a collection of commonplace books perhaps second only to that at the British Library in both extent and variety. I thank especially Stephen Parks and Earle Havens for their friendship and kindnesses in New Haven. Most of all, I was fortunate in receiving a one-year research fellowship from the Leverhulme Trust which permitted me an extended period of relief from teaching and administration in which I was able to reflect, to organise my thoughts and to write. I am therefore indebted both to the Research Awards Advisory Committee and to my own referees for making this opportunity available.

It is especially important that I also single out for acknowledgement two people I have never actually met, Max Novick and then Liz Levine, in New York City. As exceptionally supportive and encouraging publishers right from first contact through to final production, they helped greatly in bringing this book to fruition, and I am deeply grateful for everything that they have done.

Erica Wetter at Taylor and Francis and Carey Nershi at IBT Global also provided all the editorial support that I could have wanted.

Finally, I want to thank my greatest supporter, my wife Katie. She bore with characteristic good grace the apparently interminable research trips over a period of several years; and, even when our holidays together began to follow a suspicious pattern dictated by the presence of hitherto unvisited, but potentially fruitful archives and libraries, she humoured me by pretending not to notice, and willingly occupied herself in any number of unfamiliar places. Because she shared thereby in the sacrifices, as well as helping produce the two figures, it is in an important sense her book, too.

D.A.
St Andrews

Part I
Problems

1 A Question of Perspective
Scotland and England in the British Enlightenment

By the end of the eighteenth century, Scotland's cultural accomplishments were almost universally acknowledged. As one English visitor, the physician Mr Amyot, claimed in 1771, it even seemed possible to 'stand at the Market Cross of Edinburgh and take fifty men of genius and learning by the hand.'[1] In much the same vein, Tobias Smollett, Glasgow medical graduate turned Grub Street hack, had been able to boast in his comic novel *Humphry Clinker* (1771) about the same city's emergence as a 'hotbed of genius.'[2] Even George III, who in all his life never ventured across the Border, eventually understood enough about his idiosyncratic northern subjects to make knowing reference to the forbidding power of 'Scotch metaphysics.'[3] If anything, however, foreign commentators were still more loudly impressed. Jefferson contributed the magisterial pronouncement, much cited since, that in the realm of science 'no place in the World can pretend to a competition with Edinburgh.'[4] Carlo Denina, an observant Turin professor, suggested that Scotland could now be numbered among the great civilizations, having brought 'to maturity, in the cold regions of the north, what had heretofore been foolishly supposed incapable of taking root but in the warmer climes of ASIA MINOR, GREECE, and ITALY.'[5] Voltaire, meanwhile, was only too aware that there had occurred a seismic jolt in his contemporaries' orientation: 'It is from Scotland,' he wrote, the perceptible note of amusement not greatly reducing the force of the argument, 'that we receive rules of taste in all the arts, from epic poetry to gardening.'[6]

It is clear, then, that many of those best placed to judge had arrived at a quite remarkable conclusion—striking to those who perceived it precisely because, in historical terms, it was unprecedented. This was that the Scots, who understood this only too well for themselves, had recently assumed a position of extraordinary cultural and intellectual authority.[7] Such testimony, however, is not entirely unproblematic in its implications for the historian. For were we simply to take them at face value, these contemporary estimations of the Scots' primacy over other centres of emerging modern culture would, it seems certain, have far-reaching consequences for our understanding of British intellectual history as a whole.

In the first place, they would present a challenge to the rival proposition, a common notion from the eighteenth century to the early twenty-first, that it was not Scotland but England—the home, in short, of Newton and Locke, of commerce and liberty—that established the key parameters of what we now recognise as the European Enlightenment.[8] One might partially sidestep this initial difficulty, of course, by positing instead, as the late Roy Porter most recently did, some kind of creative synergy between two somehow intimately-related *British* Enlightenments.[9] But this in turn would only beg a whole series of further questions, as yet unaddressed by scholars, let alone resolved, about the extent to which a coherent intellectual culture was emerging in Great Britain during the dynamic decades following the Anglo-Scottish Union of 1707. Nor would this be all. For if contemporary claims about the decisive influence of a specifically Scottish Enlightenment are indeed to be credited, we should certainly need to find unambiguous signs of its impact having registered with particular force in Georgian England. And were such evidence to be forthcoming, then the substantial dependency of English culture upon London, an overwhelmingly derivative relationship between provinces and metropolis in terms of which most recent eighteenth-century English historiography has been couched, would itself require significant rethinking. Certainly Porter's own pronouncement that 'The *gradus ad Parnassum* from rudeness to refinement was in effect the mental journey from provinciality to London' would appear excessively simplistic, with Edinburgh above all emerging as an important alternative destination.[10]

These are the much broader questions of historical interpretation—concerning the essential coherence (or otherwise) of a British Enlightenment, and the nature of the cultural relations evolving between different parts of Great Britain—which frame this study. The present chapter, offered by way of an extended introduction, serves three more immediate purposes. In the first instance, it will reflect at some length upon recent scholarly approaches to the Scottish Enlightenment's contemporary reception. This is in fact a critical point of departure because, as we shall see, previous analysis has been so strikingly asymmetrical, far greater interest having been shown in the Scots' impact overseas than in their potential influence south of the Border. Next, it will be necessary to revisit, at least in general terms, the contours of English intellectual and literary culture, both in London and elsewhere, between approximately 1740 and 1830. This terrain has, it is true, benefited from very considerable recent surveying. Once again, however, and a determining factor behind much of what follows, it will be seen that the likely significance of the Scottish input has thus far earned only superficial comment. Finally—and absolutely necessary given the specific questions in cultural history already posed—we shall also need to confront at the outset a series of theoretical and methodological problems that it seems must inevitably be encountered by any attempt to recover the original response of a population of literate men and women to that extraordinary output of inquiries and concerns, for the most part embod-ied and conveyed in formally published materials, which was Scotland's distinctive contribution to the Enlightenment.

* * *

The wider British reception of Scottish thought and literature in the age of the Enlightenment has in fact proved surprisingly resistant to compre-hensive elucidation. This is, in its own way, a remarkable state of affairs, given the intense fascination shown by recent scholars, as by inquisitive contemporaries like Denina and Voltaire, in the broadly defined cultural renaissance that overtook Scotland between the Treaty of Union in 1707 and the death of Sir Walter Scott in 1832.[11] A number of insightful studies over the past four decades have actually taught us a great deal about the intellectual preoccupations of Georgian Scots. Particular success has been achieved in tracing the origins of the major themes or inquiries variously proposed as having characterised the period. We can, for example, appreci-ate the respective contributions of the Italian civic humanists' *virtu* and the Dutch and German natural lawyers' *jus* in the pre-history of Scottish politi-cal economy.[12] We can also assess the importance of anglicisation in gen-eral and of polite Addisonian literature in particular to the coalescence of enlightened discourse in post-Union society.[13] More recently, we have even been able to ponder the likely influence of Irish philosophical and theologi-cal debates in the early development of moral theory in Scotland.[14] No less importantly, it has proved possible to uncover a growing weight of evidence in relation to the Enlightenment's late seventeenth-century precursors and so to speculate as to whether earlier Scots such as the scientific Gregorys, Sir Robert Sibbald and Viscount Stair might have laid the essential founda-tions for the more illustrious work of Adam Smith, David Hume, Joseph Black and Lord Kames.[15] Nevertheless, it is clear that the contemporary English impact of the Scottish literati has been very much less well served.

One important obstacle to the potential study of its English reception probably lies in what might be described as the emerging internal histo-riography of the Scottish Enlightenment as an academic subject. For the overwhelming tendency has been to take for granted an essentially pro-ducer-oriented model of enlightened activity, classically seen in the seminal reading of eighteenth-century European culture offered by Peter Gay in 1967.[16] Indeed, it has been only too tempting to prioritise the investigation of a small group of authors, academics and printers at the expense of the much wider community of book buyers and readers on whose support and endorsement both the commercial viability and the cultural success of the Enlightenment must ultimately have rested. Clearly this approach, rather like those older forms of art history which emphasised the creative genius of the solitary artist above the more diffuse influences of patrons, sitters and viewers, has yielded considerable explanatory dividends in relation to individual landmark works. With specific reference to the Scottish Enlightenment, it has revealed the richly textured institutional and personal conditions in which formidable intellectual achievements such as *The Wealth of Nations*, the *Essay on the History of Civil Society* and the *Theory of the Earth* were first conceived.[17] Yet it also has significant drawbacks. Not least, it does little to discourage cynicism from those who continue to suspect that the whole phenomenon in reality comprised little more than a backslapping coterie of Edinburgh-based friends and mutual admirers surrounded by a not-much-larger outer circle who can be cast disparagingly, in Hugh Trevor-Roper's still-haunting phrase, as mere 'camp-followers.'[18] At its worst, of course, such a restrictive approach to the study of Enlightenment leaves the field open to those minded to argue, like John Lough, that, a few brilliant individuals apart, late-eighteenth-century Scotland was overwhelmingly marked by 'a narrow-minded nationalism and bigoted puritanism which have survived in part down to our own day.'[19]

A tendency to concentrate on Edinburgh, and to a much lesser extent on Glasgow and Aberdeen, has been another pronounced feature of modern scholarship on the Scottish Enlightenment.[20] An inevitable result of this, however, has been that it still remains unclear how far Scotland itself, beyond its three principal cities, was really capable of sustaining a large-scale cultural movement. Studies of urban intellectual activity in locations as significant, in contemporary demographic and economic terms, as the regional centres of Perth, Stirling and Ayr, have been notable by their absence—even though their provincial English equivalents, as we shall shortly see, have often received repeated and illuminating consideration.[21] Even more importantly, the contrast between the welcome recent attempts to open up the study of readership in eighteenth-century England—plausibly cast as the paradigmatic form of mass cultural consumption in this period—and the continuing paucity of information available on the reading habits prevalent in contemporary Scotland is particularly stark.[22] Yet arguably the most significant casualty of the producer-oriented approach to the study of enlightened Scottish culture has been the systematic underexploitation of reception as a potential focus for further research. As a result, as one recent scholar rightly complains, Scottish thought and texts have overwhelmingly been approached 'with little or no reference to . . . the reading public that consumed them.'[23] Certainly—and this is in many ways a measure of the extraordinary scale of the problem—one still looks in vain for any comprehensive account of the *Scottish* reception of the Scottish Enlightenment.

One partial corrective to these tendencies has in fact been the unintended consequence of another distinctive characteristic of recent academic studies of the Enlightenment. This is their successful colonisation by an unusually wide range of otherwise discrete scholarly communities, several of whom have *inter alia* sought to introduce elements of reception into their analysis. Of particular significance in this regard have been those specialists concerned with individual authors or bodies of Scottish thought which turned out in some way to have contributed to the formation of new academic disciplines. Thus students of the work of David Hume and Adam Smith, figures who between them greatly accelerated the development of mental philosophy, psychology and political economy, have recovered a growing diversity of contemporary reactions.[24] Such inquiries have so far been almost entirely restricted to the formal responses issued by other publicly active individuals—politicans, philosophers, historians and critics—in Britain and, perhaps especially, overseas.[25] But they do have the considerable merit of bringing us rather closer to appreciating the enlightened Scottish thinker as he may have been apprehended by at least some of his own contemporaries. They also, of course, provide a salutary reminder to the intellectual historian that the Enlightenment was actually conceived to address the concerns and questions which troubled or intrigued other eighteenth-century people in all their many locations, circumstances and guises. It certainly was *not* developed merely in an attempt to play to the very different gallery comprising the modern academic specialists who form the bulk of its latter-day audience.

More valuable still have been the attempts to trace the implications of specific bodies of Scottish thought and literature in a variety of geographical locations. Here the historiography of the Scottish Enlightenment has been especially well served by scholars whose principal interests lie largely outside British history. Those concerned with late colonial and post-Revolutionary America in particular have probably been most active.[26] The indebtedness of the American educational system to Scotland's presbyterian universities, academics and pedagogues has long been recognised, even if the full ramifications have only lately begun to be convincingly fleshed out.[27] So too has the impact of Scottish clerical eloquence and academic Whig ideology upon the political discourse of the generations responsible for the Declaration of Independence and the Constitution.[28] More recently the significance of the distinctive Scottish traditions of lecture hall and pulpit rhetoric has also been plausibly charted, going a long way towards explaining the rapid development in post-colonial America of the new university discipline of English literary studies.[29] As a result, it is possible to speak with growing confidence about the successful and creative reception of the Scottish Enlightenment across the Atlantic, as well as feeling that a number of the key mechanisms of transmission, critical evaluation and absorption have begun to be identified.[30]

A further important departure, though again significantly not the work of primarily British-oriented scholars, has been the illumination of Germany's intellectual inheritance among the civil historians, moralists and poets of enlightened Scotland. It is to this project that we owe our new appreciation of the indebtedness of the line of German-speaking philosophers culminating in Hegel to the writings of Hume, Smith and Reid.[31] It has also proved possible to trace the various implications of Scottish historical thought and literature for a number of late eighteenth-century German thinkers and men of letters such as Iselin, Lessing, Herder and Schiller.[32] This approach, however, also has its limitations. In particular, it has so far highlighted the significance of certain narrow threads of Scottish Enlightenment thought in particular countries without giving much sense of its wider European impact in the round.[33] Moreover, as Fania Oz-Salzberger has rightly insisted, the numerous linguistic and conceptual obstacles that stood between Scottish philosophers and their putative Continental disciples generated such substantial scope for variant readings and unintentional cross-purposes that, in effect, this inquiry has often of necessity had to be conducted as a study not so much in reception as in 'misreception.'[34]

It would not be fair, of course, to imply that the English reception of Scotland's contemporary thought and literature remains wholly unconsidered. For, at least in intermittent and somewhat episodic fashion, there has occasionally been work of considerable quality. One worthy exception is the study of responses to Macpherson's "Ossian." After all, the gradual unravelling of this celebrated literary imposture has not unnaturally proved compelling, whilst the role of the controversy in further enlivening Anglo-Scottish relations during the already-sensitive 1760s—the fractious decade of Bute and Wilkes—has been alluded to in several recent studies.[35] Other striking innovations have included the credible recent attempts by John Pocock to read the *Decline and Fall of the Roman Empire* in terms of Gibbon's relationship with Scottish colleagues like Robertson, Ferguson and Hume, and by Isabel Rivers to study contemporary reactions to Hume's corrosive irreligion among the Anglican and dissenting clergy.[36] Far more numerous, however, have been investigations of the posthumous impact of Scotland's Enlightenment in the decades beyond 1800, or even 1830. Here the inspiration seems to lie chiefly in the accumulating technical literature on the Scots' subsequently acknowledged role as the founders of classical political economy, of modern medical education and of historical fiction. The result has been a growing body of writing, presided over by Anand Chitnis's monograph with the revealingly disynchronous title *The Scottish Enlightenment and Early Victorian English Society* (1986), which lays bare the Scottish roots of "Manchester School" liberalism and civic intellectual activism in the nineteenth-century English cities, or else which traces the various literary consequences of the Waverley novels.[37]

Studies of this kind, it should be reiterated, have a great many virtues. In particular, they help give the lie to the more egregious insinuations that Scotland's enlightened culture in practice had little wider impact beyond the university classrooms, clubs and coffeehouses of Edinburgh, Glasgow and Aberdeen between roughly the battle of Culloden and the storming of the Bastille. They also take valuable strides towards substantiating the judgments already noted, from well-placed contemporary observers both at home and abroad, which insisted that the Scots had acquired a very major influence in the worlds of learning and letters. But explorations of its unforeseen Victorian aftershocks, just like those essentially focused outside Britain, ultimately take us not that much closer to a proper appreciation of the Scottish Enlightenment as it originally impacted upon what was unquestionably its largest and most important historical audience. This, of course, comprised those innumerable contemporaries throughout Georgian England who—as book buyers, as library members, and, above all, as readers of its newly-published texts—first encountered and, in a variety of senses, *experienced* it. It is with an attempt to explore this largely uncharted territory in the social history of eighteenth-century British ideas that the present study is concerned.

*   *   *

The contemporary English response to Scotland's increasingly remarkable cultural productivity has, as we have seen, proved largely impervious to thoroughgoing investigation. The cultural and intellectual life of England itself can, however, scarcely be considered *terra incognita*. Partly, no doubt, this is simply a natural function of the much greater size of England's modern scholarly community. Partly also it is owing to England's traditions of local and regional historiography, which are admirably extensive and deep-rooted in comparison with Scotland's. But the extraordinary nature of the story of English culture in this period probably also helps explain the relative wealth of extant literature. For the century or so separating the death of Queen Anne from the accession of George IV witnessed astonishing changes by any standards. A demographic explosion overtook English society, amongst the most important consequences of which was the growth—some would argue the creation—of a sizeable middle class.[38] No less important were a closely-related series of structural changes in the economy. These included a considerable acceleration in overseas trade, the further commercialisation of agriculture and, from the 1750s, the onset of full-blown industrialisation.[39] It is evident that the implications of these processes for the country's culture were also far-reaching. Its very nature was transformed. So too were public perceptions of both its scope and its significance. Indeed, the English increasingly gloried in their rapidly evolving culture, almost as much as in their political, economic and military triumphs. This was because they had begun to see it a vital expression of their own precocious modernity as a nation. As John Brewer has recently put it, 'It was its dynamism, variety and exuberance—not its respectability or elegance—which intoxicated them.'[40]

London's importance in these developments cannot be gainsaid. The English metropolis, by some distance Europe's largest city, contained roughly one-tenth of the country's entire population through much of the eighteenth century and encompassed nearly one million souls by 1801. It was the economic heartbeat and political master of an expanding and self-confidently imperial nation. It was also home to the leading men of letters, to the burgeoning newspaper industry and to British print culture. From its presses poured forth a vast torrent of literature, catering to an immense and diverse public stretching all the way from anglophone North American to the East India Company's stations in India and China, as well as to other educated European audiences for whom a familiarity with English writing was, decade by decade, but especially from the 1760s onwards, becoming increasingly desirable.[41] It was also for this reason, of course, that many of the most enduring new works now emerging from Scottish sources— Hume's *Treatise*, for example, in 1739–40; *The Wealth of Nations* in 1776—appeared not from the Edinburgh printers but from London's market-dominating publishing booksellers. Yet it is crucial to remember that men and women across England were deeply affected by many of the same forces that were transforming London. Nor is it true that the metropolis was ever the be-all and the end-all of national life. Indeed, were we to compare estimated population data from around 1700 with the hard evidence of the inaugural British census returns in 1801, disproportionate urban growth across most of the rest of the English landscape, usually at rates not experienced even in the heaving capital itself, would probably be the single most eye-catching trend.[42]

At the century's beginning, England had had just three other towns with more than 15,000 citizens: Norwich, Bristol and Newcastle upon Tyne. Just one hundred years later, it possessed no fewer than twenty-eight, including hitherto obscure newcomers like the Lancashire cotton town of Bolton and the busy port of Hull on the Yorkshire coast. There were also some staggering individual instances of urban growth in the English provinces, particularly in districts heavily implicated in the development of commerce and manufacturing. Manchester (with Salford), beginning with fewer than 10,000 people, had swollen to around 89,000; Liverpool from less than 7,000 to 83,000; Bristol from 21,000 to 60,000; Sheffield and Stoke-on-Trent (the latter, tellingly, a nineteenth-century coinage called into existence to describe what had once been an unremarkable group of separate Staffordshire settlements) from less than 5,000 each to 46,000 and 23,000 respectively. Even many of the old county towns, somewhat reduced in the national pecking order but in no sense redundant as commercial, administrative and recreational foci, were still expanding at the turn of the nineteenth century. They were also becoming increasingly complex in their economic and occupational structures, and, accordingly, in the scale and diversity of the cultural output and consumption that they could now sustain. Norwich, for example, the largest city in East Anglia, had around 36,000 people by 1801; Exeter, the largest in the southwest, 17,000; York and Chester, both cathedral cities and the capitals of two of the wealthiest northern counties, 16,000 each; Shrewsbury—a major regional pivot for transportation, trade and culture whose tentacles also reached deep into Wales, and, as a staging post *en route* to the Holyhead ferries, even into Ireland—at least 15,000.

Bald population statistics, however, can tell us only so much about the background to changing cultural experiences. For the economic forces propelling demographic growth and facilitating mobility and urbanisation were also transforming the social environment in England's towns and cities. Many important aspects of this process have been studied, with particularly useful synthesising accounts of the so-called 'urban renaissance' of this period coming recently from Peter Clark and Peter Borsay.[43] It is clear that physical extension and infrastructural improvement were important expressions of the age's unprecedented wealth and confidence. Countless new streets, parks and squares sprang up; salubrious new housing emerged for the expanding professional and commercial classes; new or improved civic buildings were erected to flatter the self-regard of England's urban communities as well as to meet the growing need for well-appointed public space.[44] Certain towns bent with particular success to serve the rising expectations of the affluent and the aspirant, providing a whole new social arena in which an effervescent and intensely creative culture could be focused, reformulated and disseminated. In particular, the historic spas— led, naturally, by Bath, catapulted from obscurity to be England's twelfth-largest town in 1801—came spectacularly into their own, comprehensively redesigned to offer an environment fit for the ever-increasing demands of better-off mid-Georgian people.[45]

The rapid development of the great resort towns like Bath, Brighton, Buxton and Cheltenham was itself one of the most visible manifestations of a series of social changes which had wide-ranging implications for English culture in all its diverse forms. For the same period saw both a growth and a diversification in the fashionable leisure opportunities, many of them increasingly commercialised, that were available to the public, above all in an urban setting.[46] Indeed, the choice of respectable (though also, inevitably, of nefarious) diversions came to appear virtually limitless. This was the first great age of the English turf as well as of tourism and travel.[47] Cricket flourished; theatre was in its pomp; musical performance and dancing thrived as never before.[48] A vigorous retail sector, buoyed by growing consumer affluence and underpinned by the boom in trade and manufacturing, was making shopping for the first time a recreational as much as an economic experience.[49] But of greatest significance for our own purposes, new kinds of intellectual culture also began increasingly to proliferate. Like so much else, this was made possible fundamentally by the waxing prosperity and broader social horizons of those who considered themselves—and, perhaps even more importantly, who wished to be considered by others— respectable and refined. It is also clear, however, that the unprecedented desire to be involved in the activities of learning, thinking, reading and discussion that now took root among a widening section of the English public was also stimulated and persuasively legitimised by the contemporary modification in social outlook and moral attitudes associated above all with the triumph of the concept of 'politeness.'[50]

This word, one of the most overworked in the vocabulary of Georgian men and women, carried myriad connotations for contemporaries, informed as they were by a rich literature, epitomised by Joseph Addison and Sir Richard Steele's ubiquitous *The Spectator* (1711–2), in which politeness was simultaneously defined, defended and disseminated.[51] At its most elementary, it was imagined as the outward expression of an individual's rational and tolerant personality. In practice, this entailed the urgent cultivation by each person of an educated and emollient disposition by means of which the threats otherwise posed in society by ignorance, prejudice and self-interest might be contained. In turn, this required an almost obsessive emphasis upon acquiring those skills and accomplishments which seemed to be necessary for smooth and pleasing social interaction. Such a prospectus inevitably had the most profound consequences for cultural activity. After all, the high priests of politeness insisted, just like the classical philosophers to whom they still ostentatiously deferred, that human reason, properly trained and directed by thorough exposure to sound literature and regular participation in well-informed discussion, could simultaneously reform both inward attitudes and outward behaviour.

As a result, Georgian people with serious pretensions to respectability considered it increasingly necessary to try to enrich their own discourse with ideas and insights culled from their reading: in effect, books and magazines were not only a vital tool for use in self-fashioning by status-conscious readers but also the perfect conversational topic in polite company. As *The Spectator* famously encapsulated it, what was being created across England from the early decades of the eighteenth century onwards was an environment in which 'Knowledge, instead of being bound up in Books, and kept in Libraries and retirement, is thus obtruded upon the Publick; when it is canvassed in every Assembly, and exposed upon every Table.' It was a society, indeed, in which the impact of texts upon readers was so great that authors might actually believe, as Addison himself boasted, perhaps only half in jest, that 'I will daily instil into them such sound and wholesom Sentiments, as shall have a good Effect on their Conversation for the ensuing twelve Hours.'[52]

Recent scholarship on eighteenth-century England has therefore been absolutely justified in highlighting the significance of more numerous and ever more diverse kinds of institutionalised cultural endeavour as a fundamental characteristic of a polite age increasingly defined by its belief in the transformative effects of reading and conversation. For it was precisely this potent convergence of intellectual, moral and social concerns in the pursuit of politeness that led John Callaway and a handful of other Kentish gentlemen, at an initial meeting held at the Guildhall Tavern in Canterbury on 23 September 1769, to establish a society that would allow them, as they hoped, 'to read and consult such books, make such Experiments, and debate on such matters, as shall be thought best adapted to our Instruction, Pleasure, or Amusement.'[53] As Peter Clark in particular has shown, in the decades after 1700 organisations motivated by this ambitious vision actually began to increase dramatically both in number and diversity.[54] Even the rapid expansion in the pre-existing network of masonic lodges in England's towns and cities, with their arcane rules and rituals for bringing together gentlemen, professionals and merchants, was really just one part of the same process. But perhaps the most important—and certainly the most abundant—of the new associational structures for the cultivation of politeness were those devoted specifically, like the one in Canterbury, to the facilitation of reading and discussion. As the confident subscribers of the newly-established Liverpool Library, another typical example of the species, chose to put it in May 1758: 'As many kinds of useful and polite Knowledge can no otherwise be acquired than by READING, an Attempt to furnish the Public with an ample Fund of Amusement and Improvement of this kind, at the easiest Expense, can scarcely fail of general Approbation.'[55]

Fortunately, a few examples of these quintessentially eighteenth-century voluntary institutions have now been studied in some detail. In the process, much has been revealed about the obsessive preoccupation with polite learning, pursued in an associational environment, that the profusion of local book clubs and subscription libraries both reflected and reinforced.[56] Similarly, we also have a handful of illuminating studies of the far more numerous commercial book lenders, usually described as 'circulating libraries,' that seem frequently to have arisen in their shadow.[57] This is important because one contemporary journal actually argued in 1801 that there were 'not less than one thousand' of these throughout England: certainly, as we shall later see for ourselves, the range and coverage of the circulating libraries, as well as their energy and variety, was nothing short of spectacular.[58] Whatever the true figure, however, it is at least clear that enterprises such as these must have increased still further the quantity of reading matter available to those men and women with the resources and inclination to patronise them. Not surprisingly, therefore, and at least in general terms, the extraordinary 'relish for reading' that was facilitated by the much greater accessibility of literature that the expansion and diversification of institutionalised lending seems to have afforded has lately begun to be taken rather more seriously by historians. Indeed, following the pioneering work of Richard D. Altick, and, more recently, of Isabel Rivers, Jonathan Rose and Stephen Colclough, in the history of English reading, it is now effectively a scholarly truism that the heightened enthusiasm for books among people of all descriptions was among the most interesting and most significant aspects of the gradual emergence of modern English society.[59]

There is nevertheless a strong sense in which the surface of the history of Georgian book consumption, for all the evident importance of reading in this period in particular, has barely been scratched.[60] Most of the subscription libraries for which significant records exist, and virtually all of the individual book buyers and readers whose inventories and catalogues are still extant, remain entirely unconsidered. So too, of course, do the vast majority of the circulating libraries—though, to be fair, the failure to advance very far with this particular line of inquiry probably has at least as much to do with the comparative paucity of surviving documentation, and perhaps also with its disparate locations, as it does with any lack of serious interest from scholars in what the exercise might actually reveal. At the same time, there has been much recourse to the disspiriting generalisation, as one recent literary scholar has voiced it, that 'We simply do not know and cannot find out what most readers of the past thought about a particular book.'[61] As a result, William St Clair, in a study of the reception of the Romantic book that appeared as recently as 2004, was still able to suggest, and quite plausibly, that:

> The history of reading is at the stage of astronomy before telescopes, economics before statistics, heavily reliant on a few commonly repeated traditional narratives and favourite anecdotes, but weak on the spade-work of basic empirical research, quantification, consolidation, and scrutiny of primary information, upon which both narrative history and theory ought to rest.[62]

It is because of this situation that an investigation of the reception of Scottish thought and literature in contemporary England, exploiting the considerable body of material relating to both personal and institutional book collections that has come down to us, as well as additional evidence of the way in which those books were actually *consumed* and *experienced* by individual readers, has wider significance than it might otherwise have enjoyed. For it can now be understood more widely as blazing a trail across extensive and substantially undiscovered terrain in the history of reading.[63] It also retains, however, a rather more specific role as an historical inquiry. After all, it holds out the tantalising possibility of opening up completely new perspectives on the tastes, interests and intellectual preoccupations of the literate public in this most dynamic and expansive of periods in the evolution of Britain's modern culture.

*   *   *

The study of the response of England's readers to the increasing productivity and ambition of Scottish writers and thinkers in the period of the Enlightenment, I have argued, merits our serious attention for several very good reasons. Clearly it has specific and very obvious importance to an understanding of Anglo-Scottish cultural relations in the century or so following the Treaty of Union. But it also, with reference to the crucial status of the Georgian period in particular, has real potential to illuminate some much broader issues in the currently fragmentary history of reading. At the same time, however, it forces us to confront a number of difficult methodological questions about the best way to approach any historical problem of this kind, as well as obliging us to reflect upon the fundamental implications of such inquiries for an understanding of the nature of reading itself. Indeed, the latter issues turn out to be especially thought-provoking. For they bear particularly closely upon the intensive discussions about the experience of reading that have in recent decades been taking place among literary scholars—and notably those most influenced by the theoretical insights of hermeneutics, phenomenology and sociology. Essentially, the key questions at the centre of these continuing debates about reading, and about its importance for a fuller understanding of how texts operate, have turned out to be these: How far is the meaning of texts determined at the moment of their first composition? How much, by contrast, is their significance and public import nothing more than the creation—or even the re-creation—of the readers, recipients and audiences who subsequently encounter them? And, as a consequence, what circumstances, practices and assumptions might exercise greatest influence over those readers' constructions—or, again, their reconstructions—of a text's meaning?

German critics such as Hans Robert Jauss and Wolfgang Iser, and, perhaps most prominently among the anglophone contributors, the American critic Stanley Fish, have pondered such first-order problems at sometimes extravagant length. On occasion these so-called "reception theorists" have even gestured, as we shall see, at some of the likely consequences of their observations for the future prosecution of genuinely empirical case studies in readers' actual responses to specific texts.[64] Too often, however, there has been a tendency for literary theorists in general, when probing the relationship between reading and meaning, to push to their logical limits the kinds of arguments commonly held to be encapsulated in the notorious aphorisms of the high priest of "deconstruction" Jacques Derrida (who observed that 'there is nothing outside of the text') and the post-structuralist philosopher Roland Barthes (who famously asserted that 'the birth of the reader must be at the cost of the death of the author').[65]

Indeed, such thinking, apparently exemplified by the deconstructionists' delight in offering capricious, even playful, interpretations of celebrated literary works, and closely related to their aggressive scepticism about the recoverability of the historical past through the study of texts, has encouraged the assumption that meanings are nothing more than the contingent, ephemeral and infinitely varied products of individual acts of reading: in Barthes's much-quoted words, usually taken as denying the possibility of authors exercising any lasting influence over the hermeneutic fate of their own compositions, 'writing ceaselessly posits meaning ceaselessly to evaporate it.'[66] Yet such an extreme position is clearly an exceptionally awkward starting point for anyone interested in reconciling the history of reading with the history of ideas. For were we to understand meaning as such a fluid and fleeting construct that the author's determinative role entirely vanishes, this would render almost impossible the identification of specific patterns of historical influence, classically imagined as being transmitted intentionally through a text, between its original creator and its subsequent audiences. Luckily, however, especially if we relocate this hypothetical problem within the kinds of recognisable practical contexts more likely to be of interest to the historian—something that, as suspicious commentators have increasingly noticed, has rarely been ventured by self-declared disciples of the contending literary theorists—it is far from obvious that these apparently well-favoured abstract propositions, at least in their more extreme forms, can be made to seem at all empirically plausible.[67]

It would be perfectly possible, for example, to argue that Hume's *History of England* is simply a Jacobite assault upon the cherished principles of English Whiggery—in other words, that it is a devious and dishonest work designed to undermine confidence in the secure foundations of modern political liberty and to prepare the ground for a return to the authoritarian monarchical government from which Hume's contemporaries had only lately escaped. Such, as we shall find in due course, was the unshakeable conviction of many of this text's discomfited eighteenth-century readers. On the other hand, it could equally be maintained—as most of Hume's more recent students have preferred to think—that the *History* is in fact a Whiggish philosophical tract chiefly marked by its author's deep admiration for modernity, for commerce and for secularism.[68] Were we, however, to assume that the continual reinvention of meaning by each new reader actually makes *all* readings valid—on the premise that they are not susceptible of objective evaluation by recourse either to the author's intentions or to some other extra-textual point of reference—then the practical consequences would be extraordinary. For the notion that a text means what any reader *says* that it means would not only require us to accept that *neither* of these two conflicting interpretations of Hume's *History* is fundamentally incorrect. Stranger still, it would entail us accepting that *any* interpretation is tenable, only providing that individuals can be found who are willing to advance it.

Yet it is very obvious that in reality a whole host of hypothetical constructions of a book like Hume's *History*—for example, that it is to be read as a work of Christian apologetics, or even as a feminist tract—are for all serious purposes inadmissible. Nor is it unclear why the number of credible options available to us is actually so limited. After all, reading is fundamentally a social rather than a solipsistic practice. As a result, a legitimate interpretation needs to rest upon an account of the text's meaning, based upon an analysis both of its own contents and of what can be reconstructed about the circumstances of its composition, to which at least a significant number of other competent readers, each performing similar triangulatory exercises for themselves, can be persuaded to lend their support.

Our own starting point in relation to the contemporary English reception of Scottish-authored publications is therefore a categorical insistence that writers, texts and a variety of other circumstantial factors each impose substantial constraints upon anyone seeking to create or construct meaning. Indeed, one of the defining features of a text might be said to be a capacity for prompting and directing its readers as they endeavour to arrive at an account of it that will earn at least a minimum level of wider acceptance. In this context it is especially helpful that the need to identify how meaning actually emerges within what Fish terms 'interpretive communities' has been one of the very few points on which a number of the leading theorists of reception have apparently achieved a heartening measure of agreement.[69] In Iser's influential formulation, for example, how people receive texts, and how they go about constructing meaning amidst their personal encounters with the written word, is far from abitrary. On the contrary, they are guided at all times by the operations of the 'implied reader'—a pivotal device that, he insists, is 'firmly planted in the structure of the text,' and which influences, in all manner of ways, each and every act of reading. Further described by Iser as 'both the prestructuring of the potential meaning by the text, and the reader's actualization of this potential through the reading process,' this tends to close off most hypothetical readings and leads the great majority of recipients to one of the much smaller number of interpretations that are realistically available. To put this slightly differently, by acting upon every reader during his or her encounter with the text, the 'implied reader' ultimately helps the individual to 'realise'' one or more of the possible constructions that lie latent among its distinctive 'repertoire' of potential meanings and significances.[70]

As will already be apparent, much of this discussion about the procedures involved in the reception of texts by their readers and in the consequent creation of meaning has taken place at a dizzyingly high level of abstraction. It may therefore appear to be of only limited relevance to a reasonably clearly defined empirical problem such as the English engagement with Scottish intellectual and literary culture as we have previously outlined it. Yet the sheer interpretative power of reception theory's insights into the ways in which books might actually be experienced, amid what is, in effect, a complex interplay between authors and readers that necessarily takes place in highly-individuated contexts, cannot be rejected out of hand. It is true that most literary theorists interested in such problems, at least in so far as they have deigned to offer substantial case studies, have still been more concerned to explore modern audiences' responses to landmark works of creative fiction. There appears to be no good reason, however, why we should expect the factors influencing the first readers of *Tom Jones*—one of Iser's favourite examples—to have been entirely different in kind from those affecting that work's latter-day students.

Nor is it obvious that any useful findings about the construction of meaning by eighteenth-century readers of Fielding's muscular prose would not also help us to understand how, say, the historical narratives of William Robertson, or Thomas Reid's moral philosophy, or any other contemporary Scottish work, were being construed by the same or similarly positioned individuals. In fact, especially if it were sufficiently alive, as the reception theorists in particular have argued it should be, to the collaborations that occur between authors and communities of readers wherever sense and meaning are quite literally being *made*, an investigation of readers' encounters with a group of texts such as the Scottish Enlightenment produced would potentially offer insights valuable not only to the wider history of reading but also—by virtue of its focus upon the unfolding relationship between certain sets of ideas and their eventual audiences—to the social history of ideas.

*   *   *

It is for these reasons that a fundamental focus of our own inquiries, directly addressed in Chapters 2 and 3 and then implicit in much that follows, must be the peculiar discursive environment in which readers' assumptions and preconceptions about texts—their 'horizon of expectations,' as Jauss would surely want us to call them—were actually shaped.[71] For we shall find that it was in fact the critical reviews, the newspapers, the magazines, and a number of other more or less formal mechanisms for the dissemination of appropriate judgments and the promotion of good taste, that supplied the essential frames of reference within which individual published works, including those by Scottish authors, came to be known, acquired, consumed and reflected upon. We shall then move on in the remainder of Part II to explore some of the other contexts affecting the reading public's approach to what has since come to be thought of as the Scottish Enlightenment (although it would be as well to note at this stage that, because the exact boundaries of the latter category, frequently invoked so as to bracket off certain authors from a less favoured residue, remain furiously disputed, no dogmatic position will be adopted here on the specific writers and works of Scottish origin during this period that should or should not be considered as falling strictly within its compass).[72] Accordingly Chapters 4 and 5 will be used to place under detailed scrutiny the means by which readers' encounters with books were invariably made possible—which is to say, principally the interlinked systems that were steadily evolving in England at this time to support the more widespread borrowing, browsing and buying of particular texts. At the same time, we shall also need to consider the non-institutional factors that may likewise have impacted in some way upon individuals' experiences as readers. In particular, it will be important for us to look more closely at the variety of locations in which books actually tended to be read as well as the immediate situations, both social and solitary, in which reading seems in practice to have taken place.

Part III will be concerned directly with what can ultimately be reconstructed of the personal responses of English men and women as they engaged during this period, by whatever means and in whatever circumstances, with the growing body of literature that was of Scottish origin.

In Chapter 6 the spotlight falls upon those indelible marks of textual consumption, the direct interventions onto the printed page which take the form of marginalia, annotations, emendations and other physical modifications of the original text. We shall discover that in each case these wilful acts of trespass onto the author's territory formed part of a concerted attempt by the reader to enter into a kind of dialogue with the writer—sometimes, of course, merely clarifying and amplifying, but at other times going much further, openly contradicting, contesting and refuting what had been written. In similar fashion Chapters 7 and 8 explore the remarkable (and almost entirely overlooked) evidence for the prospective historian of reading that survives within the pages of Georgian commonplace books. It will be seen that the practice of reflective self-analysis that commonplacing strongly encouraged in its exponents, and the procedures for careful and structured reading that it also called for, were to have a major impact upon the nature of individuals' experiences with the works with which they came into close contact.

Part IV will shift the focus of our attention towards some of the other implications arising from the inherently unstable and therefore often highly idiosyncratic relationship that the literate enjoy with what they happen to read. Chapters 9 and 10 duly examine a number of instances in which different individuals, their peculiar reactions frequently explicable only in terms of their own priorities and preoccupations, responded to some of the most characteristic of the ideas, themes and inquiries that, as the unforced flattery of contemporary observers like Denina and Voltaire should remind us, were even then coming increasingly to be associated with Scotland's philosophers and theorists. In particular, we shall discover that the experience of reading challenging works of the mainstream Enlightenment like *The Wealth of Nations* and Hume's *History*, but also of engaging with a less familiar and less central text like Thomas Blackwell's *Enquiry into the Life and Writings of Homer*, by no means constituted a passive form of reception, with authors simply pouring forth a predictable quantity of knowledge and understanding into inert recipients who served as little more than empty vessels. Rather it often led readers to wrestle actively and creatively with the words and ideas of each writer that they encountered—allowing them, in effect, not only to take the lead in making sense of what they were currently reading but also to begin the even more important task of making greater sense of themselves.

This empirically grounded account of how readers actually *behave* with texts, and of why they appear to respond in the ways that they do, must, of course, have wide-ranging consequences, reaching far beyond the narrower question of the contemporary English reception of the Scottish Enlightenment. Indeed, it will increasingly become clear, as will be argued by way of an extended conclusion in Part V, that it is necessary to see reading as about much more than merely the efficient transfer and accurate decipherment of the recorded observations and feelings of particular authors. On the contrary, it is a complex and essentially contingent process that impacts in innumerable ways upon the texts which form its subject as well as upon those individuals who perform it. For not only does it empower each literate person to determine afresh the meaning and significance of what those who are authors have apparently written. It also obliges them to reconsider (if only then to reaffirm) their own most cherished assumptions; it forces them to question once again (and sometimes even to repudiate) their own deeply-held opinions and beliefs. It therefore renders readers themselves subject to refashioning, with fundamental if never wholly forseeable implications for their affiliations, their affinities, their self-images, even their identities. Ultimately it was *this*—which is to say, the dramatically transformative potential of a reader's experiences with texts—that explains how literate individuals in the eighteenth and early nineteenth centuries ended up substantially making possible, though in some cases also resisting, an eventuality whose ramifications they were increasingly able to discern for themselves: the initially hesitant envisaging, and, in due course, the unambiguous identification, of a modern British culture.

Part II

Contexts

2 "The Self-Impanelled Jury of the English Court of Criticism"
Taste and the Making of the Canon

Since it forms the broader context to our own more particular inquiries, it is unfortunate, to put it mildly, that the history of reading in Georgian England has proven an especially intractable subject. Principally this seems to be because it has been all but impossible for recent scholars to approach it without becoming enmired in a complicated technical debate over the extent and impact of public literacy during this same period.[1] After all, there is no agreement as to what literacy really is, other than, when it is conceptualised at the most general level of analysis, a complex and ever-shifting combination of different reading and writing competencies. Nor is there anything approaching unanimity over its implications for the status and consumption of books. Worse still, no consensus exists even where essentially subjective judgments about the consequences of literacy are set to one side and scholars instead concern themselves simply with matters of quantification. Indeed, this crucial part of the background to any discussion of Georgian reading has tended in practice to generate infinitely more heat than light—whether in relation to precise literacy levels at any particular point in time or, for that matter, in respect of the broad trends throughout the period as a whole.

At one extreme of what has become a bitterly disputed field lies Burke's frequently quoted though alarmingly low estimate, normally taken to refer only to those individuals who regularly devoured political journalism. For what it is worth (and it may not be very much), this would give a mere eighty thousand English literates as late as 1790.[2] At the other end of the same terrain, however, we have well-known contemporary calculations, based instead on subscriptions to marriage registers, which appear to place the proportion of literates as high as 67% of men and 51% of females—or not far short of nine million people—by as early as 1839.[3] Clearly, then, we would look in vain for any straightforward starting point to our own inquiries which pretended to know just how far an ability to read and/or write might have extended across English society, as well as whether and how much it was continuing to spread among the country's inhabitants as a whole.

All that we can really say with any confidence at this stage seems to be this: that unprecedented population growth, from perhaps 5.5 million at the start of the eighteenth century to almost 9 million at its end, alongside impressive circumstantial evidence for the increasing production, diversity and affordability of printed matter (as we shall see in more detail in due course), means that there simply *must* have been significant long-term growth in the absolute number of readers alive during this period. As J. Paul Hunter sensibly formulates this tolerably safe generalisation, there was plainly emerging 'a substantial reading public, broadly based among socially, economically, occupationally and geographically diverse segments of the population.'[4] In the final analysis, it is also this situation, clearly associated in some way with widespread and growing literacy, that explains why there arose during the same period a much more determined effort by authors, publishers and a variety of other interested parties to shape the tastes of what they increasingly recognised as a sizeable and seemingly unpredictable population of readers. Any exploration of the relationship that might have emerged between the Scottish Enlightenment and those literate English contemporaries who went on to read its publications obviously needs to begin with some attempt to gauge the impact of these revolutionary attempts at the effective manipulation of mass cultural behaviour.

This would certainly require us to acknowledge the enormous power of the periodicals—newspapers, magazines and reviews alike—that blossomed so spectacularly during and after Queen Anne's reign. For it was these intentionally opinion-forming journalistic commentaries, with their substantial literary and critical content, that fuelled like nothing else the giddying sense of cultural novelty and vitality that marked what Samuel Johnson, speaking for many excited contemporaries, hailed in 1753 as 'the age of authors.'[5] Beyond the mass-circulation journals, however, which strove simultaneously to satisfy the cravings of the public and to refashion their tastes, readers were also beginning to receive instruction and advice from a number of other quarters. Of particular importance in this context was the rash of textual editing and commentary on English literature that was presided over by Johnson himself, as well as by more academically oriented arbiters like the Warton brothers. Despite its more elevated tone and avowedly scholarly purposes, this most prestigious form of criticism achieved considerable prominence in the cultural perspectives of significant numbers of academic and non-academic readers alike.

Other sources of guidance, whether operating directly or indirectly on readers' attitudes and expectations, should also be borne in mind. There were the philosophical treatises on aesthetics and taste from respected authorities like Burke and, not least importantly, from a succession of well-regarded Scots theorists: like the writings of Johnson and the Wartons, their seriousness of purpose in no way detracted from their ability to influence a wider population of sometimes excessively deferential readers. There were also descriptive travel commentaries, a genre embedded with cultural information and value-judgment that possessed more than sufficient power—which those authors who worked in it often felt keenly—to affect how its readers might subsequently perceive those other writings with which they came into contact. Indeed, there is evidence that growing knowledge of Scotland, and heightened sensitivity to the distinctive contours of Scottish culture, was increasingly influencing how contemporaries would also have approached, perceived and judged particular Scottish texts.

Conduct literature formally devoted to the practicalities of selecting books was yet another response to what Lucy Newlyn has called the 'rise of the reader' that certainly helped shape consumers' dispositions in interesting ways.[6] Nor, finally, should we neglect the far-from-neutral role of the booksellers themselves in moulding readers'—which is to say, their prospective customers'—tastes. Taken together, all of these discourses helped ensure that the literate public were subjected to a veritable barrage of advice about reading. Some, of course, was genuinely well-intentioned; much of it, almost needless to say, was merely self-interested; and by no means all of it was especially welcome or helpful to those who found themselves on the receiving end. Every bit, however, sought to prescribe the assumptions and responses of literate men and women in relation to what they might read—and not least importantly, as things transpired, to the works of the Scottish Enlightenment.

*   *   *

It would be difficult to exaggerate the extraordinary shift in the social history of culture represented by the birth of literary criticism as a popular public discourse.[7] More than any other process, this development signalled the emergence of a recognisably modern cultural economy—one, that is, characterised by never-ending negotiations between entrepreneurial producers and a largely anonymous mass of customers: 'Now learning itself is a trade,' as Johnson, one of the cynosures of this bustling new marketplace, crowed to his considerably less sanguine biographer.[8] By the 1740s, as many contemporaries recognised, readers seemed to be quickly supplanting courtly and aristocratic sponsors as the group responsible for conferring fame and success upon writers. The public, not princes or noblemen, were now the patrons of choice for a new breed of market-oriented professional authors like Hume himself, who boasted his 'Disdain of all Dependence,' as for Samuel Richardson, Oliver Goldsmith and Henry Fielding.[9]

Yet, of course, the diversity and, it was often complained, the sheer capriciousness of the literate population, also posed new kinds of problem for those who were heavily invested in the lucrative but risky business of literature. This was especially so for the creators and merchandisers of the printed word, the men (and, sometimes, the women) for whom the opportunities created by the emergence of a reading public were manifestly greatest. Indeed, they had almost immediately realised that there was a need, in Frank Donoghue's words, to 'identify and cater to the tastes of this increasing plurality of readers.'[10] It was in meeting this challenge—in attempting to manipulate the interests of the consumers of literature in ways that would be acceptable (and, which was almost the same thing, profitable) to the producers—that popular critical commentaries of various kinds, aimed at influencing the behaviour of a disparate and physically scattered community of readers, were first called into being.

The explicit priority for virtually all of those engaged in critical journalism was the definition and dissemination of something usually described as 'taste.' As Robert L. Patten insists, for the periodicals that led the campaign this meant that it was only natural that they should have 'regularly instructed their customers in the proper—that is, moral—way to read.'[11] Inevitably this enterprise could sometimes look suspiciously like a poorly disguised attempt to nudge the gullible and the suggestible towards particular commercial products. Certainly this was a common allegation levelled specifically at those trend-setting literary periodicals, notably the *Monthly Review* founded in 1749 and the *Critical Review* established in 1756, in which some of the leading publishers had financial interests.[12] Yet criticism was also a sincere endeavour to advance a broader set of values and assumptions to which, for the most part, their creators genuinely clung. Naturally, these often had political and social implications. The Whiggish affiliations of the *Monthly*, for example, and earlier of Addison himself, together with the contrasting Tory inclinations of the *Critical*, as well as of key journalistic arbiters of mid-century like Johnson and Smollett (the latter sometime editor of the *Critical*), were, after all, scarcely concealed from the public's gaze.[13]

Equally, there is no denying that the periodicals frequently sought to impose notions of female domesticity and respectability upon a readership within which women now comprised an increasingly prominent constituency.[14] Nor were overtly moral concerns capable of being completely disentangled from the project of defining and disseminating taste among readers. Making this connection unusually explicit, one commentator, writing in the first issue of the *Monthly Ledger* in 1773, insisted that his own interests as a critic would be encompassingly humanitarian and passionately moralistic rather than—as he implied previous critics had been—narrowly concerned with the technical properties of other texts: 'I mean to begin this work,' he declared emphatically, 'as I intend to continue and end it; in advocating the cause of virtue, and in attempting to promote the essential interests of mankind.'[15]

Literary and intellectual considerations were, however, predominant, precisely because these seemed to have the most profound moral implications. To quote from the same issue of the *Monthly Ledger*, and a critic who was also acutely conscious of the rising profile and potential influence of Scots authors in particular:

Error proves fatal from the pen of a Beattie, a Johnson, a Robertson or a Hume. They know not the extent of that influence which their sentiments may have in the world. These sentiments, when published, are no longer their own, but, mixed with the general mass of literature, become the property of the public, and may prove useless or injurious to thousands.[16]

This continual fear of what might happen if both authorship and public taste went unchecked by judicious and widely available criticism helps explain why, as Robert Spector has suggested, even during the wartime years between 1756 and 1763, periodical commentators held to their specifically cultural commitments so tenaciously that they were, if anything, 'more reluctant to accept aesthetic than to accept social and political changes.'[17]

Despite their boasts about influencing public manners and public morals, however, it is crucial to acknowledge that reality continually mocked the critics' pretensions to the strict dictation of literary preferences. After all, a growing and increasingly diverse population of readers, as they demonstrated time and time again, could not so easily be corralled. In fact constant complaints arose from journalists, as from the booksellers and authors with whom they were closely aligned, about consumers' seemingly undisciplined or downright wrong-headed judgments. As Vicesimus Knox complained, 'The scarcity of books, a few centuries ago, was the principal obstacle to the advancement of learning. The multitude of them is become, in the present age, scarcely less injurious to its interests, by distracting the student in his choice, and by diffusing an incorrect and undistinguishing taste.'[18] The problem of aberrant selections made by untutored (or wilfully disobedient) readers was seen most spectacularly, of course, in the inexplicable popularity of prose fiction, which, long after its initial triumph in the first half of the eighteenth century, was still discomfiting the self-appointed guardians of public taste.

Such work, insisted one in 1751 in the *Monthly Review*, had 'a tendency to mislead the understanding, or to blemish the reader's morals.'[19] Another pessimist, a York clergyman much perplexed by the spread of literacy beyond the traditional elites—as were many authorities in the turbulent years after the Napoleonic Wars—continued as late as 1819 to demand measures to 'divert the taste which has been given by the universal diffusion of the art of reading from Novels, Works of Fiction, and other pernicious Publications, and to direct it into a safe channel.'[20] Yet novels were only the most obvious of the unaccountable vices in which delinquent readers so recklessly indulged. As Spector points out, a host of literary fashions, each enthusiastically embraced by sizeable parts of the reading public but regarded with a mixture of bemusement and condescension by most right-minded commentators, attracted objections precisely because they permitted consumers to challenge the 'orthodox rules and standards' that the critics themselves had prescribed.[21]

A substantial degree of practical divergence was therefore perfectly normal between the many who read and the few who aspired to control their behaviour. Nevertheless, the waywardness of so many readers in relation to the detailed instructions they had received did not usually detract from almost everyone's acceptance of criticism, at least in principle, as an essential foundation of public taste. For not only were readers themselves often sadly deluded in their judgments. Critics too—particularly when they were also money-minded journalists rather than disinterested scholars—were not beyond well-merited criticism. As one leading practitioner freely admitted, 'there is no doubt that the number of incompetent Critics will always be great. But this affords no more foundation for a general invective against Criticism, than the number of bad philosophers or reasoners affords against reason and philosophy.'[22] In fact, as if to illustrate its omnipresence increasingly being taken for granted, by the middle of the eighteenth century, like so many other contemporary institutions, criticism had passed from being the mere subject of measured commentary—Pope's majestic *Essay on Criticism* (1711) is the finest early example—to being the instantly recognizable butt of popular satire.

This is why the bookseller Robert Dodsley argued in a piece printed in *The World* in 1753 that criticism was not only a peculiarly modern disease but also one that was 'more particularly English than any other,' whilst one of Dodsley's leading authors, Laurence Sterne, could make knowing reference in 1759 to 'your criticks and gentry of refined taste' who, having encountered his *Tristram Shandy*, would assuredly 'run it down.'[23] (Sterne, of course, was correct, at least in the short-run, with Johnson's famous dismissal in 1776—'Nothing odd will do long. Tristram Shandy did not last'—representing what was then a widely held critical opinion. Criticism only slowly and grudgingly fell into line with the reading public on the book's enduring merits.[24]) By the time that the comedy *Polly Honeycombe* was first performed the following year, its creator George Colman could safely mock 'the self-impanelled Jury of the English Court of Criticism' and tantalise his audience by reminding them that, whatever else they might think they were watching, 'I put myself on my Trial for the High Crime of writing for the Stage . . . .'[25] In 1779, Richard Sheridan's *The Critic; or, A Tragedy Rehearsed*, which introduced his own amused public to the dubious personages of Dangle and Sneer, could even make criticism, now viewed as the ever-present bane of the modern writer, the natural subject of a successful dramatic comedy.

There are also clear signs of the growing importance of criticism in the cultural experience and behaviour of the wider literate population. By the 1750s, after all, it was becoming normal for the *Monthly* and the *Critical*, as well as for other periodicals like the *Gentleman's Magazine* (the definitive miscellany of the age, founded in 1731) and its rival the *London Magazine* (which ran from 1732 to 1785), to be found in an increasing variety of public settings—where, indeed, according to Addison's famous boast about

The Spectator's circulation, a single copy might easily reach dozens of individual readers, potentially influencing and affecting the conduct of a large community of the literate.[26] This seems to have been particularly true in those institutional arenas in which reading and conversation, two seminal activities that, as we have seen, were understood to be the mainsprings of public politeness, were the main focus of attention.

Thus in Manchester in 1766, for example, the Circulating Library, in just the second year of its existence as one of that rapidly growing industrial town's leading cultural institutions, was already supplying copies of the *Gentleman's*, the *Monthly* and the *Critical* to its 126 subscribers.[27] Again, when a group of local men came together at Pulborough in Sussex in 1807 to found their own reading society, among their very first collective purchases, clearly intended to facilitate the subsequent selection of other appropriate texts, were the *Edinburgh Review* (the new century's most distinguished outlet for criticism, first established in 1802), the *Monthly Review* and the *Monthly Magazine*.[28] Similarly in the early 1820s, the Kendal Coffee Room was offering Westmorland readers ready access to copies of what were now regarded as the two most prestigious literary commentaries of the day, the *Edinburgh* and the *Quarterly Review* (its rival, founded in 1809).[29] Evidently we should take seriously Marilyn Butler's notion that journals like the *Edinburgh* 'continued that tradition to which James Thomson and Tobias Smollett had belonged, of delivering advice to the English in tones of moral and intellectual superiority.'[30] For few reading institutions by the early nineteenth century considered themselves complete without providing exposure to high-minded criticism, and so, in effect, to current journalistic guidance on all questions related to books and reading.

Widespread institutionalised provision ensured that individual copies of the critical periodicals reached the greatest possible number of readers. But it also had practical implications for those who used them. In particular, so wedded were readers to the notion that there existed—or at least that there *ought* to exist—a broad critical consensus in relation to what might be deemed 'proper' or 'correct' reading that in many institutions it was a formal requirement that proposals for new acquisitions should be accompanied by a cross-reference to criticism in a recognised journal. At the Carlisle Library, for example, which in the early nineteenth century provided copies of the *Monthly*, the *Gentleman's*, the *British Critic* and the *Monthly Magazine*, it was necessary for readers to recommend purchases by also giving 'the title, price, number of volumes, and a reference to some respectable periodical or other work for a character, if possible.'[31] At the Coventry Library in 1812, too, it was agreed that there should be 'a note left with the Librarian, referring to the Review in which such Book has been noted . . . .'[32]

That institutionalised readers endorsed the critics' insistence upon absolute propriety in the selection of books is also demonstrated by the sheer censoriousness of many of the regulations to which they willingly adhered.

Members of the Worcester Library, for example, insisted that their elected management committee should suppress any acquisitions that on closer inspection turned out to be 'indecent, and of an immoral tendency.'[33] This same formula, much repeated in critical Jeremiads against inappropriate reading even though its precise meaning and application were rarely clarified, was also echoed elsewhere, as at Pontefract in the West Riding of Yorkshire by the town's Library and News Room and at Lichfield in Staffordshire by the Permanent Library.[34] Accordingly there seems no reason to doubt that contemporary readers, especially when operating within the associational framework that, as we shall see in Chapter 4, was so important in Georgian culture, had learned to agree with the critics that careless exposure to improper texts—itself the consequence of turning a deaf ear to critical strictures—should be avoided at all costs. Indeed, it was widely believed that such ignorance was bound to wreak moral havoc, rending asunder the very fabric of polite society.

Deference towards criticism, however, was not just a herd instinct displayed only when readers flocked together in an institutional setting. Private individuals—in their homes, their drawing rooms and their bedrooms, or wherever else they chose to read—also pored with inordinate care over the judgments of the principal journalistic arbiters. Hence *The Spectator* soon achieved even greater influence than its confident creators would have dared hope. In retrospect it becomes clear that Addison and Steele had amply prepared the ground for the subsequent triumph of popular criticism, making those periodicals which followed, and which sought to emulate their winning combination of moral reflection, topical observation and critical *obiter dicta*, a necessary staple for innumerable readers. There must have been many others who trod in the footsteps of Revd John Ott, who throughout the first half of the eighteenth century, as the rector of Bexhill in Sussex, leavened his study of Anglican authorities such as Tillotson and Stillingfleet with note-taking on a variety of subjects that could be appropriately illustrated with quotations from Addison's peerless prose—including, in just the first few leaves of Ott's crowded journal, 'Admiration,' 'Advice,' 'Affectation,' and 'Ambition.'[35]

In the experience of some readers, like Thomas Holcroft, Newmarket stable boy turned radical actor and author, *The Spectator*, initially borrowed from a friend in the 1760s, fully fifty years after its debut, became the defining moment in a life of avid and increasingly well-informed reading.[36] For others, like Thomas Turner, a Sussex draper and mercer and a fervent reader in the late 1750s, 'The Spectator's criticism,' as he fondly called it in his diary, was the key contribution to a better understanding of the landmarks of English literature.[37] Occasionally, as for Charles Morgan, a young gentleman who during the late 1740s seems to have been associated with the Goddard family of Swindon, Addison played an integral part not only in an individual's recreation but also in his broader education—payments for *The Spectator* (from which, just like Turner, he transcribed

'Mr Addison's remarks on Paradise-Lost'), and for those other reliable generators of politeness, the coffee houses, occurring in Morgan's memorandum book alongside records of transactions involving his personal tutor.[38] Nor is it uncommon to find this most appealing of critical vehicles named among the precious final bequests made with the best of intentions to close family and friends. Such was the case with Elizabeth Goodall of Fowey, a Cornish reader who died in 1782, whose will left 'unto Mary Ann Coryton Daughter of my said Nephew John Coryton' a number of items including 'my Spectators in eight volumes.'[39]

The enthusiasm of individual readers for the critical periodicals that multiplied rapidly in *The Spectator*'s wake can just as easily be documented. This is clearly seen in the case of the *Critical Review*. One regular subscriber was Mathew Flinders, father of the great Australasian navigator and a learned man who ran a medical practice at Donington in Lincolnshire. In May 1782, Flinders noted that he had chosen to take the *Critical* because it served two crucial functions, appearing both 'Instructive & Entertaining.'[40] Three years later we can even catch a rare glimpse of a reader's specific susceptibility to critical guidance, Flinders confiding to himself, having just procured Alexander Hamilton's *Elements of the Practice of Midwifery* (1775), a product of Edinburgh medical expertise, that 'my inducements to purchase were the Character given of it in the Critical Review.'[41] Nor is such subservience to the *Critical* surprising in a provincial doctor. For, particularly under Smollett's direction (who, of course, possessed a Glasgow medical qualification of his own) but also continuing thereafter, it had shown a marked interest in reviewing works of interest to the profession. In 1762, for example, it had adjudicated in the on-going dispute over the first reliable investigation of the lymphatic system between two distinguished yet deeply antipathetic Scottish doctors, William Hunter and the Edinburgh professor Alexander Munro *secundus*: 'our opinion is, that his evidence is full, clear, and unquestionable,' the *Critical*'s in-house critic intoned of the former's *Medical Commentaries*, 'that his facts are apposite, and his arguments conclusive.'[42]

The *Critical Review*, however, even at the outset, was far from being the exclusive preserve of Smollett's fellow medical practitioners. Revd James Gambier, for example, was a longstanding rector of Langley in Kent. He clearly read the *Critical* extensively during the last years of its first incarnation (which ended in 1791), as well as working through old reprints of *The Spectator* and, in due course, the newly issued *Edinburgh Review*.[43] This punishing regime of criticism and literary commentary, again chiefly derived from periodical sources, seems to have helped turn Gambier, whose namesake (actually his father's cousin) was an Admiral of the Fleet and who on his mother's side was related to the Venn family of evangelical clergymen, into a notably discriminating and confident reader of the works of the Scottish Enlightenment in particular. Equally, Sir John Cullum, a Suffolk baronet, appears before his death in 1785 to have divided his attention between several different periodicals, each incorporating valuable literary and critical content—the *Critical* once again, and the *Gentleman's*, of course, but also the *Annual Register* (a yearly compendium, founded in 1758 by Dodsley and Burke, which printed excerpts from some of the latest publications) and the *St James's Chronicle* (another popular metropolitan newspaper with a significant literary element, begun in 1761).[44]

The *Monthly Review*, the *Critical*'s mirror image and slightly longer-established rival, was at least as popular. It was taken, for example, by the Gell family of Hopton in Derbyshire, who, always anxious for guidance on reading, seem also to have bought the *Monthly Magazine* after its commencement in 1796. Certainly, both of these periodicals feature extensively in the Gells' surviving notes.[45] The same two periodicals also provided vital orientation, less than twenty miles away and in a very different social milieu, for their contemporary Joseph Hunter. A Sheffield apprentice cutler, he used them to inform not only his choice of books but also, according to Stephen Colclough's recent study, his responses to what he had read.[46] Half a century earlier, Revd George Burton, rector at Elvedon in Suffolk, had seemingly been among the *Monthly*'s first readers. As he noted on the cover of his own library catalogue, again giving us an uncommon insight into periodical criticism's direct impact upon a reader's understanding of other texts, 'NB. The Persian Letters & the Causes of the aggrandizement and Declension of the Roman Empire were both wrote by President Montesquiou [sic] see the Monthly Review July 1749—p: 229.'[47]

Revd James Franks, curate of Halifax and then vicar of nearby Sowerby Bridge at the end of the eighteenth century, was yet another reader who copied out extracts from the *Monthly*. Indeed, it formed part of a rich diet of criticism from a motley assortment of other newspapers and journals—all of them again with some kind of literary coverage—such as the *Leeds Intelligencer*, the *Oxford Magazine*, the *Edinburgh Review*, the *St James's Chronicle* and the *Gentleman's*.[48] To Revd James Snowdon, meanwhile, vicar of Ponteland in Northumberland from 1762, the major periodicals represented a unique cultural lifeline, the means by which an intensely bookish Oxford-educated clergyman, marooned in a remote northern parish, stayed in touch with developments in the publishing centres of London and Edinburgh. In fact Snowdon took the *London Magazine* by preference. It was from this that he made regular entries in his diary about new works that, as he anxiously put it, he would need, by whatever means, 'to get a sight of.' It also appears more than likely that, without the constant stream of publishers' announcements and critical commentary that his chosen periodical conveyed, a man in Snowdon's isolated position simply could not have gone on to purchase quite so many books—including such key Scottish texts that he was able to describe familiarly as 'The Historical Law Tracts by Ld Kemys,' 'Sr Ja^s Stewart's—Inquiry into the Principles of Political Œconomy' and 'Dr Beattie's Treatise on Poetry & Music.'[49]

* * *

The success of popular criticism with individuals like Franks and Snowdon was not least owing to its deliberately stoking the ambitions of readers who quickly learned to look to the journals for guidance in their own selection and appreciation of published texts. As James Engell has sagely put it, in this period it really does appear not only as if literate people, unsurprisingly, 'want to read literature,' but also as if, rather more interestingly, they 'want to read about reading literature.'[50] The raging contemporary passion for reading, however, not only ensured widespread genuflection towards periodical criticism in relation to all matters of taste and judgment (even if, as the meteoric rise of the novel reminds us, its detailed prescriptions were still perfectly capable of being diplomatically ignored). It also meant that criticism was in a position to play a major role in fashioning the self-image of readers themselves.

It did this above all by imploring them to join with the critics in experiencing those responses to texts that collectively could be glossed as 'taste.' In fact, something not unlike the 'implied reader,' which, as we have seen, has been postulated by Iser as the element in a text that seeks to mould an audience's reactions, may well assist us in accounting for the quite extraordinary enthusiasm with which readers of all kinds increasingly greeted the writings of the literary journalists.[51] For critical discourse, particularly as it had developed as a popular medium by the 1740s, had one noteworthy feature above all: time and again, as Engell's comment highlights, it was the reader him or herself—not the critic, not the book, and certainly not the author—who emerged as its central protagonist.

The concerted focus of criticism upon the perceptions and responses of the reader should in one sense scarcely be surprising. Its main business, after all, was to reinforce the reader's identification with those whose judgment, and therefore whose taste, was already unimpeachable. We see this set of assumptions plainly, for example, in the approach invariably taken by the *Town and Country Magazine*, yet another popular periodical widely read throughout England. By insisting in 1776 that Thomas Pennant's second tour of Scotland 'cannot fail to please the judicious reader,' its critic was clearly signalling to his readers a series of specific expectations about their own reactions to the text that most—whether they happened to imagine themselves securely or only prospectively polite—would have been only too eager to fulfil.[52] Hume's *History*, too, was described as 'a favourite performance among the higher class of people,' leaving it open—but clearly not *that* open—as to the social category with which the individual reader, in formulating his or her own responses to that work, might wish to associate themselves.[53]

In exactly the same way, further fuelling the reader's aspirations to acknowledged respectability, an ability to share the critic's own experiences was routinely claimed to yield beneficial—and sometimes, it was even hinted, socially visible—results. It was for this very reason, no doubt, that Ferguson's *Essay on the History of Civil Society*, on its first publication, was guaranteed in one commentary to bring instantaneous elevation to the happy condition already attained by the reviewer: 'none can sit down to the perusal of it,' the *Critical's* appointed judge assured his readers in 1767, 'without rising a better man and citizen, or without finding himself improved in sense, sentiment, and stile.'[54] It would appeal, trilled the *Monthly*, no less enticingly, to 'every reader of taste.'[55]

In much the same vein, the continual use of plural pronouns and the frequent tendency to imply the existence of a polite consensus (however chimerical this may in reality have been) should be understood as merely a vigorous flexing of the critic's exceptional muscular power with which highly suggestible readers could readily be moulded in his own image: 'Sir Walter Scott is determined not to loose [his] hold upon the affections of an indulgent public,' declared one in the *Monthly Magazine* in 1820, gesturing tantalisingly at a mutuality of sentiment with his more discerning readers, and ' . . . we do not for our own parts, see why as long as there remain patrons to pay the piper, he should not merrily play on.'[56] The same confident insistence upon the possibility of convergence between readers and critics had also been embedded in the *London Magazine's* sentiments on Robertson's *Charles V* in 1769. Remarkably, this review began not, as we might expect, by commending the text's author, or even by relating the critic's own personal response. Instead it observed that 'It is with the greatest pleasure we congratulate the public on this very valuable acquisition to the world of letters . . . ': this was necessary, apparently, because Robertson's had 'not only opened an ample field of knowledge but of entertainment to his readers.'[57]

Reader-focused commentary, then, was devoured by the literate public for a number of obvious reasons. At a superficial level, criticism simply explained the latest developments in the complex and sometimes obscure world of literature, offering readers practical help in their quotidian capacities as purchasers and as borrowers: as the *Monthly Review* said of James Mackintosh's *Vindiciae Gallicae* (1791), a much-discussed Scottish contribution to the controversy over the French Revolution, it was to be hoped that it would 'induce our readers to peruse the whole of a work which we warmly recommend to their notice.'[58] Criticism, however, also did much more than this. It instructed men and women on *how* as well as *what* to read. More fundamentally still, it held out the prospect of genuine self-transformation. For it undertook to do something that, in an intensely status-conscious society in which proof of politeness was continually required, was of incomparable value. It conferred or confirmed their own membership of a prestigious club—the one formed throughout society by the discriminating and the judicious. Ultimately, this was something to which many readers of all classes and convictions desperately wanted to belong.

* * *

As will be clear, there is little doubt that the periodical critics, in all their many guises and whatever the particular postures and rhetorical strategies that they might choose to affect, were much the most influential—in part because clearly the most prolific—retailers of instruction about reading to the Georgian public at large. It follows, too, that their utterances must also have been among the factors shaping the attitudes of those English contemporaries who, from roughly the middle of the eighteenth century onwards, encountered a growing number of Scottish-authored works in particular—which, indeed, as we have already repeatedly seen, the critics often made a particular point of discussing. It is also apparent, however, that rather less transitory commentaries, themselves responding to the expanding commercial market for books throughout the anglophone world, were simultaneously making their mark upon the public's understanding of reading. Above all, serious critical scholarship in English was itself largely invented in the decades immediately before 1800, a development with potentially far-reaching consequences for readers' approaches to published texts of all types.

More than anyone else, of course, this was the life's work of Johnson himself. For he brought to the new discipline of criticism both the trenchantly expressed opinions and the unrivalled flair for generating interest and controversy that he had perfected during a long and laborious apprenticeship in literary journalism. This was why critical writing, several of whose practitioners shared Johnson's remarkable capacity for provocation, carried over from its slightly unseemly Grub Street origins an ability to reach out to a wider population of readers. It was also, though, a discourse that was informed by the rigorous concerns of professional academics, whose inspiration lay more in the older preoccupations of biblical exegesis and classical philology than in the demotic world of the magazines and the newspapers. It was arguably from this much more respectable direction that the Warton brothers—Joseph the headmaster of Winchester and Thomas the professor of poetry at Oxford—would make probably the most noteworthy contributions.[59]

What resulted inevitably differed from the style of criticism that was being pioneered and popularised in the periodicals. Its purpose, after all, was far grander in scale. Indeed, it sought nothing less than to establish a reliable and enduring framework for the interpretation and judgment of the full range of extant texts in English. Intimately bound up with this impulse towards the evaluation of an entire literary culture was the quest for an inclusive and definitive canonicity—for the secure identification, in other words, of a national tradition of authorship and creativity linking a glorious past inextricably with a richly-promising present. The near-deification of Shakespeare and the recovery and vigorous promotion of the medieval ballad tradition were among the more significant fruits of this enterprise.[60] The great editions of the bard by Johnson and by Edmond Malone (1765 and 1790), Bishop Thomas Percy's path-breaking *Reliques of Ancient English Poetry* (1765) and the brilliant but eccentric antiquarian Joseph Ritson's *Ancient English Metrical Romances* (1802) were each definitive expressions of the new English scholarship that would long endure. Yet the project of constructing an authoritative commentary upon the vast body of existing texts also exerted a powerful influence over many ordinary readers. Principally this seems to have been because, in directing attention towards the vital relationship between authors, texts and identity, critical scholarship helped ensure that certain works would increasingly be embraced by literate men and women as quintessential expressions of their own national culture.[61]

This development, it should be said, did not come entirely out of the blue. Before the decision of the Lords in 1774 to demolish the pretensions of the booksellers that they still enjoyed common law perpetual copyright under the 1710 Act, thereby transforming the market in intellectual property, budding anthologists and canonisers alike had effectively been inhibited from issuing consolidated editions of disparate texts.[62] There had still emerged, of course, an important tradition of commentary on long stretches of English, and, increasingly, of British, literary history.[63] Theophilus Cibber's *The Lives of the Poets of Great Britain and Ireland* (1753) was among the more significant examples to appear in the pre-1774 era. Another work of note, though similarly constrained by law, was Horace Walpole's humorous *Catalogue of the Royal and Noble Authors of England* (1758). So too was John Berkenhout's *Biographica Literaria* (1777), published shortly after the copyright controversy had finally been resolved.

Latterly there had also been two important attempts at canonising the texts themselves.[64] The forty-three-volume collection *The British Poets* (1773), using only works deemed to be out of statutory copyright but nonetheless bitterly resisted by the London trade, included James Thomson and, in an additional volume issued in 1776, James Beattie. John Bell's 109-volume *The Poets of Great Britain* (1776–82), meanwhile, the finer of these enterprises and the first to benefit from the new legal environment, had again incorporated Scots like Thomson and David Mallet.[65] But Johnson's *Lives of the English Poets* (1779–81), conceived by the metropolitan booksellers themselves as a series of definitive prefaces to new editions of the chosen texts, was unquestionably the greatest product of the changing perspective on the contents and ownership of British literature that was facilitated by the final undermining of perpetual copyright. In it a measured and authoritative criticism and a careful selection of works—once more including Scots like Thomson and Mallet—were at last able to walk hand-in-hand in the direction of convincing canonicity.

Over-stating the effects of Johnson's *Lives* upon the wider population of English readers would be hard. Certainly, to judge from the immense number of people who read and referred to it, it was among the most popular and influential works of the age. It also decisively affected the attitudes and judgments of innumerable individuals. Its treatment of the period's most admired Scottish poet, James Thomson, for example, triggered frantic note-taking by William Chute, M.P. for Hampshire in the 1790s, as well as by Revd Joseph Coltman, minister of Beverley in the early nineteenth century (the latter apparently being especially struck by Johnson's observation on *The Seasons* that 'This is one of those works in which blank verse seems properly used . . . ').[66] But it was not only Thomson about whom readers found much to interest them in Johnson's matchlessly opinionated pages. Revd Gambier in Kent, for example, copied out the observations on Pope's 'genius,' as again did Revd Franks at Halifax.[67] William Warren Porter, a clergyman from Clapham in Surrey, was yet another who transcribed material from the life of Pope.[68] At Micheldever in Hampshire, Robert Bristow recorded extracts from Johnson's separate work on a less fortunate writer ('To the mournful narratives, I am about to add the Life of Richard Savage . . . '), as did the Derbyshire landowner Sir William Fitzherbert.[69]

Johnson's critical judgments quickly established themselves as one of the definitive reference points for contemporary readers—whether the purple passages in question happened to come from the *Lives*, or from his other published writings, or from Boswell's *Life of Johnson*, or even, on occasion, from among the apocryphal stories that abounded about his endlessly quotable utterances. George Hibbert, M.P., West India merchant and London alderman, who, like Porter, lived at Clapham, was sufficiently moved by the *Life* that he copied out the heart-rending note from Johnson to his friend Dr Taylor following the death of the latter's wife.[70] Charlotte Broome, the wife of a Bengal army officer and daughter of Charles Burney, was among many readers fascinated by Johnson's role as a deliberate provoker of Scots anger. Thus at one point she recalled Boswell's observation that 'he expressed to his f^d Mr Windham of Norfolk his wonder at the resentment of the Scotch, at having their country described as it really was.'[71] At another point she noted Johnson's characteristically slashing criticism amid the Ossian affair ('Dr J. being asked by a believer if he thought such poems could be written by any one man now living? "yes S^r, says the Dr, by *Many* Men; Many Women & Many Children"').[72]

George Shiffner, a Sussex gentleman and merchant, seems to have been no less amused by Johnson's continually double-edged comments on all things Scottish. This was presumably why he transcribed Johnson's favourable comments about Lord Hailes's *Annals of Scotland* ('I never before read Scotch History with certainty . . . ').[73] Nor was attraction to Johnson's critical judgments confined only to the seriously moneyed. Christopher Thomson, a Hull artisan, was successively a potter, a brickyard worker, an apprentice shipwright, a sawyer, an actor and finally a painter. He nevertheless claimed to have devoured all of Johnson's writings in the early years of the nineteenth century, a formative experience apparently crucial in his metamorphosis into an ardent autodidact and campaigner for working-class education.[74]

Johnson's criticism was thus a fixture in the minds and imaginations of immense numbers of readers from the 1780s onwards. But Thomas Warton's *History of English Poetry* (1778–81), which presented a canon extending from the earliest times to the beginning of the eighteenth century, seems to have been not much less influential. Certainly large numbers read—and appear to have tried to internalise—what Warton's assured prose told them about their own cultural heritage. Library members in particular considered the *History*, like the literary periodicals, an essential tool for enhancing their own appreciation of literature. At Leicester, the Permanent Library, founded in 1800, almost immediately ordered both Warton's *History* and Johnson's *Lives*, as well as, inevitably, the *Gentleman's Magazine*, the *Edinburgh Review* and the *Monthly Review*, the better to ensure that members would be well-informed in their future purchases.[75] Nor did its utility in this capacity quickly fade. As late as August 1826, the recently established Whitehaven Library in Cumberland likewise made sure that the *History* was among its own very first acquisitions.[76]

Beyond the collective decision-making of the lending institutions, however, individual readers also continually deferred to the authority of Warton's great tome whose author, whilst admitting that 'It is not the plan of this work to comprehend the Scottish poetry,' had added, significantly for the *History*'s ability to offer a coherent vision of British literary history as a whole, that 'when I consider the close and national connection between England and Scotland in the progress of manners and literature, I am sensible I should be guilty of a partial and defective representation of the poetry of the former, was I to omit in my series a few Scottish writers . . . .'[77] Revd Coltman, who elsewhere claimed that 'The merit of Dr Johnson as a moral & critical writer is so well known that it would be superfluous to point it out' (though this did not, of course, inhibit him from transcribing Johnson's views on both Pope and Beattie), quoted Warton's work with equal relish.[78] So too did Thomas Eagles, a successful Bristol merchant and classical scholar. Indeed, Eagles was fascinated enough by this landmark study of British literary culture to produce in 1781 a forty-page 'Analysis of the 3rd Vol: of Warton's History of English Poetry' which had only just been published that same year.[79]

Warton's greatest accomplishment, however, was arguably the fact that a work of such profound scholarship was able to insinuate itself into even the most unexpected and banal of contexts—the ultimate measure, perhaps, of just how far the reach of serious canon-making critical commentary now extended. Humphrey Senhouse, for example, a Cumberland gentleman and local antiquarian who was among the founders of the library at Whitehaven, copied out from Warton's *History*, rather incongruously, the words of a favourite drinking song.[80] The eyes of Sir John Cullum, meanwhile, alighted specifically upon Warton's discussion of the obscure mediaeval poet and self-proclaimed seer Adam Davy.[81]

Nor was the elder Warton brother's status as an authority much less evident to contemporary readers. Indeed, Joseph's *An Essay on the Writings and Genius of Pope* (1756–82), important in the history of criticism not least because it commenced with a famous ranking of the major poets— from which the reputations of only Shakespeare, Milton, Spenser emerged completely unscathed—seems to have been regarded as a particularly reliable source of instruction. John Bowle, vicar of Idmiston in Wiltshire and an eminent Hispanicist and literary scholar, knew it well, the following note, which clearly used the *Essay* as a crib for insights into England's greatest seventeenth-century philosopher, appearing in his journal: 'Locke fond of Romances. *Warton* on Pope. 2.186.'[82] Gustavus Gale, too, a literary-minded early nineteenth-century Carlisle linen and woollen draper who knew the Senhouse family, was another who looked to the *Essay* for authoritative commentary. In fact, he summarised the older Warton's discussion of literature and the arts as well as copying into his own notebook more diverting material from Boswell's *Life of Johnson*.[83]

* * *

Large-scale works of literary scholarship were, then, alongside the more ephemeral periodicals, an important means by which the concerns of criticism—which is to say, the proper exercise of judgment, the wider cultivation of taste and the increasing acknowledgement of canonicity—were absorbed and assimilated by a growing number of readers. Significant in a slightly different way, however, though again with important implications for how people now approached their reading, were a series of essentially theoretical developments closely related to the advent of scholarly criticism. Indeed, both departures might be seen as a reaction to the accelerating commercialisation and diversification in the arts (in painting, engraving, theatre and music as much as the printed word) that had heightened the interest of Georgian commentators, as well as that of much of their public, in the principles underlying the operations of sound judgment.[84]

In particular, the origins and application of our notions of taste, together with the explanation of troubling phenomena like the wildly divergent preferences exhibited by different people in different circumstances, held a growing fascination. As Pope had memorably framed the central problem in the *Essay on Criticism*:

'Tis with our judgments as our watches, none
Go just alike, yet each believes his own.[85]

Yet these eternal quandaries were accompanied by more pointed questions arising specifically out of the contemporary perception of quickening social change and increasingly daring cultural experimentation: Could the tastes of the widening circle of Georgian readers be kept within the bounds of decency and decorum? In what ways (if at all) did true taste differ from the mere *ex post facto* rationalisation of the majority fashion? And did the growing number of works that flagrantly subverted established aesthetic or intellectual norms—the novel being, as we have seen, only the most offensive case in point—constitute as grave a threat to public morality as they did to public taste?

It is, of course, salient to any consideration of the approaches to Scottish authorship taken by contemporary readers that a disproportionate contribution to these debates was actually made by Scots writers themselves. Indeed, as Engell has pointed out, the latter might reasonably be categorised as 'prior to the twentieth century, the most important and cohesive group of critics in English.'[86] This proposition is lent credence by the fact that, of the seven key aesthetic theorists singled out in Patrick Parrinder's recent study of early anglophone criticism—Addison and Burke, together with Francis Hutcheson, David Hume, Lord Kames, Alexander Gerard and Archibald Alison—all but two were Scots either by birth or by heritage.[87] Hume's efforts, notably in the essay "On the Standards of Taste" (1757), were, as usual, particularly significant and have stood the test of time. Kames's interventions, however, may have been more seminal at the time. Revd Gambier in Kent, for example, was among many moved by Kames's reflections on such intractable questions as the nature of beauty and the role of the emotions in aesthetic judgment, carefully transcribing them for future contemplation.[88] In fact, in a move broadly characteristic of the Scots' contemporary contributions across several disciplines, Kames's *Elements of Criticism* (1762) had located taste firmly in a sociological and psychological context, showing that a capacity for discriminating analysis in the cultural sphere was not only the mark of the polite individual but also, when displayed by sufficient numbers, the prerequisite for a truly civilised society.[89]

In accounting for this potent Scottish addition to the sum of British critical theorising one would certainly need to acknowledge the distinctive intellectual environment of post-Union Scotland, itself the product in part of a timely transfusion of recognisably English idioms for the discussion of culture. Most importantly, it is obvious that Shaftesbury's claims about the connection between culture and morality, especially as propagandised through Addison's journalism, had acquired early and lasting currency throughout Great Britain.[90] Thus the Scottish theorists' basic assumptions and preferred vocabularies were already shared very widely among those English readers who encountered their writings. Moreover, Scots professors had also been among the first to develop the new thinking into a formal philosophy—notably Hutcheson in the 1720s and both Thomas Blackwell and George Turnbull before 1740. This in turn was why most of the best-regarded Scottish thinkers from the 1750s onwards, Kames included, tended to echo Shaftesbury's trademark argument, by now standard in all philosophical conversations about politeness, that the refinement and appreciation of the arts would help ameliorate the human condition.

This optimistic cultural theory not only provided crucial ideological impetus for the Scottish Enlightenment itself. It also ensured that the words and ideas of Scots thinkers would generally receive an appreciative hearing from English readers—from individuals like William Bulwer, for example, a Norfolk gentleman who noted down Shaftesbury's familiar teachings alongside those of his Glasgow disciple Francis Hutcheson.[91] The pioneering development of literary criticism as an academic subject was another consequence of the enduring Scottish interest in the operations of taste that had arisen to such startling effect early in the century. Smith, as is now well known, paved the way with a public lecture course offered in Edinburgh in the late 1740s.[92] It was, however, a bevy of Scots professors—Robert Watson and his successor William Barron at St Andrews, George Campbell and Gerard in Aberdeen and, above all, Blair at Edinburgh—who brought about the successful transformation of the rhetoric component in the arts curriculum into the definitive model for anglophone critical education.[93]

This important new discipline necessarily had implications far beyond Scotland's classrooms, and particularly for those English readers who from the 1760s onwards were exposed to its characteristic doctrines in published form. Ministering to the cultural anxieties of literate people everywhere in an age of increasing publication and expanding readership, academic criticism in its distinctive Scottish manifestation soon acquired a reputation not only for philosophical rigour but also for considerable practical utility. As one reviewer insisted in the *Critical Review* in 1776, in the first of three essays devoted to Campbell's newly issued *Philosophy of Rhetoric*, 'Of all the efforts of philosophical investigation, those seem not only the most arduous, but the most useful likewise, which are intended to elucidate the nature and principles of eloquence.'[94] Blair's *Lectures on Rhetoric and Belles Lettres* (1783), though, soon attained—and has always retained—even greater prestige. One early indication of its pre-eminence was that excerpts, appropriately dealing with the problem of taste, were reprinted in that year's *Annual Register*.[95] A writer in the *Gentleman's Magazine*, rightly acknowledging the widespread approval of Blair's work among his fellow critics, was also able to claim that 'The reputation of this author is much too high for our voice to be able to swell the general applause.'[96]

More tellingly still, Blair's *Lectures* became in due course another standard reference point about reading among the literate public. Gustavus Gale, for example, the Carlisle textile merchant, positively purred to himself when noting down in 1794 'a beautiful observation of Mr Blair's, that "whatever enables the genius to execute well, will enable taste to criticise justly".'[97] James Smith in Norwich, father and namesake of the famous nineteenth-century botanist and an avid student both of his own books and of those borrowed from local libraries, esteemed the *Lectures*, from which he learned much about reading, as 'exceedg good & entertaining.'[98] There may even be a fleeting image of another individual unable to resist lingering over-long on this most instructive of critical works preserved in the minutes of the Bury Library in Lancashire. Here, following the failure of a subscriber to return it, it was agreed in 1833 to write 'to Miss May of Wrigley Brook in the name of the Committee for Blair's Belles Lettres.'[99] With readers like Miss May still immersed in it fully fifty years after its first appearance, it can be no surprise that Blair's philosophical criticism had come to be seen as a foundation of serious literary studies throughout the wider English-speaking and European worlds.

* * *

Academic criticism and literary theory had apparently emerged by the early nineteenth century as prevalent influences over readers' understanding of books and their consumption. An even more overtly didactic form of discourse, however, informed by these same scholarly developments but directly addressed to the practical problem of needing to select and read appropriate texts, was also making its influence felt. The Irish clergyman Edward Mangin's *Essays on the Sources of Pleasure Received from Literary Compositions* (1813) was in many ways typical.[100] In particular, Mangin insisted that 'Our natural relish or taste . . . is susceptible of far greater improvement than may at first be supposed.' Moreover, in order to buttress this key argument, his text was larded with quotations from Scotland's theoreticians—Gerard on the sublime, for example, and Kames on 'the emotion of grandeur.'[101] The clinching evidence, however, came from Blair. Indeed, the Edinburgh professor's views about that most important quality of great literature, the sublime, seemed definitive. The *Lectures on Rhetoric and Belles Lettres* had offered 'the most plausible theory' yet to emerge: 'the theory suggested by Dr Blair,' he added, 'affords a clearer explanation and a fuller view of the subject, than any other with which I am acquainted.'[102]

Mangin's approach to popularising the study of literature as an educational practice was indebted to Scottish influences in other ways too. He praised that more recent Scots theorist, Archibald Alison, for his 'very ingenious Essays on Taste,' another work combining the exploration of aesthetic judgment with philosophical insights into the operations of the human mind.[103] Mangin's illustrative excerpts were also strongly reliant upon Scottish work, ranging from George Buchanan among the Renaissance poets to Thomson among the Hanoverians.[104] In fact, given Mangin's own enthusiasms as an unabashed proponent of Romanticism, it should not be entirely surprising that he made particular use of *The Seasons*: 'There is scarcely any person, who, in reading Thomson's Seasons,' he declared, unconsciously echoing Johnson's seminal judgment in the *Lives*, 'will not find several beauties in external nature pointed out to him, which he may perfectly recollect to have seen, though not to have attended to before; but which, now that his attention is turned to them, he feels to be productive of the most delightful emotions.'[105]

Mangin, however, was far from alone in adopting an avowedly accessible yet also unmistakably prescriptive approach to the art of reading. Rather his work stood firmly within a tradition of explicit didacticism, often directed to the edification of particular types of reader, that included tracts like the poet and essayist Hester Chapone's *Letters on the Improvement of the Mind* (1773), a work much reprinted and widely consulted by women interested in their own or their daughters' reading habits, and which was positively adamant that, because of emerging recognition of a textual canon, there needed to be 'standard books in every female library.'[106] The novelist Maria Edgeworth's *Letters for Literary Ladies* (1795), Thomas Broadhurst's *Advice to Young Ladies on the Improvement of the Mind, and the Conduct of Life* (1810) and A.S. Hunter's *Miscellanies, Designed Chiefly for the Benefit of Female Readers* (1810) were just a few among many other works that provided similar advice directed at the needs of this increasingly important and influential group of readers.

In the light of the crucial importance of reading in the formation of good character and sound judgment, however, literate men were certainly not abandoned to their fates. Indeed, the Dissenting physician John Aikin's *Letters from a Father to his Son on Various Topics Relative to Literature and the Conduct of Life* (1796) might be regarded as the masculine counterpart to the Scottish professor John Gregory's instructive classic *A Father's Legacy to his Daughter* (1774): 'At the head of all the pleasures which offer themselves to the man of liberal education,' Aikin declared, 'may confidently be placed that derived from books.'[107] Revealingly, Aikin also insisted that an important part of an individual's proficiency as a reader would be not just an improved sensibility and a greater appreciation of the principles of taste. The practiced reader would also become, as it were, a critic himself: 'Criticism,' claimed Aikin, in a sweeping generalisation that might equally have been uttered by any of the age's most ambitious periodical commentators, 'is one of the most agreeable and certainly not the least dignified employments of the mental faculties; and few topics are better adapted either to closet amusement, or to liberal and cultured conversation.'[108]

As well as books on reading that stressed its pivotal role in the cultivation of politeness in both sexes, the increasing urge to try to guide the activities of the literate also resulted in the production of manuals offering guidance specifically in the difficult task of choosing suitable texts. An excellent early example was the work of John Whiston, a London bookseller, whose anonymous *Directions for a Proper Choice of Authors to Form a Library* (1766) reflects many of the characteristic preoccupations of his trade—including the delineation of a canon upon which those who aspired to politeness were advised to concentrate their reading.[109] As Whiston put it, it was clear that there was a need for 'some directions in the choice of proper Authors, on the several subjects which would improve the understanding and correct the judgment, as well as please the imagination at the same time.'[110] Once again, moreover, an important by-product was the seamless incorporation within an emerging British canon of prominent works from Scottish pens.

Historical reading—'the most pleasing and useful study' according to Whiston—was one of the cornerstones of this putative canon.[111] Hume's *History*, for example, was 'an ingenious work,' notwithstanding 'his visible disesteem for religion, and his carelessness in some facts [which] make it not so valuable a work, as so capable an Author might have rendered it.'[112] Smollett's *History*, too, was useful, though not unproblematic: it had 'a lively style, his characters strongly painted,' Whiston cautioned, but 'his unhappy bias is too evident.'[113] Gilbert Burnet's *History of the Reformation*, although dating from the late seventeenth century, was still 'a most valuable work,' the lasting achievement of 'An author, I think, that will be more esteemed, as he is more read.'[114] As to poetry, *The Seasons* was predictably viewed as a staple, although, with a strong hint that his own readers' cultural identity as Britons was what lay behind his thinking about the wider implications of the emerging canon, Whiston suggested that there were actually 'so many valuable ones of our nation, that it would take up too much room to name them all.'[115]

Whiston was not alone in pushing the logic of canonicity to what, in the eyes of a profit-hungry bookseller, must also have appeared its potentially lucrative limits.[116] A number of other contemporary writers also attempted to offer specific guidance on the selection of supposedly 'proper' texts. In *The Oeconomist*, a Newcastle-based periodical with a wider national circulation, one contributor tried precisely this in 1799, in a volume that also contained, appropriately for the cause of canonicity, a series of extracts on the suppression of the French Templars under Philip the Fair, on Judge Jeffreys, on Richard I, on Admiral Blake and on jealousy, all taken from Hume's *History*, that definitive yet difficult modern classic.[117] Named only 'W.D.,' this bold canoniser promulgated a model inventory of the texts that a newly founded library or book club ought to acquire, as well as a separate but clearly related list aimed at private individuals and headed simply "On a Plan of Reading." The now-standard works of critical instruction, like Blair's *Lectures* and Kames's *Elements*, were essential items for any library. But a broader canon of British literature was also outlined for a lending collection that included such recent Scottish additions as the poetry of Thomson, Robertson's *Charles V*, Robert Henry's *History of Great Britain* (1771–93), Smollett's *Roderick Random* (1748), Colin Maclaurin's *A Treatise of Algebra* (1748) and the *Encyclopaedia Britannica*.[118] For personal consumption W.D. recommended a list of similarly definitive titles that now included *The Wealth of Nations* and Gilbert Stuart's *View of Society in Europe* (1778).[119]

Although issued rather late in the period, *The English Gentleman's Library Manual* (1827), written by the linguist and biblical scholar William Goodhugh, might be regarded as an exceptionally mature and expansive manifestation of this same desire to foster in readers a highly developed sense of canonicity. Here, after all, the reader would discover, if he or she were somehow still completely ignorant—or find authoritative confirmation if already reasonably well-informed—that certain books were now such an integral part of Britain's national culture as to have become virtually compulsory. Blair's *Sermons*, for example, in a phrase actually recycled by Goodhugh from the *Life of Johnson*, were 'one of the most successful theological books that has ever appeared.'[120] *Charles V*, too, was notable for its 'excellencies'; Ferguson's *History of the Roman Republic* was 'written with elegance'; and Hume's *History*, according to a judgment attributed by Goodhugh to the foremost Cambridge literary scholar Richard Farmer, was the work of 'an admirable writer; his style bold, and his reflection shrewd and uncommon; but his religious and political notions have too often warped his judgment.'[121]

The effects of such magisterial pronouncements on what to read (and, at least as importantly, *why* and *how* to read) were, in every sense, impressive. After all, they were delivered to a readership that was already strongly predisposed to credit the advice of the critics and other recognised arbiters. This is illustrated not least by the readiness with which the literate applied for themselves the increasingly familiar assumptions of canonicity. When founding a lending collection, for example, the initial acquisitions, intended to provide a sound basis for future reading, often reflected the advice of figures like Whiston, 'W.D.' and Goodhugh. Thus at Penzance, the new library, established in 1818 by the town's Edinburgh-trained physician John (later Sir John) Forbes and the local landowner (and legendary cock-fighter) Sir Rose Price of Trengwainton, began by ordering fifteen books, which duly arrived, as was then the custom, by boat from London. A few reflected distinctive local concerns (including, for instance, William Borlase's Cornish history). But they largely show the members willingly embracing a series of canonical texts, such as Hume's *History*, Smollett's *History*, Henry's *History* and Ferguson's *Rome*, as well as Johnson's works.[122]

Such obsequiousness towards the canon was not remotely exceptional among well-informed readers. Elsewhere in Cornwall, in November 1792, one of the prime movers of the so-called County Library, James Leverton of Penryn, proposed a similar block purchase, this time—probably doffing his cap to the distinctly mercantile interests of many of his fellow members—with a pronounced commercial and practical bias. Again, however, this initial core to the collection also incorporated such near-compulsory items as Adam Smith's major works, together with the latest volumes of the *Monthly* and the *Critical* (two journals that, along with the *Monthly Miscellany*, had taken the lead in encouraging readers to see *The Wealth of Nations* as an exemplary addition to the canon).[123] Exactly the same concern with canonicity—the practical corollary among polite readers of the critics' constant harping upon the existence of an approved body of literature that needed careful study and proper assimilation—also guided the Wolverhampton Library in Staffordshire when it commenced its activities in 1794.

Because the founders at Wolverhampton actually adopted the very unusual custom of assigning catalogue numbers to books in order of their accession, the priority that this particular group of readers accorded to obtaining a select group of texts would remain plain for all to see even several decades later. In effect, this cataloguing convention preserved in aspic a series of early decisions, taken in a faraway provincial industrial town, of which self-appointed literary judges like Whiston and Farmer would heartily have approved. Hume's *History*, the subject of immense critical interest and unresolved argument—a work that 'requires only to be read to be admired' according to the *Town and Country*, but one that could not be regarded as 'giving an impartial representation of facts, or exhibiting characters in just and proper colours,' in the much less favourable opinion of the *Monthly*—was accessioned as No.1.[124] Robertson's *Charles V*, the masterpiece of a less critically contentious author whom the *Annual Register*, writing of another of his works, had hymned as possessing ' . . . a felicity of illustration, a pertinence of remark, and an acuteness of observation, which betray the pen of a master,' was entered as No. 4.[125] No clearer illustration could be imagined of the power of canonicity in shaping the decisions of individual readers.

*   *   *

Criticism, as we have seen, made many extravagant claims in the dynamic era bounded by the writings of Joseph Addison and William Goodhugh. It insisted that it could discriminate accurately between good and bad work; between the practically useful and the frankly useless; between the morally beneficial and the positively harmful. More widely, it sought—and was sometimes not slow to imply that it had already made important strides towards achieving—the triumph of taste among some (or even, according to the optimists, most) of the public at large. Certainly it affected the ways in which texts were approached and consumed. It shaped readers' underlying assumptions about the status and function of literature in general terms. It affected their expectations and then their subsequent judgments as they grappled with particular texts. Probably the most important result of the influence of criticism, however, was the construction of canonicity. This occurred partly at the hands of popular periodical journalism, which was clearly the great lodestar in the cultural firmament of a substantial swathe of literate society. But it was also achieved through an unholy alliance of scholarly critics, aesthetic philosophers, avaricious booksellers and practical educators who between them increasingly lectured and hectored a generally susceptible public on *what* as well as *whether* they ought to read.

Each of these influences had specific and often demonstrable implications for the literate population at large. Given that criticism in all its forms was never embarrassed about offering trenchant opinions on a case by case basis—alternately praising and blaming individual authors and their works—the consequences of its growing profile in English culture and thus of its tightening grip on readers' minds could scarcely be insignificant for their experiences with particular pieces of literature. It is especially important, moreover, that Scots like Hume, Thomson, Ferguson and Robertson, as we have repeatedly seen, received extensive coverage. Much of this was favourable, and therefore essentially promotional in effect. Some of it (notably in Hume's case) was less kind, though this did not necessarily render its subject any less interesting. Parts of it, of course, may not have been particularly welcome to those, such as the unrepentant lovers of the cheap fictional narrative, who found themselves targeted relentlessly by an immense barrage of critical artillery. All of it, however, redounded ultimately to the potential advantage of cultural producers competing in a crowded marketplace in which the greatest barriers to status and to worldly success seemed to be not low quality but rather a low profile leading almost inevitably to low sales. Criticism, as Shaftesbury had claimed, was meant 'to assert the READER's Privilege above the Author.'[126] Yet it was also to prove a crucial precondition for meaningful engagement by readers with the publications that were produced by the Scottish Enlightenment.

3 "For Learning and for Arms Renown'd"
Scotland in the Public Mind

Criticism reached out so successfully to a large and increasingly diverse reading public because, as we have already discovered, it was the most chameleon-like of discourses, capable of taking on a bewildering variety of characters and colourings—sometimes shrilly populist and sometimes soberly scholarly; frequently engagingly humorous though just as often doggedly earnest; on occasion almost insufferably pious but at other times nakedly and joyously self-interested; seemingly perfectly at ease when offering the reader explicit instruction head-on but equally comfortable when approaching the same objective stealthily and obliquely, as if content to proceed by a series of nods and winks. Always, however, criticism served recognisably similar purposes. For its aim, widely acknowledged by both its creators and its consumers, was to disseminate a proper understanding of taste, to promote the regular exercise of correct judgment by ordinary readers and so to pre-determine in many individual instances a particular kind of cultural experience. Such ambitions, needless to say, entailed nurturing a genuine enthusiasm for literature as a desirable product in an increasingly crowded marketplace. But they also involved an attempt to cultivate a profound reverence for reading as an activity in its own right—an enterprise that, as we have found, often went hand-in-hand with a decidedly prescriptive approach to the selection and consumption of individual texts.

Above all, this was why there emerged the idea of the reader being obliged to focus upon an identifiable national canon of authors and works. Increasingly the latter was understood to include not just the likes of Shakespeare, Milton and Pope but also writers of much more recent vintage, a goodly number of them Scots like Thomson, Hume and Smith. Yet other by-products of the growing authority that criticism enjoyed also need to be considered if we are properly to understand its impact in shaping the reactions of readers to specific bodies of literature. For so great was the contribution made by the periodicals in particular in articulating and disseminating value judgments about reading, and so important were these same ragingly popular vehicles to the education and entertainment of the literate, that large numbers of individuals, especially from the middle decades of the eighteenth century onwards, could scarcely avoid having their assumptions and expectations about Scotland in general, and about the nature of Scottish culture in the round, effectively modified in a number of significant ways.

* * *

It is clear that contemporaries were inundated with a veritable flood of printed material that in broad terms cannot have failed to heighten their awareness of Scotland—and of the Scots, moreover, as an integral part of the same *British* cultural community. The expansion of news coverage, at this time a heady cocktail of official announcements, salacious gossip, pithy anecdotes, shocking criminality and tartly expressed literary criticism, was crucial to this process. It created a sense of identity and commonality among an otherwise geographically dispersed population of anglophone readers effectively located anywhere that the same printed material was being consumed. An English browser of the *London Magazine* in 1767, for example, the same year that it trumpeted the first publication of Ferguson's *Essay*, would have noted many other items with an unambiguous Scottish dimension—such as the obituary of George Drummond, Edinburgh's Lord Provost; the story of a mob in the Scottish capital that had punished a landlord who had seized the goods of an absent tenant; much material on the sensational "Douglas Cause" (one of the age's great inheritance disputes, appealed from the Edinburgh Court of Session to the Lords at Westminster); and, for good measure, on a hoary Scottish subject that by the late 1760s, following the appearance of Robertson's *History of Scotland* (1759) and the controversial tracts by Walter Goodall (1754) and William Tytler (1759), was something of a journalistic as well as a scholarly staple throughout Britain, what the *London* described—somewhat delphically it has to be admitted—as 'letters, curious ones, relative to the death of Mary Queen of Scots.'[1]

1767, however, was not an exceptional year. And nor was the *London Magazine* a remotely unusual periodical. Indeed, twelve years earlier, amongst many other things in broadly similar vein, it had informed its readers of the death of Sir John Clerk of Penicuik, the great patron of the Scottish Enlightenment, and reported the discoveries made during tumuli excavations at St Fort in Fife.[2] In 1759, too, the *London*'s readers were exposed to extensive coverage of Robertson's 'lately published' Scottish history, as well as to an attempt further to stoke interest in two of this text's main protagonists by printing a "Translation of a letter from Mary Queen of Scots to Queen Elizabeth."[3] The *Western County Magazine* in 1790, meanwhile—prominent, as the name implies, in the region centred on Bristol—printed an old anecdote about Hume's friendship with Lady Wallace, in addition to new stories on the Scots law treatment of pardoned felons and on a particularly unpleasant sexual assault in Paisley.[4] Two years later the same journal's innumerable readers would have heard of the spread of the Cheviot sheep in northern Scotland (a presage of the Clearances to come), as well as an appreciation of Beattie's poetry.[5] The *St James's Chronicle*, an even more widely read London newspaper, also acted—and, more importantly, encouraged its army of readers to act—as though Scottish events were of natural interest and concern. In 1767 alone, for example, it reported on an earthquake in Stirlingshire in its 28–30 April edition, and the manufacture in Pittenweem of a bespoke carpet for the dowager Princess of Wales in its 26–28 March edition. On 7–9 April it carried a breathless account of the £100,000 worth of goods supposedly smuggled annually into Scotland—including, apparently, tea, china and rhubarb.[6]

The *St James's* was actually one of the booksellers' favourite vehicles for disseminating literary news from the metropolis to the provinces. Accordingly its crammed columns in 1767 also included advertisements for some significant new Scottish works from the capital's presses, all of them thereby being brought to the attention of its own extensive readership, including Sir James Steuart's *Principles of Political Economy*, Henry's *History of Great Britain*, and the sixth edition of Hume's *History of England*.[7] To any of its large number of regular subscribers, therefore, like John Smith, a grain farmer from Admington in Gloucestershire, who made frequent reference to it in his journal, or Mary Madan, wife of the Bishop of Peterborough and sister-in-law of the eighteenth century's most notorious proponent of polygamy, who included many scraps from it in her notebook (including *inter alia* material from Beattie's *The Minstrel*, verses from the Edinburgh poet John Logan's "The Braes of Yarrow," and a song of Mary, Queen of Scots), the *St James's* supplied a wealth of useful information about Scotland in general and about its rich literary culture and traditions of authorship in particular.[8]

It follows, of course, that readers' initial knowledge of Scottish texts must often have been acquired in immediate proximity to a stream of much more diffuse information and anecdote about many aspects of their country of origin. This was probably how, for example, John Arden, a late eighteenth-century Cheshire gentleman who was a keen reader of the *London Chronicle*, came to transcribe the inscription from a gravestone located in Greyfriars' Churchyard in Edinburgh.[9] It may also be the reason why, in the Yale copy of Macpherson's *Fragments of Ancient Poetry* once owned by the Warwickshire poet William Shenstone, there survives a handwritten 'Epitaph In the Parish Church of Glenoxhay in North Brittain.'[10] From the 1740s onwards there was a continuous flow of such ephemeral—and, it must be confessed, preponderantly banal—material in the periodical literature that readers habitually devoured. Its cumulative impact can only have been to render the great mass of English people who were exposed to it familiar not only with Scottish culture but also with other aspects of Scottish geography, Scottish history and Scottish life. No wonder that in 1791 the *Monthly Review* could remark in passing that Scotland's past 'has been frequently considered by many able and learned gentlemen, and is sufficiently well known to most readers. . . .'[11]

By no means all of the press coverage, however, amounted merely to useful background information that gradually filled out readers' impressions about Scotland and its people. Frequently, and increasingly so as the eighteenth century progressed, the reader was also subjected to commentary that sought quite deliberately to shape his or her own attitudes towards Scottish literary culture in particular. Indeed, the factual announcements of new and impending publications, repeatedly trailed through successive editions of the same journals so that the publishing booksellers could achieve maximum exposure, were only the tip of a very substantial iceberg. One piece in the *London Magazine* in 1767—and obviously considered suitable for that periodical's overwhelmingly English readership—indicates the way in which specific messages about Scotland's culture were increasingly becoming embedded in the journalistic coverage to which regular British readers were now almost continually subjected. A poem that had first been aired at the recent opening of Edinburgh's Theatre Royal, it gushed with pride in the achievements of Scottish writers.

As one particularly emphatic stanza runs, its unfeigned pleasure at Scotland's literary and military achievements almost palpable:

Scotland, for learning and for arms renown'd,
In ancient annals is with lustre found;
And still she shares whate'er the world can yield,
Of letter'd fame, or glory in the field.[12]

Few readers in the years after the publication of the last volume of Hume's best-selling *History* and not a decade after Scottish regiments had served with distinction in the Seven Years' War could have been entirely unaware that the Scots now enjoyed an impressive reputation not only for martial but also for intellectual prowess. But just in case Scotland's heightened prominence in British culture and in the British army were still a surprise, this same point was hammered home by the poem's simultaneous appearance in the *St James's Chronicle*.[13] An anecdote printed elsewhere in the *London* in 1767 equally served to reiterate the same message, that admiration for Scottish culture, and the superiority of Scotland's learning and letters, was emerging as an accepted commonplace that readers were encouraged to acknowledge. It was remarkable, the piece observed with just a touch of smugness, that the 'Scotch, who travelled, were men of parts and learning, while the English were generally wanting in both.'[14]

*   *   *

The all-pervasive periodical press, with its pronounced emphasis upon material of largely transitory interest, was not the only tool with which readers' assumptions about Scotland were being actively reconstructed. Far more substantial works could also act in much the same way, providing contextual information about Scottish conditions in general at the same time as raising specific expectations that would tend to inform readers' responses when encountering Scottish texts. Something like this seems to have been achieved by the travel literature that burgeoned from the 1760s onwards—much of it, not coincidentally, devoted to Scotland itself.[15] It is true, of course, that these narratives were didactic in a rather more subtle way than the explicitly instructive treatises of Johnson, Blair and Alison. Nor did they seek to proffer the narrowly practical advice on reading that was available from authors like Whiston, Mangin. Their impact on readers' broader perceptions about Scottish culture, however, was always potentially at least as great, precisely because accounts of travel and exploration, in a century that saw successive triumphs for writers as different as Defoe, Anson and Cook, were now so widely respected.[16]

Thomas Pennant's *A Tour in Scotland*, first published in 1771, and his description of a second tour, the *Voyage to the Hebrides*, which followed in 1774, were two of the greatest contributions to the increasing centrality that such literature enjoyed in the minds of contemporary readers. They were also, however, an early indication of just how effectively travel literature might serve to erode ingrained English ignorance of Scotland and its distinctive culture. Indeed, Pennant himself later admitted that he had written the *Tour* specifically with this purpose in mind. As he put it with slightly misleading candour, he had wished in so writing 'to conciliate the affections of the two nations, so wickedly and studiously set at variance by evil-designing people.'[17]

Pennant delighted his readers with impressive reports of the 'thirty thousand volumes' in the Advocates' Library in Edinburgh; with sympathetic descriptions of the talents of the Scottish universities' alumni and current professors; and with explicit confirmation of the recent transformation of Scotland's clergy from inward-looking bigots to upstanding models of politeness and intellectual endeavour—'the most decent and consistent in their conduct of any set of men I ever met with of their order . . . at present much changed from the furious, illiterate, and enthusiastic teachers of old times.'[18] Pennant's purchase on the reading public's assumptions about Scotland, moreover, was reinforced by overwhelming critical approval. As the *Monthly Review* reckoned of the 1774 publication (in words that, in an act of casual piracy typical of the periodicals, were duly reprinted in the *Monthly Miscellany*), 'The numerous scenes which this ingenious traveller and voyager has visited in this excursion, are described in a faithful and entertaining manner, and cannot fail of affording pleasure to every reader of taste.'[19] So great was Pennant's authority that the *Critical* also offered no fewer than eight sizeable extracts from the second volume, promising (and again conjuring up a pleasing mutuality of response with the critic) that 'there is no doubt of receiving the same degree of pleasure experienced on two former occasions, when we traced the progress of this agreeable traveller through the interesting narrative of both his journeys.'[20]

This tendency to conceptualise Pennant's texts as a series of opportunities for readers to share vicariously in his fascination with the remarkable cultural conditions prevailing in Scotland helped in turn to structure the responses of many of those individuals who read them for themselves. Felicia Hemans, for example, herself a poet and friend of Scott and Wordsworth, was especially struck by Pennant's evocative descriptions of Scottish scenes, eagerly taking down one of them in her journal: 'The constant petition at grace of the old Highland Chieftains,' she wrote, her feelings clearly aroused by the atmospheric narration in the text, 'was delivered with great fervour, in these words—"Lord, turn the world upside down, that Christians may make bread out of it".'[21] As was so often the case, however, it was usually the episodes that spoke most directly to their own concerns that immediately attracted readers' attention as they scoured Pennant's Scottish narratives for memorable material.

Thus it was an account of religious life in the manufacturing districts of northern England in the *Voyage to the Hebrides* that was copied out by Revd James Franks at Halifax.[22] For John Bowle in rural Wiltshire, however, it was a description of funerals in Highland villages that particularly fired the sensitive clerical imagination.[23] So intriguing and so compelling were some of Pennant's observations on the peculiarities of Scottish culture that his writings on the subject seem occasionally to have acquired a special status. The proprietors of the newly established Portico Library in Manchester, for example, included Pennant's Scottish narratives in 1810 among a select group of titles that were explicitly 'not to circulate'—in other words, as works attracting unusually heavy usage and therefore reserved for in-house consultation.[24] Similar precautions would probably have been wise at Bradford. Here the library discovered in October 1814 that its dog-eared copy of Pennant's *Tour* needed urgently to be 'rebound or repaired'—another likely indication of its popularity with borrowers over many years.[25]

Useful information about Scotland and its idiosyncratic culture also seems to have been discerned by readers when they encountered the complementary publications of Johnson and Boswell, the sweet fruits of their own journey to the Western Isles in the late summer and autumn of 1773 which had itself been provoked by the great interest stirred up by Pennant's revelatory first volume. Johnson's *A Journey to the Western Islands of Scotland* (1775), taken together with his companion's *The Journal of a Tour to the Hebrides* (1785), mirrored Pennant's in their deep and lasting impact on the public's overall impression of Scotland, and particularly of its place within wider British culture. For despite the acrimony that ensued following its publication, most English eyes will not have detected in the *Journey* anything like that ungracious hostility towards his hosts which some Scots claimed to have detected. As Boswell later insisted, Johnson's true intentions, which were far more favourable to Scotland than his many Caledonian critics had acknowledged, had been 'misapprehended, even to rancour, by many of our countrymen.'[26]

Like the scholarly and inquisitive Pennant before him, Johnson was singularly well qualified to appreciate the significance of the Scots' cultural accomplishments. He reassured those English people who by the late 1770s might have been beginning to feel slightly embarrassed by their continuing ignorance on this subject: 'Scotland,' he observed, 'is little known to the greater part of those who may read these observations.'[27] He clearly sought, however, to offer an accurate and informative narrative that would convey something of the sheer wonder and sense of genuine exploration that he and Boswell had themselves experienced. As a result, the *Journey* acquired many splendid set pieces that sketch a scene or describe an event in memorable terms. Passages of this kind captured such discoveries for the two travellers—and so by extension for their mainly English readers—as the remarkable treasures in the library of Marischal College and the venerable academic traditions of the scholars and students of St Andrews and Aberdeen.[28] It is telling, perhaps, that Johnson ultimately avoided much account of Edinburgh itself. But apparently this was only because, for a growing number of readers by this time, it was actually now becoming, as he said, 'a city too well known to admit description.'[29]

The *Journey* was demonstrably a literary triumph in the most important of senses, stirring up a considerable amount of cross-border controversy and, naturally, selling very well into the bargain. It also, though, succeeded in another way. For it clearly affected its readers' perceptions of Scotland in significant respects, at once expanding their knowledge of the country and further stimulating their curiosity about its inhabitants and their peculiarities. When Revd Bowle read it, for example, he obviously thought it obligatory to transcribe a number of sections for his own future consideration. These included Johnson's intriguing observations on Hebridean funerals (expertly cross-referenced by Bowle to Pennant's remarks on the same subject) and on Scottish traditions of kingship.[30]

Boswell's *Journal* was even wider in its compass. It was also at least as influential in developing readers' understanding of his native country. In one sense a rose-tinted remembrance of things past, the *Journal* was for various reasons published only after Johnson's death. But what makes it particularly interesting for our own purposes is that it incorporated an extensive account of the part of the journey that Johnson had purposely downplayed: the pair's two substantial sojourns in Enlightenment Edinburgh. Nicely complementing his friend's greater emphasis on their travels beyond the Forth, Boswell in fact gave special attention to their occasionally prickly encounters with leading representatives of the Scottish intelligentsia—especially those whom his normally grudging companion had saluted as 'men of learning.'[31] Meetings with Lords Hailes and Monboddo, with Ferguson and Principal Robertson (who, extraordinarily, had conducted Johnson around Edinburgh whilst declaiming pertinent passages from his own *History of Scotland*), were recalled with entertaining candour though perhaps also with misleading precision. So too were the lively debates that had occurred between these giants of Anglo-Scottish literary culture on the merits of Beattie's poetry and the authenticity of "Ossian."[32]

Boswell's pride in Scotland and in its cultural achievements, however, clearly came across unmistakably to his many readers. One of them was John Dickenson, a Manchester merchant with houses at Rusholme and in London. In this case it was the *Journal*'s anecdote of William Robertson's letter being read to Edmund Burke (the historian having suggested that Johnson's remarks on the Scots were poured down 'like excellent oil, and break not the head,' the Irishman responding that the comments were rather like 'Oil of vitriol!') that earned pride of place in the early pages of Dickenson's own memorandum book.[33] Another reader, anonymous but clearly also present in London at the turn of the nineteenth century, went further. He too made transcriptions from the *Journal* at the very beginning of his notebook. But he also bothered to add his own tabulation of the 'Rout taken by Johnson and Boswell in their Tour to the Hebrides,' beginning with 'Edinburgh to Leith' and ending at Mauchlin and Auchinleck.[34] Neither of these creative responses to an encounter with Boswell's compelling account of Scotland, actively appropriating parts of it for their own private reconsideration, seems to have been especially out of line with how others probably approached it. After all, we might recall that it was once again the *Journal*, along with Cowper's poetry and the *Life of Johnson*, which apparently provided the focus of intense discussion and debate between the young Jane Austen and her bookish father.[35] In short, the Scottish tour of 1773, because of the remarkable textual immortalising that it soon received, would turn out to have ramifications for large numbers of readers who had never visited the country for themselves and who had never met either of its principals.

So popular and so influential was Scottish-related travel literature of this kind apparently becoming that the *Critical Review*, in discussing Edward Topham's *Letters From Edinburgh* in 1776, no longer thought it unreasonable to suggest (the phraseology again implying awareness of an overwhelmingly English audience) that, at least as far as Scotland was concerned, 'it might be presumed that any further account of that country could not much engage the attention of the public, at least for some time.'[36] The previous year's *Monthly Miscellany* had even joked that, given readers' seemingly boundless hunger for narratives on this particular subject, excursions north of the Border were in danger of becoming a compulsory experience for all properly educated Britons: 'Scotland seems to be daily so much increasing in consideration with her sister-kingdom,' it mocked, when reviewing Johnson's *Journey*, 'that tours to the Highlands, and voyages to the isles, will possibly become the fashionable "routes" of our virtuosi, and those who travel for mere amusement.'[37]

As we shall later see, this was not very far wide of the mark. Many English travellers would indeed wish to visit Scotland for themselves, and would do so with an understandable determination to see it as if through the eyes of the leading travel-writers whose works they had already acquired, read, enjoyed and internalised. As with the rise of literary criticism, so also with the popularity of travel literature, it was perhaps inevitable that the satirists, always alive to the emergence of another high-profile target, would seek to enter the lists. Fittingly, the most successful product of this realisation was itself the work of a Scottish pen—Smollett's own much-loved final masterpiece *Humphry Clinker*, an epistolary narrative replete with cleverly contrived opportunities for further instructing the reader about the unusual culture and society obtaining in this particular corner of the recently-united island of Great Britain.

The glib claim that Enlightenment Edinburgh was 'a hotbed of genius,' supposedly descriptive of the city during this golden age of cultural achievement, has subsequently been anthologised out of all context. Smollett's wider narrative, however, had a more immediate function for its original, and very largely English, audience. For it achieved, as Leith Davis has recently argued, the 'simultaneous representation and imaginative integration of political difference in the cultural realm.'[38] In other words, *Clinker* helped draw the sympathetic attention of Smollett's contemporary readers to precisely those post-Union developments—the universities' unvarying excellence, the remarkable cerebral power of the Scots lawyers, the unprecedented moderation and unparalleled learning of the established clergy— that were acknowledged by real visitors like Pennant and his disciples.[39] All of this, indeed, seemed conclusive proof not only of Scotland's new cultural eminence but also of its vital contribution to Britain's burgeoning sense of its own cultural supremacy. As a writer in the *Annual Register* remarked in 1791, clearly irritated by the fact that not everyone yet accepted the arguments of Smollett and other well-informed and fair-minded authors, 'The people of Scotland are confessedly not so far advanced in all the arts which tend to promote the comforts and luxuries of life as their wealthier neighbours of England, but are certainly much more in a state of civilization than some partial writers, biased by the littleness of national prejudice, wish us to conceive.'[40]

Clinker's mixture of good humour and judicious instruction was, needless to say, an instant hit in England. Indeed, its publication was even accorded special critical privileges, at least if we are to believe the claims of certain commentators. The response of the *Town and Country Magazine* was representative of the sympathetic coverage that it received from the major arbiters (encouraged no doubt by the knowledge that its author, Grub Street hack as well as Scottish man of letters, was very much one of their own):

> We seldom make Extracts from printed Books, as our Intention is to furnish our Readers with original Matter, a Plan never before attempted; but the singular merit of Humphry Clinker (by the Author of Roderick Random) has made us so far deviate from our general Plan

as to present our Readers with the following satirical Descriptions of London and Bath, which we doubt not will to them be agreeable and entertaining.'[41]

The *Critical Review*, which Smollett had formerly edited, had similar thoughts, its observer confessing (whilst again hinting that its own readers already possessed sufficient critical acumen to arrive independently at the same conclusion) that '[W]e should have indulged ourselves in extracting more copiously from it, were we not certain that the original must come into the hands of all such as are readers of taste, by whom we may venture to affirm it will be ranked among the most entertaining performances of the kind . . .'[42] Assisted by such aggressive ramping and back-slapping, it is not difficult to imagine how Smollett's satire—the most engaging and amusing of narratives even on its own terms—can only further have encouraged his immense public to approach Scotland and its contemporary culture, rendered at once endearingly familiar and enticingly different, with the very highest of expectations.

※   ※   ※

Critics and other cultural commentators were responsible for most of the frames of reference within which contemporary readers perceived those products of Scotland's intellectual life that they personally encountered. It would obviously be wrong, however, to ignore those individuals who in the most immediate sense actually made the public's reading experiences possible in the first place. For it was the bookseller—as the publisher as well as the retailer of books was at this time invariably known—whose business depended upon the successful placing of certain texts with significant numbers of consumers. Everywhere the imperatives of this trade were the same. Above all, there was a pressing need for these latter-day patrons of literature to achieve two closely related objectives. One, inevitably, was to bring the texts with which they were commercially concerned to the attention of the reading public—mainly through advertising and promotional activities of one kind or another. The second, of course, was to have some of them actually *buy* those books.

As we have already noticed, the periodical press made a conspicuous contribution to the achievement of both of these aims. Indeed, it was this, more than anything else, which facilitated the eighteenth-century expansion in the sheer quantity of information not only about literature but also about its creators and its producers. Many popular outlets, like the *Gentleman's*, the *London* and the reviews, listed the latest publications, a service to potential customers that, as we have found, readers like Revd Snowdon at Ponteland and Dr Flinders in rural Lincolnshire greatly appreciated. Excerpts and extracts, of the kind carried by both the *Gentleman's* and the *Annual Register*, served similar purposes. In effect, they offered tempting foretastes of what was purchasable in its entirety (though, as the *Monthly Ledger* did in 1774 when reprinting that part of 'Dr Robertson's celebrated History of Scotland' which summarised John Knox's life and works, it might be claimed, highly implausibly, that this was not a cunning marketing ploy but rather a charitable aid to 'such as may not have many books').[43]

More explicit forms of marketing, where direct attempts were made to manipulate the decision-making of individual readers, were also devised. Most importantly, newspapers began routinely to carry advertisements from London's (and, increasingly, from Edinburgh's and other provincial centres') publishers.[44] Indeed, the booksellers themselves, not only in London but also in the provinces, frequently had interests in the production of newspapers, another feature of the printing trade at this time which allowed powerful creative synergies to operate between different parts of the same businesses. That newspapers should go out of their way to try to sell particular books and authors to their own readers, as well as providing information about the literary world in general, was therefore as automatic as night following day.

Anyone regularly perusing the *London Chronicle* in 1759, for example, would have heard expeditiously first of the appearance and then of the early successes of Robertson's *Scotland* (though they may or may not also have known that a proprietor of the *Chronicle* was none other than William Strahan, that book's publisher).[45] Robertson's work was initially advertised in the edition for 16–18 January, along with Smollett's *History of England* (which had actually been in print for some time). Its availability was also strenuously talked up in the edition for 24–27 February, in this case with the additional feature of a quite shameless disclaimer about any pretensions to influencing the reader's own response:

> Sensible of the impropriety of attempting to anticipate the determination of the reader on the merits of a work of this nature, we shall only observe that the writer appears to us to be possessed of just discernment, sound judgment, and a good heart; and that his language is clear, nervous, correct, and unaffected.

By the edition of 3–5 April, the *Chronicle* was even to be found broadcasting advance news of a decision to produce a second edition of Robertson's work (which duly appeared that same year, with a third, once again cashing in on the success of this sophisticated marketing and merchandising strategy, swiftly following in 1760).

This kind of rolling coverage of a book's appearance and availability (and invariably, given the stark commercial imperatives, unembarrassed repeat announcements of the same news over succeeding weeks and months) was a ready means by which the publisher could hope to reach the greatest possible number of potential customers. Yet other expedients were available too. Some booksellers printed advertisements for other works within the books they had themselves produced. Thus the reader of the first edition of George Fordyce's *Elements of the Practice of Physic* (1770) would have discovered facing the end-paper an advertisement for John Hunter's soon-to-be-published *The History of the Human Teeth*, a production by the same metropolitan bookseller, Joseph Johnson, a well-known issuer of scientific and medical works by Scottish authors who worked from premises in St Paul's Churchyard.[46]

Individual traders across the country, especially where they actually held significant retail stock but were not themselves much involved in publishing books, were also able to issue their own catalogues. A good example comes from the bookshop run by Thomas Richardson and Harper Handford in the Market Place at Derby. In 1823, these men published a catalogue of what—again with one eye on the public's susceptibility to notions of canonicity—they called 'Standard Books on Sale.' In this case they included a rich stock of what were then still the popular texts of the day, among them Hume's *Essays and Treatises* and almost inevitably the *History*, and Beattie's *The Minstrel*, as well as key works on taste and reading like Johnson's *Lives* and Blair's *Lectures*.[47] Although not universal, this practice was by no means uncommon. Certainly Samuel Mountfort had employed it sixty years earlier at Worcester: indeed, this is the only reason why we know that his shop near the Guildhall in 1760 stocked a copy of a newly published text by a Glasgow professor, Smith's *Theory of Moral Sentiments* (1759).[48]

It is necessarily difficult to gauge the precise impact upon readers of such diverse sources of information, much of it clearly overtly promotional in intention. After all, except in very rare cases like Flinders and Snowden who actually recorded their own thought processes as book buyers, how can we ever be sure that marketing stimulated a particular purchase by an individual customer? There is much evidence, however, to suggest that lists of desirable books were increasingly being compiled by Georgian readers themselves—exactly the kind of response among potential customers that any self-respecting bookseller would have wished to encourage (as indeed had authors like Addison himself, who in *The Spectator* had even gone so far as to provide model reading lists for the typical polite female).[49]

We have already met Humphrey Senhouse, a well-heeled Cumberland book lover. It was he who around the turn of the nineteenth century drew up an inventory of those texts that he most wanted to read—including, it would appear, important Scottish works such as the ever-growing *Encyclopaedia Britannica* (first issued in numbers in 1768), Alison's *Essay on Taste* (1790) and the Edinburgh minister Robert Wallace's controversial demographic treatise, much argued over with Hume, the *Dissertation on the Numbers of Mankind* (1753).[50] His contemporary Isaac Stockton Clark of Whitby did exactly the same, compiling around 1810 a note of 'Books which I intend [to] purchase when capable': this was a very short tabulation, suggesting that Clark, whose occupation and personal details remain obscure, may have lacked Senhouse's means, though it did include that reliable Scottish staple for the determinedly pious, the writings of Beattie.[51] So, apparently, did John Scott of Bungay in Suffolk, a tanner's son and Cambridge undergraduate, who drew up a 'Rough list of books and plays' in 1807.[52] A member of the Beldam family in Hertfordshire employed the same device in December 1821. Here a household diary had added to it a column headed simply 'Books to buy when Convenient.' In due course this included the title (replete with tell-tale information on the booksellers responsible for its manufacture and sale) 'Medical Royal Society of Edinburgh [sic], Printed by Cadell & davies of D° 1805.'[53]

Behind each of these readers' personal lists clearly lay their relentless exposure to the literary gossip, booksellers' information and hard-edged critical comment customarily carried by the periodical press. Occasionally, however, it is possible to find even more direct evidence of marketing and promotional activities impacting on individual readers. Horace Walpole, for example, maintained a private collection of newspaper and periodical cuttings that confirm his avid interest in the latest publishers' announcements. To give just one example of how Walpole seems to have used them to keep track of literary developments, one clipping that he retained, evidently from the *Public Advertiser* of 18 March 1771, ran as follows: 'Speedily will be published. In one Volume Twelves, Price 2s. 6d. sewed, The Man of Feeling: A Novel Printed for T. Cadell in the Strand.'[54]

Presumably for similar reasons, an anonymous individual known only as E.D., who lived somewhere along the River Dove on the Staffordshire-Derbyshire border in mid-century, noted down the press announcements of a succession of major works, and particularly those puffed by the *Gentleman's Magazine*. There were several significant titles of Scottish provenance in E.D.'s compilation, including, for example, David Fordyce's *Elements of Moral Philosophy* in April 1754; the first volume of Hume's *History* that same November; and then Hutcheson's *System of Moral Philosophy* in April of the following year.[55] Other readers, too, seem to have found ways to hoard this vital information. Charles Curwen, who lived just outside Workington (and whose family provided a daughter for Wordsworth's son John), long retained among his papers an 1805 advertisement from James Wallis, the London bookseller, publicising, amongst other things, the availability of an illustrated edition of Hume and Smollett's histories as well as three new editions of *The Seasons*.[56] Another reader in the 1750s preserved a printed leaflet itemising the literary wares available for purchase from Miss Ward, a bookseller at Ashby-de-la-Zouche in Leicestershire: these included, predictably enough, those key opinion-forming critical vehicles, the *London Magazine* and the *Monthly Review*.[57]

An important distinction in the *modus operandi* of different kinds of English bookseller, especially those located in the smaller provincial towns, may also help us better to understand what individuals like Charles Curwen and E.D. were doing in thus envisaging their own future reading. The first, of course, was noting down what was being advertised by a metropolitan bookseller; the second, by contrast, was compiling a list of works mentioned in his own periodical of choice. Both, however, were clearly trying to provide themselves, as was Revd Snowdon at Ponteland when compiling his diary entries, with an *aide memoire* in circumstances in which their own physical access to books for sale was disappointingly limited. For we should remember that a sizeable body of texts might only be inspected first-hand in a minority of bookshops. James Lackington's Temple of the Muses in Finsbury Square, in the early 1790s the largest outlet in England, was utterly exceptional in the retail experience it provided.[58] As a result, the keeping of lists, based on advertisements and announcements and perhaps rounded out with further items spotted in lending libraries or in the homes of friends and neighbours, may have been an absolute necessity for most Georgian readers, whose purchases generally had to be ordered, usually sight-unseen, from a geographically distant supplier.

This was the situation that clearly faced the loyal customers of Abraham Dent, a general shopkeeper at Kirkby Stephen in Westmorland. Dent kept a number of used books, probably, like so many were, acquired at the auctions usually held on the death or insolvency of their existing owners. These, after all, were the means through which, right across eighteenth-century England, antiquated but still-valued texts were routinely recycled, often within a reasonably limited local area. In July 1762, for example, Dent was able to despatch a bundle of familiar older works, including Robert Ainsworth's *Dictionary* (1736) and James Hervey's *Meditations* (1746-7), both of which had been requested by his neighbour, Mr James Highmoor of Flitholme.[59] But Dent was also a bookseller in the practical sense that he undertook to order the newest publications for his customers, to whom, indeed, they might initially be provided on a credit rather than a cash basis. In other words, whilst Samuel Mountfort's clientele at Worcester may have been able to inspect a respectable range of contemporary literature on his premises, and perhaps to browse at least some of their chosen books before they actually purchased them, those who relied upon small-time booksellers like Abraham Dent were very largely dependent upon other methods for monitoring the latest literary developments. It was surely for this reason, if for no other, that many readers found it necessary to mimic the critics and the canonisers by compiling lists of what they wanted to read.

* * *

Attempts by individuals to list the titles that they wished to read can therefore be seen as the ultimate vindication of the book trade's endeavours in forming and fashioning the private behaviour of the reading public. For publishers, and the far greater number who were engaged in selling books for a living, were compelled to disseminate information about texts, and so to heighten interest in reading them, among the wider population. This was the *sine qua non* of commercial viability for the trade as a whole in an age of rapidly expanding publication and an increasingly volatile market comprising essentially faceless book-buying customers and innumerable ordinary readers. Indeed, without the periodicals, the reviews and the newspapers, without the advertisements and announcements, without the conduct literature, literary treatises and other advice on selecting and reading books, and without those literary forms that provided the public with their broader expectations and assumptions about culture, this increasingly complex economy could never have operated so satisfyingly for most of its participants and so lucratively for many of those whose own livelihoods depended upon it.

Nor, we might add, would the great mass of readers have behaved in the way that they demonstrably did when choosing and reading books. Their understanding of the wider world, including of Scotland and its distinctive literary culture, as well as of other places outside their parishes and increasingly also of distant lands beyond the oceans, was to a large extent the product of the vast body of relevant information that was now being moved quite deliberately in their direction. As a result, their appreciation of authorship and publishing—of what was being printed, by whom and at what cost—was continually being augmented. Most important of all, their growing sense of themselves as readers—discriminating, proficient, respectable, and, not least, polite—was being shaped by the same critics and commentators who claimed to empower them as individuals, but who also, with greater or lesser success, manipulated and moulded them as consumers. Yet individual encounters with books, and not least with the works of the Scottish Enlightenment, remained, as we shall see, appropriately complicated affairs. Principally this is because those experiences were necessarily shaped by a number of more immediate and more personalised contexts. It is therefore to some of the places and circumstances in which readers' engagement with books actually occurred that we must turn next.

4 "An Ample Fund of Amusement and Improvement"
Institutional Frameworks for Reading and Reception

Literacy and its implications for the historical study of reading are likely to remain, as we have already noted, the focus of intense scholarly disagreement. It is also far from common—though as the cases of readers like Mathew Flinders and Revd Snowdon demonstrate, it is sometimes still just about possible—for us to be able to establish the precise consequences of critical discourse and processes of canonisation for the choices made by literate individuals. Few would deny, however, that the most important physical context associated with the consumption of books, and indeed one that was talked about again and again by contemporaries, was the 'library.' It follows that this particular venue needs to play a central role in any serious exploration of readers' experiences at this time. Nevertheless, this is not an entirely straightforward enterprise, given that Georgian use of the word 'library' turned out to cover a multitude of bookish sins. Indeed, in practice it connoted a considerable variety of different places and situations in which relationships between individual readers and specific groups of texts were able to unfold.

On the one hand, a library might, for example, comprise only a handful of mouldering books left on a parsonage shelf for the convenience of a clergyman like Revd Franks or Revd Bowle. But on the other it might imply a great country house collection belonging to a spectacularly privileged reader like Horace Walpole, holding literally thousands of calf-bound and gilt-lettered volumes in accommodation that was as lavishly spacious as it was purposely gracious. Nor were these the only possibilities. For exactly the same word might describe a cupboard-full of texts bought by a group of friends for their short-term gratification and subsequent disposal. It might apply equally to a prestigious institutionalised collection, like those of the Carlisle and Penzance libraries we have already encountered. In this context, of course, a 'library' would have a substantial membership, a permanent collection, detailed protocols governing lending practices and even its own premises (the latter also termed a 'library,' though now in an even more corporeal sense). Yet the same term could just as easily be applied to a nakedly profit-making retail operation run from a bookseller's shop, like Lackington's in London, whose users were, as they well knew, nothing more or less than paying customers.

As if such drastic differences in scale, scope and purpose were not sufficient, other parts of the nomenclature surrounding the Georgian library are also seriously confusing. In fact, the terminology often appears to have been downright ambiguous at best, and, in not a few cases, deliberately dishonest in its application.[1] It is with this set of problems very much in the forefront of our minds that we need to begin by considering two closely connected types of lending collection, habitually at this time distinguished from one another as the 'book club' and the 'subscription library' but both of which, as befits an age that was passionately interested in voluntarism and polite sociability, also amounted to one form or another of membership-based association. In short, in our search for some of the key locations in which English readers might actually have encountered the published works of the Scottish Enlightenment, we should turn first to those quintessentially Georgian institutions that had been created and were still directly controlled by those who used them.

*   *   *

Despite its being the very simplest form of lending facility that evolved during the eighteenth century to meet readers' growing demand for books, it is emblematic of the serious difficulties in making sense of this subject that the 'book club' did not always choose to be so described. In fact, as we shall see, a book club sometimes preferred to call itself, with a discernible hint of *hauteur*, a 'book society.' In other cases, nicely emphasising the high literacy levels of its members rather than the exact nature of its physical property, the label 'reading society' proved an even more attractive soubriquet. Whatever the chosen moniker, however, all of these terms remained effectively synonymous. And they were conventionally attached to what was recognisably a single type of lending institution—one whose participants had undertaken to act together in order to purchase, read and then, crucially, dispose of books. Indeed, it was probably with the latter eventuality in mind that the term 'library,' which to most ears hinted at an enduring and fully institutionalised body of reading materials, was, despite readers' boundless appetite for terminological inexactitude, generally avoided.

Other defining characteristics of the book club were closely related to these original peculiarities of form and function. Perhaps the most obvious was simply one of size. For the great majority of book clubs had no fewer than fifteen and no more than thirty members, with an average probably towards the lower end of this range. The Pulborough Reading Society in Sussex, for example, founded in 1807 by eighteen local men, seems to have been in statistical terms close to both mode and mean.[2] So too was the Woodstock Book Society in Oxfordshire, whose first rule, promulgated in 1822, actually stated that 'The Society [is] to consist of twenty Ladies and Gentlemen

Inhabitants of the Town. . . '[3] The Botesdale Book Society, active in a small Suffolk rural community from 1778, when it had just twelve subscribers, and the Barnard Castle Book Society in County Durham, which had exactly the same number on its foundation in 1819, had slightly fewer participants at the outset, before growth subsequently occurred.[4] The Middlewich Book Club, based in a Cheshire community made rich by salt mining, was, if anything, on the large side of average, with twenty-seven members in 1801, this again within a year of its first meeting.[5]

Based as they were on face-to-face relations between readers who were usually also friends, kinsfolk, colleagues or neighbours of one another, virtually all book clubs must therefore have been unassuming gatherings indeed, at least when compared with the much larger scale routinely attained by the second type of associational lending institution, generally described as the 'subscription library' or the 'permanent library.' In fact, the latter usually had many times more members—as well as, in numerous instances, a truly daunting concentration of the local great and good. The subscription library at York, for example, had no fewer than 477 members by 1823, led, predictably enough, by the Archbishop, the Dean and the minster canons—with sixty-five clergymen all told.[6] At Norwich, too, the proprietors included the Bishop, fifty-five other reverend gentlemen, six baronets and two earls, and had a membership of 456 in 1792.[7] In Liverpool, meanwhile, there were eventually two such institutions. The Liverpool Library (subsequently The Lyceum) capped its membership at 893 even before 1800—though among them were many of the city's mercantile leadership—while The Athenaeum had a very impressive 502 members just twenty years later.[8] Even at Whitby, a much smaller community on the east coast of Yorkshire, there were eighty members in the fourteen-year-old local subscription library in 1789.[9] Such figures for full-blown permanent libraries suggest that the book club's limited size was almost as much of a defining feature as its emphasis upon selling off rather than accumulating the books that it had bought.

A further characteristic of the book club—and, interestingly, a factor greatly affecting its ability to bring groups of readers into contact with particular kinds of literature—was linked to its generally modest scale. This was its capacity for taking root even in comparatively obscure locations. The latter certainly included many places that would never have been able to sustain a subscription library. At Hartington, for example, a small town in the hills of northern Derbyshire, a dozen readers were meeting each month around the turn of the nineteenth century in order to choose and circulate their own book purchases.[10] Furthermore, the book club would in many places of this kind have been the most important—because usually the *only*—cultural institution active in the locality, the parish church made an exception. At Kibworth in Leicestershire, for example, texts like Hugh Blair's *Sermons* (bought in 1790 at the request of Revd Arnold) and *Mary Queen of Scots: A Tragedy* (feeding the late eighteenth-century frenzy of interest in her, and acquired the previous year on the suggestion of a 'Mrs Maior') would probably never have been seen by so many local readers without the existence of the book club that repeatedly enabled significant works of literature to pass through their appreciative hands.[11]

Also related to the quite remarkable geographical coverage eventually achieved by the book club phenomenon—since the well-documented Kibworth example could easily be multiplied dozens or even hundreds of times over, right across England—was the significantly broader social range of readers for whom this most basic of associational structures was able to offer a meaningful cultural focus. Certainly there is much evidence that the book clubs were able to reach beyond the boundaries of gender and status delimited by the beneficed Anglican clergy, the members of the traditional urban mercantile and professional elites and the gentry and nobility from the surrounding rural hinterland—the people who, especially in the great regional centres and major county towns like York and Norwich, tended naturally to set the social tone of the subscription libraries.

The Sheffield Book Society, for example, founded in December 1806 as 'a society for the circulation of books,' included among its early subscribers one Robert Ernest, a local apothecary, who would go on to request books like Dugald Stewart's *Philosophical Essays* (1810), and Joseph Ward, a tailor, who, apparently possessing a strongly poetic temperament, later proposed Gerard's *Essay on Taste* as well as the works of Burns, the second part of Beattie's *The Minstrel*, and two new works by Walter Scott, *The Lord of the Isles* (1815) and *The Bridal of Triermain* (1813).[12] At Penzance, too, there was a Ladies' Book Club from 1770 whose twenty-four founders were so determined to preserve it as a single-sex forum that they decreed (an exceptionally unusual instance of an explicit gender bar) 'That no gentleman be admitted a member.'[13] Other all-female book clubs also arose in locations as scattered as Bishop Wearmouth in Durham, Saffron Waldon in Suffolk and, not least, Chawton in Hampshire, where Jane Austen was a member.[14] Clearly, then, this smaller, simpler and rather looser type of association had among its peculiar advantages the fact that it provided a haven for large numbers of enthusiastic readers who also looked somewhat different from those patricians, prelates and prosperous urban oligarchs who dominated the larger subscription libraries.

This does not mean, however, that the subscription library itself was closed to readers who did not belong to the business elite, to the squirearchy or to the old literate professions. Virtually all subscription libraries in fact went out of their way to stress that they were amenable to women members in particular, and most lived up to this promise, at least to a degree. At Lichfield, for example, there were nineteen ladies among the 119 subscribers in 1815.[15] At Lewes in Sussex, too, there were twelve among ninety-four subscribers to the Library Society by the late 1820s.[16] Especially by the end of our period, there were also a small number of subscription libraries that specifically served the needs of humbler readers—a famous example being the Artisans' Library, founded in 1824 in Smithy Row, Nottingham, run for the benefit of the industrious apprentices of this burgeoning manufacturing centre—as well as comparable institutions for the edification of readers drawn from an increasingly diverse urban middle class—the Blackburn Subscription Library, for example, had been founded in 1770 and by 1825 had a varied membership that included five local solicitors, three 'druggists,' a bookseller and two ladies.[17]

By the 1820s, the mechanics' institutes, which, because of their permanent collections, might be thought of as a further extension of the subscription library model, were also emerging. And although they obviously lie towards the chronological limits of our own period, it is worth noting that, in places like Liverpool, where Hume's *History* was among the very first books borrowed from the Mechanics' Institute (on 1 March 1824 by an otherwise unknown local cabinetmaker named Hugh Campbell), they too seem to have afforded unprecedented opportunities for tradesmen and craftsmen, and other readers who would never have had the opportunity or the means to join an orthodox subscription library, to get hold of and to engage with some of the age's most important and most challenging texts.[18]

Revealing first-hand reports from inside the otherwise opaque cultural world of the literate Georgian artisan—whose library membership was as often funded by an employer or other well-wisher as by himself—have occasionally been preserved. Usually these crop up in the autobiographies of early nineteenth-century working-class writers like William Heaton, a Methodist tanner's son from Luddenden near Halifax. Labouring locally as a weaver and eventually publishing some of his own poetry, Heaton later remembered how he and his friends, all of them utterly fascinated by lepidoptery, had 'formed a library, and bought a number of the best books we could find on the subject.'[19] Yet for all of these achievements in the direction of greater inclusivity, and the evidence that the permanent book collection within an associational framework was indeed capable in some circumstances of catering for the literate female and even for poorer and less privileged readers, it is clear that it was not the subscription library *sensu strictu* but rather the book club that by its nature was best suited to the aspirations—because, fundamentally, to the pockets—of people such as these.

Another interesting feature of the book club, and once more an aspect closely linked to its relatively limited size and aspirations, was its adaptability to specialised needs, some of which also had important implications for the way in which certain types of literature might have come to the attention of particular classes of reader. The most striking manifestation of this trend was the plethora of occupational book clubs that eventually emerged, most often formed to circulate professional texts between subscribing physicians, lawyers or clergymen. A good example was the Medical Book Club in Newcastle upon Tyne, active during the 1790s, whose thirteen founders agreed to 'contribute annually one guinea for the purchase of books.' Applying to themselves what were already the tried-and-trusted conventions of the book club format, they also resolved to meet 'at each others houses in rotation on the 3rd Wednesday every month,' with each member in his turn 'to receive a new book first & circulate in rotation.'[20]

The Nottingham Medical Book Society was similarly inspired, open from the outset to those local gentlemen who possessed either a medical doctorate, membership of the Royal College of Surgeons or the status of licensed apothecary.[21] By the late 1820s it had twenty-two subscribers, and was an important resource for the dissemination of current medical knowledge among Nottingham's practitioners, circulating such important sources of new insights as the *Edinburgh Physical and Surgical Journal*.[22] Specialist responsibilities, however, were never the exclusive preserve of the book club. A comparable focus, at least where the resources and the demand existed, was also sustained by a small number of true subscription libraries—as at Sunderland, where a Medical Library emerged in 1814, allowing local physicians to borrow copies of key texts by leading Scottish bulwarks of the medical establishment, like William Cullen's *First Lines of the Practice of Physic* (1777–84), generally regarded as its author's greatest work; Alexander Monro *primus*'s *Anatomy of Human Bones* (1726); and John Hunter's *Treatise on the Blood, Inflammation, and Gunshot Wounds* (1794).[23]

Another important characteristic of the book club stemmed directly from the transience of its holdings. As will be clear, regular disposals in effect granted participants the opportunity to secure personal ownership of significantly discounted copies of recent publications—often including, in the process, titles from among the Scottish Enlightenment's principal works—whilst at the same time materially enhancing their collective capacity for purchasing yet more items for future reading. There were doubtless many members like Mr Charlesworth, of the Newark Book Society in Nottinghamshire, who acquired a cheap copy of Robertson's *America*, recently bought at his own suggestion, when it was sold off in 1783, or like Mr Pocklington, who that same year acquired what seems to have been the same club's already surplus copy of Blair's new *Lectures*.[24] Ultimately, it was this practice, as vital to the club's financial viability as it was advantageous to individual members, that in due course enabled the Newark Book Society to replace its earlier titles with fresh offerings from the Edinburgh presses, like *The Mirror* (1779–80), bought in 1784 (again on Mr Pocklington's recommendation, perhaps again with an eye on subsequently acquiring it for himself?), and *The Lounger* (1785), acquired in 1786 (this time proposed by Mr Charlesworth).[25]

Again this should not be seen as proof that the subscription libraries, despite their distinguishing commitment to permanent holdings, were completely different in practice. The Amicable Society Library at Lancaster, for example, perennially on the brink of economic disaster and chronically short of room because of an overly aggressive acquisitions policy, paid for its sins by being obliged to sanction regular disposals: 'Ossians Poems 2 vols' fell victim to this expedient in 1771, falling thereby into the lap of a grateful member; in similar circumstances the minutes also record that 'Hume's Essays 2 Vols [was] sold to L[eonard]. Clarkson for 5s. 9d.' in 1774.[26] When the same action was performed by a book club, however, it was no emergency measure. Instead it represented a normal, even a desirable, state of affairs. The continual dispersal of texts like Hume's *Essays* or Blair's *Lectures* was therefore simply another aspect of the book club's role as an association conceived so as to allow readers to share more literature between themselves—and, it goes without saying, to do so more cheaply and more extensively—than would have been feasible if they had each continued to act alone.

The scattering of surplus books was not, however, the only phenomenon that often in practice—though never quite in theory—united the two principal types of associational collection. Contemporaries would ordinarily have understood what, according to strict definition, a subscription library was actually meant to be, even though complete disambiguation was hardly aided by the fact that, from place to place, it might variously seek to identify itself as 'permanent' (as in the Hereford Permanent Library), 'circulating' (as in the Manchester New Circulating Library, though unhelpfully, as we shall see, this particular adjective more commonly signified something quite different), or even 'public' (as in the Ipswich Public Library—indicating, rather confusingly to later ears, not universal free access but openness to anyone who could afford membership). Yet a subscription library was also what might well have come into existence by default once an unusually successful book club, previously just a convenient vehicle for sharing books between readers, had attained the necessary critical mass of members and begun to acquire a semi-permanent stock.

In Cornwall, for example, the Penzance Library, formally founded in 1818 and still functioning today as the Morrab Library, grew naturally out of the Gentleman's Subscription News Room that had been operating since 1799.[27] In Lancashire, too, the Liverpool Library, first established in 1758, was simply the legatee of several prior book clubs in that increasingly prosperous and rapidly expanding port.[28] Such metamorphoses, with their pleasing implication of newfound solidity and greater social prestige, were most commonly triggered by steadily rising membership rolls and by a consequent increase in the financial resources available for more adventurous purchases. Yet awareness of a welcome surge in the number of fellow-subscribers also seems to have been capable of effectively changing the psychological mood among groups of readers, simultaneously boosting their collective confidence and heightening their aspirations both as consumers of literature and, more widely, as convincing actors on the contemporary cultural stage.

*   *   *

To some extent the palpable sense of ambition embodied in so many of the subscription libraries was fuelled by a cocktail of local pride and public-spiritedness—such as that which, in the decades following its foundation in November 1768, inspired the members of one to boast that 'the rapid extension of the CARLISLE LIBRARY. . . may be placed foremost in the list of the many judicious and salutary improvements which, within a few years past, have been carried into effect in Carlisle, much to the comfort and convenience of the inhabitants.'[29] It is plain, however, that the determination of certain classes of readers to be affiliated with a substantial and permanent lending library also reflected the profound desire among the self-consciously respectable to be involved in the replication of established and well-regarded cultural practices that appeared in effect to confirm, to reinforce and even to celebrate their own unqualified politeness.

It may thus be especially revealing as to the widely perceived moral and social implications of reading that book-lending institutions so often seem to have involved themselves in the shameless mimicry of similar endeavours already underway elsewhere. A natural inclination to emulate existing forms, and hence to claim a share in some of the accumulated cultural capital built up by the successful activities of other readers, presumably helps explain why a variety of libraries with the enticing word 'amicable' in their titles eventually cropped up—for example, at Northampton (a book club, from 1779); at Ratcliff in Middlesex (a book club, from 1809); but also, as we have seen, at Lancaster (seemingly the earliest example, a true subscription library founded in 1769), as well as further down the Lancashire coast in Liverpool (yet another book club, from 1812).[30]

A compulsive urge to co-opt rather than to challenge the familiar conventions of polite associationalism also explains the frequency with which the rulebooks adumbrated by institutionalised readers relied conspicuously upon ideas and phraseologies borrowed from elsewhere. It was no accident that the Shrewsbury Subscription Library required of any proposed new acquisition that 'when its price, and the review in which it is noticed can be mentioned, attention to these circumstances is required,' and that the founders of the Hereford Permanent Library, subsequently formed in the principal town of the adjacent county, likewise stipulated that 'when its size, number of volumes, price, and the Review in which it is noticed, can be mentioned, attention to those circumstances is requested.'[31] It is also symptomatic of the determination of the prospectively-polite to follow where the already polite had led that the first thing that a group of ambitious Nottingham book lovers did in 1816 when founding their own library was to compile an initial order of titles based directly on the published catalogue of the long-established and highly regarded Liverpool Athenaeum.[32]

Unembarrassed imitation of cultural precedent by those with serious polite aspirations—the principal means by which the relentless spread of enlightened values and modes of behaviour throughout society was achieved—was not confined to the denizens of the more substantial subscription libraries. Even in the book clubs, with their usually more limited horizons, the same vaguely obsessive concern with the emulation of existing models of polite endeavour was sometimes only too evident. In Lincolnshire, for example, there survives a draft of the proposed rulebook for a new early nineteenth-century book-lending institution. It actually takes the form of an old copy of the *Rules and Orders of the Book-Club-Society, at Market-Rasen*, however, with the original printed place name amended in handwriting, sufficient for the immediate purposes of the fledgling institution, to read 'Great Grimsby.'[33] Such expropriations are so revealing, of course, because they confirm that associational reading, whether taking place in modest book clubs or in the famous subscription libraries in the major towns, was simply too important for the structures and procedures that nurtured and sustained it—even, perhaps, for their basic nomenclature and their trademark rhetorical claims—continually to be reinvented afresh.

Another important feature shared in practice by all of the associational lending institutions was a keen interest in providing opportunities for sociable interaction as well as for borrowing and reading. This too was an assumption easily traceable to the core principles of polite culture that were such an important foundation of the British Enlightenment: as Shaftesbury, one of its prophets, had observed, 'We polish one another, and rub off our corners and rough sides by a sort of amicable collision.'[34] At its most extreme this saw book-lending facilities fully integrated within larger associations that sometimes espoused the broadest and loftiest of cultural ambitions. At Derby, for example, a substantial library perfectly complemented the wider aims of the Literary and Philosophical Society, an organisation that explicitly sought to stimulate local interest, it proclaimed, in 'questions on subjects in Philosophy, Literature, or Natural History.'[35]

Indeed, Dr Richard Forester, president of the Derby Literary and Philosophical Society in 1810, had insisted upon the far-reaching cultural benefits of what he called 'a superstructure, which in an increasing town like this, may eventually reflect credit on its founders, and gradually diffuse, with habits of observation and attentive reading, an active spirit of investigation and research, to which mere book clubs do not afford an adequate stimulus.' Interestingly, however, Forester went on to confess that he had actually been inspired in his own idealistic vision for this increasingly populous and prosperous Midlands industrial town, where supportive institutions would encourage both judicious reading and edifying social interaction, by the singular example of the northern British capital. In fact, betraying a keen awareness of the Scottish Enlightenment, he argued, in justifying the Derby enterprise, that 'the establishment of the Medical, Speculative, and other well known, and well organised Societies in Edinburgh, has largely contributed to advance the cause of Learning and Philosophy, and to give celebrity to that University.'[36]

Such sentiments, clearly situating the borrowing and reading of books at the heart of a programme of wider cultural improvement associated in particular respects with the Scottish Enlightenment, were not in fact confined to Derby. Indeed, the founders of the Liverpool Mechanics and Apprentices Library acknowledged broadly similar inspiration as they attempted to cultivate an enthusiasm for learning and literature in the local population. As they declared in 1824:

> Scotland affords a gratifying example of the blessings of education when placed within the reach of all classes of the community: its effects are there proudly exhibited in the orderly, moral, and industrious character of her peasantry and mechanics, than whom, as a body, there exist not better men or better subjects.[37]

Nor was Derby alone in witnessing attempts to orchestrate the act of reading and the conduct of discussion in the formation of an all-encompassing voluntary association committed to the generation of a truly polite and enlightened community.

Newcastle upon Tyne, already the greatest town in the industrialising northeast, gave rise to a recognisably similar cultural project around the turn of the nineteenth century. Here the Literary and Philosophical Society sought to provide a structured framework for scientific and scholarly debate—in characteristically polite vein, it was also stated that 'Religion, the practical branches of Law and Physic, *British* Politics, and indeed *all* Politics of the day. . . shall be deemed prohibited subjects'—as well as maintaining an extensive book collection for what by 1819 were already more than five hundred subscribing citizens.[38] The Liverpool Literary and Philosophical Society was yet another civic institution with comparable aspirations. With its impressive library and provision for the delivery and discussion of learned papers, it confidently pursued the same manifesto as at Derby, with reading and conversation the parallel routes to genuine politeness. In Cambridge, too, the Society for Promoting Useful Knowledge, founded in 1784 and soon in possession of a substantial lending collection, declared that its intention was 'to read, debate, and converse upon such subjects as are calculated to improve our moral and intellectual faculties, and to advance the best interests of man.'[39]

Less distinguished institutions, however, frequently accommodated comparable expectations about the axiomatic relationship between the consumption of appropriate books and collective engagement in intelligent debate. At Lancaster, the nascent Amicable, still a small subscription library, agreed on 3 December 1772 'That as the Society has for some time allowed discourses to be held on a Variety of Subjects by them. . . a Committee be appointed to regulate the said Conversation Clubs.'[40] In Lincolnshire, too, in 1804, the Boston Literary Society agreed that, in addition to the borrowing of books, they should also meet together to 'read passages or pieces of their own composition; except any thing of a political or an immoral tendency.'[41] And at Hackney in Middlesex the gentleman and ladies who conceived the idea in 1815 of forming a local learned institution for the purpose of 'the acquisition and dissemination of Literature & Science' made a telling decision, explicitly fusing the practical functions of reading and learning, when they named it the Hackney Literary Institution and Subscription Library.[42]

Nor should we doubt that both books and vocal discussion were what this ambitious cultural organisation to the north of London actually provided for its participants. For along with early orders for Robertson's *America*, Henry Mackenzie's report on the authenticity of the Ossian poems and Scott's recently published *Waverley* and *Guy Mannering*—all of them requested by members in the first few weeks of operation—the subscribers soon found themselves listening on two separate occasions to a lengthy and controversial paper by John Clennell in which, as the minutes recorded, some of his colleagues identified much to dispute:

> Mr Lumby made some observations on the subject of the Essay, and vindicated the character of Dr Johnston [sic], which he conceived to have been in some degree aspersed by the Essayist, with the view, as he thought, of invalidating the testimony of the Doctor, who had argued against the authenticity of the poems; and brought forward some charges against the general character of Mr McPherson, the translator of the poems, which he considered as tending to invalidate his testimony in favour of their authenticity.

> Mr Wright, and also Mr Smallfield differed from Mr Lumby in his ideas of the character of Doctor Johnston; and altho' they considered him as one of the brightest ornaments in English Literature, could not avoid ascribing to him many violent prejudices & eccentricities; several observations were made by different persons present and the conversation closed.[43]

The evidence suggests, incidentally, that Middlesex's suburban intelligentsia had an alarming tendency to involve themselves in violent disputation, to the obvious detriment of their new institution. Within just two short years it had been dissolved, its assets ultimately being divided among the warring subscribers. Apparently this had been the result of another badly received talk by the argumentative Mr Lumby, the outspoken sceptic about Ossian, who this time, as the minutes laconically record, had 'produced his promised Essay on the character of the female heart.'[44]

At Sheffield, meanwhile, another similar society, initially established in 1810, published a list of the conundrums that its subscribers hoped to clarify through conversation and debate. It too neatly captures the intimate connection between discussion and reading that polite culture, particularly in its associational form, so strongly emphasised. And as at Hackney, it also highlights questions and issues that surely only a thorough working knowledge of leading recent works by Scottish authors could have suggested:

66. Are the Poems ascribed to Ossian his production, and worthy the reputation they claim?. . .

80. Was there any real magnanimity in the act by which Charles V resigned his dominions to his son?. . .

86. The Theory of Money. . .

93. The best method of studying History. . .

109. Is Mary Queen of Scots to be considered as an accomplice in the murder of her husband, Henry Darnley?. . .

170. Does Robertson, Gibbon, or Hume rank the highest as an historian?. . . [45]

It seems reasonable to conclude that readers at Sheffield who were already familiar with *Fingal*, *Charles V*, *The Wealth of Nations*, Robertson's *Scotland* or Hume's *History* would have had many useful observations to contribute.

*   *   *

Despite its evident success in engaging men and women in cultural activity of several different kinds, voluntary associationalism was not the only means by which people were able to increase their own access to books. Surprising as it may seem, the parish library was another crucial resource, at least for certain categories of English reader.[46] Unfortunately, however, both the origins and the function of the parish libraries actually differed markedly from place to place, making nationwide generalisations hard to formulate. In some instances they were certainly little more than a small bequest left for his successors by a previous incumbent. To borrow the self-explanatory title of a document from one Norfolk parish around 1760, a simple parish library might take the form of 'A Catalogue of the Books given by the Revd. Dr Hooper to the Rectory of Fakenham For Ever.'[47] Alternatively, the donor might be a pious layperson like Elizabeth Crompton of Broseley in Shropshire, who on her death in 1765 left books for the curates of Stone in neighbouring Staffordshire.[48] Indeed, this assumption that local church libraries were primarily for clerical use only mirrored the situation in the English cathedrals, where the collections were usually aimed specifically at the chapter and local clergy (though in fact lay readers often intruded: Coleridge, for example, used both Carlisle and Durham, Sterne the collection at York Minster, and Johnson, including on his last visit, the library at Lichfield).[49]

In other cases, however, it is clear that the parish library had a rather different function. In fact, it was sometimes a genuinely public facility, available not only to the parsons and their fellow clergy but also to others, such as the churchwardens and other literate lay people in the locality. Shropshire and Suffolk, for example, where the Georgian position can be reconstructed using modern catalogue evidence, had many libraries with substantial stocks of books that were meant, at least in part, for more general use.[50] There were also well-intentioned founders like Thomas, 2nd Baron Trevor, in rural Bedfordshire in 1740, who gifted a set of books explicitly 'for the use of the Minister and Parish of Bromham.'[51] The collection at St George's, Doncaster, too, established by a group of local clergymen for their own personal use but soon recast for wider benefit, was actually described as 'a common public library.'[52] At Chirbury in Shropshire a seventeenth-century parish library had been expressly founded 'for the Use of the Schoolmaster or any other of the Parishioners who shall desire to read them,' while the Chetham group of libraries in and around Manchester likewise operated avowedly 'for the edification of the common people.'[53] Again there were parallels in the cathedrals, since at Chichester, where the library continued to receive new stock throughout the eighteenth century, it served as a sort of public lending library to readers in western Sussex.[54]

The established church's educational responsibilities had also given rise to what may in fact have been the only truly "public" libraries in England at this time. For unlike the so-called Suffolk Public Library at Bury St Edmunds (which like a number of others with similar titles, was in reality a subscription-funded private association), book collections that were owned by town corporations and grammar schools were often available for use by at least some sections of the wider population. Indeed, it is clear that both the Leicester Town Library, created in 1587 for the use of the clergy and then falling under civic control, and the Old Town Library at Ipswich, founded in 1599 for the parish but then taken under the auspices of the corporation, had become properly public both in their formal management and in their practical function by our own period.[55]

Grammar school collections, usually originating in intensely Protestant notions about education but subsequently broadening out in function to encompass adult readers from outside their host institution, offered another form of meaningfully public provision that was more or less under the control of church and corporation. At Guildford, for example, the town's grammar school library, largely the product of a lavish donation by a sixteenth-century Bishop of Norwich, was tellingly known as the 'town library,' whilst elsewhere in Surrey the collection at Lewisham grammar school was likewise described significantly as the province of 'the clergy and gentlemen in the Hundred of Blackheath.'[56] At Hawkshead in Lancashire, too, the school collection, so far from being the preserve of the masters and pupils alone, was expressly open to 'Gentlemen of Education in the Neighbourhood who may wish it.'[57]

Whatever may sometimes have been implied by the institution's many critics, the parish library, in its narrower sense, was in no sense dormant or moribund in this period. In fact, the unchecked rise of New Dissent, the continuing problem of Old Dissent, and the pressing need for the Anglican church to respond effectively to these challenges, stimulated renewed creativity in the provision for reading. The Church of England's preferred prescription was, broadly speaking, more of the same. Under the assiduous direction of energetic and dynamic clergymen, notably Revd Thomas Bray and his Associates, but also of the Society for the Propagation of Christian Knowledge, the foundation of additional parish libraries, in the belief that this alone would deliver sufficiently educated pastors and, by extension, a suitably pious flock, was the predominant strategy.[58] Thus at places like Dullingham in Cambridgeshire in 1712, Streatley in Bedfordshire in 1729, and Poulton-le-Sands in Lancashire in 1757, parish libraries sprang to life where none had hitherto existed.[59] At the same time, generous individuals continued to leave their own mark on the cultural life of particular parishes in the time-honoured fashion. In 1744, for example, Revd William Standfast, rector of Clifton in Nottinghamshire, bequeathed a library to the county town, with the intention, he claimed, of benefiting future generations of local clergymen, lawyers and physicians.[60]

New kinds of church library were also devised during this period as its nervous supporters struggled vainly to maintain the historic dominance of Anglicanism. This essentially defensive posture resulted in such splendid institutions as the Norwich and Norfolk Clerical Society, created in 1828 under the auspices of the Bishop of Norwich for the ministers of a substantial part of this important diocese.[61] But the same motives also produced rather more ferocious sounding institutions with explicitly sectarian purposes. At Ashbourne in Derbyshire, for example, the Moral and Religious Permanent Library, founded in 1819 for the use of Anglican communicants, forbad the admission of 'Books or Tracts hostile to the Established Church, or at variance with its Doctrines, or professedly controversial.'[62] The Church and King Library at Bolton in Lancashire, established in 1794, similarly demanded that any new borrower should 'declare himself to be bona-fide a member of the Established Church': this appears, incidentally, a distinctly odd stipulation, given that readers were thereby gaining access to shelves that positively groaned with secular literature, including such works as Hume's *History*, a text universally known to be entirely at odds with Anglican teachings, and even Dugald Stewart's cerebral *Philosophical Essays*, a difficult work which voiced its author's characteristically Scottish confidence in the possibility of inculcating polite and polished behaviour through a comprehensive programme of philosophical education.[63]

The Church of England's various rivals, protected by rising levels of practical toleration and spurred on by their own success in attracting adherents, were not slow to pursue a similar strategy in relation to reading. The Unitarians were particularly active—even if, unlike the parishes of a well-endowed and legally privileged established church, their lending had to rely upon regular cash payments by individual readers. The book club format, given its proven effectiveness among like-minded people, was unsurprisingly a favourite expedient, a good example being the one established by twenty-four Unitarians at Northiam in Sussex at Christmas-tide 1808 (where Beattie's *Evidences of the Christian Religion* (1786), the most famous apologetical work from a contemporary Scottish source, was among the first acquisitions).[64] This most highbrow of denominations also spawned many fully-fledged libraries with permanent collections. These included one run from the vestry of the Westgate Chapel in Lewes from 1808, which initially had just twenty-four enrolled members, and another at the chapel in Portsmouth, founded in 1816.[65] In early nineteenth-century Norwich, meanwhile, there was a Unitarian library in the Octagon Chapel that, conveniently enough, opened after each Sunday service (when, amongst other texts, they would have found a copy of Blair's ever popular and helpfully non-sectarian *Sermons*).[66]

Other dissenters followed where the Unitarians had led and where, since the late seventeenth century, the Quakers, with their custom of lodging books in the Friends' Meeting House, had also long since been headed.[67] At Great Yarmouth, for example, there emerged the Methodist Subscription Library.[68] In Bristol, the local Baptists founded Broadmead Vestry Library in 1820, following a meeting 'for the purpose of forming a library consisting of instructive religious works to be lent to such persons belonging to the Church and Congregation at Broadmead, whether Subscribers or Non-Subscribers, as may be disposed to read them.'[69] At Blackburn in Lancashire, the local Congregationalists founded a library in 1809, again noting that 'all meetings for Business [should] be convened by Public notice from the Pulpit, in the Afternoon and Evening of the preceding Sabbath.'[70] Many of these institutions were clear that their *raison d'être* was to reinforce distinctive theological identities. In Newcastle upon Tyne, for example, one library even declared that 'Persons desirous of making themselves thoroughly acquainted with the genuine Doctrines of the New Jerusalem Church are very respectfully requested to Read attentively the works mentioned in the subjoined Catalogue.'[71]

It is important to underline, however, that, despite the accusation that the Anglican parish libraries in particular were basically useless for the purposes of the general reader—a complaint first formalised by the Public Libraries Committee of the House of Commons in 1849 and most influentially repeated by Altick—this actually seems rather too harsh a judgment.[72] It is certainly true that the readership of most of the chapel and church collections was numerically quite limited. It is also undeniable that religiously based provision exhibited a bias towards divinity. Indeed, in the Anglican parishes, as in the collections run by town corporations and grammar schools, this was not least because so many had been endowed with no means of purchasing new works that their holdings often became, as a matter of course, more and more fossilised over time. Moreover, in the words of one Victorian observer, the seventeenth and early eighteenth centuries in particular had been 'days of vast and intense ecclesiastical enthusiasm and controversial acerbity.' The result was that 'the effusions of bitter antagonists on well-nigh every conceivable religious tenet from men of well-nigh every party crowd the shelves of the church libraries.'[73]

Yet the evidence suggests that the unappetising stereotype of the arcane and dusty religious library, heavy with recondite contributions to long-forgotten theological disputes, requires significant modification. For while 'dusty, shabby and out-of-date' they may generally have been, utterly irrelevant to the concerns of Georgian readers these institutions were certainly not.[74] Some secular texts, including a number at the cutting-edge of contemporary fashion, were likely to be encountered by those readers with both the opportunity and the inclination to delve into their local church collection. Moreover, where evidence of borrowing also survives, such texts seem to have found a welcome among those people who regularly used these libraries.

At Chichester in the last decades of the eighteenth century, the cathedral library actually offered the town's inhabitants access to copies of many recently published works, including those of the Scottish Enlightenment. Among them were, for example, first editions of Robertson's *Scotland* and *Charles V*.[75] Ipswich Old Town Library likewise offered Hume's *History* to its readers, along with key philosophical works by Locke, Bayle and Descartes; Hume's *History* was also available from the grammar school library at Hawkshead, while the school collection at Guildford provided Smollett's *History of England* and the libraries at Faversham in Kent and at Leeds in Yorkshire provided convenient access to that paragon among modern essayists and cultural theorists, Addison.[76]

This level of availability was certainly not merely incidental to what Georgian readers actually consulted, at least if the contemporary lending records that survive from the cathedral libraries are any guide. Furthermore, this has direct implications for our understanding of the way in which the Scottish Enlightenment in particular would have intruded into the reading experiences of ordinary users of the church collections. Paul Kaufman has demonstrated that the cathedral's copy of Hume's *History*, for example, was borrowed no fewer than thirty times at Canterbury and twenty-four at Durham; Ferguson's *Civil Society* (1767), meanwhile, was loaned out on five occasions from Durham; Robert Henry's *History of Great Britain* (1771–93) was lent eight times from Gloucester and twenty-two from Winchester; and George Ridpath's *Border History of Scotland and England* (1776), appropriately enough given its regionally-specific subject-matter, left the safe keeping of Carlisle's historic library on at least six separate occasions.[77]

Perhaps more surprisingly, similar scholarly interests among local readers, often naturally embracing recent Scottish works as they appeared, must also have been served by some of the parish collections. At Whitchurch in Shropshire, the library owned Hume's *History*, as well as, clearly only suitable for the more adventurous reader, the *Essays and Treatises on Several Subjects*.[78] At nearby Bridgnorth, the philosophically inclined parishioner would also have found Hutcheson's *Essay on the Passions* (1728) and Dugald Stewart's *Philosophy of the Human Mind* (1792–1827), as well as, slightly more digestibly, a copy of Robertson's *Charles V.*[79] At Norbury in Staffordshire, meanwhile, any interested reader in the local community would have found that the church's library held a copy of Sir John Dalrymple's thought-provoking work of historical jurisprudence, the *Essay Towards a General History of Feudal Property* (1758).[80]

Nor were the dissenters slow in recognising the advantages of making available to readers an attractive range of modern secular literature. Thus the Yarmouth Methodist Subscription Library offered Smollett's *History of England* and the complete historical works of Robertson.[81] The Brunswick Library, at the Pitt Street Methodist Chapel in Liverpool, provided its sixty-five subscribers with intellectually demanding works like Reid's *Essays on the Intellectual Powers of Man* (1785) and *Essays on the Active Powers of Man* (1788), alongside the comprehensively humane but only occasionally spiritual Boswell's *Life of Johnson*.[82] At Newcastle in 1808, too, the newly established Brunswick Chapel Library for local Methodists, which immediately purchased Robertson's *America* and *Charles V* and Smollett's *England*, openly admitted that 'it is not meant to be exclusively a Religious Library, and useful Books, containing nothing inimical to the interests of Religion, will readily be admitted'—as would in particular 'any of those works which tend to improve the mind.'[83] And even the collection at Portsmouth's Unitarian Chapel, supposedly made up 'chiefly, but not exclusively, of religious books,' in practice soon found space not only for Robertson's popular histories but also for Kames's *Elements*, with its well-known treatment of taste, Reid's *Inquiry* (1764), famous for its consoling rebuttal of Hume's scepticism, Henry's innovatively thematic *Great Britain*, and, in due course, Walter Scott's complete poetic and prose works.[84]

* * *

Clearly we need properly to acknowledge the potentially important role of primarily religious libraries in exposing certain readers to the Scottish Enlightenment—including, as we have seen, some of its more technically complex texts. It was undeniably profit rather than piety, however, that was much the greatest boon to the man or woman in search of books. For the fee-charging 'circulating libraries' were in fact by far the most significant providers of books for loan. The spectacular growth of these commercial operations, and in many locations also the dense concentrations that swiftly emerged, is truly remarkable. And this, it should be noted, was despite the quite extraordinary barrage of criticism to which the circulating library was routinely subjected by hostile commentators who feared its impact upon public morality as well as the established social order.

In Birmingham alone, between around 1740 and 1830, the most conservative guess would now place the number of separate commercial lenders somewhere in the vicinity of fifty.[85] For Manchester, "Cottonopolis" itself, a comparable estimate would be forty; for Norwich, a large county town and regional hub, again around forty; for Bristol, the great port city of the west, eighty; for Liverpool, gateway to Ireland and the world, around ninety; and for London, the Behemoth of the book trade and by far the most populous urban centre in England and Europe, perhaps two hundred. It would be wrong, however, to think that this phenomenon was confined to the industrialising cities and the major conurbations where so many readers congregated together. Indeed, in virtually every small country town, at least one commercial lender operated at some time during this period. Kettering in Northamptonshire, a small town known for footwear and velvet manufacturing, could stand for many. It supported at least three separate circulating libraries during the late eighteenth and early nineteenth centuries—Downing's, Waters' and Watson's—a fact that may go some way towards explaining why a local weaver called John Leatherland could by the 1830s apparently indulge in well-informed workplace conversations arising from a close reading of Thomas Reid's philosophy.[86]

Active competition between rival commercial providers seems to have been increasingly normal. Alnwick, the tiny Northumberland market town in the shadow of an immense medieval castle, sustained at least four circulating libraries during the 1790s and early 1800s alone—respectively Catnach's, Graham's, Davison's and Smith's. Cockermouth in Cumberland, where Wordsworth was born and raised towards the end of the eighteenth century, had a minimum of eight. Stamford in Lincolnshire, neither a county town nor even a significant manufacturing centre, had at least ten commercial lenders, as well as a thriving subscription library. Such was the profusion right across the country that one almost begins to wonder whether the much-quoted contemporary estimate in the *Monthly Magazine* of 'not less than one thousand' in 1801, albeit a mere snap-shot of a single moment in the circulating library's relentless rise, might not actually be unnecessarily cautious.[87]

Circulating libraries, just like the associational institutions that arose in parallel and which commercial proprietors often deliberately aped, quickly took on a great diversity of forms. In particular, their size soon varied considerably. A recently opened library in a smaller town might only have had very limited holdings—as, for instance, did the Cockermouth establishment of Edward Banks in the early nineteenth century, which held just 226 volumes, or John Brown's library at Wigan in Lancashire which in 1821 was offering a collection of just 378 titles.[88] Yet many other owners numbered their books in four figures—as did William Marriott, for example, whose library on Full Street in Derby in the 1790s boasted a large and diverse collection running to more than two thousand volumes.[89] By late in our period, indeed, holdings five times larger even than Marriott's were not unknown. London's famous Minerva Library on Leadenhall Street, run by William Lane, had ten thousand volumes in 1792, whilst Thomas Hookham, a celebrated proprietor operating on Old Bond Street, offered almost nine thousand in 1794.[90]

Some commercial lenders even managed to mimic the most alluring aspects of the book club format. This might mean dangling before readers the delicious prospect of ultimate ownership—as, for example, did John Rutter in Dorset, owner of the ambiguously named Shaftesbury Subscription Library for Circulation and Reference, who tantalised his customers with the promise that they would 'be at liberty to order any work of general interest in the English, French or Italian languages, not previously added to the library, on taking the work so ordered, after its circulation for one clear year, at half its published price.'[91] Alternatively, simulating the privileges of associational participation might entail customers choosing at least some of the books for themselves: thus did Joseph Lansdown of Bristol advertise in 1807 that his own subscribers might 'once a year order one Book or Set of Books, provided the amount does not exceed the annual subscription. . . '[92]

Again like the voluntary institutions, to which they must often have represented supplementary rather than rival lending provision, the circulating libraries displayed a striking adaptability to the requirements of different kinds of reader. Bespoke provision was especially common by 1800. Music circulating libraries hawked their wares at Binfield in Berkshire, Barnstaple in Devon, the cathedral city of Lincoln and the university town of Cambridge. John Anderson on West Smithfield and Samuel Highley on Fleet Street both ran medical circulating libraries in early nineteenth-century London. Children's libraries also emerged, ranging from Nathaniel Hailes' business on Piccadilly, active from around 1817, to the 'Juvenile Circulating Library run at Dover by the bookseller Thomas Williams.[93]

Market segmentation was also a sign of the commercial sector's increasing maturity. As an early nineteenth-century guide to Brighton suggested, most of that resort's miscellaneous visitors, from whichever occupational or social group they hailed, would find circulating libraries specifically tailored to their own needs. Robert Loder's, for example, on North Street, was 'an old and capital concern, embracing above twenty thousand volumes in every branch of science. Hither may the student resort, secure from the interruptions of the giddy and the gay. . . '[94] At the Royal Marine Library on Marine Parade, by contrast, there was 'every popular work, especially such as are calculated for the fair sex.'[95] The Royal Colonade Library, on the corner of North Street and New Road, was different again. Run by Edwin Wright, it held a royal appointment and so, not surprisingly, was 'particularly patronized and frequented by the army, navy, and clergy.'[96] But Wright also ran the Royal Esplanade Circulating Library on King's Road, 'an establishment well worthy the distinguished patronage it receives from all the Nobility and Gentry, residents and visitors of the Western part of Brighton.'[97]

The strong emphasis upon polite interactions that was such a feature of associational institutions was also ruthlessly plagiarised by the circulating libraries. Indeed, some of the more imaginative proprietors clearly appreciated the competitive advantages of trading upon the presumed affinity between reading and sociability. The most significant consequence of such thinking was the so-called 'newsroom,' many examples of which were probably like the one run by the Moore family on The Crescent at Buxton, the Derbyshire spa town, by the 1790s. Their customers had the opportunity to sit and read a range of current periodicals, including the *Monthly*, the *Critical* and the *Gentleman's*, the better to sharpen their own powers of critical discrimination. They also had access to a large lending collection (the Moores accentuated the illusion of associationalism by calling it a 'subscription' library), where they would find works such as Blair's *Sermons*, Robertson's *Scotland* and, in due course, Scott's novels.[98] The Assembly News Rooms at Newcastle similarly linked accommodation for reading and social mixing with a substantial lending library that boasted a number of texts germane to readers' understanding of literary taste, like Blair's *Lectures* and Johnson's *Lives*.[99] In both cases, moreover, coffee and other refreshments would also have been available, further enhancing the essentially social pleasures associated by contemporaries with the personal experience of reading.

Entrepreneurial creativity of this kind makes it all the more regrettable that the precise composition of the circulating libraries' Georgian customer base is almost impossible to reconstruct. For there is a desperate shortage of systematic information—as opposed to merely anecdotal evidence—on those who actually *read* the books that commercial lenders made available. In almost all cases, we lack the names of borrowers. This is itself unsurprising, because, unlike the status-obsessed and historically aware participants in the subscription libraries, the typical circulating library's clientele never developed any coherent collective identity. Nor did individual proprietors have occasion to publish a list of their own customers. As a result, too much modern scholarship has been forced to credit the unhelpful myth that the circulating libraries were overwhelmingly the haunt of weak-minded women and insubordinate servants: 'A circulating library in a town,' declares an obviously outraged Sir Anthony Absolute in Sheridan's *The Rivals* (1775), 'is as an evergreen tree of diabolical knowledge!'[100]

Even the tiny handful of customer records that survive is of severely limited wider value. They may tell us that subscribers to James Marshall's Circulating Library on Milsom Street in Bath in the period 1793–9 included the Prince of Wales, Mrs Piozzi, Dr Herschel, the Duke of Ancaster, the Duke and Duchess of Richmond, the Duchesses of Devonshire and Cumberland, the Marquis of Bath, the Earl and Countess of Suffolk, the Earl and Countess of Haddington, Lord and Lady Howe, Lord Romney, and the Bishops of Salisbury and Cloyne.[101] They also tell us that at George Williams's Library in Cheltenham's High Street in 1815, the customers included a succession of military worthies, such as Admiral Dixon and Lieutenant-Colonels Lowe and Henry.[102] The evidence even confirms that both institutions actually accommodated a healthy social range, as well as a significant number, but always a minority, of female readers (at Marshall's, around one-third of the total).[103] Yet apart from confirming that Marshall and Williams owned exceptionally large and singularly well-favoured establishments in the wholly untypical environment of two of the premier resorts for retirement and leisure, such data offer little help in characterising that vast army of English readers who were reliant upon the great mass of more humdrum circulating libraries.

The surviving evidence, overwhelmingly printed catalogues, provides rather better insights into the circulating libraries' holdings. And these once again place in serious doubt the familiar accusation that the commercial collections were largely restricted to prose fiction. This is not to say, of course, that no library pandered to this dispiriting stereotype. Samuel Russell, for example, a Guildford library proprietor whose stock was inventoried in May 1829, had owned what were described simply as '5640 Vols. Of Novels, Poems, Plays & Miscellanies.'[104] Meanwhile, Jan Fergus's well-known study of Samuel Clay at Warwick showed that novels and belles lettres dominated his lending.[105] Yet a much wider trawl through the extant catalogues gives very strong indications that the situation on the ground across England was actually much less uniform than might initially be expected.

Commercial lending in fact seems to have been far more varied, probably rather more complicated, and without doubt much less threatening to public taste and decency, than was long believed.[106] The Waters family's library at Kettering in 1813, for example, probably represents the typical position. One can only imagine that they arranged their words with care when describing their own offerings as 'Consisting of History, Travels and the Most Approved Novels'—in short, as a collection including but by no means confined to the narrative fiction that enjoyed particular public favour. Texts such as Gibbon's *Decline and Fall* and Thomson's *The Seasons* helped lend substance to such rhetorical reassurance.[107] Thomas Collinson, who traded from the Market Place at Wirksworth in Derbyshire, was no less keen to convince readers that he could satisfy a diversity of interests, advertising in 1805 that it offered 'History, Biography, Voyages, Novels, Travels, Plays &c.'—as indeed it did, with Blair's *Rhetoric* and Robertson's *Charles V* and *America* actually on the shelves.[108] John Rutter at Shaftesbury in Dorset made equally expansive claims, fully backed up by what his library contained. In fact, he declared in 1827 that his business provided readers with 'a regular supply of new and interesting works, chiefly confined to History, Voyages, Travels, Biography, Arts and Sciences, General Literature, Poetry and the passing publications of the day, together with the superior class of Works of Fiction.'[109]

The strategy of Christopher Wright, who traded on Chapel Bar in Nottingham, was even more revealing. In a new catalogue issued in 1821, he presented exactly the same sort of all-embracing lending collection, with novels effectively counter-balanced by a fine selection of historical and philosophical texts. Indeed, Wright's library achieved the quite astonishing (and, one suspects, commercially risky) feat, especially given its date, of carrying not a single work by that era's most bankable novelist (Walter Scott—though Wright did offer some of his poetry) while, as far as the Scottish Enlightenment was concerned, potentially providing Nottingham's readers with a whole series of full-length studies by the likes of Hume (the *History*) and Robertson (*Charles V, Scotland* and *America*).[110]

Accordingly, and as was bravely suggested by John Feather more than twenty years ago, it may well have been not unknown in practice for circulating libraries to be as rounded in their holdings as that of Ann Ireland at Leicester, who in 1789, as Feather noted, owned 2,500 lending items, barely 5% of them actually novels.[111] In this context, small-town proprietors like John Brown at Wigan, whose 378 titles in 1821 comprised approximately 70% fiction but who also provided many key works of intellectual substance such as Robertson's *Scotland* and Boswell's *Journal of a Tour to the Hebrides*, may well have been much more typical than they might at first appear.[112] This re-assessment also helps make sense of the fact that it was in a Bath circulating library that David Ricardo first encountered *The Wealth of Nations*, and another in the same town that, for broadly similar reasons, earned the soubriquet 'Southey's Bodleian.'[113] Such experiences may have been far more common than was once thought possible. At the very least, there is every reason to believe that entrepreneurs like John Rutter and Christopher Wright—whatever the critics and the carpers suggested—did indeed help in constructing and sustaining the more serious and stimulating reading tastes of contemporary men and women.

* * *

Libraries, as we have seen, played a crucial role in bringing Georgian readers potentially into contact with a body of literature that was as varied as it was vast. More particularly, whether mere book clubs or the grandest of subscription libraries, whether commercial collections, the disparate forms of charitable provision associated with the parishes, chapels and cathedrals, or even the venerable town and grammar school collections, institutionalised lending afforded contemporaries—few as famous as Ricardo or Southey—the opportunity to engage with the works of writers like Hume, Smollett, Smith, Beattie, Reid and Robertson. Not all reading, however, was dependent upon lending by institutions. Nor, obviously, was it the case that all books that were read had had to be borrowed. Indeed, as we shall see in the next chapter, book ownership by individual readers, as well as a range of other factors that shaped and structured the intensely personalised experience of reading, actually had at least as much bearing upon how contemporaries were ultimately able to engage with the ideas and idioms of the Scottish Enlightenment.

5 Readers and Their Books
Why, Where, and How Did Reading Happen?

By contrast with some of the meaner parish collections, dustier school libraries and basic commercial operations to which many readers were nevertheless very grateful to have access, the *Bibliotheca Beauclerkiana*, on Great Russell Street in London in the 1770s, was one of the real wonders of the age. Some saw it as a statement entirely befitting an era of Enlightenment. To Boswell, it was truly a 'great library'; '. . . it reaches halfway to Highgate,' joked an equally impressed Walpole of the accommodation that Robert Adam, no less, had been retained to erect, 'Everybody goes to see it.'[1] When auctioned off in 1781, this quite extraordinary collection, the property of Topham Beauclerk, extended to more than nine thousand separate titles across more than 350 catalogue pages.[2] In fact, in order to dispose of a library of such uncommon magnitude—'upwards of thirty thousand volumes,' as the same catalogue proudly boasted—the auctioneer, Samuel Paterson, Johnson's great friend, set aside fifty days of his own time. Nor, in the event, did the collection disappoint. Indeed, it eventually fetched the colossal sum of £5,000.

Beauclerk was, of course, typical of no one but himself. He was, by any measure, no ordinary reader. A grandson of one duke (St Albans) and son-in-law of another (Marlborough), he was, despite lacking an aristocratic title of his own, an impeccably well-connected member of the social and political elite. As a denizen of Johnson's Club and a Fellow of the Royal Society, he had both earned and gloried in his status as a leading cultural light in mid-eighteenth-century London.[3] Beauclerk's collecting of books had also known no bounds, either of finance (since he was formidably wealthy) or, apparently, of self-restraint (for he was, by his own confession, an incurable bibliophile). The library that gradually emerged, however, among the many insights it affords us into the nature of individual bookownership in mid-Georgian England, is useful for one very particular reason. In effect, it provides an exceptional instance of the way in which different kinds of works by Scottish authors, and especially some of the recent works associated with the Scottish Enlightenment, might occupy, in the most conducive of circumstances, a significant place in the life of a contemporary English reader.

*   *   *

One measure of Topham Beauclerk's complete familiarity with Scottish authorship was closely related to his tendency to seek out not only the fullest possible range of individual books, but also—and this characteristic feature of Victorian collecting seems to have been less common at this juncture—multiple editions of the same title, as well as duplicate copies of a single edition. In fact, with Richard Heber, the greatest hoarder of books in the early nineteenth century, Beauclerk might well have protested that 'No gentleman can be without three copies of a book: one for show, one for use, and one for borrowers.'[4] Thus he procured two editions, for example, of Hutcheson's *Inquiry* (1725) (and he also held copies of all of Hutcheson's other published works). There were also two editions of Hume's *History* (dated 1762 and 1773) and three each of Thomson's *The Seasons* and Smith's *Theory of Moral Sentiments*.[5] Even minor Scottish works, rather less well remembered today, like George Fordyce's *Elements of Agriculture* (1765), were sometimes held in two copies, whilst James Wallace's *Orkney*, acquired in both the 1693 and 1700 editions—obviously, like so much else in personal as well as institutionalised collections, picked up from second-hand sources—was typical of Beauclerk's sensitivity to Scotland's literary output not only during the Enlightenment but also in the immediate pre-Enlightenment period.[6]

A closely connected aspect of Beauclerk's purchasing was his determination, as a true bibliophile, to build a collection in which contemporary literature of whatever kind could be viewed in the much longer perspective of printing and publishing history. Accordingly he was alive not only to the achievements of contemporary Scots like Hume and Smith but also, presumably again through assiduous activity in the second-hand and auction markets, to the richness of Scotland's native traditions of classical and religious scholarship stretching far back into the Reformation era. In fact, Beauclerk managed to gather together work by most of the main Scottish authors from this earlier period, like George Buchanan (the great *History of Scotland* (1582) as well as the poems and tragedies), John Spottiswoode (the *History of the Church of Scotland* (1655)) and, especially, the voluminous output of Gilbert Burnet, East Lothian minister and Glasgow divine-turned-Anglican bishop.[7]

Beauclerk, however, was hardly remiss when it came to texts by comparatively minor Scots writers from those more obscure times. Seventeenth-century works in his collection included those by Robert Monro (*Monro His Expedition* (1637)) and Sir Thomas Craig (notably the *Jus Feudale* (1603)). For similar reasons Beauclerk owned a number of texts, by both Scots and English authors, concerned with what in the years after 1750 had become the fashionable historical controversy—fuelled, as we have observed, by repeated periodical and press coverage—surrounding Mary, Queen of Scots. Illustrative of the long-term evolution of the arguments over Mary's merits, which had recently shifted from broad disapproval to genuine sympathy, these included the recent contributions of Walter Goodall and William Tytler as well as the rather older works of Robert Freebairn and Sir William Sanderson.[8]

It is clear, then, that Beauclerk was fully alert to the wider Scottish cultural heritage of which the Enlightenment was itself in some respects the brilliant culmination. At the same time, however, his passionate bibliophilia led him to seek out whole groups of works in certain specialist disciplines—not always so central to the Enlightenment as it has subsequently been perceived—in which he himself maintained a close interest. Some acquisitions, for example, were drawn from local and regional topography and historiography, a significant area of Scottish output between the 1730s and 1790s (as one critic in the *Monthly Review* felt moved to tell his readers in 1791, 'The fashionable study (for there are *fashions* in *study*,) of topography, poligraphy, and partial history, has begun to make its appearance in the northern capital of our island').[9] William Nimmo's *History of Stirlingshire* (1777), Lachlan Shaw's *History of the Province of Moray* (1775), John McUre's *History of Glasgow* (1736) and Hugo Arnot's *History of Edinburgh* (1779) were among them, although, Arnot perhaps excepted, most were largely unknown to other English readers, were rarely found in institutionalised collections south of the Border and have been little studied since by scholars of Enlightenment culture.[10]

Fittingly for a man who possessed his own private laboratory facilities, Beauclerk was also much concerned with scientific and medical texts of which Enlightenment Edinburgh had happily emerged as a major provider—a pointed reminder, too, that, had Johnson's fancy for refounding the University of St Andrews ever come to fruition, Beauclerk would have been elected professor of natural philosophy *sans pareil*.[11] William Cullen's *Of the Cold Produced by Evaporating Fluids* (1756), William Hunter's *Medical Commentaries* (1762–4), John Hunter's *Natural History of the Human Teeth* (1771), Joseph Black's *Explanation of the Effects of Lime Upon Alkaline Salts* (1756), Colin Maclaurin's *Geometry* (1720) and *A Treatise of Algebra* (1748), and William Smellie's *Thesaurus Medicus* (1778–85) were among the great number of works that Beauclerk sooner or later acquired—and to judge from the dates of publication, most if not all (Maclaurin's work is the only likely exception) were probably bought as new.[12] Indeed, it appears almost as if a later critic's thoughts when reviewing one of Smellie's subsequent publications, the *Philosophy of Natural History* (1791), had already been vindicated by Beauclerk's behaviour in acquiring every one of these texts. Each, after all, was 'useful to everyone whose mind is sufficiently at leisure, and fully disposed, to acquire the information that it conveys. . . for the well-instructed naturalist is already a philosopher.'[13]

As will by now be clear, the case of Topham Beauclerk is in many ways illustrative of how the evidence of personal book buying can be used to help reconstruct an individual's tastes. He certainly confirms how familiar with Scottish literature it was now possible for an English reader potentially to become, even without regard to the unprecedented further opportunities that the explosion of institutionalised lending were now opening up. It will be obvious, however, that there were tensions and contradictions in Beauclerk's collecting. For appreciating books as artefacts for collection and display, as the owner of the *Bibliotheca Beauclerkiana* certainly did, might well encourage a far more aggressive approach to purchasing than would typically be exhibited by a reader guided mainly or exclusively by an interest in devouring the texts that particular books happen to contain. Moreover, were we to advance a very rough rule of thumb, the same impulses would have to be suspected in most if not all owners whose holdings ran well into the high-four figures. Certainly it seems undeniable that a collector like Heber, the age's most prolific book purchaser and reputedly by the late 1820s the possessor of almost 150,000 volumes, had a library extending in practice far beyond the levels at which meaningful skimming, let alone proper absorption, of every title would have been remotely feasible.[14]

Nor were libraries such as those amassed by men like Heber and Beauclerk so utterly exceptional that this interpretative problem can safely be moved to the periphery of a history of Georgian reading. Indeed, they were common enough to form a significant subset within the surviving documentary record. Thus we should have to concede that the personal libraries of, for example, Revd Thomas Crofts, former chancellor of the diocese of Peterborough, which amounted to 8,219 titles in 1783, and of Revd Thomas Clarke, former vicar of Trinity Church in Hull, which, when it was sold at York in 1798, included 5,450 titles, would be equally difficult to interpret as straightforward evidence of their owners' reading preferences.[15] On the contrary, both because of certain peculiarities of approach (Clarke's, for example, included four different editions of Hume's *History* and two each of Robertson's *Charles V, Scotland* and *America*) and because of the sheer number of volumes that they finally accommodated, these collections hint once again at owners who were constructing a prized collection of intrinsically previous *objets* not for reading and inward reflection but for proprietorship, for aesthetic enjoyment and for outward display.[16]

Far more numerous than bibliophile owners like Beauclerk, Crofts and Clarke, however, whose collections clearly raise a series of more complex questions in relation to reading habits, were relatively ordinary readers who bought books—many, especially in an age of middle-class expansion, drawn from the burgeoning literate professions. These were normally owners of books on a substantially more human scale, their holdings typically numbering in the far more manageable hundreds of titles. In illustration of what was undoubtedly a relatively widespread cultural experience, especially by the latter part of our period and particularly among those non-landed persons who were less likely to benefit from the sometimes very substantial inherited collections found in a great house, we might usefully consider a group of near contemporaries from the eastern part of Derbyshire, in the district abutting upon Sheffield, whose books were eventually listed in a series of printed sale catalogues.

Ebenezer Rhodes is the first, a master cutler who, when his library was dispersed in 1828, owned 217 books, including Blair's *Sermons* and *Lectures*, the ubiquitous Hume's *History* and Robertson's not-much-less popular *Scotland*.[17] For his part Revd Francis Gisborn, minister of Staveley, was a fairly typical country parson. He owned just 209 titles in 1822, although these included (intriguingly for, as we shall see, it was a text that some clergymen found absolutely spellbinding) a copy of *The Wealth of Nations* as well as the first forty-eight volumes of the *Edinburgh Review*.[18] Wootton Thomas, meanwhile, was a gentleman farmer from near Chesterfield. He too was clearly interested in books. In his case, however, this meant eventually owning 160 titles, including, like Rhodes, a copy of Blair's *Sermons*, but also a somewhat scarcer item of Scottish provenance, the Aberdeen professor Thomas Blackwell's *Memoirs of the Court of Augustus* (1753).[19] John Longden of Ashbourne, by contrast, was a businessman. But, unwittingly making it hard to pigeon-hole him as Mr Gradgrind, he had by 1827 amassed a collection of around five hundred books. These included Gilbert Stuart's *View of Society in Europe* (1782), William Cullen's *Practice of Physic* (1776), and Scott's best-selling novel *Waverley* (1814)—it may even have been a first edition, though the evidence is unclear—but also, appropriately, a copy of Scott's only Derbyshire-based narrative, *Peveril of the Peak* (1822).[20]

Collections such as these, full of recent publications as well as of the continually recycled auction-house staples that were so important in Georgian book purchasing, were, needless to say, entirely capable of being read through from end to end, and perhaps repeatedly so over the years, by those who had bought them. Certainly with Ebenezer Rhodes, who also has a reasonable claim to recognition as a man of letters in his own right (his *Peak Scenery* (1818–24) was briefly definitive in an admittedly narrow field), we might feel confident in supposing that a copy of Hume's *History* would have received a serious amount of scrutiny over time. Yet equally, in the same attempt to link an individual's known choice of books with their broader outlook on life, it is hard not to find oneself imagining a country landowner like Christopher Beauchamp, who lived near Great Gransden in Huntingdonshire in the early 1790s, thumbing with particular eagerness and excitement through at least some of the three hundred titles that he owned—such as the *Sporting Magazine* (1792-) and other squire-friendly titles like *Jockey Club, Returning From the Races*, and *Duck Shooting*.

With Beauchamp, of course, even if we are rightly wary of judging books by their covers, it would be almost irresistibly tempting to epitomise an individual's character by reference to the texts that he or she can be shown to have possessed. Despite the fact that he does indeed seem to have borne a passable resemblance to Squire Western, who was excessively enamoured of 'his guns, dogs, and horses,' it would need to be added, however, that Beauchamp also owned some much more intellectually stimulating texts.[21] And as far as the Scottish components of his collection are concerned—works such as Blair's *Sermons*, Maclaurin's cerebral *Algebra* and *Newton*, and Hume's complex and challenging *History*—it would clearly be much less easy for us to reconcile them simplistically with Beauchamp's apparent status as a bluff fox-hunting country gentleman.[22] Once again, then, evidence of personal ownership may have its limitations for the historian of reading. For how could we *really* be sure that all the books that a person owned would actually have been read—much less that the same reader came eventually to know them well, to understand them and to appreciate them?

Notwithstanding these very significant reservations, it is still occasionally possible to see something of the role that private collections of books, and even single volumes within them, might well have played in the lives of the person or persons who owned them. In particular, it is clear that certain texts formed part of the immediate physical environment in which people's daily existence was acted out—not least in the country houses, most of them replete with dedicated accommodation both for storing and for reading books.[23] It is in this context that we can begin to glimpse the way in which at least some books from the Scottish Enlightenment may have contributed to the unusual internal layout of a residence, and so to the distinctive activities that took place in certain homes. Above all, this is because, as one keen reader, Revd James Ashton, an Oxfordshire parson, wrote in his own notebook in the 1790s, it was becoming ever more obvious in this period that 'Many persons Esteem Books, as they do Furniture, to set off & adorn their Rooms.'[24]

This adage would certainly have struck a chord with Ashton's contemporary Sir Michael le Fleming, 4th Baronet, M.P., and a man justly described as having 'a great love of literature.'[25] It was around 1803 that a record was made of some of the books in Fleming's drawing room at Rydal Hall in Westmorland. It appears, moreover, that these had been placed apart from the main library precisely in order to create an atmosphere conducive to the conversations which family members and their guests were expected to undertake in that particular room. The forty items selected undoubtedly had a specific resonance in common. Biassed towards the literary and the historical—in other words, towards genres favoured by the most polite and polished readers—they included such prime examples of the contemporary Scottish commitment to moralistic literature as *The Mirror* in three volumes and, further elevating the uplifting tone to which this particular domestic space clearly aspired, Blair's *Sermons*, a work that on its first appearance in 1777 the *Gentleman's Magazine* had recommended to readers like le Fleming as 'These excellent discourses, of which we know not which most to admire, the sentiments or the language. . . .'[26]

Physical separation of a private book collection into discrete parts was by no means uncommon in larger houses. As at Rydal Hall, this arrangement might effectively encode certain assumptions about the particular atmosphere that would emerge when a wall was bedecked with aptly chosen titles: 'This work deserves a place in the library of every young student,' as the *Critical Review* observed of the Scots preacher James Fordyce's *Advice to Young Men*, 'and in the splendid bookcase of every macaroni'—a remark that plainly acknowledges that specific texts might indeed make an eloquent statement about those who had placed them on open display.[27] Such distinctions, however, might equally well reveal an owner's tacit expectations about slightly more practical matters. Certainly this seems to have been the case at Grove Park in Warwickshire, home of Charles, 9th Baron Dormer. For his books were split between a main library and a 'Small Library,' adjacent to Lord Dormer's own room, which was graced with a pair of mahogany bookcases and a 'Reading Stand.'[28] The implication here was presumably that books reserved for Dormer's use, rather than for display in a more public space, might well be kept here.

Interestingly for our own purposes, this part of the collection included copies of Hume's *Essays*, Alexander Tytler's *Elements of General History* (1801) and Cullen's *Lectures on the Materia Medica* (1772) (the latter an important work on practical remedies), making it difficult not to suspect that, at least at certain times, these titles did form part of Dormer's own private reading regime.[29] A similar arrangement obtained at Hackwood in Hampshire. Here the Orde-Powlett family separated their books into four discrete groups, housed either in two spaces that were more likely to receive visitors—namely the North Library and the South Library—or in two rooms reserved for private use—the Saloon and Breakfast Room, and the Study. Again, it is hard not to wonder why certain texts, notably a group of Scottish sermons (some by John Drysdale as well as the more familiar Blair), a key work of Scottish moral philosophy by Dugald Stewart (the *Outlines of Moral Philosophy* (1793)), and Gilbert Burnet's *History of His Own Time* (1723–34), came to be located in this rather less public space.[30] The most likely explanation may be the family's awareness of distinct uses, or at least distinct intentions, in relation to particular titles, with those liable to be used most frequently being assigned to the rooms designated for reading and private discussion.

There can be no doubt that great care was often taken in the storage, presentation and organisation of private book collections—even when the over-riding priority was simply a requirement for easy retrieval when required. In some cases, however, the arrangement of a library may have been informed by more complex reasoning based on the relative importance or perceived value of certain texts. At Mark's Hall, south of Great

Dunmow, for example, the home of Filmer Honywood, a collection of just 491 titles in 1786 was probably organised so that the most intensively used books were in the most accessible and most visible positions.[31] According to a surviving plan, which helpfully identifies each shelf with an alphanumerical reference, there were two tall bookcases against a wall on either side of a fireplace, both of them containing five shelves (Figure 5.1).

Within this system, what may have been the more popular items, such as recent narrative histories, were placed around eye-level, on the second or third shelves of a case—as were, for example, those familiar Scottish mainstays, Robertson's *Charles V* and *Scotland*, and Henry's *History*. By contrast, most of the older or more specialised texts, likely on balance to be consulted rather less often—including in this case Scottish texts such as Burnet's *Memoirs of the Dukes of Hamilton* (1676), the political writings of Andrew Fletcher of Saltoun, and Lockhart of Carnwath's *Memoirs of the Affairs of Scotland* (1714)—were located either below or above the viewer's immediate line of sight, on the first or the fifth shelves of their designated bookcase.[32]

Honywood, who was an Essex gentleman and M.P., was certainly not alone in adopting a peculiar storage system of this kind. At Cottesbrooke Hall near Northampton, for example, Sir James Langham, who died in 1795, apparently used his books' physical arrangement in much the same way, so as to convey the affinities, at least in his own mind, between specific titles (Figure 5.2).[33] Thus Blair's *Sermons* was kept on Case 14 Shelf 3, even as other great preachers from earlier times were consigned to the opposite end of the collection, in the shelves of Case 1. By marked contrast, because this text had been placed within Case 14, Blair was clearly in the company not of other divines and pulpit orators but rather of the very recent authors of polite literature, such as William Shenstone, and not far from Addison and Steele (*The Spectator* resided in Case 11) and the poetry of Thomson (in Case 12).

Langham's library arrangement is also interesting because it married in one place the popular historical and philosophical works of the Scottish Enlightenment whilst divorcing them physically from older kinds of scholarship ostensibly devoted to the same topics. Hence Hume's *History* (together, interestingly, with the *Essays*), was on Case 9 Shelf 5, alongside Robertson's *America* and *Scotland*, but far away from other earlier histories of England, such as those by Milton (Case 6) and William Howell (Case 4).[34] On the other hand, Hume and Robertson were accommodated with those of recent compatriots like Robert Watson (whose studies had recently been puffed in the *Gentleman's*, as Langham may have known, as the achievements of 'an accurate and spirited historian') rather than with historical works from different eras, such as those by pre-Enlightenment Scottish writers like George Buchanan, John Spottiswoode and John Lesley.[35] Here, then, neither alphabetical order nor formal genre nor

	E	F	G	H
5	Thomson, <u>The Seasons</u>		Fletcher, <u>Political Works</u>; Lockhart, <u>Memoirs</u>	
4				
3				
2	Smith, <u>Wealth of Nations</u>	Henry, <u>History of Great Britain</u>	Robertson, <u>Charles V</u>; Robertson, <u>Scotland</u>; Watson, <u>Philip II</u>	
1			Burnet, <u>History of His Own Times</u>	Burnet, <u>Dukes of Hamilton</u>

FIREPLACE

	A	B	C	D
5				
4				
3				Ramsay, <u>Travels of Cyrus</u>
2				
1				

Figure 5.1 The Library of Filmer Honywood, Mark's Hall, Essex, 1786.

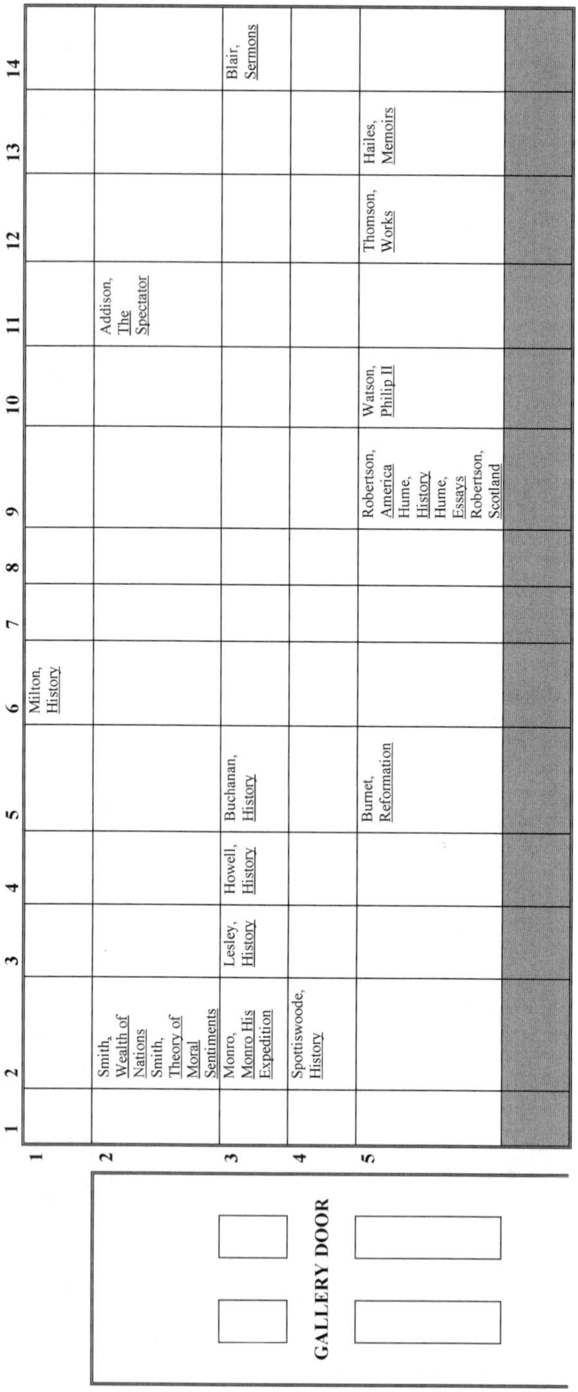
1 2 3 4 5 6 7 8 9 10 11 12 13 14
1
2
3
4
5
Milton, History
Smith, Wealth of Nations
Smith, Theory of Moral Sentiments
Addison, The Spectator
Monro, Monro His Expedition
Lesley, History
Howell, History
Buchanan, History
Blair, Sermons
Spottiswoode, History
Burnet, Reformation
Robertson, America
Hume, History
Hume, Essays
Robertson, Scotland
Watson, Philip II
Thomson, Works
Hailes, Memoirs
GALLERY DOOR

Figure 5.2 The Library of Sir James Langham, Cottesbrooke Hall, Northants, 1791.

even specific subject was the main organising principle. Rather it appears to have been Langham's awareness of broader changes in literary fashion as well as of the personal characteristics and affinities of individual authors and groups of texts.

It will be equally obvious, however, that many book collections were simply too small to make their internal arrangement, much less their ostentatious display, a serious consideration. After all, there were increasing numbers of readers in this period who could hope to put together a set of books for personal use—perhaps no more than a few dozen titles at one end of the spectrum, barely a half-dozen at the other—who, if we accept James Raven's plausible estimate, may have done so on the basis of an annual income of as little as £50 each.[36] Occasionally the reading interests of such people are given colour by the chance survival of documentary evidence, such as that which lists the books of Mary Cowgill, a Methodist woman in Ribblesdale in the North Riding of Yorkshire some time after 1800. This is why we know that she eventually owned seventy-three titles, mainly spiritual in character, including the work of the Scottish clergyman and minor poet Robert Blair (both his famous religious meditation *The Grave* (1743) and his collected verse) and (though this is scored out, presumably having left her possession) James Beattie's poems.[37]

An extant inventory also tells us that Sarah Long, who lived at Prospect Place in Chelsea, owned just sixty-one books at her death in 1797, among them a copy of Robertson's *Scotland*.[38] William Barnard, meanwhile, yeoman and leaseholder of Harlow Bury Farm in Essex in the early nineteenth century, whilst listing his horses in his journal ('Prince, 7 yrs old black gelding, 16 hands high'), also itemised a small collection of twenty-one titles, which included Tytler's *Elements*, while George Bowden, a shoemaker at Taunton in the early 1760s—whose personal collection is know about only because he had as an unusually observant apprentice the future bookseller and compulsive self-publicist James Lackington—amassed a grand total of just seven books.[39]

It needs to be recognised, of course, that, even in these most limited of book collections, not every item had necessarily been chosen by its owner. Some, indeed, came as gifts from benevolent superiors. William Dodd, for example, who worked in a woollen mill at Kendal in the 1820s, was fortunate in this regard. His employers were Isaac and William Wilson, a pair of Quakers, who, following an industrial accident, allowed Dodd to leave work early for a time 'in order that I might improve myself,' as well as giving him 'a few presents of books' that became for him 'the foundations of what I now consider a tolerable education.'[40]

There was therefore never a straightforward linear relationship between an individual's own tastes, their potential purchasing power and the nature and extent of what he or she ended up owning. Not least, there was the striking irony that those with the greatest disposable incomes were also most likely to receive books for free. This was particularly true as far as authorial donations were concerned. *Eminenti* such as Horace Walpole, who received an autographed presentation copy of Lord Hailes's *Annals of Scotland* (1776), and Thomas Pelham, 1st Earl of Chichester, who got hold of his copy of Blackwell's *Memoirs of the Court of Augustus* by the same route, were the periodic recipients of complimentary books, including those representing the Scottish Enlightenment, in a way that would surely have astonished cash-strapped readers like Mary Cowgill or William Dodd.[41]

The accidental effects of inheritance also shaped individuals' ownership of books. For most of the largest collections were in practice the product of decades, even centuries, of zealous purchasing within often-byzantine kinship groupings. Philip Stanhope, for example, 5th Earl of Chesterfield and in June 1778 just twenty-three years old, may have owned, at his magnificent seat in Buckinghamshire, an impressive private library, particularly strong on pre-Enlightenment texts and on older historical work—including Spottiswoode and several of Burnet's writings.[42] It is also clear, however, that the library at Eythorpe, notably deficient in recent philosophy and science, was essentially the collection left by his late cousin, godfather and mentor, the recently deceased 4th Earl, the celebrated statesman, wit, correspondent and literary patron, who in turn had inherited many of the same volumes—especially those published during the seventeenth century—from his own ardently book-loving predecessors.

Nor was this tendency for books to cascade advantageously down the generations, and so for some individuals to find themselves in possession of texts that they had neither chosen nor bought (nor, we might occasionally suspect, even wanted or liked), merely a peculiarity of the great landed proprietors. Henry Dalton was a member of a Baptist family from Whitehaven in the 1820s. A keen reader, he also made a note entitled simply 'A List of Books Which I Got From My Wife's Share of Her Mother Palmer's Library. . . ': predictably, the bequest from Mary Dalton's mother, herself the daughter of Thomas Palmer, a celebrated non-conformist Cumberland minister, chiefly comprised antiquated religious and devotional works.[43] Similarly, when John Randle of Breaston in Derbyshire prepared his will late in the eighteenth century, he decreed that his bible, an unnamed 10-volume history of England (perhaps *The New and Impartial History* (1763–4) by John Barrow?), and also his books on architecture, should pass to his brother's daughter Martha.[44] We can, however, only guess what this young woman, these books' undoubted possessor thereafter, would have made of this last act of generosity from her departed uncle.

*   *   *

Personal book collections were, as we have observed, the spaces within which texts were habitually contained—in the sense of physical confinement as well as of convenient storage. Indeed, the same fundamental constraints applied to the books that belonged in the homes of their owners as they did to those that crowded the shelves of the various institutionalised collections that were accessible to far greater numbers. It is a crucial aspect of the use of books, however, that they generally have to leave these places before they can actually begin to be read. Happily, we do not have to rely upon our own experiences to tell us that this must also have been so for the Georgian reader. There is considerable evidence that texts were at this time carried—and in due course consumed, nay devoured—far beyond the physical spaces in which they were ordinarily housed, with important consequences for how they were approached, read and absorbed. Perhaps the most striking of these extra-mural contexts was the result simply of travel. In fact, many texts, including works that have come to be seen as central components of the Scottish Enlightenment, eventually found their way overseas in the company of individual readers who voyaged to the far-flung limits of the wider British world.

Francis Russell went out to Calcutta with the East India Company in the early 1730s. His family, back home at Chequers in Buckinghamshire, thereafter despatched regular consignments of items that he had requested. These included the supply of the good-quality writing materials badly needed by a literate young man in the East—some Dutch foolscap and some quills were sent out in November 1731. But among them were also certain of Russell's own books, including seventeen 'Political pamphlets in one parcel,' copies of the fashionable periodical *The Craftsman* in 1731, a copy of the *Life of John Tillotson* (1717), *An Impartial History of Michael Servetus* (1723) and some volumes of the Royal Society's *Philosophical Transactions* in February 1736.[45]

Such fodder—topical, traditional and devotional in roughly equal measure—says much about the tastes of a pious and polite Englishman abroad in the 1730s. As the decades passed, however, specifically Scottish work of much more recent provenance may very often have come to form a significant part of any such list. Eighty years later, Peter Cherry of Denford in Berkshire found himself in a similar position to Russell, working for the Company and awaiting receipt in Madras in 1814 of a mixed collection of books that comprised works recently bequeathed him by his father George. These included the *Encyclopaedia Britannica*, *The Wealth of Nations* and *The Spectator*, all previously housed in the family library, and a second group that had apparently been stored in the interim in boxes in the loft above the stables, among them that peerless authority on taste and reading, and one of the Scottish Enlightenment's canonical works, Kames's *Elements of Criticism*.[46]

India was not the only destination likely to draw an individual's books temporarily or permanently into foreign fields, where they might even turn out to be read carefully and repeatedly for want of regular new supplies. Lieutenant George Hopper of the 89th Regiment, for example, stationed successively in the Mediterranean and in North America during the Napoleonic Wars, was a book lover who seems to have kept himself furnished with favourite literature, much of it probably sent out from home, some of it perhaps borrowed locally. Thus it was that Hopper was able to quote Scott's *Lay of the Last Minstrel* at Gibraltar in 1810; to speculate at Malaga about the veracity of Ossian, citing as evidence for the prosecution Gibbon's sage reservations; to copy out several of Burns' poems, which, as we shall later see, he greatly enjoyed; and, when at Halifax, Nova Scotia, in 1813, to note down information in Hume's *History* on various aspects of England's medieval history.[47]

A better-known traveller with only slightly more control over her own peregrinations was Lady Mary Wortley, who left London and her husband in 1739 to live in Italy. With her into self-imposed exile she took what we can probably safely presume were her own favourite books. They included the lately published *The Seasons*, of which she seems to have been a great admirer, and, perhaps as a memento of another traveller recently exiled in Europe, that fitting culmination of Scotland's pre-Enlightenment historiographical tradition, Burnet's *History of His Own Time*.[48] A Gloucestershire man, George Whitmore of Lower Slaughter, who went to France in 1785 in the hope that it would improve his health (it did not, and he died there), similarly took with him just seven books. Reflecting the emergence of the Scottish Enlightenment, the clear majority had obvious connections with Scotland, for they included Hume's *History*, Robertson's *Scotland* and *Charles V*, Ridpath's *Border History* and Smollett's *History of the World*.[49] The transportation of favourite books overseas, whether Scottish or not, was even a sufficiently familiar practice by the next century to invite gentle satirising: the unsophisticated Colonel Thomas Newcome, according to Thackeray, always travelled abroad with *The Spectator* on the reasoning that he liked 'to be in the company of gentlemen.'[50]

A rather different circumstance in which books might travel elsewhere for reading is also a useful reminder that lending was never exclusively the prerogative of institutionalised collections, whether commercial, charitable or associational. Indeed, inter-personal loans were extremely common in an age in which books were still prohibitively expensive for many who were desperate to read them.[51] Again, the evidence is patchy; but just enough survives to confirm the importance for many readers of private borrowing. Thus we find the London physician Dr John Ash of Bond Street writing to Sir Joseph Banks to thank him 'for the favor of reading Dr Cullen's new Edit: of his Material Medica.' Having been lent this book by Banks, Ash had concluded, with obvious sympathy for the author's intentions, that 'the whole [is] a glorious effort to get rid of the whole doctrine of Humoral Pathology. . . .'[52] Dr Charles Burney also seems to have allowed John Callcott, a composer and music lecturer although not a close personal friend, to use his private collection. This contained an immense body of technical literature relevant to both of them: in October 1799, for example, Callcott was reassured that 'I and my Lib^y will be at your Service—when we will talk ab^t a future visit & the books you want.'[53]

Members of an apparently very different social universe, for whom alternatives routes to reading were potentially even more circumscribed, also benefited. Thomas Carter, apprenticed to a Colchester tailor around the end of the Napoleonic Wars, gained access to a number of what became his most beloved texts, including *The Seasons*, when his employer gave him the run of his own small collection—as indeed, two hundred miles to the north, did Thomas Bewick, then indentured to a Newcastle engraver, and as in the West Country did John Cannon, a Somerset butcher's son and grazier, who borrowed from the local gardener's collection.[54]

William Brown, who enjoyed a colourful career as a Devon servant, a London errand boy and an apprentice pawnbroker in Sheffield before becoming a soldier and then a Yorkshire schoolmaster, was also blessed with supportive patrons. It was from Revd John Reynolds at Middleham in the North Riding that he got Locke's *Essay Concerning Human Understanding*, from which he subsequently graduated to reading—it is hard not to think that Hume must have been among them—what he later called the 'other infidels of the day.'[55] John Jones, a Bath domestic servant, confirms what we might otherwise merely have suspected, that not all private loans occurred with the owner's consent—or even knowledge. Jones later recalled that it was his furtive use of his employer's books that had furnished him with much of his early reading: 'there was a bookcase in the dining room which was left open,' he confessed, 'and by this means I was enabled to spend many a delightful hour at it. . . .'[56]

Given that such liberties were simply too tempting for some readers to resist, it can hardly be surprising that many book owners, like Wordsworth at Rydal Mount, should have kept detailed records of borrowings, lest an unfortunate lapse of memory or an unsavoury dispute in the future, to say nothing of the alarming possibility of unlicensed borrowing by visitors or by light-fingered servants, should denude the library of a much-loved work.[57] Thus Edward Sheldon Constable, a gentleman in the East Riding of Yorkshire around 1800, scrupulously noted down the volumes he had lent to one 'Mr de Villedeuil,' including copies of both the *Monthly* and the *Critical*.[58] William Beldam, meanwhile, who lived near Royston in Hertfordshire, discovered the awkwardness and extra work that resulted when care was not taken with a collection of books. A notebook, dated 1823 and probably written by Beldam himself in the third person, reports that 'Mr W. Beldam has been writing to or seeing all the persons to whom he lent any of his Uncle's books, it being in his opinion an indispensable duty to return what has been borrowed. . . .'[59]

*   *   *

Reading, as we have already seen, was inherently a social activity. Not least this was because, in a culture fixated upon notions of politeness, proficient textual consumption was thought to be essential to the creation of a socially acceptable personality. It was therefore no disadvantage when lending institutions offered ready-made opportunities for conversation and conviviality between the like-minded. Yet reading was a communal act in other ways too. To take only two of the most obvious and thoroughly ritualised examples, the sermon, which still remained central to English Protestantism, was generally a performance in which a reader delivered a spoken exposition of a prepared text, just as the biblical lesson, its close cousin, entailed the public reading of scripture to a captive audience.

The underlying assumption, that reading could thus be a social rather than a private activity, was reinforced by other considerations. Above all, a combination of the relative scarcity and expense of books, the technical constraints imposed by limited literacy and unquestioning belief in the benefits of familiarity with certain texts greatly strengthened the conviction that, if only in particular places and at particular times, it would make both economic and practical sense for an individual to read aloud to other people. In short, as Naomi Tadmor summarises the situation, reading remained necessarily in many circumstances a 'sociable rather than a solitary experience.'[60]

This fact in turn affected not only how reading was sometimes performed but also the purposes for which it might be undertaken. For there were a whole range of situations, as Jane Austen herself acknowledged in *Mansfield Park* (1814), in which an ability to vocalise one's reading, with 'a clear manner, and good delivery,' as she put it, was not merely a desirable social accomplishment but an absolutely vital social skill.[61] Above all, reading aloud remained part of normal educational activity, a convention certainly familiar to Henrietta Maria Bowdler, the unmarried sister of the now notorious Shakespearian editor Thomas, who in 1812 described to a friend, Mrs Pares, how, when considering historiography in particular:

> I am always happy when I can give my Mother's sentiments on any subject, & I know she thought it very important to devote a considerable portion of time to that study after what is commonly call'd education was nearly finished, & she wish'd it to be done by reading aloud for two or three hours in the day, wth a judicious friend, who w^d encourage the making remarks, & talking over the Book. . . [62]

Interrogative reading, seen as enhancing the inexperienced reader's understanding of the text through structured dialogue with a more skilful companion, seems to have been a common pedagogical tool. Mary Chorley, a spirited young Quaker woman and the daughter of a Liverpool merchant, who during the 1770s was living with her aunts at Lancaster, was clearly engaged in a private education in which reading aloud played a pivotal role.

Chorley's extensive diaries describe her tutor regularly having passages read to him both for his expert correction of her enunciation and for their mutual discussion of the contents of each book—a highly organised procedure that prefigured Mary Wollstonecraft's advice in *The Female Reader* (1789) that girls should be encouraged to 'read with propriety' and to 'exercise the voice' (and which also provides a less momentous counterpoint to the reve- latory experience of Thomas Jefferson Hogg and Percy Shelley at Oxford a generation later, who achieved their own famously independent-minded education by precisely the same means, reading aloud and vigorously dis- cussing Hume's *Essays* and other similarly challenging texts 'until the early hours of the morning').[63]

On 31 January 1776, for example, Mary Chorley reported that 'upon reading the history of England &c. my master... made some beaut- tiful remark remark [sic] on it.'[64] Whether the object of their study on this occasion was actually Hume's *History*, which, as we shall later see, was an increasingly desirable part of some women's educations by this time, is unclear. But we can be certain that works by prominent Scottish authors were an integral feature of Chorley's formal education, as well as of her religious instruction. On 15 December of the same year, a benefi- cial encounter with a devotional text, this time shared with an older rela- tive, occurred when, as young Mary recorded, 'My aunt Mary read one of Fordice's sermons on piety which I admire extremely.'[65] James Fordyce, who had long since left Aberdeen for London and a fruitful association with Dr Johnson's circle, was in fact a fine choice for this purpose, one of the few preachers from Scotland to have won a substantial English audi- ence by the mid-1770s.

A similar approach to reading, and again one that casts the encounter with certain kinds of Scottish text as an experience that was capable of being shared simultaneously and advantageously between a number of peo- ple, was revealed in the 1790s by the East family, who lived at Hall Place near Maidenhead.[66] Lady East in particular is a most engaging personality. Unselfconsciously hypochondriac, her diary records the daily consumption of heroic quantities of rhubarb in the unlikely expectation that it would remedy her constant stomach complaints. Both she and her husband Sir William were also avid readers of books that it is very clear they read out aloud, to each other as well as to others.

Ordinarily they read books to each other at bedtime (for example, Gib- bon's *Decline and Fall* through the early weeks of 1791, and the *Life of Johnson*, which on 30 October of the same year she 'read aloud... till eleven o'clock & had a very good nights rest'). They did this with special relish to the assembled family in the evenings, here preferring works of piety and explicit moral instruction. Interestingly, the Easts, who seem to have been orthodox, church-going Anglicans of an entirely unremarkable kind, were especially fond of reading out Blair's *Sermons* to the household, particularly on the Sabbath. On Sunday 6 May 1792, Lady East recorded that 'Sir William read prayer & a sermon Blair's first [sic] to the family this evening & intends to continue it with prayers in the morning each week day'; on Sunday 13 May, 'Sir W. read the second Sermon of Blair'; and on Sunday 20 May, yet again, 'Sir William read the 3d of Blair's Sermons.'[67]

Here, then, is a striking instance of one of the period's most highly regarded Scottish texts—influentially hymned by the *Critical* as 'distinguished by an air of superior genius, by an extraordinary elevation of sentiment, and by a remarkable spirit and elegance of language'—taking on a specific function for certain people by virtue of the peculiar reading practices through which they approached it and the distinctive occasions and settings in which they encountered it.[68] At least in this case, moreover, the reading of Blair's *Sermons* had become a *performance* in the most literal of senses—in other words, the text's burden played out, and its Edinburgh-based author given proximate voice, by Sir William East himself, sitting grave and eloquent (as we can probably safely imagine him) in the midst of his children in a drawing room or beside the hearth in rural Berkshire.

There is also good reason to suspect that sermons, as the Easts' communal use of Blair's work hints, may have been a particularly popular genre for active vocalisation, especially in a domestic setting. Peggy Turner and her husband Thomas, the Sussex shopkeeper, for instance, were fond of declaiming Archbishop Tillotson's pulpit oratory to each other in much the same way, as indeed was William Byrd II, the American landowner whose private reading habits have recently been explored.[69] As Alison Scott has argued, reading aloud and listening to religious texts was a crucial unifying experience for many people, which served 'to reinforce their faith in the religion they shared and collectively demonstrated their membership in a larger community of believers.'[70]

Sermons, however, were not the only focus for reading aloud. Mary Chorley, for example, recorded a quite different collective experience on 18 May 1778 when she noted down an encounter with probably the most popular Scottish novel of the century: 'We are much entertained,' she gushed, 'in reading the expedition of Humphry Clinker.'[71] Elizabeth Montagu, too, who lived at Sandleford Priory in Berkshire, wrote in July 1803 to her husband Matthew, a Pittite M.P., describing just what she and the children had got up to with a diverting volume recently borrowed from a local book club: 'We have got Kotzebue's Exile from the Newbury Club,' Montagu reported of a popular recent work on Britain by a German writer, 'which amuses your sons & myself after our supper.'[72] In the household of Richard Lovell Edgeworth, meanwhile, a stern Anglo-Irish patriarch, even more challenging texts were given air. His daughter Maria tells us that *The Wealth of Nations* and Hume's *Treatise of Human Nature* were prominent among the works that were read out aloud during Edgeworth's concerted attempts to foist his own deep respect for intelligent and useful learning upon the family.[73]

Several of the great sages of early- and mid-Victorian England were also familiar with such experiences, later recalling the habit of reading aloud in their childhood homes. It was shortly after 1800 that Thomas Babington Macaulay reckoned he had acquired his lifelong love (and, not coincidentally, his formidable skill at memorisation) of Burnet's historical writings,

The Lounger, The Mirror and the poetry of Walter Scott, in each case having heard them declaimed repeatedly at the family fireside.[74] Twenty years
later Ruskin heard his own father reading to his mother most of the works,
including those of Shakespeare, Addison and Johnson, but not least the
poems of Walter Scott, that would subsequently dominate his own literary
outlook: 'His sense of the strength and wisdom of true meaning,' the son
remembered, 'and of the force of rightly ordered syllables, made his delivery
of Hamlet, Lear, Caesar, or Marmion, melodiously grand and just. . . .'[75]

As these witnesses testify, the specifically social contexts to reading,
especially when they also brought together family, friends or workmates,
could very strongly influence a text's impact on the individual—how much
it was enjoyed, how readily it was internalised, the particular meanings
and associations it acquired, even the longevity of its effects. Yet the desire
to act out a performance that would display to an audience both the proficiency of the reader and the merits of a particular text could have even
more public expressions. Some, indeed, reflected the expectations about
the profitable relationship between reading and discussion that were, as we
know, encouraged by the contemporary preoccupation with politeness. A
striking instance is provided by the Liverpool Literary and Philosophical
Society in the 1820s, whose stalwarts clearly shared a desire to exhibit to
their friends and associates their own carefully honed skills as the readers
and explicators of complex scholarly works.

One was William Jevons, a Unitarian master nailmaker and iron merchant. It was Jevons who in January 1822 delivered a talk in which he dis-
sected with smooth competence the philosophical writings of Hutcheson,
Beattie, Hume, Smith, Reid and Stewart in what he called 'the enquiry
respecting the true theory of morals.'[76] Another speaker, this time in
December 1817 and on the technical subject of 'the faculties of Conception
& Imagination' as found in Stewart and in the third section of the second
chapter of Reid's *Inquiry*, was William Tartt—again, notwithstanding his
efforts to impress his rapt listeners, no professional moralist, but merely a
keen and inquisitive reader of the Scottish Enlightenment's philosophers
and, by occupation, corresponding clerk at Ewart, Myers' Brokers, one of
Liverpool's great cotton trading houses.[77]

Quoting, summarising and analysing a book such as Reid's *Inquiry* could
clearly lead to reading becoming in every sense a public performance, even
an *occasion*, quite different in kind from the more constrained readings
routinely undertaken by the Easts or the Montagus in the privacy of their
own homes. Yet it should be underlined that even the silent consumption
of a book by an individual, which surely remained much the most common
reading experience in this period, could sometimes structure and shape
responses to a text in striking ways, simultaneously enhancing its impact
and imbuing it with additional layers of meaning. In particular, if private
reading took place out of doors, this might well take the individual into an
environment with the potential to affect the manner in which certain texts,

especially those many works in this period that were concerned with natural or religious themes, could strike an impressionable reader.

The life-changing rapture with which a thirteen-year-old John Clare, son of a Northamptonshire agricultural labourer, experienced his own encounter with *The Seasons* in 1808, has long been known. Previously unable to buy a copy at Stamford, he was later successful, and, on his way back home, he could contain himself no longer and 'clumb over the wall into Burghley Park, and nestled in a lawn at the wall side.'[78] A no less familiar episode in the history of auto-didacticism, this time atop a Surrey haystack, allowed the fourteen-year-old William Cobbett, who would later also devour the works of Thomson and Blair, to enjoy the precious copy of Swift's *A Tale of a Tub* that he had bought for three pence.[79]

Much less well known, however, though better representing the experiences of very many obscure men and women in this period, particularly of the poorer sort, who took books out into rural settings, are the cases that can only be reconstructed from chance later remarks or as a result of the lucky survival of manuscript evidence. John Strickland, for example, was a farm labourer and household servant from near Wareham in Dorset whose conversion to Catholicism and then to Methodism was prefigured in his habit, dictated by a want of domestic privacy, of *al fresco* reading: 'I lived near a very large wood,' he subsequently recalled, 'this stump was my seat, and over my head waved the branches of other trees and bushes. . . I made a little dry grass for my cushion; on this I bent my knees often, and laid open the good book before me.'[80] William Dodd, the Kendal mill-worker, also frequently read outdoors: 'It was customary for me,' he remembered, 'in the summer months, to take a book, and a crust of bread in my pocket, on a Sunday morning, and go to a very retired and secluded wood, and there I spent the day alone, on the banks of a rivulet. . . .'[81] Another incident that could probably stand for many others involved Letitia Napier, a Somerset teenager, around the turn of the nineteenth century. In her jottings, recording the deeds of England's medieval kings from Egbert to John, she added to her summary notes on Henry II—obviously derived from Hume's *History* or another of the canonical works in this field—the illuminating words 'written by moonlight at Linecar Cottage, July 10th 1799.'[82]

Even where both the location and the circumstance were a little less picturesque, the context of the reading experience could greatly affect an individual's perceptions of a book. Sometimes the very purpose of reading was actually to copy out a passage. Thus when a member of the Bridgeman household in Hertfordshire elected to take down a succession of extracts from the *Encyclopaedia Britannica*—'Sea-dragon,' 'Sea-water,' 'Seamanship,' 'Seamen,' 'Sepoys,' etc.—the reading of this particular text had plainly been undertaken with the intention of deferring its proper absorption until later, when those same notes could be revisited and more fully reflected upon.[83] Some books were not read sequentially at all, readers instead devouring particular sections whilst spurning others. This is suggested, for instance, by a British Library copy of the 1800 edition of Hume's *Essays and Treatises on Several Subjects*, bearing highlighting marks in the margins which imply that certain essays were studied assiduously—notably "Of Refinement in the Arts" and "Of the Standard of Taste"—whilst other parts—"Of the Idea of the Perfect Commonwealth," for example, together with the two *Enquiries*—were virtually ignored.[84] Nor should we be surprised or offended if readers were clearly attracted by just one part of a much larger text. As Dr Johnson, not a man lightly accused of adopting a cavalier approach, snapped at an incredulous Boswell, 'A book may be good for nothing, or there may be only one thing in it worth knowing; are we to read it all through?'[85]

By contrast, other readers actually worked steadily and methodically through the entirety of a text, page by page and one line at a time, apparently thinking and evaluating, more or less continuously, as they went. They must also have repeatedly stopped in the process, however, whether for breaks or to deal with interruptions. It was perfectly possible in such circumstances that they might feel it necessary to remark upon what they had read to another person, either at the time or later, a transitory response for which no material evidence would usually survive. Alternatively they might want to write a comment on the printed page or in a notebook kept especially for the purpose—a happy decision for the later historian who, as we shall see in the following chapters, can thereby hope to some extent to retrace their footsteps through the text. Indeed, for every case in which reading occurred in a striking or spectacular setting—in solitude on a country haystack, or out loud in front of a learned society, or even in a European cantonment in India—there were many more encounters with texts that must have unfolded in these apparently straightforward and least exceptional of contexts.

Most commonly, we may be sure, reading will have taken place somewhere as mundane as a study, a bedroom, by a fireside or in a lending library. The experience will also have been solitary, and in a sense invisible, or at least inaudible. At all times, however, as we shall see again and again, the infinitely varied reading practices adopted by individual men and women were never unimportant to the nature and implications of the experience. As William Godwin, who understood the protean significance of context better than most, insisted in his revealing essay "Of Choice in Reading," 'the impression we derive from a book, depends much less upon its real content, than upon the temper of mind and preparation with which we read it.'[86] This, ultimately, is why a multiplicity of factors, often intensely personalised both in origin and in character, would turn out to be so fundamental in shaping the responses among English readers that different parts of the Scottish Enlightenment would elicit.

Part III
Contingencies

6 "One Longs to Say Something"
English Readers, Scottish Authors, and the Contested Text

In the experience of Georgian England's substantial literate population—indeed, there is every reason to think, for people in all places and all periods—reading was clearly an activity that was profoundly affected by context. One potential influence, however, although it was not always a factor, had particularly serious implications for those reading experiences which it touched. This was the determination of certain readers in certain situations, in fact the positive compulsion of a small number of literate people, to write in the books that they owned or had borrowed. The resulting annotations, physical links with past reading experiences, are obviously welcome news for the historian. For they provide a uniquely eloquent account of how particular encounters with texts, undertaken by a long-dead man or woman, might actually have unfolded. It is to the uncommon willingness of at least some contemporaries literally to make their *own* mark on what they were reading, and, as we shall see, to exert an unusual measure of personal control over the meaning and significance of some of the major works of the Scottish Enlightenment, that the present chapter is devoted.

* * *

The defacement of books—to give this set of practices its straightforwardly pejorative name—has ever been a fact of life, at least for a minority of readers. This arguably makes it all the more disappointing that until recently the deliberate marking of printed pages had attracted virtually no attention, either from intellectual historians or from literary scholars. Thankfully this is no longer the case. A growing number of researchers have discovered the value of annotations for the reconstruction of reading experiences. The late Renaissance period of the late fifteenth and sixteenth centuries, the golden age of textual emendation by philologically trained scholars, has been especially productive. Joseph Scaliger and Guillaume Budé, for instance, can now be seen for what they were—exceptionally skilful and confident interlocutors engaging in a conversation, albeit staggered over nearly fifteen-hundred years, with the revered authors of key classical texts.[1] Gabriel Harvey, too, the Tudor humanist and teacher, has been revealed as Livy's adept and enormously well-informed admirer.[2] Indeed for the early modern period it has proved possible to exploit hand-written additions to printed books so as to shed unprecedented light upon the inner thoughts of several English readers.[3]

Such studies, it is only fair to point out, have shown encouraging signs of being helpful in the study of the Georgian period too. As we might expect, the technical and philological preoccupations of earlier readers, principally manifested in glosses, rubrics and scholia, had begun to give way to a greater interest, increasingly influenced by eighteenth-century literary criticism, in observations upon the truthfulness, aptness and aesthetic charm of an author's original words.

The overwhelming focus for this later period, however, as for earlier ages, has remained upon those readers who were also celebrities—which is to say, people ultimately of continuing interest for reasons other than what can be reconstructed of their reading. A particularly fruitful example has been Samuel Taylor Coleridge. The great Romantic theorist was actually a compulsive writer in printed texts and, as we shall see, an outstandingly sophisticated commentator on several of the Scottish Enlightenment's minor philosophical works. Indeed, it has been plausibly claimed that, at least among extant English annotations, there is 'nothing comparable with Coleridge's in range and variety and in the sensitiveness, scope and depth of his reaction to what he was reading'—an editorial assessment that presumably explains the decision to devote no fewer than six volumes in the *Collected Works* project to the poet's prolific marginalia.[4]

Almost as thought-provoking, though in the same narrowly literary-biographical vein, have been Hester Piozzi's annotations: 'I have a Trick of writing in the Margins of my Books,' she confessed, clearly aware of the practice's moral ambiguities; 'it is not a good Trick, but one longs to say something . . . .'[5] Widely found in her surviving books, her comments have helped portray Dr Johnson's close female friend, *confidant* and biographer in a strikingly new light.[6] Nor is this all. Building on pioneering attempts to compile catalogues of annotated books as a necessary precursor to more systematic research, broader studies of marginalia have also lately begun to be ventured, notably by Steven Zwicker and W.E. Slights for the humanist period, and, especially, by Heather Jackson for the practice in general.[7] Yet there has still been no substantial attempt to integrate the analysis of book marking into an account of the wider reception of a coherent literary or intellectual movement among an historical reading public. It is therefore partly by way of an exploration of what might be feasible that this chapter's investigation of the different contemporary approaches to the defacement of the works of the Scottish Enlightenment proceeds.

It would also be best for us to be clear at the outset about the great diversity of forms actually taken by this practice—or, perhaps we should say, practices.[8] We should certainly not underestimate the interpretative difficulties likely to be encountered. For whilst virtually all annotational systems tend to fit into one of two very broad categories, the implications of neither are quite as they might initially seem. The first is apparently by some distance the easier for us to explain. It comprises simply words, phrases and sentences—occasionally even whole paragraphs of the reader's own creation—that present themselves in much the same way as the authorial text around which, or even into which, they have been fitted. Taken at face value, these are semantically meaningful formations of words and sentences that seem straightforwardly to document a person's reactions to the text in a relatively precise fashion.

Partly because they are frequently elliptical in style, however, and partly because they are not always the product of mature reflection, an individual reader's additions to the page, even if they are couched in apparently familiar terms, are at least as capable of taking on a whole range of variant meanings and implications as any author's printed text. An outstanding example occurs in the manuscript notes on Burnet's *History of His Own Times*, written on separate sheets that were kept with (or conceivably even inside) his own copy of the first volume of the first edition, by Daniel Finch, 2nd Earl of Nottingham and 6th Earl of Winchilsea, at some point between the work's publication in 1724 and his own death in 1730.[9] In fact, these jottings comprise a close commentary on Burnet's deeply controversial narrative, here capturing the reactions of a singularly privileged reader—an individual who, as a leading Tory politician during the Glorious Revolution and a man who had personally known its key participants, had himself been intimately involved in the events that the text was meant to explain.

Even so, and for all their seeming precision as a reader's response to the *History*, the exact meaning of Nottingham's words to us—we should probably give him the benefit of the doubt and assume that they meant something to him—often remains frustratingly obscure. Does the comment 'p. 538. Sydney tryd me. But I was not so submissive a hearer,' for example, listed under the heading 'Of Himself,' indicate that Nottingham considered that Burnet had erred by introducing his own experiences to an historical narrative; or does it mean that Nottingham doubted the author's self-advancing claim not to have been easily led by figures like Sidney?[10] Again, does the note 'p. 390 Pepys,' which appears under his barbed classification of some of Burnet's points as 'Assertions wʰout proof,' mean that Nottingham was challenging the text's veracity (which here asserted Pepys' role in guiding royal policy in 1677); or was he merely objecting to its author's preference for sometimes offering statements (as Burnet was wont to do) without presenting corroborating evidence?[11] In such instances, ellipsis and terseness, the familiar friend of the annotator on intimate terms with the printed text, are also the mortal enemy of unambiguous clarity for the posthumous interpreter.

In contrast with this superficially intelligible style of annotation, however, the second type of mark makes no pretence at being meaningful to the independent observer. Indeed, comprising a wide variety of non-linguistic notations—underlining, parentheses, exclamation marks, asterisks, crosses, and so forth—they are in practice virtually impossible to translate. Does underlining, for example, mean approval or reproof? Does an asterisk signify inward pleasure or exquisite pain—or even merely amusement or condescension? And how should we distinguish between the annotations in the same hand and on the same pages that, particularly with the increasing use of coloured drawing pencils in this period, appear in a splendid variety of hues? As we shall see, it is only in the broader contemporary context—including, above all, what we can discover about how other readers might have responded to the same text—that interpretative salvation, if it lies anywhere, is likely to be found.

Occasionally the historian encounters a cryptic annotator who nevertheless set down a key to his or her own notations. We have already met Revd James Gambier, rector of Langley in Kent—and we shall find in due course that he was an unusually attentive reader of *The Wealth of Nations*, among many other important works of the Scottish Enlightenment. In the second volume of his commonplace book, however, which he began in 1789, he added to the inside of the front cover a fascinating note headed simply 'Marks in Books.' There is, of course, no reason to suppose that he was strictly representative of other readers in the way in which he invested various symbols with specific meanings. Yet Gambier's elaborate system is worth quoting for the insights it affords into the subtle differentiations that even non-verbal marks could evidently sustain in the mind of a habitual annotator:

= Worthy of Observation in a general way, without any particular regard to its excellency, truth, or utility. This refers chiefly to a single sentence.

! Excellent ¡ Surprise in a bad sense. Surprise in a middle sense Ϙ Ϙ

+ Assent. This regards the truth of an Observation or Assertion, without respect to its utility.

? Doubt or negation.

X Important to the point in hand; or proved; or a good Argument to prove the point.

‖ Not to the point or not proved.

Ѳ— Refer to a Note on the Subj^t either in a collect^n of remarks on that partic^r Work or in the Common Place Book Ѳ—

R Read over again ⎫ These refer to the whole
NB Read over again as of especial ⎬ passages not to a single
importance ⎭ sentence

≡ More worthy of Observ^n as being useful &c. A degree below!

.ᴎ ᴄ. A passage which seems unintelligible![12]

His tabulation makes it clear that Gambier wanted to be able to distinguish accurately and consistently between his various marks. For implicit throughout his extended repertoire of standard responses was his expectation that, since he almost certainly owned the books he was annotating, he would be able to return to them easily enough on future occasions. It was when doing so that his marks would come into their own, transformed from meaningless symbols into articulate signposts and providing him—like Theseus following Ariadne's golden thread—with reliable yet economical routemarking through an otherwise labyrinthine text.

Unfortunately, none of Gambier's books is known to survive. Accordingly we can only guess that some of them eventually came to be covered with this curiously expressive private language. It is certain, however, that very few books will have been written, even in this period, with these bizarre marking practices actually in the author's or the publisher's mind. Yet the occasional published work did, as it happens, encourage the contemporary reader to write in it, to intrude upon its normally sacred spaces. Easily the most interesting example associated with the Scottish Enlightenment is James Beattie's *Scoticisms Arranged in Alphabetical Order* (1779). This sought directly to exploit the urge to annotate, offering itself as a text to whose aims—which is to say, the elimination of characteristic Scots terms and turns of phrase—the individual would be invited to make their own active contribution. Hence it came with ready-made 'blank spaces,' as the text put it, 'which the reader may fill up at his leisure.'[13]

One surviving British Library copy of the 1811 Edinburgh edition duly bears the annotations made in just the manner that Beattie had envisaged. At the end of the 'A' section of the text, for example, this reader inserted the following useful notes:

A design is afoot not on Foot—At least it is better so.
I apprehend—for I understand—is used in good Authors
Abstract—for withdraw—is not in Johnston [sic].
Adhibit (for apply) is in Johnston [sic]
Apparent for seeming, is in Johnson.[14]

As if to confirm the vigour with which this particular reader had set about fulfilling Beattie's expectations, the same copy contains no fewer than thirty-six additional leaves of manuscript notes, serving to rectify a succession of supposed Scots solecisms: for example, 'I was judged worthy—not adjudged' and 'I had rather walk than ride should be would rather etc..'[15] Such systematic self-correction was, it seems reasonable to suppose, exactly what Beattie must have had in mind when he remarked that 'The following is incomplete in many respects; and may be very much enlarged by one who attends to these matters.'[16]

At the opposite extreme from these articulate and perfectly intelligible interventions by one of Beattie's careful readers, no author could surely have imagined the system of marginal commentary that would be created by one owner of Maclaurin's *Algebra*, whose copy is also preserved in the

British Library. Beside Maclaurin's observation that 'Algebra is a general Method of Computation by certain Signs and symbols which have been contrived for this Purpose, and found convenient,' for example, the reader wrote simply:

$$\text{⌐ | ƒ ⌐ ꓪ ꭥ ꭥ ⏌ ⌐ ⏌,— ꭥ / ⏌ . . . . .}^{17}$$

This appropriation of shorthand techniques so as to condense one's own annotations was in many ways a thoroughly rational response by an itchy-fingered reader to the problem posed by the inflexible confines of the printed page. It was also an ingenious exploitation of the rapid advances then being made in shorthand systems, in particular by Samuel Taylor (whose *An Essay Intended to Establish an Universal System of Stenography* appeared in 1786).[18] Whatever form they took, however, and whatever the reasons for a particular type of mark being applied, all annotations by readers had at least one set of functions in common. Everywhere they effected the permanent alteration of a book as it had originally been printed. This in turn rendered it more relevant, more acceptable, and, in a sense, more useable, to the reader—as well as, at least potentially, to anyone else who subsequently opened it.

* * *

The most rudimentary (and excusible) reason why readers write in printed books is simply to correct the text. Sometimes these alterations are occasioned by clear evidence of faulty typography. In other words, realising that the printer has introduced an error, or perhaps that the author has failed to check the proofs, the reader feels compelled to intervene in order to set things to rights. In other cases, however, the impulse arises in slightly more complicated circumstances. After all, once one is willing to interfere with the text's original presentation, one can almost as easily justify the modification of the author's own words, particularly his poor grammar or inappropriate vocabulary, intolerable sins which the long-suffering reader, acting as the self-appointed guardian of proper usage, cannot resist the temptation to adjust. In still other situations, the urge is triggered less by a need to correct than by the reader's sense that further illumination or amplification would be useful—even in the form of changes which the author might theoretically have welcomed. Yet again, the reader might simply want to produce a superior rendition of the author's words and ideas—thus placing multiple editions side-by-side and collating them so as to manufacture a definitive version.

In each of these situations, any intrusion onto the printed page obviously represents a shift in the normal balance of power, a clear transgression by the reader onto hallowed territory conventionally seen as the exclusive domain of the writer. It is clear, too, that this role reversal would have had particular resonance in the innovative and invigorating literary environment in which, as we have seen, Georgian men and women operated. After all, by the very act of applying pen to printed page, the reader had necessarily assumed greater responsibility for how the text was to be approached, in exactly the way advocated in the contemporary reification of the reader by forward-looking critics and other commentators. Indeed, in an important sense, modifying a text has always involved the reader in issuing an overt challenge to the final authority of the writer and printer over its meaning—in declaring an intention to play a more visible and more audible part in the hermeneutic process. In John Kerrigan's description of the wider consequences of these interventions by readers, 'one kind of emendation quickly ran into others.'[19] To this extent, the insertion even of the simplest correction, let alone of a substantial comment, permits us, if only we would listen to it, to eavesdrop on an historical dialogue that unfolded between an author and a reader over the interpretation and significance of a given text. As Charles Lamb revealed to his great friend Coleridge, though surely speaking unintentionally for annotators everywhere: 'I can converse with you by letter, and with the dead in their books.'[20]

As some individual readers' responses to certain Scottish texts reveal only too plainly, the desire to correct a flawed text often arises straightforwardly out of an unsympathetic disposition towards its author. A far from benevolent attempt to modify perceived deficiencies in Hume's writing occurs, for example, in one early composite copy of the *History of England*, which is now at Chetham's Library in Manchester. The reader's identity is unfortunately not known, although it is possible that he was the otherwise unidentified Patrick Murdoch whose name appears on the title page of the 1754 volume (then named *History of Great Britain*) in an obviously eighteenth-century autograph hand. Whoever he was, however, this individual's brusque handling of Hume's prose can only have been the product of a deep-rooted antipathy.

When reading the 1757 volume he had clearly concluded that the description of William and Mary's declaration as monarchs of England, France and Ireland was erroneous, whether because of Hume's poor command of the constitutional facts or because of an unaccountable slip by the printer. Impatiently underlining the word 'France,' he added beside it the curt rhetorical question 'Should not this be—Scotland?.'[21] In fact, in this case it is the reader who was confused, the text being accurate as it stands. But the reader also seems to have concluded that Hume was on occasion guilty of another stylistic solecism, the needless repetition of the obvious. One instance arises where Hume's text in the 1762 volume noted how John de Warenne, Earl of Surrey, had claimed in 1275 that the Conqueror had originally taken England on behalf of *his* ancestor too. This observation earned the reader's pencilled rebuke, indicating his growing frustration with Hume's narrative technique: 'this has been stated before,' he snapped impatiently from the margin.[22]

Another early encounter with the same text, although this time far more reverential, is documented by the extensive technical annotations in the Bodleian Library's first edition copy of the version entitled *History of Great Britain*. Particularly interesting here is the fact that the anonymous reader appears to have had a sound knowledge of the *History*'s second edition, from which he had determined to amend—to improve further, as he saw it—the text of the original. Hume's discussion of Elizabeth's death in 1603, for example, leads to a bracketing off of the entire passage and the insertion of the self-explanatory note 'left out in ye 2^d edition.'[23] Other parts of the text are similarly modified, sometimes for expression and, to a degree at least, for minor aspects of sense.

The intention, however, is always to reconcile the original with Hume's own revisions. About James I, where the text simply reports 'Peace was his favorite passion,' it would, if the interpolated amendment were incorporated, subsequently say 'The love of peace was his ruling passion.'[24] More adjustments, again indicating meticulous study of two parallel versions, include one relating to Prince Henry, of whom Hume had noted that 'his merit seems to have been very extraordinary' but with the reader, once more guided by Hume's careful amendments in later editions, having scored through the word 'very.'[25] Robert Carr, too, the Jacobean courtier, described initially as having 'an easy air and mien,' would become instead, by comparison with the second edition, a man with 'an easy air and graceful demeanour.'[26] Nor was this most assiduous of readers uninterested in accommodating even some of Hume's minor changes to the scholarly apparatus. Hence new footnotes were also added to the comments of the Duke of Sully on James I and to Sir John Fortescue.[27]

A similar process of emendation, revealing a reader's determination to improve one version of an author's work in the light of another, befell a copy of the first (or 1783) edition of Blair's *Lectures*, now in the British Library. Strict collation, page by page, between the copy in hand, probably owned by the annotator, and another copy that had perhaps been borrowed, is strongly implied. On page 362, for example, the intrusions read 'End of the First Volume' and '456,' clearly a reference to the second or 1785 edition's pagination.[28] Blair had also observed early in the 1783 edition that 'Of those who peruse the following lectures, some, by the profession to which they addict themselves, or in consequence of their prevailing inclination, may have the view of being employed in composition, or in public speaking': the comment is altered by the reader, who has struck through the phrase 'by the profession to which they addict themselves, or in consequence' and, linked by a cross mark inserted before this phrase in the text, has created a marginal note containing a variant reading running 'in consequence either of their profession, or.'[29]

Typographical and grammatical corrections, often based on detailed analysis of the evolving phraseology of later editions but sometimes also on the reader's own estimation of how best the text might be sympathetically improved, were a particular avocation of those who read the Scottish Enlightenment's medical works. Presumably this reflects the specialist expertise of medical men, and the continual processes of investigation and improvement to which their profession was intrinsically committed, which might well have encouraged the reader to venture helpful and entirely constructive emendations. The results are well seen in one copy of George Fordyce's *Elements of the Practice of Physic*, an important work written by a former pupil of Cullen at Edinburgh who had then worked and lectured for many years at St Thomas's Hospital in London, where he became a member of Johnson's Club and an F.R.S..[30] Here the handwritten changes to Fordyce's original prescriptions seem to reflect subsequent developments in medical knowledge of which an anonymous reader was clearly aware: a tamarind-based cure for catarrh and a potential treatment for the plague using relaxants were among the recommendations modified in this pragmatic way.[31]

A broadly similar response, with the reader's corrections almost certainly inspired by recent advances, is seen in the changes made to a British Library copy of a different and even more popular Scottish medical text, Cullen's *Synopsis Nosologiae Methodicae* (1769), a work that classified diseases— famously emphasising observable symptoms rather than underlying pathologies—and which was intended, in keeping with its origins in its author's Edinburgh teaching, to aid practitioners in the process of systematic diagnosis. Indeed, here Cullen's notes in Latin are copiously annotated in the same language. New conditions are neatly interpolated—'Dysorexia,' for example, the class of illnesses which incorporates the eating disorders, is inserted among the headings, and then a list of specific conditions is added, including 'Bulimia,' 'Polydipsia,' 'Pica,' 'Nymphomania' and 'Nostalgia.'[32] Old conditions are also renamed. Arthritis, for example, is struck through and instead becomes 'Podagra' (which is to say, 'gout').[33] The over-arching logical structure of Cullen's nosology is also corrected in the light of the reader's superior knowledge, the lists of conditions even being renumbered so as to reflect the new material.

One group of texts that is especially suggestive of this essentially progressive and pragmatic approach to favoured medical texts now forms part of Exeter Cathedral Library, though it clearly belonged in the nineteenth century to the town's Medical Library and before that its constituent parts may well have belonged to individual local physicians. Not surprisingly, these works include several of the principal treatises produced by Scotland's influential scholar–physicians. Several of the volumes also show signs of having been extensively consulted, reflected upon—and, most importantly, creatively revised—by the contemporary practitioners who used them.

Some, such as a copy of Alexander Monro's seminal *Anatomy of the Human Bones* (1763) and one of John Hunter's *Treatise on the Venereal Disease* (1786), carry a great deal of relatively straightforward manual highlighting, a practice familiar enough today in the well-worn standard textbooks of any university library: it can reliably be taken as evidence that at some point a reader has identified the relevant passages as being particularly apposite to their own concerns.[34] Hunter's *Treatise*, however, also bears a set of amplifying notes which serve to underline the understanding and general acceptance of his arguments by at least one of his early Exeter readers. Where the author asserts, for example, that the venereal diseases cannot 'mix' with other infections, the reader dutifully places in the margin a neat and effective summary of his own which reinforces this key diagnostic principle—'no two diseases in same part & same time.'[35]

Two copies of Cullen's *Synopsis Nosologiae Methodicae*, in the Edinburgh editions respectively of 1780 and 1785, are also richly annotated, presumably by near contemporary Devon physicians keen to reinforce, or even perhaps to push further, the author's distinctive approach to disease classification. The later edition has conspicuously well-informed marginal referencing to other relevant products of Scottish medical expertise—to Pringle's *Diseases of the Army* on aspects of opthalmology, for instance, and to Fordyce's *Practice of Physic* on gonorrhoea—again with the clear intention of improving its value and enhancing its meaning by tying its discussion into other authoritative treatments.[36] The 1780 edition, meanwhile, also has lavish marking in both red crayon and black ink—additional evidence of a reader's confident identification of pertinent passages—as well as cross-references to the *Edinburgh Medical Essays* that serve nicely to expand Cullen's original advice on conditions such as apoplexy and colic.[37] Both copies, in short, are exemplary instances of readers' sensitivity to inter-textuality, and a reminder that individual texts, especially when being read and interpreted, do not function in an isolated fashion but rather in relation to wider discourses.[38]

Some of these expert early readers of Cullen might themselves have been drawn to this generally approving response by themselves being graduates of the Edinburgh Medical School. This is at least strongly hinted at by the presence in the same Exeter collection of a heavily marked copy of *The Art of Puffing; an Inaugural Oration* (1765), an anonymous attack upon the great professor himself. Its knowing annotations, again providing helpful amplification of the printed text, certainly seem to rely upon first-hand insights into the murky internal politics of mid-century Edinburgh medicine. At one point, for example, the comments reflect upon the author's mockery of Cullens's distinctive oral delivery, remarking that this was 'Said to be ye stile in w^h Dr. C. talked of himself—certainly a Character which he deserved.'[39] Elsewhere the same reader inserted his own footnote to the text, observing that 'Dr. C. first lectured in English & when the novelty of his Doctrines first excited attention refused to be judged of by partial hearers.'[40]

This same circumstance, of an unusually well-informed reader supplying annotations that better explain an author's original purposes, also underlies one person's response to an early copy of John Witherspoon's *Ecclesiastical Characteristicks* (1763). An extended satire on the Moderate clergymen written by one of their most talented and convincing evangelical presbyterian opponents, this work took aim at both the cultural milieu and the personal foibles of ministers whom Witherspoon regarded as intolerably liberal and secular-minded.[41] Yet Witherspoon had still found it necessary to disguise the explicit personal criticism of his colleagues, adopting as a consequence the elliptical style preferred by so many aggressive eighteenth-century satirists.

At least one reader, however, was more than capable of filling in the gaps for himself. From the cryptic dedication to 'Mr——, Minister in——,' where the annotations added were 'Ramsay' and 'Kelso,' and the early reference to the writings of 'Mr——' ('David Hume') and his '<u>adversary</u>' (this being footnoted in manuscript to 'Mr: Balfour Professor of Moral Phil^y: in Edinburgh'), the reader provided his own illumination throughout.[42] Even the amusing culmination of the text, a marvellous mock-manifesto that Witherspoon had invented in parody of the Creed, was subjected to enlightening annotation. 'In fine,' had joked Witherspoon, mischievously presenting himself as the confident mouthpiece of Moderatism, 'I believe in the divinity of L^d. S——, the saintship of Marcus Antoninus, the perspicuity and sublimity of A——e, and the perpetual duration of Mr. H——n's works, notwithstanding their present tendency to oblivion. Amen.' His erudite reader, however, again inserted the missing names, effectively laying bare on the page the various objects of Witherspoon's raillery: the 3rd Earl of Shaftesbury, Mark Akenside and Francis Hutcheson.[43]

* * *

A closely related form of technical correction, again aiding the reader's appreciation of an author's work, may suggest itself when a text contains distinctive language that is by its nature not easily comprehensible. Such responses among eighteenth-century readers were, of course, particularly likely when they were faced by those unfamiliar or obscure literary traditions with which Enlightenment authors and editors sometimes deliberately entangled themselves. Problems of this kind raised by the recovery and representation of Lowland Scots poetry, a project integral to the Scottish Enlightenment in particular, can be seen especially starkly in some of the early English reactions to Allan Ramsay's work. One copy of the 1733 edition of his *Tea-Table Miscellany*, for example, now in the British Library, was extensively annotated—apparently by an individual named Reeves who already owned the book in May 1734.[44]

Those attributable to Ramsay himself, such as 'The Cordial,' 'The Malt-Man' and 'The Widow' were marked simply 'R'; but 'The Bush aboon Traquair,' for example, was noted as being 'By Robert Crawford,' 'The Faithful Shepherd' was by 'By Alex Drummond Esq. afterwards British consul at Aleppo,' 'Sandy and Betty' was by 'Sir William Bennet of Grubbet,' and of 'Lucky Nansy' it was recorded that 'This was written by Duncan

Forbes, afterwards Lord Advocate and Lord President of the Session.'[45] Evidently the purpose was to improve Reeves's experience of reading Ramsay's text by supplying useful notes illuminating provenance as well as context.

No less revealing annotations, with no doubt equally benevolent motives, survive in a copy of the 1755 edition of Ramsay's *The Gentle Shepherd* that once belonged to the poet William Shenstone. Like the Scot, with whom he had developed an understandable affinity, Shentone was both artist and antiquarian, a more-than-proficient composer of his own pastoral verse but also an avid collector and preserver of older English poetry. Deep interest in vernacular tradition, however, seems also to have been vital to Shenstone when, particularly through Ramsay's pathbreaking publications, he encountered Scotland's native literary heritage, itself conceived and presented as the expression of an age-old peasant society that was now finally in the process of disappearing.

This was surely why Shenstone annotated *The Gentle Shepherd* so extensively with manuscript notes on interleaved pages, thereby providing himself with a private glossary to the otherwise impenetrable argot that Ramsay had utilised. Along with what he called 'Some General Rules for Understanding the Scotch Language,' Shenstone added an 'Explanation of Scotch Words &c. in the Gentle Shepherd' that eventually included translations of such characteristic Scots terms as 'Hartsome' (rendered by Shenstone as 'Heartsome, Heartcheering, Joyfull'), 'Halesome' (simply glossed as 'Wholesome, Healthfull') and 'Chirm' (which he nicely explained, with due deference to more conventional forms of philological investigation, as 'To Chirp or Sing like birds, either from the Sound or from the Fr. & Eng. Charm from Lat. Carmen').[46]

The gratification that Shenstone derived from the encounter with Ramsay's work can also be seen in the confident opinion that he added in pencil at the end of the poem:

> I read this May ye 23 with extraordinary Pleasure: having seldom or never read a Poem of this length, where the simplicity both of <u>Sentiment</u> & <u>Language</u> is so well sustained—The metre is generally harmonious, & many words of ye old Scotch Dialect have an extremely good effect. Good-sense expressed naturally; in a Phrase easy, perspicuous & musical, & not utterly devoid of ornament, seems the Talent of Mr Ramsay; whose <u>taste</u> in composit^n seems more remarkable y^n his Genius—And whom great <u>Fire</u> & <u>Invention</u> would only have prevented from writing the gentle Shepherd with so much Propriety.[47]

Clearly Shenstone's own evaluation of *The Gentle Shepherd* also echoed that offered in published criticism, such as the assessment subsequently printed in the *Critical*: 'The beautiful simplicity of the Gentle Shepherd is such as can hardly be preserved entire in any variation of the language. Though the present modernisation of it therefore may prove more intelligible to an English reader than the original, we may venture to affirm, that much of the spirit has unavoidably been lost in the transfusion, and that to a native of Scotland, who is endowed with taste, the pastoral, as it now appears, is greatly inferior in point of merit, to the inimitable dramatic poem which for upwards of half a century has been the delight of the inhabitants of the North.'[48] Despite the technical hurdles, therefore, Shenstone's reading of Scots verse, assisted by the necessary process of illuminating the printed page with his own scholarly apparatus, had resulted in what criticism in general hoped would be the outcome for all competent English readers: which is to say, deep admiration of its unsuspected but undeniable literary power.[49]

Similar kinds of annotation, shedding light upon the interpretative problems raised by Anglo-Scottish cultural engagement and providing vital additional illumination for the reader, were, not surprisingly, a likely consequence of encounters with the Ossianic works of James Macpherson. At their most basic, these interventions might simply involve the reader adding a manuscript note concerning the perplexing question of Macpherson's trustworthiness as a purported translator of ancient Gaelic epic. Joseph Ritson, for instance, who, like Shenstone, was prominently involved in the burgeoning field of British literary antiquarianism, was also understandably keen to facilitate his own study of an exotic poetic tradition. Hence in his own copy of a 1773 edition of the *Poems of Ossian* Ritson inserted on the flyleaf a transcription of the famous letter on this subject from Hume to Gibbon, dated 18 March 1776 and subsequently published in the latter's memoirs ('I see you entertain a great Doubt with regard to the Authenticity of the Poems of Ossian. You are certainly right in so doing').[50]

Much the same approach, this time rather earlier in date and, significantly, more favourable to Macpherson, left its mark upon Shenstone's own copy of the *Fragments of Ancient Poetry* (1760). Copied in his own hand onto blank leaves there is an extract from a letter written in 1760 by Thomas Bruce, the 5th Earl of Elgin's brother, who had sent the book to Shenstone as a gift. By placing these words within Macpherson's book, the English poet evidently intended that his own future reading of it should be enhanced by recalling—as Bruce's letter reassuringly noted—that:

> It is translated from an old highland Poem by one M[r] M'Pherson, a Minister in y[e] Highlands. There are great numbers of these elegies all over y[e] Highlands which they sing to mournfull tunes in y[e] evening over their Fires. M[r] M'Pherson has I hear translated [some?] more of them which I fancy will soon be published. . . . It will be needless to say any thing in praise of y[e] Poem, as I think it can sufficiently recommend itself. The Translation has a great deal of Merit. I think it is one of y[e] best I ever saw . . . [51]

Scottish poetry, cast in a strange language, was, however, only the most obvious candidate for explanatory annotation. Indeed, wherever those readers who encountered them suffered from anxiety about their own lack of familiarity with the material in question, even the major prose works of the Scottish Enlightenment might sometimes require elements of the same approach.

This is certainly what befell yet another surviving copy of the first edition of Hume's *History*, this time belonging to successive generations of the Hudson family at Wanlip Hall in Leicestershire. It contains the bookplate of Sir Charles Grave Hudson, a South Sea Company director and London merchant who died in 1813. But his son and heir having changed the family name, the book eventually acquired a manuscript note, pasted inside the front cover, probably written by its then-owner George Joseph Palmer, grandson of Sir Charles, who succeeded to the baronetcy in 1827.[52] This was intended to help make sense of Hume's political vocabulary, the origins and implications of which it was clearly feared would not be quite so readily decipherable by this date. Indeed, Palmer's note is most instructive for what he seems to have considered it would be useful for the *History*'s latter-day readers—including himself and other family members—to know about the lost world that it so engagingly described:

> Whig is a Scottish, or Irish word for Whig or sour milk; When the duke of York took refuge in Scotland, his party being strongest, oppressed the opposite one, who were forced to retire into the Mountains & lived on Milk, for <u>wch</u> they were reviled by their opposers & called Whigs; they retaliated, & stiled <u>tories</u> or robbers.—Burnet says the word Whig arose from a march to Edinburgh <u>wch</u> Argyle headed called the Whiggamore's Inroad, from the word Whiggam used in driving their horses by the Leith corn carriers.[53]

On such necessary information, if Palmer's assessment of this most complex and controversial of texts was correct, a reader's chances of developing a proper appreciation of Hume's narrative might well have depended.

*   *   *

It was by no means unknown, then, for contemporaries to subject aspects of the Scottish Enlightenment, as they appeared in printed form, to correction or even to amplification in a number of what were still essentially straightforwardly technical senses. Such interventions were evidently intended, for the most part, to *improve* the experience of reading, now and in the future. It was also possible, however, for both rather more elaborate and far less positive responses to take shape. For the practice of annotating a printed book created more than sufficient scope for what Steven Zwicker has called 'contestative reading,' entailing the development of a hostile reaction by readers not remotely sympathetic to a text's presumed meanings and implications.[54] Indeed, once the momentous decision has been taken to despoil the pristine printed page, literate individuals are likely to find themselves perfectly positioned to grapple on their own terms with an author's intolerable utterances. In other words, the process of annotation by its nature demarcates a space on the page in which a reader is able, quite literally, to have his or her own say, and thus to enjoy the singular privilege of interrupting or even of refuting the author's own line of argument.

William Robertson was, of course, an exceptionally popular writer, much praised by critical opinion. Yet particularly in his capacity as spokesman for the Scots presbyterian tradition, Robertson was also perfectly capable of provoking a somewhat quizzical response from parts of his wider British audience. Evidence of this occurs in one copy of *The Situation of the World at the Time of Christ's Appearance* (1759), now in the British Library. Significantly, this was soon bound together into a single volume, which juxtaposed it with sermons by William Crowe (on Charles I's martyrdom, published in 1724) and George Horne (on the same anniversary, from 1761). This expedient may in turn indicate that this copy of Robertson's text was owned by a reader whose interests lay in the pulpit oratory of the High Anglican clergy. He was, however, clearly dissatisfied with Robertson's speculative approach to the history of religion. For he took immediate issue with those arguments which seemed to demonstrate that Christianity had emerged at the time and place in human history best suited to receive it.

Where Robertson says, for example, that 'no sooner had the tyranny of the *Roman* Emperors removed this restraint, by subverting liberty, than superstition made its advances on the world by sudden and mighty steps,' this reader interjects angrily in the margin: 'Did superstition in fact prevail in the world after it was subdued [by?] the Romans? I think not.'[55] Again, Robertson's argument that the mildness of modern life was not due to 'the influence of better instituted governments; for in legislative wisdom the antients far excelled us,' provokes this reader's hostility. Evidently suspicious that the Scots clergyman was guilty of exaggerating the political virtues of the ancients for rhetorical effect, he responds by asserting, with self-conscious patriotism, that 'This is not entirely true, for no form of government is equal to our own.'[56] In other words, what was frequently believed by mid-eighteenth-century commentators—namely that modern Britain's constitution was superior to all previous historical models—meant that Robertson's apparent preference for the Roman polity, an increasingly untenable and slightly old-fashioned view, could simply not be allowed to stand.

Hume, unsurprisingly, was an even more obvious target for belligerent readings, as individuals sought actively to confront and hopefully also to nullify the unsettling implications of his work. One hostile reader of the *History* was Arthur Onslow, M.P. for Surrey and longstanding Speaker of the House of Commons.[57] Onslow had serious scholarly credentials on which to found an informed critique of Hume's account of recent British politics: indeed, he even published his own notes on Gilbert Burnet's work. Yet it was clearly Onslow's profoundly Whiggish political affiliations that most strongly guided his pen when, in the early 1760s, he scrawled his thoughts onto the pages of his copy of the *History*, which survives today at Harvard.

Some of Onslow's annotations, often tied to the relevant text by precisely positioned cross symbols, make what are in one sense merely technical corrections. Even these, however, frequently arose out of his sense that an author whose motives were so disreputable had failed to do justice to specific points of principle. Where the *History* provides an appendix on the declaration of rights and the condemnation of James VII's dispensing powers, for instance, the validity of the printed words is placed directly in question by Onslow's aggressive objection that 'The author has not stated this important matter so accurately as he might and ought to have done': this readerly intervention was in fact buttressed with references to Burnet and to the *Commons Journal* (a text with which Onslow happened to be intimately familiar); and it was neatly concluded with a self-justificatory note confirming an exceptionally knowledgeable individual's awareness of the revisions found in subsequent editions—'This the author in his late new Edition has observed, and corrected.'[58] Similarly Hume's observation that the claims of Henry VII's family to the throne of England had been 'omitted' in parliamentary legitimation of their properties was greeted by Onslow, effectively deploying his own superior knowledge of the facts, with the tart marginal comment, flatly rebutting the suggestion of legislative failings in this matter, 'It was expressly excepted.'[59]

Some of Onslow's tussles with Hume, however, were plainly not just a question of removing factual errors. For, in what was clearly an intensely ideological reading of the *History* that, as we shall later discover, was by no means uncommon among Hume's English contemporaries, Onslow also seems to have believed that the narrative was shot through with a dangerously Tory—if not a treasonably Jacobite—commitment to absolute royal authority. Such doctrines, of course, were diametrically opposed to the Speaker's own politics, and an affront to those twin pillars of the Hanoverian constitution, parliamentary sovereignty and accountable government. As a result, where Hume asserted, for example, that convention had provided 'certain irregular checks' to the powers of Parliament, Onslow fell upon the comment with obvious glee, marking it with another cross which was then tied to his own ripely Whiggish riposte in the margin: 'I guess the author's meaning; but good Government is the best check.'[60]

This was not all. Beside the remark that the convening of the medieval parliaments had not been 'frequent'—implying, Onslow suspected, that Parliament had not been the enduring embodiment of English liberties that eighteenth-century Whigs liked to believe—he parried Hume's thrust this time by underlining the offending word and then inserting his own reference to an authoritative refutation, reading simply 'See the Rolls of parl^t for the contrary.'[61] On the next page, too, Onslow found it impossible to swallow Hume's glib assertion that the crown had recently been 'diminished of its antient powers.' Proud as the guardian of Parliament's institutional authority, and also reluctant as a Whig to accept that the crown's wide-ranging traditional prerogatives had ever enjoyed unquestioning acceptance, Onslow underlined the entire problematical phrase before inserting his own terse contradiction in the margin: 'not Rights.'[62] In short, Onslow was confident that there had always been a world of difference between the powers that sovereigns had once exercised and the rights to which they had strictly been entitled.

Another reader who responded with articulate displeasure to what he perceived as the violent but veiled Toryism of some of the Scottish Enlightenment's leading historians was Horace Walpole. Walpole in fact reserved especially scornful treatment for his presentation copy of Lord Hailes' *Annals of Scotland* (1776), a work that revised many crucial but hitherto uncertain episodes in Scotland's earlier history. Above all, his reading seems to have focused in particular upon what he interpreted as Hailes's cravenness and credulity in the face of historical claims to royal authority, a political deficiency that he viewed not merely as incidental but actually as a worryingly characteristic feature of Scottish authorship in general.

Hailes, for example, had discussed William of Malmesbury's account of Queen Matilda, observing in passing that 'I have somewhere read of a country that never had but *two* popular Kings, and they were *both* vitious and debauched': Walpole, uncomfortable with anything that sounded like uncritical veneration of royal foibles, noted acidly in the margin 'I suppose he means Edward 4th & Charles 2d of England,' then adding, in mockery of what he considered was Hailes's naive approach to the merits of individual monarchs, 'Who were the Good Kings that We have had & not liked, except King William! I suppose the Author means Charles 1st.'[63] Again, where Hailes had described a ball at Jedburgh for the ill-fated Alexander III in 1285 on his marriage to Yolande of Dreux, and had recounted the story that a ghost had danced at it, Walpole, ever the modern-minded pricker of credulous antiquarian balloons, could not resist voicing his private disapproval. Hence he inserted his own comparison in the margin, neatly undermining the repellent mixture of sentimentalism and royalism in Hailes' discussion: 'A like story was told in the reign of Charles 6th of France,' he scoffed, 'and assigned as the Cause of his Frenzy, as if a King coud not be made mad but by a miracle.'[64]

Yet another example of an openly hostile response is again a useful reminder that strong dissatisfaction with an author's text could readily co-exist alongside other kinds of reaction. An essentially two-pronged approach, successfully combining helpfulness in relation to technical questions with a capacity for pointed criticism of a work's substantive failings, is nicely illustrated in a surviving copy of John Pinkerton's *Dissertation on the Origin and Progress of the Scythians or Goths* (1787), which once belonged to the radical politician and linguist John Horne Tooke but which now resides at Yale. Pinkerton's text, reworking stadialism and conjectural history in an entirely new way, was one of the most controversial and divisive that the Scottish Enlightenment would produce. In particular, it had achieved instant notoriety for its claim that the Scots were descended from the noble Scythian race, and were thus a Gothic or Germanic people, rather than from the feckless Celts.[65] In Horne Tooke, however, Pinkerton had found the least compliant of readers. As an expert philologist—a man who had actually published a work (*A Letter to Mr Dunning on the English Particle* (1778)) that attempted the unlikely feat of a grammatical proof that the legal indictment that had led to his own convictiction for libel was invalid—he was more than capable of responding to the technical challenges posed by Pinkerton's fiendishly complex analysis.

Like so many of this work's other readers, Horne Tooke disagreed strongly with most of the *Dissertation*'s more unorthodox deductions. As Jackson has observed, Horne Tooke was one of those late eighteenth-century readers who would 'pounce on careless or inaccurate remarks with obvious relish . . . all part of the intellectual contest between them and the authors.'[66] Consequently he set himself the task of understanding the evidence on which the *Dissertation*'s remarkable conclusions ultimately appeared to rest. Indeed, the depth of his engagement with Pinkerton's eccentric arguments is made abundantly clear even on the title page, the place where Horne Tooke, almost as if seeking to remind himself of his own knowledge of the languages in which Scotland's ancient inhabitants had first been described, decided to list a number of variant Greek renderings of the key word 'Scyths'—such as 'Σκυθ,' 'Σγνθ,' and 'Σγοθ.'[67]

Horne Tooke's subsequent analysis of Pinkerton's thesis gave rise to an enormously detailed series of annotations that constituted his own running commentary on the sources the author had originally consulted. Certain items in Pinkerton's bibliography, like Burton's *De Veteri Lingua Persica* (1720) and John Chamberlayne's *Oratio Dominica . . .* (1715), for example, are marked with crosses, probably indicating that Horne Tooke had checked them, or at least intended to check them, for himself.[68] He also marked Pinkerton's reference to the ancient geographical writer Solinus's *Collectanea Rerum Memorabilium*, adding what may have been another demonstration to himself of his own scholarly virtuosity: 'The time when Solinus wrote could not be discovered by Erasmus, the Scaligers, Lipsius, Grotius, Salmasius, &c., in short, by all, from the revival of letters to this hour. There must be witchcraft in the case, for nothing is more easy . . . he clearly wrote between 230 and 250, say 240 . . . .'[69] Key arguments and phrases are also highlighted. Pinkerton's ringing declaration 'Nor let us, deceived by vulgar blindness, esteem it a disgrace to be called by our real name of GOTHS, but rather exult in the glorious title' is marked in this way, thereby distinguishing within the text one of the *Dissertation*'s principal rhetorical claims.[70] Also picked out is Pinkerton's important but essentially unsubstantiated assertion that 'words more shortened,' such as much of the vocabulary of the gutteral Anglo-Saxon and other Germanic languages, are 'a grand mark of a polished tongue, as long words are of a rude and primitive one.'[71]

Even so, Pinkerton's extreme opinions combined frequently to reduce Horne Tooke not exactly to bemused silence but at least to wordless exclamation at the author's outrageous sleight-of-hand. Pinkerton claimed at one point, for example, that 'The physical reason for the Northern nations using V for P, or pronouncing P as V, may be, that the cold contracts their organs, for V is only a less open pronunciation of P': this distinctly unlikely explanation earned from Horne Tooke only a laconic but wonderfully eloquent '?' in the margin.[72] In much the same fashion, Pinkerton at one point launched an extraordinary attack upon the Celtic pronunciation of 'Mhic' as 'Wic,' actually describing this peculiarity as 'A strange and horrible absurdity! as it conceals every rule of language; and must shew a confused and dark understanding in the people who use it, nay even to speak it must *ex post facto* throw a mist over the mind.' Horne Tooke responded to this intemperate outburst first by underlining the entire passage, then by adding parenthetic highlighting beside the text so as further to emphasise the singularity of its sentiments, and finally by adding a note of his own reactions in the margin—in this case consummately articulate even when expressed simply as '!!' and '!!!.'[73] Pinkerton's *Dissertation* was, of course, by any standards an exceptionally demanding text. But in this case some of its most violent rhetoric, launched by a Scottish writer against those normally considered the ancestors of Scotland's modern population, had plainly left even this most expert and engaged of English readers quite literally lost for words.

* * *

By no means all annotations were motivated by fear, suspicion or outright hostility towards the claims of particular authors. In fact, it may always be more common for individuals to find affirmation of existing viewpoints, even a measure of self-justification, in what they read. Furthermore, it is far from clear that constructive responses would in principle be less likely to give rise to a lasting mark on the printed page. Some of the latter, of course, might involve no more than an indication of general satisfaction, like a tick in the margin. Others would justify more elaborate interventions, such as marginal notes specifying the grounds for agreement or exploring at greater length some of its various implications. Whatever the chosen technique, annotation provided a means by which a record was created of the manner in which an encounter with a text had become simultaneously an act of self-discovery. Nor, as we have already seen, is this an exclusively one-dimensional process. Rather than a mute recipient passively absorbing an author's words, reading has always had the potential to reflect and to reinforce its exponent's own attitudes and commitments—in essence, providing the unique validation conferred by the higher authority of the printed word.

Hester Piozzi's reading seems to have been impelled by just such a yearning for experiences with texts that would be comfortingly affirmatory. Certainly her responses to the intellectual tussles between Hume and Beattie—for many readers the key dispute framed by the mature Scottish Enlightenment—leave little room for doubt as to her own instinctive preferences (further coloured, no doubt, by her personal acquaintance with Beattie).[74] As she worked through the 1776 edition of Beattie's *Essays*, in a copy formerly belonging to Dr Johnson, the habits of a compulsive annotator frequently allowed her to vent her sympathy for the Aberdonian's bold stance against philosohical error. Beattie had observed, in a notable rhetorical flourish, that reason is 'the instrument of seducing and bewildering mankind, and of rendering philosophy contemptible.' Beside this expression of a consoling Christian orthodoxy that had been offered in specific rebuttal of Hume's dangerous pretensions, she wrote, simply but revealingly, 'That is all very truly & very sweetly said.'[75]

She also willingly signalled her identification with Beattie's other attacks upon Hume. To the sceptic's claim that 'concerning the cause of the universe we can form no rational conclusion at all' she responded instantly with all the self-righteous hostility that Beattie's deliberately unsympathetic gloss had invited: 'Gross Absurdity not worth confuting!,' she snapped in obvious irritation at Hume's pretensions.[76] Similarly, Beattie's tendentious presentation of Hume's argument that the continued fluxions of the tides were simply 'a logical deduction of a conclusion from premises' produced the equally outraged response that 'Mr Hume might as well have said he had eat & drank forty years, *therefore* He should eat and drink forty years more. What nonsense!.'[77] Equally, where Beattie discussed atheism and mentioned Hume again by name, this was yet another red rag to Piozzi's defiantly orthodox bull: 'The Infidel's Creed,' she spat, 'is the hardest Creed of all: & Satan's Servitude the most galling of all Yokes.'[78]

Where the printed text expanded upon the principles of piety and common sense, however, Piozzi, conservative in her own opinions and determined to bolster her sense of her own Anglican rectitude with appropriate reactions to the two warring philosophers, positively purred her approval of Beattie's strategy from the sidelines.[79] One discussion of religious faith provoked the obviously discontented comment, which also serves to date at least one of Piozzi's encounters with this page, that 'We have seen since this book was written the precious effects of Infidelity & Scepticism; France has bled at every Vein in Consequence of the new Philosophy, & is not tired of her Sufferings yet. 1801.'[80] She also responded by seconding Beattie's fears—it is tempting to imagine her discussing them during his visits to her Streatham home—about the difficulty of refuting the sceptics' claims in relation to the narrow limits of human knowledge, noting soberly that 'It cannot I fear be confuted, but it is no nearer the Truth for that.'[81] If anything, her only concern about Beattie's otherwise reassuring position was that, by its nature, it might share some of the same vulnerabilities that the sceptics' doctrines possessed: 'Beattie's System,' she wrote anxiously, her shrewdness as a reader momentarily getting the better of her partisanship as a believer, 'is good, & his Motives pure; yet many of his Arguments may be resisted—and some—confuted.'[82]

Piozzi's close identification with Beattie's polemical defence of orthodoxy also seems to have reinforced her admiration of his personal character—a facet of her natural tendency towards hero-worship that was in many ways, but above all in her relationship with Johnson, a determining feature of her life.[83] Certainly this is suggested by the annotations in her 1807 copy of Sir William Forbes's *Life of James Beattie*. Indeed, the retelling of Beattie' life story provided Piozzi with many opportunities to identify a comforting reflection of her own beliefs and attitudes in his work, whilst at the same time engaging in what appears on occasion to have been a blunt but thoroughly self-vindicating dialogue with Forbes about a biographical subject whom she had not only known personally but had also once joked to Johnson that she might marry.[84]

Forbes's text claimed, for example, that Beattie's life 'furnishes no unuseful lesson, and no mean incentive, to men of genius': to this Piozzi simply indicated her own agreement by writing in the margin 'Certainly.'[85] Elsewhere, again addressing her approval to Forbes himself, she wrote 'what an amiable Character is this of Beattie from beginning to end.'[86] Piozzi also used the experience of reading the *Life* to underscore once more her own orthodox piety. She did this by disagreeing with John Gregory, successively professor in both Aberdeen and Edinburgh, who had claimed in a letter to Beattie in 1767 that until very recently no-one had really managed to debunk natural religion: 'Oh yes sure,' Piozzi mocked incredulously, 'Shaftesbury, Bolingbroke, & a too long Etcetera.'[87] Beattie's admirable personal character was another constant refrain kept up from the margins. Beside an account of Beattie's letter to Thomas Blacklock, for example, in which the former had remarked that the *Essay on Truth* would see him 'animated, without losing my temper, and keen, without injury to good manners,' Piozzi noted compliantly '& so he is.'[88]

Less prolix but probably no less clear-cut in their endorsement of the mainstream tradition of eighteenth-century Scottish moral philosophy are the annotations left by another anonymous contemporary in a copy of the first edition of Adam Ferguson's *Principles of Moral and Political Science* (1792). Here again the reader was able to isolate key passages in which a broadly conventional account of human morality and understanding had been asserted. Ferguson's discussion of 'Goodness,' for example, earned a simple but thoroughly eloquent tick in pencil, indicating this reader's approval of the discussion.[89] So too did Ferguson's measured treatment of 'felicity & veracity,' a section with which the text's owner, by choosing to place another tick, was again presumably more than happy.[90]

There was also, however, a quite different way of marking the page so as to indicate agreement between author and reader. This was to introduce extracts from other work that might reinforce essentially the same arguments—exactly what one reader of Dugald Stewart's *Philosophy of the Human Mind* (1792–1827) chose to do. For this owner actually bound into the front of his copy of Stewart's work, now in the British Library, two manuscript sheets which were, perhaps, a slightly unusual way of attempting to associate its explicit claims with other statements of conventional piety. In fact, they contained, first, the poetry of that most saintly and pious of sixteenth-century English men of letters, Robert Southwell, and second, an extract from Beattie's *Essays on Poetry and Music*.[91]

Coleridge was yet another reader who found in some of the publications of the Scottish Enlightenment the perfect opportunity to corroborate his own fundamental ideas and beliefs. In particular, he was to show himself a sympathetic student of a metaphysical work not now much noticed by historians of philosophy but, according to Coleridge, who annotated it between May 1808 and October 1810, one which had nevertheless served as a helpful bridge between the experiential methodology for which eighteenth-century British thinkers had already become famous and the critical rationalism advanced so successfully by Kant and his European successors. This work was James Hutton's *Investigation of the Principles of Knowledge* (1794), a major philosophical treatise written by the pioneering Edinburgh geologist.[92]

On the title page of his own copy, an appreciative Coleridge recorded his own recognition of Hutton's achievement, though, significantly, he was not unaware of its limitations:

> "I can not walk <u>with</u> them, because I could walk <u>in</u> them," said a Wag of a very much too large Pair of Shoes. Something of the sort might be applied to this Work. There is great metaphysical Talent displayed in it; and the writer had made an important step beyond Locke, Berkeley & Hartley, and was clearly on the [?] of the Critical Philosophy with which & the previous Treatises of Kant he appears to have had no acquaintance. In short, there is Sense, and strong Sense; but it loses itself in its own enormous House, in the wilderness of the multitudinous Chambers & Passages . . . [93]

As an expert reader in this field, Coleridge was well able to locate Hutton's arguments in the longer tradition of modern epistemology. He was also keen to document his approval at least of Hutton's motives in seeking to develop his inquiry beyond the point successfully reached by David Hartley (whom Coleridge, of course, venerated to the extent of naming his eldest son after the philosopher). Hutton had, however, fallen short of the destination towards which he had apparently been travelling.

Another Scottish text elicited a similarly complicated response from Coleridge—part warm affirmation, part mild rebuke. This was the work of Duncan Forbes of Culloden.[94] The latter's remarkable metaphysical system—inspired by his admiration for John Hutchinson, whose *Moses Principia* (1724) had attacked both Newton and the advocates of natural religion and had claimed instead that the Hebrew Old Testament contained a symbolic representation of a revealed natural philosophy—was in fact treated by Coleridge to as careful and, ultimately, as ambivalent a reading as he had earlier given to Hutton's *Investigations*. On the one hand he praised Forbes as 'so good and wise a man . . . and so calm and sober a reasoner'; but on the other, a note written by Coleridge in August 1817 on a blank leaf facing page 262 at the end of the first volume that contained Forbes's "Thoughts Concerning Religion, Natural and Revealed" also observed that the author should have 'explained himself more at large, concerning the position, p. 99, that by the Light of Nature men might have learnt the benignity and mercifulness of the God of Nature but could not have deduced that he would pardon a Sinner sincerely and effectively penitent—μεταγοδγτα. Doubtless, he had weighty grounds for this affirmation, of the importance of which he himself seems to have been fully sensible.'[95] Coleridge, in other words, had noticed Forbes's difficulties in finessing a classic problem in all Hutchinsonian thinking. For like many others, Forbes had failed to explain how it would be possible to reconcile acquiescence in the deists' claim that certain general religious principles could be demonstrated in Nature with Hutchinson's absolute insistence that other more specifically Christian doctrines—such as redemption and salvation—were only discoverable by revelation.

Interestingly, the copy of Forbes's writings to which Coleridge had added these misgivings was not in fact his own. This is clear because he actually offered an apology, and a partial explanation, for having so rudely defaced someone else's book—in this case, that of his friend George Frere:

> The desire to record this regret of mine has tempted me to the liberty of disfiguring this leaf in a Book of yours. You or your brother may perhaps be led to some solution of this problem, the assertion contradicted by Duncan Forbes being one of the main foundation-stones of the Deists, whether simply Deists simply [sic], or Unitarians—For my own part I feel inclined to agree with D.F. in the second or negative position, but doubt the first—viz. that by the light of Nature, as contradistinguished from all Revelations, man could have learnt any of the moral attributes of God.

In short, Coleridge claimed that he had written not self-indulgently but merely for the benefit of his friend, whom it is possible had already raised this particular philosophical problem with him. When highlighting an author's failures in such an important matter as the evidential basis for religious faith, marking the pages, it would seem, was quite literally a service to others.

This ability to appropriate a text for the more pragmatic purpose of reflecting upon and reinforcing one's own beliefs is also seen in the reading of James Leigh of Blackrod, a Lancashire gentleman, when tackling Robertson's *History of Scotland*, of which he owned the 1759 first edition.[96] Leigh seems to have gone through this text on more than one occasion, pausing to underline in red, for example, those passages in the early parts of the narrative that dealt with feudal society, clanship and the weakness of the Scottish crown in its long-running contest with an over-mighty nobility.[97] Other passages that struck him also seem to have stimulated a desire to mark the page—as with the section describing the machinations of the Guise and Lorraine factions in bringing about the betrothal of Mary, Queen of Scots, to the Dauphin, or as with Robertson's description of the Scots' yearning for religious purification (indeed, as if to emphasise their enthusiasm for spiritual renewal, Leigh actually underlines the key word 'rage' in grey pencil).[98] In other words, simply having been intrigued by a particular passage or turn of phrase, and evidently finding it interesting or amusing, seemed more than sufficient reason for Leigh to make his own contribution to the printed page.

It was, however, this text's capacity for being read not as a neutral history of sixteenth-century Scotland but as a polemical defence of Protestantism and a systematic critique of Catholicism that particularly seems to have warmed the cockles of Leigh's heart. His annotations perceptibly increased in density and grew much more pointed and acerbic wherever opportunities arose to flourish his own prejudices. Important words and phrases were underlined in red, highlighting, for example, Robertson's discussions of the 'independent spirit' of Scots Protestantism, or of the 'inflamed' state into which the righteous populace had been pushed under the repressive Guise regime.[99] The same treatment, indicating Leigh's endorsement, was meted out to Robertson's reference to the 'encroaching and sanguinary spirit of Popery.'[100]

That the Reformation had been a challenge to feudal power and that it had brought about a greater attachment in Scotland to what Robertson called the 'exquisite models of free government' pioneered in Greece and Rome seems to have occurred to Leigh, who evidently approached this whole question from the position of a lofty Hanoverian Whiggery. His contemporary frame of reference when reading Robertson was further underlined by his unprovoked attack in the margins upon another author. William Mitford, a Tory M.P., had in his popular *History of Greece* (1784–1810) positioned himself as an openly unsympathetic historian of the classical democracies: 'What do you say to this Mr Mitford?,' asked Leigh, where Robertson's discussion (obviously written long before Mitford's work) asserted the superiority of more widely representative polities.[101] A passionate commitment to the 'great end' of liberty (again Leigh frantically underlined Robertson's idealistic words at this point) was evidently the aspect of his own Protestantism and Englishness that this particular reader believed he could hear strongly echoed in the ultimately successful struggles of the sixteenth-century Scots reformers.[102]

*   *   *

Annotations, as we have seen, provide an exceptionally revealing window through which we can view aspects of readers's experiences with individual texts. As diverse in significance as they are varied in form, marks left on the printed page allow us to make useful progress towards the reconstruction of contemporary responses to the Scottish Enlightenment in particular. Much of the time, of course, annotation seems to have been a matter only of offering different kinds of correction—amending the author's text for the sake of clarity, or expanding helpfully upon his claims, or even adjusting the pages of one edition so as to reconcile them with a later version. Yet the practice actually reveals more than merely the willing involvement of readers, as Charles Lamb suggested, in a private conversation with the author. It also provides clear proof of the utter determination of some readers either to exploit or to subvert the authority of the printed text for their own purposes, and to trespass wilfully and profitably onto territory conventionally viewed as being under the sole and exclusive proprietorship of its original creator.

Whatever else its importance might be, therefore, a decision to mark the page necessarily represents an attempt, fundamentally creative in character, to wrest control of the meaning and significance of a text. It confirms, in the final analysis, the lengths to which some readers will go in seeking to render what they have in front of them not only acceptable but also useful to themselves—an act of unembarrassed appropriation with immediate implications for the self-image of each reader, as well as a performance for which the printed page, a potentially contested space that also enjoys immense cultural prestige, is in many respects the ideal arena. Annotations, however, are only one insight, and by no means the most expansive or communicative kind, into the manner in which books successfully draw forth responses from those who encounter them. It is to other forms of evidence for readers' experiences of the Scottish Enlightenment, in no way so confined by the boundaries of the printed page, that we now turn.

7 "Many Sketches & Scraps of Sentiments"
Commonplacing and the Art of Reading

Annotations are, of course, only one means by which the historian might subsequently be able to track the halting progress of a reader through a text. A separate notebook documenting aspects of one's experiences with a text—in short, the manufacturing of what has long been known as a 'commonplace book'—is another means by which lasting evidence of reading might emerge.[1] Indeed, this has always been a popular expedient, being both less constrained and also significantly more versatile in its applications than mere annotation. After all, liberated from the need to cramp one's own contributions around and within the author's printed efforts, the act of writing in a commonplace book necessarily affords greater scope for articulating complex reactions to what is being read. Because of this possibility, as well as because in its most basic form commonplacing also allows the virtually cost-free permanent reproduction of favourite pieces of text (and in the eighteenth century did so when the number and variety of works for short-term borrowing was rapidly expanding), the popularity of commonplacing among Georgian readers should hardly be surprising. It follows naturally that this factor must also be an important focus in any attempt to reconstruct English contemporaries' responses to the Scottish Enlightenment.

* * *

As with reading itself, so was the business of commonplacing hedged round in the Georgian period with customs, assumptions and technical expectations that exerted considerable influence upon individual practitioners. Not least this was because the commonplace book, even if it enjoyed unprecedented esteem in the eighteenth century, was no radical new invention.[2] On the contrary, it had roots in the ideas about philosophical, literary and rhetorical education first advanced by seminal ancient authorities like Aristotle, Cicero, Quintilian and the younger Seneca. In particular, the identification of valuable truths and pertinent observations—formally described as *sententiae*—had long since been accepted as an essential element in the process of constructing robust propositions and persuasive arguments. Frequently, this had led on to the production of manuscript works that supplied a ready-made fund of wise and informative extracts. In the later middle ages this culminated in the rich tradition of *florilegia*—literally 'books of flowers'—that offered readers a highly structured compendium of useful philosophical and, above all, scriptural and patristic quotations.

From this point it was but a short further step to the Renaissance humanist's heightened interest in studying and memorising elegant *sententiae*.[3] By the sixteenth century this often justified the publication of printed collections that promoted the spread first of correct Latin and Greek usage and then, subsequently, of the appreciation of vernacular literature. Ben Jonson in England, Desiderius Erasmus in the Netherlands and Octavianus Mirandula in Italy were among the noteworthy contributors to this tradition. The modern literary anthology and the multi-disciplinary encyclopaedia might even be considered among its more important long-term consequences.[4] Yet as public literacy improved and the self-confidence of the literate also grew, the same notions finally began to encourage the creation of manuscript commonplace books by readers themselves.

In one sense these were empty vessels into which any knowledge or wisdom that was encountered could conveniently be poured. They were also treasured as personal collections of *bon mots*, anecdotes and favourite extracts, as well as places in which it was possible to reflect upon and to learn from one's own experiences as a reader. Accordingly, by the end of the seventeenth century the future of commonplacing lay in the hands of the individual reader more than those of the published author.[5] Locke's *A New Method of Making Common-Place-Books* (1686), which appeared posthumously in 1706, was therefore not aimed at a small coterie of educators and professional scholars. Instead, with considerable and enduring success, it was pitched at the growing population of men and women who felt themselves to be in need of practical guidance when starting to compose manuscript commonplaces of their own.[6]

Given the tradition's august heritage and yet its evident adaptability to a great range of different cultural circumstances, it is extraordinary that so little scholarly interest has been shown in the modern history of commonplacing from around 1700 onwards. As Earle Havens has argued, this period has unfortunately been 'the subject of little research and less debate,' apparently because it has been assumed that 'general interest in commonplace books declined in the centuries following the Renaissance.'[7] This is the implication to which even Ann Moss's excellent study of the sixteenth-century printed commonplace book tends. It later fell into decline, she suggests, reduced to 'a rather lowly form of life, adapted to simple tasks, and confined to the backwaters of intellectual activity.'[8] As should be clear from the substantial number of manuscript commonplace books that actually survive from this period, however, in England the Georgian era witnessed not the slow withering but the vigorous flourishing of commonplacing as a feature of the reading lives of many people. Indeed, rather than the classics and scripture, those old staples of the genre, slipping rapidly from view, dragging the commonplace book with them into an abyss, the Enlightenment in fact triggered a rejuvenation of interest in systematic note taking by fusing a continuing fascination with these conventional preoccupations together with a fashionable concern for a much greater range of modern and vernacular texts that increasingly seemed worthy of comparable attention.

Nor did the very notion of a select canon of approved and quotable authors, that had previously done so much to inspire and sustain commonplacing, suddenly vanish, rendered redundant by new cultural forces and new literary trends. Instead, as we saw in Chapters 2 and 3, critical commentary in the Augustan period actually accelerated the process of canonisation so that, as the concept was eagerly embraced by the reading public, it also accommodated more recent British literature—including, as it turned out, much that was unmistakably Scottish in provenance. Consequently, growing numbers of people were able both to take up and to modify further the time-honoured conventions of commonplacing. In fact, what had once been a cornerstone of a supposedly static and largely closed scholarly culture now appeared the perfect vehicle for the expression and exploration of English readers' own idiosyncratic and endlessly changing sensibilities.

The commonplace book was thus not only a highly regarded but also an increasingly ubiquitous presence in eighteenth-century England. But it was also one that prospered precisely because of its considerable versatility in both form and purpose. For it is the ever-increasing diversity rather than the rigid uniformity of commonplacing that probably most marks out this period. Above all, where once it had been the prerogative of a narrow circle of humanists, scholars, secretaries and courtiers, it was now the everyday diversion of a much wider cross-section of society. Military men, politicians and merchants increasingly kept them. Indeed, notable surviving examples were compiled by readers as diverse as Thomas Binns, a Quaker merchant from Liverpool; the parliamentarians (and friends of Horace Walpole) William Chute, who, a neighbour of the Austen household, sat for Hampshire, and Joseph Gulston, who represented nearby Poole and compiled a commonplace book with the incomparably uplifting title "Effusions of Fancy and Fun"; the serious-minded Lancashire schoolmaster Thomas Wilson was also an active commonplacer; and so, apparently, was Edward Columbine, naval commodore and later African colonial administrator.[9]

Even more interestingly, increasing numbers of women—and particularly, it has to be said, *young* women—seem to have manufactured commonplace books of their own. To judge from the examples which eventually found their way across the Atlantic into the academic libraries of New England, female commonplacers from this period included the poet Felicia Hemans; the inimitable annotator Hester Piozzi (one of whose journals laboured under the unique title "Minced Meat for Pyes"); an unnamed daughter of Revd Robert Hunter, rector of Okeford Fitzpaine in Dorset (though possibly his eldest, Maria Eliza); and two otherwise unknown ladies, Anne Milbanke and Anna Maria Sharpe.[10]

Nor, it should be added, was the manuscript commonplace book always compiled for the use of its creator. Some certainly served as the precious gift of one person to another, offered in the hope that they would provide edification and instruction to their grateful recipient. This was, for example, the thinking behind the decision of James Dalloway, a Gloucestershire banker, to prepare a commonplace book for his son (also James), which he subsequently explained in a few telling words written out at the front: 'My Dear Boy, Within these Covers (which will most probably fall into your hands) you will find many Sketches & scraps of Sentiments promiscuously inserted without order or Method, occasionally pen'd down to help a bad Memory . . . .'[11]

Some of the traditional functions of the commonplace book, which, as Dalloway's self-deprecating comments recall, had served fundamentally as an aid to memory and learning, seemed to have continued much as before. Thus materials for sermons, reflections on scripture and copies of lectures and speeches remained important components of many readers' notes. Good examples of this tendency would be the extensive sermon notes and sketches compiled by Edward Williams, an Independent minister in late eighteenth-century Oswestry on the Welsh border, or, also demonstrating that this preoccupation was by no means confined to the academically-trained clergy, the voluminous notes on scripture and sermons made by Mrs Jane Pateshall, an intensely bookish, but also extremely pious landed gentleman's wife from Weston in Herefordshire.[12]

Meditative commonplacing encouraged by religious devotion, however, sometimes showed clear signs of catching the philosophical mood of an age of Enlightenment. Indeed, it was often capable of embracing the fashionable idioms promoted to readers through popularising accounts of technical questions such as the 'moral sense' (a recurrent topic in the *Monthly Review* through the second half of the eighteenth century) and in critical discussions of writers, many closely associated with the Scottish Enlightenment, like Hume (whose philosophical works were several times examined in that most widely read and most influential of contemporary commentaries, the *Gentleman's*).[13]

This is surely why James Moore, for example, an attorney at East Dereham in Norfolk in the 1790s, became so obsessed with the 'passions'—fear, love, jealousy and the like. He explored them in a commonplace book filled with evidence of his having pored over popular works as diverse as the Scottish physician William Buchan's *Domestic Medicine* (whose *bon mots* on visceral emotions like grief and anger Moore eagerly transcribed) and Boswell's *Life of Johnson*.[14] No less preoccupied with mankind's base instincts, and in a language that interestingly mingled traditional piety and contemporary philosophical controversies, was the note taking of Benjamin Howlett, non-conformist minister at Olney in Buckinghamshire—the parish indelibly linked which Cowper, the age's finest devotional poet—in the early nineteenth century. Howlett added lengthy ruminations on the 'Passions' to his own commonplace book.[15]

Revd James Gambier in Kent, that compulsive writer in printed books, was also not immune to this specific set of concerns, as central to the Enlightenment as to older Christian debates, with the unpredictable consequences of our peculiar psychological construction. He added to his commonplace book a summary of part of Kames's *Elements of Criticism* on the social instincts ('Lord Kaim [sic] makes the difference between <u>Emotion</u> & <u>Passion</u> to consist in the latter's being accompanied by <u>desire</u> . . . ').[16] He also made a précis of Blair's discussion in the *Lectures on Rhetoric and Belles Lettres* that, although drawing upon Quintilian's rhetorical theories, had again captured something of the deep-rooted Christian suspicion of the unruly passions: 'The Language of Passion is plain, & simple; abounding indeed with those Figures, which can express a disturbed & impetuous state of Mind, such as Interrogations, Exclamations, and Apostrophes; but never employing those which belong to the mere embellishment & parade of Speech.'[17] Kames was, of course, a particularly ready source of edifying thoughts on psychology, as a late eighteenth-century note taker in the East Riding of Yorkshire demonstrated. This anonymous reader actually made his own summary of exactly the same passage from the *Elements* as Gambier had chosen: this he now called 'Lord Kaime's [sic] Division of Emotions,' noting, crucially, that emotions were 'those feelings which are antecedent to passion, & seem ye causes of passion.'[18]

By no means all of the inspiration for commonplacing, however, was religious or philosophical in origin. Indeed, anecdotes and medical and culinary recipes, immediately practical subjects that had already proven attractive to note takers in the seventeenth century, remained key preoccupations for compilers in the eighteenth and early nineteenth. The former were, if anything, an even greater obsession than before, their availability and topicality having increased as magazines and newspapers filled with entertaining material of this kind. Revd Howlett, for example, took obvious pleasure in culling from the *Eclectic Review* the famous story of Lord Charlemont's description of Scotland's most notorious philosopher—'Nature I believe never formed any man more unlike his real character than David Hume . . . .'[19] The breathlessly gossipy commonplace book of Miss Hunter, meanwhile, was stuffed with tales of Samuel Johnson, the Duke of Hamilton and, most interestingly, Colonel Ewart of Dumfries's experience of Robert Burns: 'he spoke of him as a man of very coarse unpleasant manners,' this Dorset reader wrote, '& very satirical in conversation, sparing no one, especially his superiors.'[20]

Less amusing, perhaps, but also no less conventionally practical, was the keen interest of note takers in those medical subjects in which Scottish authors now played such a prominent part. At Coughton in Warwickshire, Sir Charles Throckmorton was evidently a determined reader of medical texts, including the same works of Alexander Hamilton, Edinburgh professor of midwifery, whom we have seen that Mathew Flinders in Lincolnshire also esteemed.[21] William Chute, at his family home at The Vyne in

Hampshire, was another admirer of the sayings and saws of the Scottish physicians. Hence he transcribed Pringle's advice on preparing an elixir for the cough, a prescription for 'putridity' from Sir William Fordyce (brother of the divines James and David), and other gleanings on subjects such as insanity, as well as, beneath the heading 'Economicks,' a recipe for beef and vegetable soup—this concoction, as Chute added, specifically 'for the poor.'[22]

Its role as a pivotal site in its owner's unfolding relationship with a range of printed texts, and so by extension with the experience of reading, was also affirmed by the other kinds of material with which a man or woman might now fill their own commonplace book. Sometimes this might mean nothing more than a list of books that the compiler either had already read or wanted to read in future. As we have already noted, Humphrey Senhouse, a Cumberland gentleman, incorporated one in his commonplace book at the turn of the nineteenth century.[23] James Smith, too, the Norwich wool merchant and Unitarian, prepared what he called 'A Catalogue of Title Pages of Books Read . . . 1762–1786' which reveals him as having already worked through Hume's *Political Discourses* and the *History*, Robertson's *Scotland*, Gilbert Stuart's *History of the Reformation in Scotland* (1780) and Dalrymple's *Memoirs*.[24]

More often, however, it was the contents rather than the mere existence of certain books that led a reader to commonplace. A fine example of what might result was the work of Thomas Sutton of Great Yarmouth, who towards the end of the eighteenth century copied out an article in the *Encyclopaedia Britannica*'s that provided a satisfyingly complete chronology of historical events all the way from 4008 BC to 1783.[25] Among those committed not merely to transcribing but actually to the much more demanding process of combining accurate précis with discriminating evaluation—which, in an age of criticism and self-conscious striving for good taste, seemed more important than ever—James Smith of nearby Norwich is again a paragon. His splendidly acute analysis of Robertson's *Charles V* displays an impressively keen eye and ear for the distinctive literary manner of the leading Scottish historians: 'entertaining & well wrote,' Smith confidently judged, 'very much in the manner of Hume's History of England, which is a peculiar one, & more amusing than solid, & rather like a discourse or dissertation then an accurate relation of facts . . . .'[26]

Historical writing was in fact by some distance the preponderant genre in English readers' engagement with the Scottish Enlightenment, and so was almost inevitably to the fore as an inspiration for commonplacing. Occasionally it seemed almost to exclude the possibility of a reader actually having meaningful contact with any other kind of literature. An extensive summary of a passage from Henry's recently published *History of Great Britain*, for example, which the *Town and Country Magazine* had straightaway recommended as a work of 'much judgment' and 'a concise account of the most interesting events that have occurred in this kingdom, since it was invaded by Julius Caesar,' eventually formed the entire subject of a commonplace book compiled by George Norman, a timber merchant at Bromley in Kent in the mid-1770s.[27] Equally taken with Henry's work was William Barton, a Lancashire parson who before Cambridge and ordination studied medicine both at Edinburgh and in Vienna. In fact, Barton began his own commonplace book with an account of ancient British history attributed directly to 'Dr Henry in his history.'[28]

Other Scottish historians were at least as popular as Henry. Malcolm Laing's recently published *History of Scotland* (1800), for example, provided the notes on 'Scotland from the Union of the Crowns to the Union of the Kingdoms' written down by George Ashby, former President of St John's College, Cambridge.[29] The antiquary Thomas Astle, meanwhile, summarised around 1760 parts of Lord Kames's *Historical Law Tracts* (appropriately, perhaps, since Astle had trained as an attorney), which he also noted had been published by Millar as recently as April 1759.[30] Astle was evidently a fervent reader of Enlightenment historiography, elsewhere producing a neat condensation of parts of another Scottish text:

Gillis History of Greece 2. Vols 4to
London 1786
Vol. 1.
Chap. 2. Page 36 Religion Governm^t. [?]
Manners & character
Chap. 3. p. 80. The origin of Grecian Oracles
particularly that at Delphi
91. Lycurgus collected Homer's Poems in Ionia or
Aeolia, & carried them to Sparta & arranged the
sev^l parts see pag: 498.
171 to 181 Of Grecian Music, worthy of attention
The Greeks had arrived at the heighth of musical perfec:
:tion in the beginning of the 6th Century before Christ . . . [31]

Not all readers were as assiduous as Astle in documenting their engagement with recent historical scholarship. The forty-eight-page summarisation of Elizabeth I's reign taken down by Anne Orlebar, a Bedfordshire woman in the 1790s, can only have rested upon her knowledge of one of the period's popular historians, possibly Hume or Smollett or Henry (the latter being another of Astle's favourite quarries), even if she neglected to identify the source.[32] Like Orlebar, a member of the Beldam family in Cambridgeshire in the 1780s made extensive notes on English history, unfortunately leaving no hints as to their provenance.[33] Despite this, however, these laborious attempts to capture the burden of a favourite text undoubtedly underline the importance of the basic level of historical knowledge that was increasingly considered necessary by any reader with serious intellectual pretensions.

Another traditional feature of the commonplace book that was pushed in entirely new directions at this time was its practical role as a secure storehouse of favourite text. For the exponential growth of the topical press meant that most commonplacers from the 1750s onwards—who were usually also sufficiently wealthy to buy newspapers and magazines for themselves—were also likely to be able to accumulate significant quantities of clippings. Indeed, the advent of comparatively affordable as well as disposable print, at least from the more ephemeral publications, encouraged the effective transformation of the commonplace book into what we would today recognise simply as a scrapbook. At its simplest, this hunger for the physical perpetuation of printed material might lead, for example, to an image of a bust of David Hume being cut out from *Cooke's Pocket Edition of Hume* by one of the Heselrige family from Noseley in Leicestershire.[34] More likely, however, it would involve pasting select items into a commonplace book.

Horace Walpole was a particularly enthusiastic hoarder of material from the contemporary press. But what he selected was evidently much influenced by his literary and intellectual interests. Certainly a lot of his gleanings cast useful light upon what he had already read or bought. From the *Public Advertiser* in January 1777, for example, he took an item concerning the King's Fool and the treatment of this subject in Robertson's *Scotland*.[35] Abrasive Whiggery, meanwhile, must have been what led someone in the early 1770s—not Walpole himself although the resulting clipping did subsequently find its way into the Walpole Library at Farmington—to retain an item in the *Public Advertiser* which alleged that Dalrymple's *Memoirs*, because of the Scottish author's blind attachment to George III and the Tories, had effectively destroyed the reputations of the Whig martyrs Russell and Sidney.[36]

The copying out of poetry, a practice that looked back to the origins of the commonplace book in the memorisation and rote learning of elegant phrases and passages, also provided an important focus for contemporary readers' note taking. But two trends in particular should be highlighted. First, British poetry rapidly came to dominate, effectively relegating the classical verse that had been popular among commonplacing readers in the decades either side of 1700. This seminal development might in turn be regarded as simply additional evidence among an increasingly critically aware readership of that growing emphasis upon an essentially *British* literature that we have already examined. Furthermore, in a person like Revd Robert Martin, an early nineteenth-century Leicestershire vicar whose poetic transcriptions now focused very much on authors like Cowper, Byron, Keats and Shakespeare rather than on the Latin and Greek poets whom his Augustan predecessors had still favoured, we might even discern a process by which the natural instincts of modern commonplacers to follow explicit critical guidance was reaching its apogee.[37]

Second, commonplace books simultaneously came to reflect an important corollary of the self-confident literacy of so many Georgian readers by providing them with encouragement to produce creative compositions of their own. In fact, many now felt emboldened to venture their own 'poetic trifles' (as Johnson's friend the musicologist Charles Burney called his own efforts), exploiting the unusual combination of privacy and freedom afforded by the commonplace book to document a deeply felt response to experience—and not least to the peculiarly personal experience of reading. Burney, for example, penned an 'Elegy, addressed to Dr. Beattie, on perusing his Poems and Elegys.'[38] Thomas Stevens, too, a West Country dissenting minister in the early 1780s, intermingled his own compositions with favourite extracts from Thomson's *The Seasons*.[39] In each case, moreover, it is seems likely that commonplace verses, whether copied from an eminent author's works or simply the original product of the reader's own muse, were often intended not for silent rereading but for the sort of outward recitation—within a family or other social circle—that poetry in particular almost demands.

Perhaps the most striking evidence of the English reader-as-poet who was willing to reflect creatively upon the implications of a Scottish text is a short piece written by the younger James Dalloway, the recipient of his father and namesake's well-meant advice. As it happens, this was emphatically not created with public recitation in mind. Written for his sister Martha following their mother's death and bearing the title 'J.D. Jun[r] to his Sister, with Dr Gregory's Legacy,' it stressed the lessons that John Gregory had insisted upon in his much loved *A Father's Legacy to his Daughter* (1774)—a copy of which Dalloway had also given to her:

> Take from a Brother's hand, this moral Page,
> A gift well suited to thy tender age,
> For here around no brilliant fictions stray,
> To lead thy fascinated heart astray,
> But, the pure dictates of parental love;
> And such, thy Mother living would approve.[40]

Eventually preserved in a commonplace book that James's son Joseph gifted in turn to his own wife Catherine, this poem also perfectly captures the significance of reading in the minds of so many contemporaries. Firmly encouraged by the selection of an exemplary text that was, of course, especially meaningful in the circumstances (*A Father's Legacy* had been written for Gregory's own daughter following her mother's death), reading was clearly an experience that was expected—and as successive generations of the Dalloway family certainly hoped—to make a person not just wiser but also better.

* * *

Of all the functions it performed, the commonplace book may have been most important for its Georgian exponents as a tool in the construction of the polite and cultivated individual. As John Brewer has underlined, 'the literature of politeness emphasized self-fashioning,' and 'keeping a journal or diary' of one's experiences and reactions, not least for the reader, seemed particularly advantageous when 'seeking to fashion him or herself as a cultured person.'[41] This may, of course, be partly why contemporary readers turned to commonplacing even more readily than they did to annotation. For above all, the commonplace book provided a way of achieving a high degree of personal identification with specific beliefs, opinions and values articulated in printed texts. The most dramatic consequence in so far as engagement with the Scottish Enlightenment was concerned is probably the extraordinary eagerness with which many readers seem to have bolstered their own identities by using their commonplacing so as to delineate (and, often quite consciously, to document for posterity) a fundamentally antagonistic response to the philosophy of David Hume.

In one sense this is scarcely an inexplicable strategy among readers concerned at some level or other with questions of personal identity. As Stephen Greenblatt points out, self-fashioning is especially successful when worked out 'in relation to something perceived as alien, strange, or hostile.'[42] It is therefore important that Hume was also an author who tested the patience and the intellect in roughly equal measure. Above all, it was this ability to vex his readers that eventually saw him subjected to as much mischief-making and apocryphal anecdotalising as any literary figure of the period. It also gave him an unusual place within contemporary culture. For Hume in effect came to serve more as a touchstone or totem in relation to which the parameters of an individual's own orthodoxy could be clearly demarcated than as a man of flesh and blood whose writings could be evaluated openmindedly and without drawing upon a whole host of generally negative preconceptions and prejudgments.

Certainly Hume's visibility in commonplace books from the 1750s onwards can only be explained by the extraordinary mixture of fascination and revulsion that his ideas (real or imagined) tended to provoke. The readerly musings preserved in one surviving commonplace book, now at Yale, which appears to date from the early 1780s, make this very clear. Almost certainly a well-educated male, this reader combined an interest in two of the century's most distinguished authors with an endearing propensity for impromptu versification of questionable quality.

The resulting composition is headed 'Written in August on a hot day in company, upon a Deist (who greatly admir'd D. Hume) saying th[t] Dr. Johnson for his pride deservd to be the Devil's secretary.' It reveals a strong partiality towards Johnson as a model of pious rectitude but also an equal and opposite dislike of Hume (a bias that doubtless befits a reader whose commonplace book was also full of material from the book of Isaiah):

Twas in mid August, & at burning noon
Beneath the Willows by my River laid

I dreamd me thought I was buried soon
On wide-winged Griffon to the Stygian shade.[43]

Having first encountered Lucifer and his minions, the writer subsequently imagines seeing two men dragged unceremoniously into Satan's presence—'Sam Johnson one, & t'other David Hume.' Satan, in the poet's reverie, discovers that the religious pride of the former is 'more imperious than my own,' and so is by far the 'feircest [sic] of my foes.' As a result, in Johnson's words as he departs the scene in understandable haste, it is Hume who 'will serve [thee?] with a faithfull heart.'

Caricature of Hume's spiritual affiliations, however, existed alongside systematic denigration of his personal integrity, this focus for readers' criticism invariably deriving in part from unsympathetic (and, for the most part, wholly apocryphal) anecdotes. Miss Hunter, for example, the Dorset parson's daughter, took malicious pleasure in recording the blatantly false account of Hume's deathbed recantation of his doubts—'his mental agonies were dreadful—that he had a Prayer Book constantly by him—which he always hid under the the the [sic] bedclothes, when his philosopher friends came to see him'—a story which, Miss Hunter noted with obvious relish, appeared to refute Smith's exculpatory essay on his friend's Stoical departure which she had also read when it was printed as an appendix to her own father's now-burned copy of Hume's *History*.[44]

Charles Bracebridge, an early nineteenth-century Warwickshire gentleman, was another whose violent distaste for Hume, based on the standard equation of scepticism with irreligion and so with immorality, was rendered fully explicit through his commonplacing:

> David Hume, a very good Man in practice, was, as every Man knows, a perfect unbeliever. It had been the endeavour of his literary life to undermine and shake those opinions of a future state, which are often the support of Virtue—, the last hope of the unfortunate—, the only counterpoise of absolute evil in this world—, and which furnish the only explanation of which it is susceptible.'[45]

Even Gustavus Gale, the Carlisle draper, broadly agreed with Bracebridge, finding Hume's doubts about the afterlife utterly repellent. 'What mind but views with horror,' Gale complained in 1794, 'so dismal a prospect as that of total annihilation, and revolts at so uncheering a doctrine, whether it discovers itself under the fascinating charms of ancient eloquence, or pollutes the modern writings of a *Hume*.'[46]

William Chute was equally motivated by a perceived obligation to help contain this strikingly dangerous product of the Scots' penchant for unconstrained philosophising. Here, however, rather like Hester Piozzi, Beattie's Common Sense riposte was invoked as an effective antidote to the sheer toxicity of the sceptic's arguments. Chute noted in his commonplace book, under the terse heading 'Hume,' the following definition-by-antonym: 'Whose uncomfortable & unintelligible system of Pyrrhonism has been exposed with great spirit & eloquence in Dr Beattie's Essay on the nature and immutability of truth . . . .' Reuse of the same heading subsequently created an opportunity for Chute to renew his own private assault upon Hume. But this time it involved some damaging accusations that revolved, as Beattie in particular had suggested, around the injuries inflicted by scepticism upon our confidence in the accuracy of perception and understanding: 'Most ingeniously reasoning us out of every ground of certainty & every criterion of truth,' Chute ruminated bitterly to himself, 'involving self evident actions in obscurity & confusion & intangling our understandings in the gloomy intricacies of scholastic subtlety & metaphysical abstraction. Giving an air of speciousness, to the wildest singularities, by the most exquisite graces of composition.'[47]

As Chute's analysis here makes plain, when not confining their thinking to Hume himself, readers were also able to identify with other, far less dangerous aspects of the Scottish Enlightenment's philosophical debates. Indeed, they seem frequently to have found it desirable to enlist Scotland's talented philosophers in the continuing endeavour of validating their own assumptions, expectations and identities as orthodox believers—explicitly sympathising, in other words, with the sentiments expressed by authors like Beattie, Reid and Stewart, and, as Patricia Meyer Spacks has suggested is the consequence of such potent psychological strategies, almost becoming 'imaginatively part of the same community.'[48]

Hutcheson was an unsurprising focus for some approaches of this kind, as is seen in the response of William Mildmay, who lived at Moulsham Hall in Essex in the mid-eighteenth century. Mildmay undoubtedly had eclectic tastes not only as a reader but also as a commentator on his own reading—taking down interesting notes in history, ecclesiastical affairs, theology and architecture, as well as, rather less attractively, carping at Catholicism at every available opportunity. But it was clearly his interest in defending conventional religious and moral principles that led him to embrace so enthusiastically Hutcheson's widely respected and, as it seemed to him, eminently sensible reasoning. In deferring to the 'Author of the Inquiry into the Original of our Ideas &c.,' indeed, Mildmay apparently came to believe that Hutcheson's arguments were authoritative not least because he 'hath taken great pains to explain his Meaning in a proper manner.' Yet it was the claim that 'wherever there is any Regularity in a System capable of many other Positions, there must have been Design in the Cause' that particularly drew his attention.[49] As Mildmay wrote in his commonplace book, it seemed possible to make this principle not only 'applicable to Natural Philosophy' but also 'likewise an Argument against those who pretend to Doubt the Creation of the World by a Divine Agent.'[50]

William Bulwer, who lived at Heydon in neighbouring Norfolk, had essentially similar attitudes to Mildmay. Certainly he viewed Hutcheson as the obvious point of reference when recalibrating his own orthodoxy in matters of morality, perception and belief—in the 'affirmation of ordinary life,' as Charles Taylor has called this integral element in self-construction, to which reading and reflection upon it actually contributes so prodigiously.[51] Bulwer was especially alert to the way in which Hutcheson's "moral sense" could be applied to the defence of common sense understanding, both in its metaphysical and in its everyday manifestations. In fact, he produced an elaborate précis of the *Inquiry*'s handling of the question of the reliability of aesthetic judgments in which 'The Author of Nature' played the decisive reassuring role—God having 'mov'd to make such connection between regular objects and the pleasure which accompanies the perception of them.'[52]

A comparable self-defining response to another aspect of the emerging Scottish "Common Sense" tradition—again with Hume conveniently identified as its antithesis—was experienced by a Lancashire schoolmaster, Thomas Wilson. On the first page of his own commonplace book, compiled around 1769, Wilson discussed the concept of an 'Idea,' alighting significantly upon the disputes between Hume and Reid over what he called (actually using the latter's phrase in the *Inquiry*) 'the Principles of Common Sense.' But Wilson was especially perturbed by the notion, so threatening to his own and to everyone else's sense of themselves, '"that Sensation and Thought may be without a Sentient Being",' for Hume, 'although his whole System is built upon it, never offers the least proof of it.' In despatching the profoundly troubling implications of this proposition, however, Wilson borrowed the remarkable critique recently supplied by Reid's work: 'It seems therefore, this Notion however strange is closely connected with the received Doctrines of Ideas, and we must either admit the Conclusion or call in Question the premises—Reid.'[53]

Wilson was not alone in articulating his own orthodoxy by warmly embracing Reid's pivotal contribution to the Scottish Enlightenment. Identical concerns, and much the same qualms about Hume's role in the debate, led William Chute to compile his own notes on 'Philosophy, Dr Reid's,' in which he observed that Reid's unpicking of Locke's empiricism in the Introduction and Conclusion of the *Inquiry*, a necessary part of his famous rescue of common sense from encroaching scepticism, rested on precisely this point: 'Dr R.,' Chute observed, 'thinks it the greatest blemish in Mr Locke's essay that the word idea is used ambiguously, sometimes to signify thought, sometimes the internal objects of thought.'[54] James Franks at Halifax was another who appreciated Reid's importance to the defence of conventional psychology and morality. This role had been best performed, according to Franks, in the *Inquiry*'s sixth chapter, from which he duly appropriated a germane passage for his own commonplace book.[55]

Much the same willingness to borrow Reid's comforting arguments is seen in a discussion of the 'Evidence of the senses, defended' noted down by Benjamin Howlett, the Buckinghamshire minister, who, even if Reid was not mentioned, clearly looked back fondly to the *Inquiry* when observing how 'Descartes, and most of the modern metaphysicians, have joined in the same complaint, of the fallacy of the senses; a doctrine well suited to that system, which represented the perfection of philosophy as consisting in doubt.' It was in fact obvious, added a much reassured Howlett, that 'the active part of mankind, in all ages, from the beginning of the world, have rested their most important concerns upon the testimony of sense' and, as a result, it was 'difficult to reconcile their conduct, with this so generally received opinion of the fallacy of the senses . . . .'[56]

Franks and Howlett may well have been among a significant number of English clergy for whom a careful reading of the raging epistemological debates in Edinburgh, Glasgow and Aberdeen came to serve as an important focus for their thinking about the foundations of their own and other people's perceptions and behaviour. Interests of this kind certainly seem to have informed many other clerics, as they did, for example, a member of the Betts family of Suffolk clergymen. He too fashioned an extensive commonplace note on 'Common sense' that plainly acknowledged the interdependence of everyday understanding and conventional moral and religious principles upon which most Scottish theorists were now insisting:

> Bright & sparkling parts are like Diamonds, which may adorn the Proprietor, but are not necessary for the good of the World: whereas common sense is like current Coin; we have every Day in the ordinary occurrences of Life, occasion for it: & if we would but call it into action, it would carry us much greater lengths than we seem to be aware of. Men may extol, as much as they please, fine, exalted & superior sense; yet Common Sense if attended with humility & industry, is the best guide to beneficial truth, & the best preservative against any fatal error in knowledge.[57]

In the composition of personality, and in both intellectual and social life, the role of Common Sense—that most instantly recognisable of philosophical achievements associated with the mainstream Scottish Enlightenment—had seemingly become axiomatic by the second half of the eighteenth century among a growing and increasingly disparate population of readers.

*   *   *

Appropriating material in such a way as to help reaffirm one's own piety and moral respectability was, however, but one way in which individuals exploited the various opportunities for meaningful self-fashioning that encounters with the Scottish Enlightenment opened up. Indeed, the very act of copying, or of documenting a response to the printed text, permitted readers—as Chartier has said, leaning heavily upon the insights of Paul Ricoeur—to achieve 'the "effectuation" or "actualisation" of the semantic possibilities of the text' as well as managing 'to reach self-comprehension and construct reality' for themselves.[58] Yet creative imitation, rather than verbatim transcription, is surely the sincerest form of flattery—and certainly the most intimate form of engagement with any text—in which the genuinely sympathetic reader can indulge. It is therefore highly significant that this too seems to have been the outcome when at least some readers found themselves confronted with the works of certain authors.

An outstanding example of such an inventive response to the Scottish Enlightenment in particular is the work of two young Essex friends, Benjamin Strutt and Jacob Pattison. The former was a schoolmaster's son from near Colchester who, by the end of a long life, would have become a central figure in that town's civic politics, as well as a noted eccentric. He cultivated wide-ranging interests in music, painting and literature; befriended and supported the prince of East Anglian landscapists, John Constable; avowed vegetarianism; and even became in due course the local theatrical impresario.[59] For his part, Pattison came from nearby Witham. It was to there that he returned during the vacations that punctuated his medical education at Edinburgh between 1779 and his early death in 1782. No true commonplace books survive for Strutt or Pattison. But fortunately, part of their correspondence does. This reveals how, with the two of them using letters in much the same way as a single person might use a commonplace book, they not only recorded but also explored and experimented with the implications of what each had been reading.

The letters are also useful in a further sense. For both men were blessed with the *gauche* self-confidence of young men intensely aware that they lived in an age of Enlightenment. Accordingly, they used their writing in order to assist in establishing their intellectual credentials, their politeness and their possession of acute critical faculties. In fact, their discussions represent an unusual twist upon the accepted conventions of commonplacing, since their easy-going intimacy permitted the essential privacy of this genre, and the exceptional scope for improvisation that it afforded, to be carried over in a series of profoundly self-revelatory letters. This makes it all the more intriguing that their reading had clearly brought both of them into close and sympathetic contact with some of the most distinctive and influential discussions generated by the Scottish Enlightenment.

One of their key intellectual interests certainly appears to have been the tradition of moral and aesthetic theory which had its Scottish roots in the early reception of Lord Shaftesbury's teachings, but which, as we noted in Chapter 2, had subsequently been widely disseminated by professors like Hutcheson, Blackwell and Turnbull, as well as by non-academic philosophers like Hume and Kames—a group whose collective legacy, indeed, Pattison in particular would have personally experienced at Edinburgh. In a letter from Pattison, undated but apparently written on a Monday in 1778, Shaftesbury, for example, was singled out for praise, evidently because of his exemplary observations on 'perceiving ill,' a classic crux for those Scottish theorists concerned with the relationship between the psychological mechanisms for evaluating virtue and beauty.[60]

This was followed on a 'Friday morning' by Pattison's thoughtful analysis of Kames's opinions on a related question, which seemed to provide a clear restatement of Shaftesbury's trademark insistence on the links between the aesthetic and the moral sense: 'Lord Kaims somewhere in his philosophic Essays asserts,' Pattison declared, 'that "If the perception of Beauty & Deformity in external Existence be natural to man the perception of Beauty and Deformity of right & wrong in actions must be equally so".'[61] Strutt—whose correspondence here is missing—had seemingly asked for clarification on this seminal point, perhaps reflecting his acknowledgment that Pattison was the one now benefiting from a Scottish university education and so best placed to offer the definitive judgment. Certainly Pattison continued this letter by imploring Strutt to embrace the argument, authoritatively enunciated by Kames, that 'this is rational and convincing if it is fixed upon the base of Experience no criticism can ever affect it. it is one of those many Truths which must stand quasi [sic] by a necessity of Nature and to this perception do I appeal from the anxious Queries of my friend.'

At the same time, however, and closely related to this shared interest in a technical controversy upon which Scottish thinkers had offered the greatest illumination, the two friends also shared a powerfully affecting response to James Macpherson's highly distinctive poetry. Again, this appears to have been a sincere attachment, and one that they felt able to flaunt to each other by strewing their communications with obviously parodic phrases conceived in the recognised *argot* of the Ossianic corpus. Hence Pattison prefaced his comments on Kames's philosophy with a series of these artful imitations. But Strutt too, undeterred by being in the east of England rather than the west of Scotland, littered his letters with *faux* Celticism: 'From their Airy Hall descended his fathers . . . ,' began one passage written on 28 May 1778; 'Does he ride upon the Gold-skirted cloud . . . ,' Strutt asked again on 3 June; 'the gloomy woods at distance bend their green Heads . . . ,' he moaned later on that summer.[62]

Back from Pattison came a series of equally accomplished homages to the singular genius of Ossian. Containing some striking geographical references, they might almost have been designed to jolt Strutt's mind back from the ancient Hebrides to contemporary Essex and Suffolk, promiscuously mingling Macpherson's distant mythic landscape with the familiar scenes of their own corner of late eighteenth-century East Anglia: 'But Grief rises in the Soul of Uvorn's son,' Pattison wrote at one point, 'he is compelled this morning with the Dawn to pursue the boars of Mist on the Clouds of the East, Ipswich with its Plains, thy native fields O sun of Uvorn & Kennet's flowery heath. . . .'[63]

The motivation of these two young gentlemen in their respective imitations of Macpherson's characteristic idiom and imagination is clear. Indeed, there can be no doubt from their philosophical reflections that Strutt and

Pattison had already been persuaded that ethical and aesthetic judgment were mutually reinforcing, in precisely the way that respected Scottish teachers like Kames had argued. It was in this context that they took such pleasure in reading the Ossianic translations, a genuine thrill that was then carried over into their heartfelt mimicry of his work. Here, in the sublime and unashamedly sentimental outpourings of a Celtic bard, they considered that they had found the distilled essence of a rare and precious sensibility, one that was exceptionally direct and natural. It was also one that—if only they could manage fully to embrace and emulate it—might permit them to experience for themselves what Charles Taylor calls 'the right impulse or sentiment' that was increasingly seen, because of the legacy of Shaftesbury and Hutcheson in particular, as among the most definitively *human* aspects of human nature.[64]

As Strutt reassured Pattison in a letter from August or September 1778:

> Ossian the prince of Sentiment (notwithstanding Mr [blank] Shandy's claim to the Title) has more true Copies of such Evenings as you describe, than any Writer whatever, he no doubt enjoyed the beauty of nature, & was susceptible of its sublimity—How pathetic & sentimental many of his passages are . . . .'[65]

Their surviving correspondence, with Pattison back in Edinburgh, continues into the autumn of that year, and takes the form of further rumination on a closely-related philosophical problem, of which Ossian's protean sensibility, curiously transcending the Dark Age gloom, may again have provided a thought-provoking case in point—whether 'natural affections,' or an ability to apprehend beauty, were 'inherent' in men or simply acquired by personal experience.[66] Evidently both men remained closely engaged— and, crucially, had already established through their writing an immediate personal identification—with some of the most problematic and yet suggestive writings of the Scottish Enlightenment.

Richard Barham, later author of the *Ingoldsby Legends*, indulged privately in youthful mimicry much like that shared between Strutt and Pattison. Whilst at Brasenose College, Oxford, around 1807, he too copied down, only now into a proper commonplace book, a convincing imitation of some of the materials that he had been reading, here headed simply 'Ballad after the manner of Walter Scott.' The resulting verse, though quite different from the efforts of the Essex men, again caught the distinctive flavour of an especially evocative verse narrative:

> What shadowy form thus dimly seen
> Glides slowly on with noiseless tread
> O'er mouldering graves and hillocks green
> Where rest in peace the mighty dead?

What glimmering light amidst the gloom
Like some false meteor's trembling ray
Shines faintly on th' escutcheon'd tomb
And gleams athwart the churchyard way
Is yon the form of Ulric brave
Who fell by dark Helvellyn's spear
Return'd to weep o'er Imma's grave
And mourn beside her sable bier . . . [67]

Whatever else Barham thought that he was doing in penning this parody of Scott's poetry, with its tell-tale Gothic settings and sense of mythic drama, it is clear that imitation afforded him, like almost no other exercise in which he might have immersed himself, the opportunity as an English reader to don the mantle of a famous Scottish author, simultaneously embracing and yet also gently mocking the raw power of the original text.

It would be difficult to find a reader less like Strutt, Pattison or Barham, than Revd Thomas Spedding. For Spedding was no brash young interloper in the world of letters, no instinctive follower of the newest literary fashions. An elderly and somewhat earnest Cumberland minister, he was the long-serving vicar of the newly founded St James's Chapel in Whitehaven between 1753 and 1783. A surviving family notebook, containing much that was copied out by Spedding himself, suggests that part of this time was devoted to the sober task of documenting his family's history. Yet he was also plainly a great lover of verse—a fact which should remind us, as we have already seen, that poetry was throughout this period a central facet of the emerging British canon to which clerics in particular long were deeply attached.

Spedding was also perfectly capable of creative responses to what he was reading. It is this particular impulse that lies behind a verse entitled "On Thompson's Seasons—by the Revd Thos. Spedding," which is preserved in the same family manuscript. As it begins:

Hail, Nature's Poet, whom she taught alone
To sing her Works, in numbers like her own;
Sweet as the Thrush, that warbles in the Dale,
And soft as Philomena's tender tale . . . [68]

The choice of imagery, like the tone which is simultaneously reverential and strongly declamatory, certainly recalls Thomson's high poetic manner: 'Hail, mildly pleasing Solitude,' begins one of Thomson's best-known works; 'Hail! Power Divine . . . ' runs another.[69] But Spedding was in fact being economical with the truth in passing off this work as his own. For it had been composed by Revd William Thomson, Fellow of The Queen's College, Oxford, even appearing in print, in the *Annual Register* of 1781 and then subsequently in the *Gentleman's*.[70] All that can be said, then, is that Spedding's admiration for the Scottish poet had led him to perpetrate the most blatant act of literary larceny that any reader might commit. In effect, he had expropriated someone else's poetic homage, passing it off as the finest fruit of his own idiosyncratic muse.

Quite different again from readers like Strutt and Pattison, or even from Revd Spedding, was Stephen Simpson, a weaver who lived and worked on the High Street in Coventry in the middle years of the eighteenth century. Yet in preparing what he called 'a choice Farrago of new Poems,' Simpson relentlessly parodied a succession of canonical British poets, Milton and Pope among them—even apparently sending at least one of his efforts to the *Town and Country Magazine* in 1771 (though, as he later lamented, it was 'not inserted').[71]

One of his most intriguing productions, however, was a verse almost certainly conceived in imitation of Beattie's *The Minstrel*. Written on or shortly before 21 April 1774—the year in which the long-awaited second part of *The Minstrel* was published—Simpson's verse, although suitably deferential towards its esteemed subject, is also disappointingly stilted and wooden. It does, however, convey the burden of Beattie's tale with perhaps more convincing rusticity than the Aberdeen professor had himself achieved:

Edwin

1. A Steady Mind, a friendly soul
   Young Edwin long had shown
   Nor e'er did Nature give a grace
   He made not soon his own

2. The strictest tie that binds on earth
   (His word as firmly giv'n)
   Could not tho sacred hold more fast
   Than he was bound to heav'n . . . [72]

Simpson's verse continues to develop almost as a précis of *The Minstrel*, telling Beattie's story in a simpler and more authentically rustic manner:

9. The Rage of passion once appeas'd
   Alas poor Edwin say
   How droopt thy Soul as Reasons strength
   Resum'd her cutting sway . . .

The parody is undoubtedly made more effective, of course, because whereas Beattie had for the most part composed his verse in formal iambic pentameters, Simpson's poetry alternated between simple tetrameters and trimesters, a comparatively crude stanza form, particularly suited to the reiteration of straightforward rhymes, that Johnson himself had cruelly mocked for its lack of sophistication ('I put my hat upon my head . . . ').[73]

* * *

Commonplacing, as we have seen, took a great variety of forms. Certainly to conceptualise it as merely a passive response, and thus by implication as essentially unilluminating about the underlying experience of reading, would be a grave mistake. Indeed, the commonplace book shaped and structured by the tastes and judgments of literate individuals, preserving like no other kind of evidence their decisions, preferences and reactions when confronting and engaging with printed texts. The opportunities that commonplacing gave to develop a range of more complicated responses to what had been read should also not be overlooked. These factors, moreover, are what has already allowed us to use surviving commonplace books to map some of the main contours of English readers' reactions to some of the most significant works of the age—including a widespread love of Scottish historiography, the complex reception given to Scottish metaphysics and the veneration evidently felt for the writings of individual Scottish authors as different as Robertson, Hutcheson, Reid, Macpherson and Beattie. It is to some of the further ramifications of these personal encounters with the Scottish Enlightenment, again documented through the peculiar practices of commonplacing, that we now turn.

8 Copying and Co-Opting
Owning the Text

Imitative composition of the kind indulged in by people like Jacob Pattison and Stephen Simpson was only the most dramatic of the reactions to reading that the habits of commonplacing could sometimes call forth. More often, individuals responded simply by copying materials from a text. This too, however, was revealing, not least because it generated enduring evidence of the experience not only of narrow interest to the historian of reading but also useful for the much broader social history of ideas. Indeed, given the dominant place that straightforward transcriptions occupied in most Georgian commonplace books, the particular selections made may well provide unique insights into contemporaries' attitudes towards particular authors, works and genres at this time. Certainly they ought to illuminate the whole question of readers' literary and intellectual preferences rather more effectively than the study of surviving marginalia (which are simply too scarce to be properly representative).[1] Most significantly for our own purposes, a better sense of what was actually commonplaced, and of the ways in which this process was usually being approached, might allow us to begin to see both how and why certain individuals came to engage with aspects of the Scottish Enlightenment in particular.

* * *

James Thomson, the son of a Roxburghshire manse, was predictably pervasive in his hold over contemporary English commonplacing—the *Critical Review*, in considering an edition of his poetry published in 1762, speaking for most arbiters, and for large numbers of readers, when insisting that 'A just taste, a delicate sensibility to the beauties of nature, an overflowing benevolence, and that subdued piety which ever accompanies innocence of manners and sound understanding render the memory of this favourite son of the muses, equally dear to posterity, as his person was to his contemporaries.'[2] It is worth noting, however, that *The Seasons*, whilst certainly Thomson's most celebrated text among contemporaries, was not his only work to register a significant impact with notetakers. Indeed, it was actually the verse-drama *Sophonisba* (1730) that supplied Gertrude Savile, for example, sister of Sir George Savile, a Nottinghamshire baronet, with numerous excerpts deemed best to illustrate the states of 'Love,' 'Content, Ease, or Relief' and 'Pain or Grief' when she considered each of these conditions in turn in her commonplace book.[3]

Her near neighbour, Mary Acklom of Wiston, was similarly impressed with another less well-remembered work by Thomson, the patriotic masque *Alfred* (1740). Here, however, it was the sententious words 'Attach thee firmly to the virtuous deeds and offices of life' that seemed to encapsulate a moral principle well worth recording and attempting to follow—an extract that Burns appropriated in a letter of 1792, and which he aptly introduced by remarking, in a manner nicely reflecting the thought processes of a commonplacer: 'Do you know, I pick up favourite quotations, & store them in my mind, as ready as armour, offensive or defensive, amid the struggle of this turbulent existence.'[4] Lady Horatia Waldegrave, by contrast, one of the "Three Ladies Waldegrave" in Reynolds' famous painting, had a strong personal preference for Thomson's *Tancred and Sigismunda* (1745).[5] It was chiefly from this that she bolstered her commonplace book with dramatically worded quotations, including the set-piece opening declamation of Sigismunda, the heroine ('The death of those distinguish'd by their Station,/ But by their Virtue more, awakes the Mind . . . '), and the same character's subsequent melodramatic lament ('Hopes I have none!—Those by this fatal Day/Are blasted all—But from my Soul to banish . . . .'[6]

Despite this often intense interest in a wide range of his other works, however, nothing could disturb the unruffled pre-eminence of *The Seasons* as Thomson's most widely loved work, among commonplacers in particular as among readers in general. It was quoted from almost endlessly, at great length and also by transcribers of all descriptions. At the same time—as Hazlitt appreciated when discovering a battered copy at an inn at Lynton on the north Devon coast, Coleridge duly exclaiming 'That is true fame!'—*The Seasons* was also so popular that it could be encountered in all manner of unusual contexts, each lending it a slightly different significance in the minds of those who came across it.[7] Weston Yonge, for example, a squire who lived at Charnes Hall near Eccleshall in Staffordshire in the early nineteenth century, was a great admirer of James Macpherson, with whose naturalistic descriptions and bold declamations he filled his commonplace book. But he also seems to have been keenly aware of the suppositious Gaelic translator's close affinity with Thomson. In fact, Yonge evidently considered that *The Seasons* had prefigured this apparently very different poetry from north of the Border, placing an extract from the final element of Thomson's text, "The Hymn to the Seasons," essentially a rendering of Psalm 139, amongst his many jottings from Ossian:

> Should fate command me to the farthest verge
> Of the green earth, to distant barbarous climes,
> Rivers unknown to song, where first the sun

Gilds Indian mountains, or his setting beam
Flames on the Atlantic isles. . . . [8]

Certainly at a general level Yonge appears to have considered the careful attention to the interactions of landscape and climate for which Thomson was so admired a significant foreshadowing of Macpherson's later efforts.

Different assumptions probably explain the response of Yonge's contemporary, Revd Thomas Stevens, the West Country clergyman, who transcribed into his commonplace book in 1779 the passage from *The Seasons* dealing with 'the lovely young Lavinia.' Indeed, this extract was sufficiently lengthy as to suggest that it may have been intended to form the basis of a future recitation to an audience: Stevens, moreover, appears to have been particularly touched by the poetry of sentimental piety, as witness his also copying out parts of Edward Young's *Night Thoughts*, and this may well help explain what he saw in Thomson's work.[9] Again, the words of Mary Cornwallis, the wife of a Kentish clergyman who around the turn of the nineteenth century compiled a commonplace book specifically for her daughters, might perhaps be taken as representative of many other readers' understandings of this seminal text and of its peculiar significance: 'Thomson's Seasons are very beautiful,' Cornwallis asserted, 'we cannot but love the man who possess'd such general phylanthropy [sic]—whilst we admire the poet who could display all nature in such pleasing & lively colors . . . .'[10]

Another well-to-do family, the Claytons, who lived at Sandybrook Hall near Ashbourne in Derbyshire, were no less enthusiastic about Thomson's gift for combining humane and devotional concerns with the skilful evocation of nature, a winning poetic strategy which, in investing the familiar English landscape with a deep pious resonance, had successfully imbued his own verse with what has been called an 'acute but morally disciplined sensibility.'[11] The Claytons seem greatly to have appreciated this quality, adding to their commonplace book a substantial letter that had originally accompanied a copy of *The Seasons* given to them as a present which, in implying that reading Thomson was itself a quasi-religious experience, seemed to sum up their own unrestrained passion for this particular work and this particular author: 'A Vol. on which Reason bestows as many Beauties as Imagination; Tis a Subject that our first Parents would have sung in Paradice had they never been seduced by the Syren Flattery of False knowledge to forsake Humility and Innocence . . . Such Writings give Dignity to Leisure & exalt Entertainment & Amusements into Devotion . . . .'[12]

The Seasons, as befitted its central place in a canon that was being actively promoted by authorities like Johnson, was thus a particularly frequent source of commonplace extracts, especially where readers conceived of parts of Thomson's text as speaking directly to their own present circumstances. The conceit that in so borrowing a poet's words the reader took on not only the perspective but even something of the persona of their creator—thereby

acquiring momentarily an ability to reflect back with unprecedented eloquence and insight upon his or her own position—may well have been present in many people's minds: 'When I read Thomson,' claimed the radical
philosopher William Godwin, articulating this assumption unusually viv-
idly, 'I become Thomson . . . I find myself a sort of intellectual chamelion,
assuming the colour of the substances on which I rest.'[13]

The elder James Dalloway's commonplace book certainly reflects this
notion where it incorporated quotations from Thomson on the subjects
of retirement and the simple life. The latter seemed a particularly fitting theme on which to descant in what Dalloway clearly meant to be
a continuing guide from beyond the grave to his son James, the book's
recipient:

> Oh knew he but his Happiness of men
> The Happiest he! who far from publick rage,
> Deep in the Vale, with a choice few retir'd
> Drinks the pure pleasures of the Rural life.[14]

John Tompkins, tenant of Woodhouse Farm at Poling in Sussex, evidently
read the same text as Dalloway. He did so, however, thinking as a farmer
and occupant of the countryside rather than as a worried father. This in
turn led him to prefer Thomson's evocative naturalistic descriptions to his
equally fluent didactic philosophising. In short, Tompkins was as keen as
Dalloway to render Thomson's words relevant to his own circumstances,
and so to appropriate the poet's sensibility for himself.

It is clear that Tompkins found in *The Seasons*—above all its description
of landscapes and ordinary country life—something especially pertinent
to his own lot on a working farm situated beside an exposed coastline:

> The cattle from th'untasted fields return
> And ask, with meaning low, their wonted stalls,
> Or ruminate in the contiguous shade.
> Thither the household feathery people crowd,
> The crested cock, with all his female train,
> Pensive and dripping; while the cottage-hind
> Hangs o'er the enlivening blaze, and taleful there
> Recounts his simple frolic: much he talks,
> And much he laughs, nor recks the storm that blows
> Without, and rattles on his humble roof.[15]

Tompkins also seems to have been greatly attached to the famous passage in "Winter" describing a snowstorm, where Thomson implores the
reader, as Mary Jane Scott has recently argued, to exercise his or her own
Hutchesonian moral sense and thus to feel compassion for the shepherd
who tragically becomes its victim.[16]

As Tompkins noted by way of introduction to this key passage, effectively explaining to himself the poet's ostensible point at this key moment:

Thomson Book IVth Pag.151
Prognosticating a storm, he says:
"Retiring from the downs, where all day long
They picked their scanty fare, a blackening train
Of clamorous rooks thick-urge their weary flight,
And seek the closing shelter of the grove.
Assiduous, in his bower, the wailing owl
Plies his sad song. The cormorant on high
Wheels from the deep, and screams along the land.
Loud shrieks the soaring hern; and with the wild wing
The circling sea-fowl cleave the flaky clouds.[17]

Tompkins's response to *The Seasons*, in other words, was to personalise the implications of what the Scottish poet had cast into memorable verse, using his commonplacing to take literal possession of it for his own distinctive purposes.

Like John Griffin, a Kentish contemporary whose notetaking focused upon Thomson's description of a comet ('Reviving moisture on the numerous orbs/Through which his long ellipsis winds . . . '), Tompkins had in a sense found in *The Seasons* only what he had wished to see—an evocative description of a symbolic natural phenomenon that already interested him.[18] But this approach also read into the text a context-specific meaning of which Thomson, however much he may have sought to encourage his readers to treat the poem as a series of discrete episodes, could not really have been fully aware. For her part, Elizabeth Carpenter, writing to her friend, twenty-two-year-old Jemima, the Marchioness Grey (wife of Philip Yorke, 2nd Earl of Hardwick), in August 1744, had more than an inkling of this intensely personal dimension to reading that the complementary act of writing served both to encourage and to document. Certainly she was aware of what reading it might be *doing* to a text's meaning. Acknowledging her own low spirits, she confessed, in a moment of striking parenthetic self-revelation, that 'a melancholy story, a Night Thought, or a line of Thompsons (which I perhaps apply differently from what he has done) unravels all again.'[19]

On the evidence of the commonplacing tradition, Beattie's *The Minstrel* was also by some distance its author's most popular work among English readers, more even than the *Essay on Truth*—something, incidentally, that lends credence to a commentator's observation in the *Critical Review* that 'The moral reflexions of this author are just and nervous; and his imagery deserves as much praise for the effects which it produces, as for its propriety and animation. It excites love of innocence, nature, and virtue.'[20] That a number of printed copies survive in family papers is surely significant.

These include texts owned in the eighteenth and early nineteenth centuries by the Trevelyans of Nettlecomb in Somerset and by the Martins of Anstey in Leicestershire.[21] From the 1760s onwards, moreover, *The Minstrel* was consistently among the most frequently commonplaced items whenever individuals transcribed their favourite passages. As with *The Seasons*, it was the naturalistic descriptions, the insistence upon homely virtues, and, above all, the sentimental piety of Beattie's poetry that especially entranced his early readers, a disproportionate number of whom seem to have been women.

These aspects of *The Minstrel* certainly appealed in 1785 to Harriet Anne Bisshopp, a young Gloucestershire woman recently married to the Sussex landowner Sir Cecil Bisshopp: 'And be it so, let those deplore their doom,' she copied down, evidently struck by the melancholy religiosity of Beattie's words, 'Whose hope still grovels in this dark sojourn . . . .'[22] Illustrating a significant trend among similarly susceptible readers, the same passage, laden with pious gloom, also registered an impact upon Augusta Leigh, Byron's half-sister, who quoted it in her own commonplace book, begun in August 1805, along with two other extracts from *The Minstrel*, with the opening lines 'O how canst thou renounce the boundless store . . .' and 'In truth he was a strange & wayward Wight . . . .'[23] In both cases it was clearly the exquisite sentimentality with which Beattie had expressed his religious sentiments that had singled out these particular passages for special attention at the hands of these contemporary female admirers.

This is not to suggest, of course, that *The Minstrel*'s charms were lost on men. The Liverpool merchant Thomas Binns, for instance, had great affection for the poem and its author, leading him to the labour of love that was the manual transcription of the entire text in fully 63 pages, a painstaking exercise capped with an epitaph "To Dr. Beattie" that may in many ways have epitomised the peculiar hold exerted by *The Minstrel* over so many readers at this time:

> Hail thou, whose Muse contemning Grandeur's Bowr's,
> bewhile in native Dignity array'd,
> An artless 'shepherd Boy's' unfolding Powr's,
> And bright romantic Reveries display'd . . . .'[24]

It is not hard, perhaps, to imagine Binns using the complete transcript for a recital of at least certain excerpts from the poem before an audience of friends and family. But the strictly private reading of A.E. Smith, a West Country gentleman who lived at the Down House near Blandford in Dorset in the 1820s, was, if anything, even more dominated by the same poem. In fact, *The Minstrel* was the single most important source of material for Smith's commonplacing. Exercising a preference often exhibited by those compiling manuscript miscellanies, he focused in particular upon passages in which Beattie had coined an epigrammatic phrase to express a valuable quasi-philosophical truism—for example, the excerpts beginning with the lines 'Liberal, not lavish, is kind Nature's hand;/ Nor was perfection made for man below' and 'Of chance or change oh let not man complain . . . .'[25]

* * *

From the late 1780s onwards Burns's poetry would prove no less adaptable than that of Thomson and Beattie to the peculiar needs and interests of those who now encountered it. Edward Hussey of Scotney was among them. It must have been around 1820 that this young Kentish gentleman, probably then still in his late teens, transcribed some of Burns's most famous poems into his commonplace book, including ever-popular pieces like "Scots Wha Hae" (also copied, as it happens, by Matthew Lewis, the M.P. and Gothic novelist) and "Life is But a Day at Most."[26] Another anonymous contemporary, allegedly a mariner whose vessel carried Byron to Greece and certainly an admirer of Byron's poetry, revealed much the same partiality specifically for Burns's romantic lyrics. In this case "The Parting Kiss" and "Epistle to Dr Blacklock," full of passionate sentiments about love and separation, provided extracts that spoke strongly and eloquently to the reader.[27] More interestingly, Thomas Howitt of Heanor, a devout Quaker in early nineteenth-century Derbyshire, gloried in the almost masochistic "Despondency: An Ode" ('Oppress'd with grief, oppress'd with care,/A burden more than I can bear'). Howitt, like the young Cumberland reader Charles Curwen around 1830, apparently saw more than enough in this depressing verse to justify its careful commonplacing.[28]

A not dissimilar response to Burns's more pensive work arose in that great admirer of Beattie's sentimental piety, A.E. Smith. The latter extracted from the Kilmarnock Edition a fair quantity of what he described as 'Scraps from Burns's poems,' including extracts from "Despondency" as well as from one of the poet's best-known early verses in which Burns had exploited his knowledge of animals—"The Twa Dogs." Smith also included a significant portion of the most famous and philosophically charged of the poems in which an animal provides a focus for potent reflections on the human condition:[29]

> But Mousie, thou art no thy lane,
> In proving foresight may be vain:
> The best-laid schemes o' mice an' men
>   Gang aft a-gley,
> An lea'e us nought but grief an' pain,
>   For promised joy.
> Still thou art blest compared wi' me!
> The present only toucheth thee:
> But och! I backward cast my e'e
>   On prospects drear! . . . [30]

As will be clear from his other poetic tastes, Smith's interest in "To a Mouse" lay in its encapsulating man's unique awareness of his own vulnerabilities. Such humbling perspectives probably appealed especially to the more devout. Certainly both William Chute and Charles Holte Bracebridge were similarly touched by Burns's gift for mingling the mundane with the profound so as to emphasise the limitations of man's position. Each as a result copied out the text of "To a Mouse" (Bracebridge doing so immediately after a rumination on mortality stimulated by reading a description of Hume's monument in Edinburgh).[31] So too, appropriately, did Charles Curwen, who incorporated "To a Mouse" among many mournful dirges and religious reflections.[32]

Another facet of Burns's work to which commonplacers particularly responded was his role in the emergence of an avowedly plain speaking and consequently more authentic strain of poetry that was seemingly validated by its deep roots in a rapidly disappearing peasant culture. For understandable reasons, such perceptions may well have been unusually prevalent among working-class readers (and, occasionally, writers) for whom the literary employment of everyday idioms and a related emphasis upon the experiences of ordinary country people appeared a particularly significant development. Joseph Blacket, for example, erstwhile shoemaker, avid reader and prole-tarian poet, who at Seaham in County Durham enjoyed the patronage and encouragement of the Milbanke family, found it hard not to see a reflec-tion of his own experiences in the meteoric but ultimately tragic career of Scotland's peasant bard. Blacket, indeed, speaking perhaps for many other humble readers of Burns, claimed that 'This ill-starred genius and myself have shaken hands together frequently, while I have been perusing his inter-esting life . . . On reading his last letter, I think I am perusing the history of my feelings and sufferings . . . .'[33]

Burns's fluency in a language that was simultaneously indigenous and unashamedly colloquial also elevated him in the estimate of some readers to the status of an icon of Britain's own distinctive cultural heritage. This in turn may explain his peculiar place in the affections of those who found themselves far from home. George Hopper, for example, who served with the 89th Regiment in the Napoleonic Wars, recorded in his commonplace book, when stationed on Malaga on 26th November 1811, the simple biographical note 'Robert Burns the Poet was born in Ayrshire in the year 1759, and died in the town of Dumfries in July 1796.'[34]

Hopper's factual statement, which presumably helped provide some use-ful context on the Scottish poet, was followed by a suitably martial extract from Burns, the opening stanza of "The Song of Death":

A field of battle—Time of the day evening—the wounded dying of the victorious army are supposed to join in the following song.

Farewell, thou fair, thou green earth, and ye skies,
Now gay with the broad setting sun!

> Farewell, loves and friendships, ye dear tender ties!
> Our race of existence is run![35]

A further virtue of Burns for readers overseas may have been, of course, that his loftier sentiments seemed emphatically universal in their application but also, because of the Lowland Scots culture out of which they clearly grew, highly particular in their affiliations. Of all Burns's efforts, it was accordingly "Auld Lang Syne" that was most likely to provide them with a means to celebrate and re-assert their own insular origins. Hence at a masonic meeting held in Calcutta on St Andrew's Day 1815, the familiar refrain was sung out loud by the assembled brethren in suitably amended form—'The honest hearts ayont the Cape/ The frien's o'lang syne.'[36]

By the early nineteenth century, then, the selective appropriation of Burns's verse was an acceptable way for a reader to express proper identification with sincere piety, with common humanity or even with one kind of patriotic Britishness. Yet during precisely the same period, Walter Scott's burgeoning reputation was also beginning, with dramatic consequences, to make itself felt. This may have been especially true among women commonplacers, who apparently found the copying of Scott's verse a means by which personal feelings could be both focussed and expressed. Emma Knight of Dodington, a keen reader of Byron and Southey, was typical in this respect. She copied out Scott's article on Byron in the *Edinburgh*, thereby melding two of her favourite literary interests at one fell swoop. She also transcribed an extract, nicely capturing the bittersweet recollection of departed friends, taken from the second canto of Scott's *Marmion* and beginning

> When musing on companions gone
> We doubly feel ourselves alone
> Something, my friend, we yet may gain;
> There is a pleasure in this pain. . . . [37]

The Lay of the Last Minstrel, among the early nineteenth century's most popular Scottish texts, actually seems to have provided certain readers with a startling experience when first encountered. Robert Story, for example, a Northumberland shepherd, was one who was forcefully struck by its deliberately Romantic effects, noting in particular the raw affective power in what he called its 'uncontrolled barbarism . . . harsh, puerile, and fantastic.'[38] "Monk" Lewis was another admirer of Scott's work, transcribing several passages from *The Lay* into his own scrapbook.[39] But, at least to judge from its considerable prominence in commonplacing—which, given the poem's declamatory form and powerful rhyme and rhythm, may well hint again at its particular popularity as a text for recital aloud—it also appealed especially to female readers who seem to have found its heady brew of historical evocation, naturalism, romance and chivalry positively intoxicating.

Jane Nelson placed excerpts from the fifth canto in her notebook around 1822.[40] At almost exactly the same time, Mrs Elizabeth Scott (later Mrs Williamson), who lived at different times near Bristol and at Sydenham in Kent, transcribed the lines from the same canto beginning 'True love's the gift which God has given/ To man alone beneath the heaven . . . .'[41] Augusta Leigh, meanwhile, placed a number of selections from *The Lay* in her own commonplace book.[42] And in a letter of March 1808 to John Higgins at Turney Abbey in Bedfordshire, young Charlotte Beattie, then at Brighton, summed up the sense of complete contentment, nicely complemented by eager anticipation of further pleasure, that must have warmed the hearts of many of this work's early readers. 'Can you recommend me any thing to read,' she begged, 'I have just now the Battle of Flodden (Marmion) written by Mr Walter Scott; if it is equal to his Lay of the Last Minstrel it will give general satisfaction.'[43]

Charlotte Beattie was far from unusual, however, in plunging headlong into *Marmion*, if that is indeed what she went on to do. For this poem too had innumerable admirers, some active commonplacers, among them Edward Hussey, Gustavus Gale, and Augusta Leigh.[44] Despite being a narrative set amid the early sixteenth-century Anglo-Scottish wars, this martial verse was actually at least as attractive to the female as to the male reader—with its rollicking pace, acute descriptions of nature and ear for powerfully emotive exchanges between its characters not only add-ing further layers of meaning but also increasing the text's obvious poten-tial for dramatic recitation to an enthralled audience (like Ruskin's father declaiming from this very work, 'melodiously grand and just').[45] This is well seen in the response of Anne Rushout, who lived at Northwick Park in Worcestershire and whose notetaking reveals her contented immersion in the imaginary world Scott had fabricated in *Marmion*. In particular, she copied out the first thirty-two lines of the fifth canto, with its masterly evo-cation of winter's cold and dreary scenes ('When dark December glooms the day . . . ').[46]

Rushout was also enraptured by Scott's other poems, avidly taking down extracts from works as different as *The Bridal of Triermain* (from which she took the colourful description of a beautiful woman—'They praised thy diamonds lustre rare . . . ') and *The Field of Waterloo* (1815) (here noting Scott's dramatic request to the reader to recall the reasons for the grief experienced by so many British people—'but think on Water-loo!').[47] Another woman from the West Midlands, this time an anonymous reader in Warwickshire around 1810, perhaps a member of the family of the Revd Clement Newsham of Harbury, shared Rushout's unquenchable ardour for Scott's ability to frame universal-seeming sentiments on life and love in flowing verse. She copied enthusiastically from *The Vision of Don Roderick* (1811), whilst elsewhere noting down pertinent lines from *The*

Lady of the Lake describing a daughter's acknowledgement of her duty to her father, which this female commonplacer (conscious of her own filial duties?) considered worth preserving precisely because they were 'beautiful': 'Some feelings are to mortals given/With less of earth in them than Heaven . . . .'[48]

By its nature narrative prose fiction sits less easily with the tried-and-trusted conventions of commonplacing. Poetry, after all, even when composed in a longer form, tends naturally to be subdivided by line, couplet or stanza—a great boon for those minded to engage in selective copying from a much larger whole. Moreover, with its assertive use of metre and rhyme, poetry is usually also better suited both to memorisation and to recitation. Accordingly, it has always been more likely than a continuous prose narrative to yield a brief extract, substantially complete in itself, for convenient transcription. It should not therefore be surprising that, by contrast with his verse, Scott's novels scarcely impacted upon the contemporary English commonplace book—notwithstanding their immense popularity with readers, which soon made *Waverley* and its successor novels, as Cruse has written, 'like the Bible and Shakespeare . . . part of the Englishman's inheritance,' as well as a fixed feature of the English canon for nineteenth-century readers of all classes and inclinations, like the young Ruskin, who later admitted that, along with Pope's *Iliad*, Scott's prose was the foundation of his own juvenile reading.[49]

Even so, there are a few suggestive hints in the commonplacing record at the wide and devoted audience, among women as well as men, that Scott's historical fiction instantly acquired. Predictably, given commonplacing's fixation with the declamatory, it was only the most dramatic passages—powerful and emotional direct speech by leading characters, and rarely the narrator's own descriptive voice—that caught the notetaker's eye. Elizabeth Scott, for example, copied out some material from *The Pirate* (1821). This comprised the words of the half-crazed Norna of the Fiftul-head to Minna Troil, conveying an essentially sentimental message in highly metaphorical terms about the bodily effects of lost love: 'The heart—aye the heart—touch that, and the eye grows dim, the pulse fails, the wholesome stream of our blood is choked and troubled, our limbs decay like sapless seaweed in a summer's sun; our better views of existence are past and gone; what remains is the dream of lost happiness, or the fear of inevitable evil.'[50]

The ability of readers to conceive of a new context for a particular passage, and to imbue them with specific local significance, was, as we have seen, intrinsic to acts of appropriation. Scott's novels certainly contained material that could be adapted so as to suit the circumstances in which they were now being read. Sir Richard Hoare, antiquarian and resident at Stourhead, recorded his own response to *The Fortunes of Nigel* (1822). But in doing so he made it abundantly clear that he believed the chosen passage to be directly applicable to his own situation:

I was forcibly struck with the following passage

"My young friend, when you attain possession of your inheritance, I trust you will not add one to the idle followers of the Court, but reside on your patrimonial estate, cherish your ancient tenants, relieve and assist your poor kinsmen, protect the poor against subaltern oppression, and do what our fathers used to do, with fewer lights, and with less means than we have."

To my Son Henry Hoare for his perusal—
reflection—
and I hope, execution,
and I regret his not having taken more interest in his paternal and
    country Estate

April 1823   RCH[51]

Bearing on the reverse the explanation 'Walter Scott's most excellent advice to <u>all</u> young men of landed prop^y' (the underlining reinforcing what Hoare considered the peculiar relevance of the text), this extract—wise advice from the Earl of Huntinglen to Nigel Olifaunt—was intended to provide his own son with posthumous guidance. Coming, in truth, from one of England's great banking dynasts, whose wealth rested upon prodigious commercial success in the City of London, the suggestion that Henry Hoare actually sprang from ancient landed stock, and needed to act accordingly, is an odd one—though, perhaps, not much more so than Scott's casting Huntinglen, elsewhere confessedly 'an ancient and constant ornament of the Court,' as a proponent of virtuous seclusion.[52] Sadly, however, son predeceased father. Thus Scott's vicarious instructions, extracted by Sir Richard in the vain hope that they might serve a very particular instructive purpose, would turn out to have been tragically redundant.

*   *   *

Scottish poetry, and very occasionally the Scottish novel, yielded extracts for commonplacing not least because, like its English equivalent, it dressed up truths in elegant language. The Scottish Enlightenment, however, also supplied other kinds of inspiration to readers. Indeed, after copying passages from works of creative literature, their most widespread response as commonplacers was the transcription of authoritative information or personal opinion. The thinking behind such actions, of course, varied substantially. Sometimes it was to clarify significant questions of fact. At other times, as with verse, it set out simply to preserve well-used words. But most importantly, perhaps, it captured statements of beliefs and values with which the reader clearly wished to be aligned.

Hume's *History*, not surprisingly, seems to have attracted attention for all three reasons. At the most basic level, it served very successfully simply as a standard source of facts about the English past. To that Whiggish patriot William Chute, for example, part of Hume's treatment of Alfred the Great, the greatest of early English kings, seemed entirely deserving of transcription. In fact, under the simple but significant heading 'England,' Chute wrote 'Alfred, says Mr Hume, declared in express terms, in his last will, that it was just the English should be as free as their own thoughts.'[53] Likewise Sir William Fitzherbert, a Derbyshire politician and author of *Dialogue on the Revenue Laws*, perceived in Hume an unusually pertinent piece of information that he recorded under the heading 'Taxes': 'Hume even acknowledges,' wrote Fitzherbert accordingly, 'the Sovereign has encroached upon the People in Subsidys, Tho' he says they have encroached upon the prerogative of the Sovereign.'[54]

Another reader, probably William Legge, 2nd Earl of Dartmouth, also interrogated Hume for historical information germane to his own interests. A government minister during the 1760s and 1770s, he used the *History*'s account of the sixteenth and seventeenth centuries, along with Burnet and Dalrymple, as the basis for what he described as a 'plan for reading Modern History,' which was in fact heavily skewed towards political events with whose long-term implications he was, as a mid-Hanoverian statesman, still directly concerned.[55] Richard Neville, another Whiggish M.P., looked to Hume for evidence on the growth of parliamentary checks upon executive power, a topic that once again can only have interested him from his own experience. Indeed, Neville even expanded what had been only a passing reference in the *History* so as to produce the rather more illuminating note that 'Ld Mountjoy was the only peer in Hen. 8's time, who dared protest to any bill brought into par^lt. His protest was then against the act whereby the kings proclamations had the force of Statutes; It is as extraordinary that his L^dshp did not lose his head for his patriotism.'[56]

Clearly even some of those strongly Whiggish contemporaries who were most likely to find Hume's ideological stance difficult to swallow found that they could use the *History* in this way—in short, as a definitive point of reference for evidence on those aspects of English history that most intrigued them. It should be less surprising, however, that Hume also enjoyed a similarly positive reception as a basic canonical text among the wider population of contemporary readers.

One anonymous commonplace book, probably from Surrey, hints at the sheer reverence with which Hume's work could be regarded by readers merely wanting (as they saw it) simple answers to simple historical questions. In pursuit of information on a wide range of topics, this individual looked to the *History* without any apparent hesitation when tackling, as he put it, the problem of 'Alderman, ye original of it':

Alderman originally implied one of Age & experience, who coud assist ye Prince with his council, & advice, The 3 Estates of ye kingdom were divided into Atheling which included the nobility, Alderman the

2^d Rank & <u>Thane</u> ye last. Note. There was one <u>Athelstan,</u> mentioned in the Reign of ye King of y^t Name who is called Alderman of all England, & is said to be half <u>King</u>; tho' ye Monarch himself was a prince of Valour & Abilities.
See Hume's Hist. Vol 1st P. 196. [57]

The same quest for evidential certainty compelled John Griffin from Kent to ransack the *History* at the end of the eighteenth century for material on such things as Sir William Waller the Parliamentarian general, the thirty thousand dependents of the Earl of Warwick in the Wars of the Roses, and a summary of the fluctuating career of Cardinal Wolsey.[58] On each subject Hume was plainly as much an acceptable as he was an obvious arbiter.

Clearly, Hume's famously loaded interpretation of the English past was something beyond which many readers ultimately found it possible to look—or even to downplay. Hence Revd Robert Pickering, a Northamptonshire clergyman in the early nineteenth century, transcribed a passage that also illustrates how the *History*'s potentially explosive burden could be defused, not least by the very process of reducing a larger text to a brief commonplace entry. The lines used dealt with the Crusades, a topic on which Hume's conclusions were, of course, less than flattering to the Christian cause. But, once decontextualised from the wider narrative, Hume's message in this short excerpt sounded almost pious, consistent with an emphasis upon humility and the recognition of human weakness:

> When Saladin, the Emperor of the East, (who fought so many Battles with the Christian Princes during the time of the Crusade to the Holy Land) lay upon his death bed at Damascus, he ordered his winding sheet to be carried as a standard through every street of the City, while a crier went before and proclaimed with a loud voice—This is all that remains of the mighty Saladin, the Conqueror of the East. Hume Hist. Of Eng. Vol II—Page 22—An. Dom. 1192.[59]

Much the same reasoning probably explains why Lieutenant George Hopper came to cite the *History* on a bewildering range of questions—many no doubt of concern to a patriotic and pious army officer based overseas who was evidently interested in the development of England's distinctive political institutions, economic progress and military achievements down the ages. Stationed at Halifax, Nova Scotia, in January 1813, he busied himself through the harsh Canadian winter by reading a copy of Hume's work—perhaps borrowed from a local lending collection—and compiling his own notes on such different matters as the origin of the practice of widow's thirds in Magna Carta; King John's granting of annually elected mayors and other civic representation in London; the first parliament under Henry III; the chartering of Newcastle's coal supplies; the heroic death of Sir Philip Sidney at Zutphen; and the scale and manpower of the Spanish Armada.[60]

If such a problematic and contentious text could obviously be rendered so instructive and so harmless, particularly when subjected to the processes of ruthless dissection and radical recontextualisation that commonplacing invariably involved, then less controversial texts from the Scottish Enlightenment proved able to serve no less enlightening and reassuring functions for those contemporaries who encountered them. This was especially true of historiography, clearly a major intellectual preoccupation among Georgian readers in general. Henry's *History of Great Britain*, for instance, was particularly well-favoured, being widely seen as a thoroughgoing modern account of Britain's development. It was in just this spirit that one notetaker, probably Revd Joseph Coltman, minister of Beverley at the turn of the nineteenth century, used Henry as a source for his own jottings on the medieval origins of higher education: 'Between 1216 and 1399,' Coltman wrote, 'a very great & advantageous change in the state of our universities took place . . . .'[61]

Revd Coltman was in fact a magpie-like reader of the historical works of the Scottish Enlightenment, as his treatment of Robertson's *Charles V* demonstrates. It was chiefly used as a quarry for intriguing material that, as he put it, neatly delineated another of his own interests, 'respecting the Jesuits': 'As the constitutions of the order vest in the General absolute dominion over all its members,' Coltman wrote, copying Robertson's text word for word, 'they carefully provide for his being perfectly informed with respect to the character and abilities of his subjects.'[62] Indeed, the impressively versatile, widely praised and hence hugely authoritative Robertson was a particularly popular source for commonplacers fascinated by a great range of questions.

For Sir John Cullum at Hardwick in Suffolk, an antiquary, botanist and divine, *Charles V* was the obvious place to look for information on the Crusades, his commonplace book as a consequence incorporating Robertson's striking insistence that these adventures had been 'the only common enterprise in which the European Nations ever engaged . . . .'[63] Cullum, whose wide-ranging interests may have been especially well served by the compendious scope of *Charles V*, and particularly its panoptic introductory "A View of Society in Europe," also plundered it for intriguing facts on the medieval practice of trials by combat and endurance, on the meeting of Henry VIII and Francis I in 1520, on the Peace of Cambrai in 1529, and on Martin Luther's will, each matters by which he had clearly found his own curiosity strongly aroused.[64]

Such obsessive concern with *minutiae*, and a tendency to seek verification for them in Robertson's majestic historical narratives, seems to have been far from unusual among contemporary readers. "Monk" Lewis, for example, had a particular interest in the nuggets of information, many touching on religious matters, that *Charles V* contained. Doubtless this was why he transcribed material on Tetzel's indulgences, on the Catholic doctrine of good works, on the Munster Anabaptists, on Charles's receipt of Naples from the Papacy and on the origins of the term "Huguenot," as well as proving a keen student of Henry's *History*.[65] Another reader in the same generation as Lewis, sadly unidentifiable though his commonplace book now forms Huntington Library 34804, showed essentially similar interests in sixteenth-century religious history, carefully copying out Robertson's discussion of indulgences as a trigger to the Reformation.[66]

Sir Charles Throckmorton, who came from one of Warwickshire's most recalcitrant recusant families, read the same work in much the same way—in other words, in search of interesting facts. Here *Charles V* stimulated notes with headings as diverse as 'Commerce,' 'Paper,' and the 'Feudal System.'[67] But Throckmorton, like many of Robertson's contemporary readers, was also a close and attentive student of the writings of less famous historians. Indeed, he appears to have been especially enamoured of the sharp eye for the interactions of landscape, culture and human endeavour that many of the minor Scottish historical writers, influenced by the stadialist theories of the leading literati, frequently exhibited. William Maitland's and Hugo Arnot's works, for example, each entitled *History of Edinburgh* (1753 and 1779 respectively), supplied Throckmorton with a mass of intriguing information on the local antiquities and topography.[68] As a result, one is left wondering whether the only viable explanation for this English reader's deep interest in the Scottish capital and its environs is either that he had already visited the city or else that, like so many other readers in the wake of Pennant and Johnson, he had simply conceived an irresistible desire to do so.

If relatively prosaic facts were capable of motivating readers to create notes that addressed their own unremarkable fascinations and preoccupations, then an interest in the exotic could also be served by close attention to the works of the Scottish Enlightenment. Robertson's *India*, recently described as 'exhilarating in the breadth of its concerns,' certainly stimulated considerable excitement in Robert Cater Oakley, an officer in the 20th Regiment, who between 1811 and 1833 was stationed successively in Heligoland, Ireland, Spain, France and St Helena.[69] In fact, although Oakley does not appear to have served in India himself, he was intrigued by southern Asia and its penetration by Europeans. The works of the orientalist Sir William Jones were one focus for his commonplacing; but so too was Robertson's text, which eventually stimulated notes on Phoenician, Greek and Italian trade with India, as well as informing Oakley's own discussion of the caste system ('Dr Robertson reckons only four Castes in India . . .').[70]

In what was clearly a précis of one of the key claims at the heart of Robertson's *India*, Oakley also noted how greater knowledge of the Hindu deities had begun to shed light upon the wider development of human religions: 'Dr Robertson. . . . ,' Oakley wrote, evidently alive to the potential significance of this principal tenet of Enlightenment conjecturalism, 'observes that a striking uniformity of features may be recognized in the systems of superstition established throughout every part of the earth, that the less men have advanced towards a state of civilization, the fewer have been their divinities, and as their knowledge has extended the objects of their veneration have multiplied—over every movement in the natural world and every function in domestic & Civil Life . . . .'[71]

This tendency for commonplacing to help isolate information and assertions which particularly struck the individual practitioner as interesting or pertinent, and to transform them into a focus for private analysis and subsequent reflection, is again especially well seen in the reading of William Chute, that most bookish of Georgian parliamentarians. From Ferguson's *Civil Society*, for example, Chute extracted, under the heading 'Society Civil Ferguson,' several pages from the critical first section of Part I which emphasised the essential sociability of mankind. Accordingly, Chute's commonplace book incorporated Ferguson's now-famous lines declaring that 'Mankind are always to be taken in groupes, as they have always subsisted. The history of the individual is but a detail of the sentiments and thoughts he has entertained in the view of his species: and every experiment relative to this subject should be made with entire societies, not with single men.'[72]

From Lord Monboddo's *Of the Origin and Progress of Language* (1773–92), too, Chute gleaned evidence on the vocal habits of 'savages' and the linguistic skills of the early Germanic peoples.[73] Indeed, Monboddo's reputation as a difficult and quixotic author does not seem to have deterred readers from using his work in exactly the same way as those of Hume and Robertson—which is to say, as an intellectually respectable source of important facts. A good example is the anonymous contemporary who compiled Huntington Library 34804, transcribing in the process Monboddo's discussion of the origins of Sanskrit and the roots of the Greek language in ancient India.[74] Thomas Eagles, meanwhile, a prosperous Bristol merchant in the 1780s who was also an accomplished amateur musician, painter and classical scholar (some of his translations of Athenaeus were published posthumously in *Blackwood's Magazine* in 1818 and 1819), was another who found much instruction in Monboddo's dense scholarship.

Indeed, Eagles seems to have judged *Antient Metaphysics* (1779–99), which was then in the process of appearing, a reliable account of classical religious beliefs. Hence he recorded in his own commonplace book, evidently for future reference when rereading the text, the various contents of Monboddo's first volume.

The Introduction gives the Design of the Work—viz. to revive antient Theism particularly the theism of Plato & Aristotle—the difference between antient & modern theists—the Moderns make their System of Nature too mechanised—though they allow that <u>Mind</u> was necessary at first to produce this Universe, and set it a going . . . [75]

Anna Larpent, however, the wife of a civil servant and theatre censor whose extensive experiences with books, recorded in a diary over many years, have recently been reconstructed by John Brewer, was rather more ambivalent about Monboddo's idiosyncratic claims. She was 'entertained and instructed' by *Origin and Progress of Language*, which she read during a summer visit to Aston House in Oxfordshire, and was suitably impressed by its author's 'infinite display of learning.' But she was also suspicious—justifiably in the opinion of most later critics—about 'the many erroneous and yet plausible arguments on which it is founded.'[76]

*   *   *

Historiography was only the most popular terrain on which English readers responded creatively to the works of the Scottish Enlightenment, by extracting material that they deemed useful, illuminating or thought-provoking. But other subjects to which Scotland's authors had contributed also attracted notetakers in search of information and instruction. Science was among them, and, reflecting the innate intellectual eclecticism of Enlightenment culture, it apparently provoked interest from some readers who were already immersed in the study of philosophy and history. Charles Bracebridge, for example, who in the 1820s was, as we have seen, bristlingly hostile towards Hume's scepticism, was sufficiently interested in certain aspects of modern scientific research to copy out a discussion of James Hutton's findings in the *Edinburgh Review* of 1822. Indeed, Bracebridge's reaction to this particular text is striking, revealing a strange mixture of intellectual fascination and genuine fear at what the new geological theories emanating from Scotland might betoken: 'The imagination stands appalled,' an edgy Bracebridge wrote, 'on the brink of this Abyss of time, where human reason dares to lead us.'[77]

Yet Scottish science of various kinds did exercise a grip on many intellectually curious readers, despite their understandable ambivalence both about its potential ramifications and about the increasing technical complexity that was gradually rendering parts of it less accessible to the non-specialist. We have already noted a number who greatly appreciated Scottish medical expertise. But other practical considerations might also recommend certain texts to particular readers. One of the Jervoises of Herriard in Hampshire, for example, was seriously impressed, probably as an eager student of estate management, when reading the Edinburgh professor Francis Home's newly published *Treatise on Agriculture and Vegetation* in June 1757. In fact, this reader was presumably able to share in the author's pleasant surprise at some very recent experimental advances. One of Home's own textual amendments was what was duly noted down—'P. 174. Since these Papers were wrote, I have read three Volumes of Experiments publish'd by Dr Hamel . . . They are distinct, exact, conclusive so far as They have gone, and stand a Model for Experiments in Agriculture.'[78]

Readers' spiritual sensibilities could also be reflected in the way in which they read some of the religious publications associated with the Scottish Enlightenment. Frances ("Fanny") Throckmorton, for instance, the niece of Sir Charles, clearly approved of the relentlessly uplifting observations that characterised Blair's much-loved *Sermons*. She was especially moved by the Edinburgh minister's encouragement of humility in the face of praise. Indeed, for all that she was a member of a distinguished Catholic dynasty (the ecumenical Blair would surely have been delighted that his lessons were reaching so easily across the religious divide), Fanny duly incorporated these blameless effusions of polite presbyterianism into her personal commonplace book: 'No man ever gained lasting fame,' she noted, 'who did not on several occasions contradict the prejudices of popular opinion.'[79]

Similarly appreciative eyes and ears for Blair's skilful sermonising were those of Anna Grenville, Duchess of Buckingham and Chandos. This was presumably why she transcribed the somewhat maudlin observation that

> Solitude is the hallowed ground which religion hath in every age chosen for her own—There her inspiration is felt & her secret mysteries elevate the Soul—There falls the tear of contrition, there rises toward heaven the sigh of the Heart; there melts the soul with all the tenderness of devotion, & pours itself forth before him who made, & him who redeemed it . . . [80]

Anna Grenville's choice of extract, of course, like Fanny Throckmorton's, may well suggest that what some of Blair's contemporary critics most disliked about his style—his shameless sentimentalisation of the language of piety and morality—was precisely the aspect to which many readers were powerfully and all-too-willingly drawn.

Henry Mackenzie, the secular counterpart of the "Moderate" clergy in their capacity as moralists and social observers, was another safe Scottish source of reassuring truisms from which the appreciative reader could readily draw succour. This was especially true of *The Mirror* and *The Lounger*, together the most successful platforms for the dissemination of Mackenzie's (and arguably, by extension, the Moderates') views: 'The undue severity wh [sic] appeared in some of our reformers is rather to be attributed to the age in which they lived and the dark system of Popery from which they could not entirely free themselves than to any defect in the opinions they adopted or any sanguinary or unchristian spirit in them,' were the words noted down around 1810 by Miss Ann Bletchley, a pious spinster who lived at Stoke Newington in Middlesex.[81]

Bletchley, indeed, seems to have been especially fond of Scotland's orthodox Christian apologists and moralists For in an earlier notebook Bletchley had already condensed for her own private use—and deploying much the same commonplacing technique as Thomas Eagles had used when summarising Monboddo's *Antient Metaphysics*—what she clearly believed to be the extremely beneficial burden of Beattie's seminal *Evidences of the Christian Religion*:

Chap 1ˢᵗ Revelation useful & necessary

2ᵈ The Gospel History, true

Sect 1ˢᵗ The Gospel considered as a part of anᵗ Hisy

2ᵈ Arguments from Prophecy

3ᵈ The Faith of the first disciples not from weakness, but well provided conviction

4 The excellence & singular nature of Christianity a proof of its Truth

3d Objections answered

1,2 From the numbers, abilities, & virtues of unbelievers

3 From the obscurity of particular passages

4 from the supposed inconsistencies of the gospel—Of inspiration—

5 from the supposed unsuitableness of Xᵗʸ to the course of human affairs

6 From its supposed inefficacy in reforming

7 From the apparent insignificance of the human race compared with the universe

Very good & I think suitable—[82]

Such a response to Beattie is, of course, revealing. For it underlines what, beyond even the collecting of facts and interesting information that was so prevalent, was undoubtedly the Scottish Enlightenment's most significant function for ordinary literate men and women. This was the ability of well-regarded writers—such as those that Scotland was now providing in striking abundance—to provide an apposite restatement of the views and beliefs already possessed by the individual reader.

*　　*　　*

Like Joseph Coltman at Beverley, who perceptively noted down, *apropos* the success of the Beattie's *Essay on Truth*, how much 'Common sense has in Modern times been used by philosophers,' it is clear that Ann Bletchley, whose response could stand for many other readers, was fully able to appreciate just how useful certain texts actually were for the task of fixing a recognisable point in relation to which one's own ideas, opinions and values might be delineated.[83] For the most proficient exponents, indeed, the act of reading, particularly when repeated and continually reinforced by commonplacing, may have become central to the construction of individuals' own personalities. After all, it was precisely the ability to reflect intelligently and insightfully upon the texts that they had encountered—'I am now in the Country,' claimed one contributor in *The Spectator*, 'and employ most of my Time in reading, or thinking upon what I have read'—which created the opportunity for individuals to define their own positions with regard not only to the works of the Scottish Enlightenment but also to fundamental questions of morality, truth and identity.[84]

Part IV

Constructions

9 Reading and Meaning
History, Travel and Political Economy

Whether commonplacing or annotating, English readers, as we have seen, responded in an immense variety of ways to their experiences with the texts associated with the Scottish Enlightenment. Some attempted to refute what they read. Others were inspired, usually with the best of intentions, to try to enhance what had actually been written. Most often, though, readers sought to identify in some sense with the words and ideas they had encountered—even, on occasion, venturing parody or imitation of the author's peculiarities. It may therefore be that we should conceptualise reading not merely as a passive experience but as an active performance in which texts come to be appropriated by individuals for essentially personal and, it would appear, invariably highly specific purposes. Yet if this is fair, it would also be necessary to add the crucial rider that taking possession of what an author has written never leaves the person who embarks upon it completely unmoved.

Indeed, not only does the reader, in engaging with it, necessarily *do* things to a text. Engaging with a text also *does* things to readers, assisting them in focussing their attention on particular questions and concerns, and, no less inevitably, leading them first to evaluate and then either to validate or (less commonly) to modify their own beliefs, self-images and identities. Ultimately *this* is why it seems reasonable to suppose that there is a fundamentally reciprocal relationship between a book and its reader, one which, by its nature, leaves neither quite as it was before—and, moreover, one which it is must also be the objective of any satisfactory history of reading to document, understand and explain. Accordingly, the following chapter continues to explore surviving evidence for these genuinely creative encounters. In particular, it probes more closely certain experiences with texts connected with the Scottish Enlightenment that not only clearly affected the distinctive meanings and uses that some readers attributed to them but also, as we shall see, had complex implications for the individuals concerned.

*   *   *

Readers, as we have observed time and again, imbue the printed word with a variety of implications and significances. This in turn requires that we should consider the meanings of texts not as pre-determined and immutable but as context-specific and necessarily contingent—and, as a consequence, as always subject to further and not entirely predictable processes of revision and redefinition. Given the essentially circular relationship between readers and texts, however, it is important that we also give closer thought to that other transformational aspect of reading, profoundly significant for the individual reader, which Stephen Greenblatt describes as 'self-fashioning.'[1] Unsurprisingly, this is an especially fruitful notion with which to explore the experiences of those English readers among whom the writings of the Scottish Enlightenment received their earliest and most extensive reception. After all, the changing cultural conditions of the Georgian period in particular—with the reader increasingly repositioned centre stage as the subject of an unceasing flow of advice, satire and judgment about reading from the likes of Addison, Johnson and the periodical journalists—ensured that responses to texts were becoming more important than ever before in the construction of the self.

Such possibilities were certainly realised by the founding members of the Gentlemen's Library at Wigton in Cumberland, who captured this dramatic sense of the sheer power of reading over the formation of personality in a phrase positioned, for all to see, on the title page of their 1806 catalogue: 'We are here humanized without Suffering,' they wrote, undaunted by the extreme magnitude of the claims, 'we become acquainted with the Manners of Nations; acquire a fine polish without Travelling; and without the trouble of Study, imbibe the most pleasing, most useful Lessons.'[2] Another seminal commentator on the role of reading and reflection in the formation of the self had already had the same thought. It was Shaftesbury who, in recommending what he called 'SOLILOQUY or *Self-discourse*,' asserted that this was what allowed us to 'form within our-selves what in the polite World is call'd *a Relish*, or *Good* TASTE,' whilst also serving to 'teach us the Turns of *Humour* and *Passion*, the Variety of *Manners*, the Justness of *Characters*, and TRUTH of Things . . . .'[3]

There were several corollaries to this growing awareness that reading might play a dominant part in constructing the moral values, the social performances, and the political and religious attitudes, of those engaging in it. Not least, as Wigton's readers evidently understood, was the identification of specific responses to the experience as constitutive of a person's own character. As Patricia Meyer Spacks has argued, this may help explain the contemporaneous rise of the novel, that most manipulative of genres, since its great architects, like Fielding and Sterne, prospered precisely because they 'assume the reader's active engagement in an imaginative process and his possession of intellectual capacities (wit, judgment), social attitudes (eg., high regard for money and fame), and moral convictions (kindness is preferable to cruelty, openness to hypocrisy) that are felt to be more or less universal.'[4] Expectation of such beneficial outcomes to reading was also implicit in certain people's behaviour—for example, when donating books, the whole point of this action being, in effect, to improve the recipient by creating the opportunity for an appropriate response to be experienced. For similar reasons, parents, guardians and friends were anxious to encourage younger people—those, not coincidentally, with the most malleable characters—to respond correctly to certain texts, and helpful gifts played an obvious part in bringing these aspirations to fruition.

Such assumptions, as we have already seen, lay behind the younger James Dalloway's presentation of Gregory's *A Father's Legacy* to his sister following their mother's untimely death. It was doubtless this same idea that had motivated whoever gave a copy of *The Seasons* to the Clayton family in Derbyshire. Both gifts, to judge from the remarks made at the time, were presumed to be useful to their recipients because they would stimulate piety and reinforce acceptable moral values—providing, of course, that they were properly reflected upon. It follows that the more experienced and discerning reader, able to display greater independence in his or her own continuing education, could be no less aware of reading's prodigious constructive potential. Such thoughts seem to have guided Anna Larpent, for example, as she scrupulously noted down her responses to what she had just finished reading. Indeed, Larpent was always conscious of the significance of encounters with texts in the formation and expression of her own personality, continually striving to demonstrate to her own satisfaction a level of competence and authority as judge and critic.[5]

A further corollary of wide public acceptance of the formative role of reading was that instructions on the selection of appropriate texts were frequently both sought and given—and particularly, as we would expect, in those communications which passed between more and less experienced practitioners. Hence the formal guidance on reading issued to the literate public by authorities like John Whiston and William Goodhugh repeatedly found their informal counterpoint in the private correspondence of large numbers of literate contemporaries. It was this determination to emphasise the constructive power of reading, and its potential for moulding and improving the participants, that led, for example, to a note sent in the early years of the nineteenth century to Sarah Ann Philips, wife of George Philips (later Sir George, 1st Baronet) of Weston in Warwickshire. Probably from her friend Mrs Sharp, and clearly based on the sender's previous discussions with other readers, it was headed 'Course of History recommended to Lady Philips,' and it confirms the instinctive deference to expert knowledge—from friends, from family, or just from other proficient readers—that guided so many individuals in their selection of appropriate texts. The contents are impressively specific, nicely mimicking the express encouragement to historical study offered by published guides like *A Father's Legacy* and Chapone's *Letters* (the first of which had reassured the nervous that 'There is no impropriety in you reading history,' the second concurring that 'The principal study I would recommend, is history. I know of nothing equally proper to entertain and improve at the same time, or that is so likely to form and strengthen your judgement . . . ').[6]

As we might have hoped, the Scottish Enlightenment was a key source of texts deemed appropriate for the Lady Philips' personal development. On ancient Roman history, Mrs Sharp recommended 'Hume's Essay on the Populousness of the Romans & Gibbon Chap. 1, 2, 3, and 9.'[7] The next stage, concerned with the 'Feudal System,' comprised 'Montesquieu, Millar, [?], Robertson & Stewart' (presumably Gilbert Stuart).[8] Following this Lady Philips was to occupy herself with Stuart on 'Chivalry,' although, according to Mrs Sharp, she should also note that 'Liberty does not immediately succeed the Barbarian conquest. read Robertson's dissertation. Charles V' (a text that again Chapone had specifically advised her own readers to consult).[9]

Thereafter Philips's intellectual fashioning would progress to 'England . . . their code of laws similar to that of the other barbarians Wilkins, Hume's 1st Appendix, Rapin . . . ' (the latter a cornerstone of women's reading at least since Sophia Western had devoured it in *Tom Jones*), and thence to 'Millar on the English constitution'; but she should also 'Observe the disagreement between Hume & other historians as to the origin of our constitution.'[10] Robertson would then provide the necessary background on early French history, whilst for Spain Philips should 'read Robertson's introduction to Charles V.' Specifically for Castile, pausing to recognise that the 'Barons have too much power,' she should 'read Robertson and Watson.'[11]

Sensitivity to the potential complications introduced by Hume's polemical intentions was also important because of reading's influence in forming a person's attitudes and values. As a consequence, Sharp, who may have been mindful of Chapone's claim that on British history Hume's treatment was the 'most entertaining,' advised extreme caution with regard to his handling of Edward III in particular: 'Hume says the king avowed his power, pleaded the necessity of the case & the consent of the prelates Barons & some of the commons,' Sharp advised, 'but he omits the latter part of the answer, which says "The King wishes that such impositions be not drawn into consequence."'[12] Moreover, as she continued,

> Hume & Rapin differ widely in their account of the character of Richard II. Hume says he imposed no taxes, Rapin that he did. Rapin is here correct. When the articles were exhibited against Richard II, the Bishop of Carlisle alone spoke for the king. The speech is given in Brady, but Hume by adding to it prejudices us against the Barons. Compare Hume & Rapin & wherever they differ in their conclusions refer to the original documents.'[13]

Nor was this laborious programme of medieval historical education the end of the matter. Sharp's instructions continued in similar vein deep into the eighteenth century and the unresolved conflicts between Whigs and Tories that she and Philips well knew from personal experience.

How realistic this rigorous prescription of wide-ranging reading and meticulous cross-checking with original documentary sources might have been in practice—even for a Warwickshire baronet's wife with extensive leisure time and unfettered access to serious book collections—remains unclear. It was, however, certainly not a unique expectation on the part of a friendly advisor with a susceptible reader's best interests at heart. Henrietta Maria Bowdler's letter to her friend Mrs Pares in 1812 clearly contained comparable guidance on the texts that would need to be worked through by anyone wishing eventually to play convincingly the role of the polished and polite reader:

> Virtot's Knights of Malta & the 1st Vol: of Robertson's Charles 5, give you a good account of the Middle Ages. I shd strongly recommend Henry's History of England as far preferable to all others, but it must be follow'd by Hume, who must always be read wth caution, for there is always a conceal'd [?] to lessen the respect due to religion & to religious men . . . [14]

What is most important about Bowdler's well-intentioned advice, as about that from Mrs Sharp, is the underlying assumption, pretty much identical with that of the critics and commentators, that reading certain passages of particular texts—disproportionately drawn from the leading Scottish authors—would instil exactly the sort of expertise that could be relied upon to impress in respectable and learned circles. The implication that a rounded and well-read person would need to display a good working knowledge of a prescribed body of literature is also clear proof of the critics' success in entrenching notions of canonicity—in other words, of what really *needed* to be read—among the wider literate population.

This palpable sense of urgency in embracing a canon whose proper digestion was conceived as necessary for the construction of a polite and respectable social personality also explains why Mary Cornwallis, wife of the rector of Wittersham in Kent in the early nineteenth century, prepared such strict guidance for her own children. Her commonplace book was produced, like James Dalloway's, purposely for the benefit of the next generation. Towards the end of it, Cornwallis focused, like so many other people concerned with defining appropriate reading experiences, on prescribing a textual diet from which her daughters would benefit. As in Lady Philips' prospective regime, history formed a key part of the programme for the Cornwallis girls, and Scotland's contribution to this part of the canon, as viewed from the perspective of a keen reader, was once again everything that we might have anticipated: of the twenty historical items listed by Mary Cornwallis, fully one quarter—Hume's *History*, Robertson's *Scotland* and *Charles V*, and Watson's *Philip II* and *Philip III*—had Scottish origins.[15]

Like Mrs Sharp, Cornwallis also saw the need to warn against uncritical absorption of certain texts, particularly, in this case, by the vulnerable female offspring of an upstanding pillar of the local community. Thus she added (surely unreasonably in the precise distinction between literary manner and intellectual content that her advice assumed) that 'Hume & Gibbons [sic] are both of them free thinkers—you must therefore take care to avoid the pernicious influence of their principles whilst you do justice to the beauty of their language & the excellence of their historic compositions.' In short, it was not merely correct texts but also an appropriate personal relationship with them—and so a suitable outlook and set of attitudes informed by them—that was assumed to be constitutive of polite respectability. Cornwallis's list, touching such genres as poetry, novels, drama, tracts, devotional literature and memoirs, actually contained few surprises, and pointed towards very much the same destination: *The Seasons*, Mackenzie's *Man of Feeling* and *Man of the World*, Home's *Douglas*, Blair's *Sermons*, the Highland tours of Boswell and Johnson, and the biographical *tour de force* that was Boswell's *Johnson*, were all specified, Cornwallis acknowledging their increasingly canonical status as works promoting the correct feelings and sympathies, and hence helping to remould character and personality, among those prepared to read them.[16]

Friendly correspondence describing one's own responses to reading to another person was another recourse as individuals sought out forms of self-fashioning that would simultaneously help define themselves and encourage and assist other individuals. These processes are strongly hinted at in a letter from Lady Margaret Heathcote, the wife of Sir Gilbert Heathcote, a Rutland baronet, to her sister-in-law Jemima, Marchioness Grey, written in June 1759, in which the former described her own response to a very recent encounter with Hume's *History*:

I have just finished Hume's hist: of the Tudors, wch is an entertaining Book, particularly his account of Q. Elizabeth, wch exactly answers my Idea of her; (for my part I had much rather have George the 2^d for any king;) in some respects I cannot bear her, & even some of the best parts of her Character proceed but from a very middling foundation; her firmness was in great measure obstinacy & arbitrariness; her Religion was certainly Policy, as her title to the Crown depended upon it; & her Good nature was for the most part Dissimulation: But does not Mr Hume give, in some respects, rather too favourable an account of M.Q. of Scots? He does not indeed pretend to defend the murder of her Husband, nor her affair with Bothwell; but in general he seems to wish me not to think too ill of her, & absolutely denies the truth of the scandalous report of her & Rezio [sic]; but I suppose that is for K. James's sake, whom he seems mighty fond of: I take it for granted he does not himself belong to the kirk of Scotland, as he does not seem at all favourable to that party—I shall now read Robertson's Scotch history, from wch I expect much entertainment.[17]

Evidently Heathcote was a particularly self-aware reader, discriminating clearly in her own mind between her private construction of meaning and what may have been an author's quite different intentions. Here, indeed, the advice ostensibly offered to a friend seems very much about self-examination by the reader herself. In effect, she uses the opportunity of recounting her experience with the *History* to clarify her own pathway through the dense thicket of potential interpretations that grew so profusely out of Hume's multi-faceted book.

In certain circumstances, however, the most expert and most privileged readers, fully alive to the potential consequences of particular texts, even offered advice directly to authors on how they might more reliably wish the requisite effects upon their audiences. This was what happened when Thomas Hyde, 6th Earl of Clarendon, first encountered the recently published *The Lay of the Last Minstrel*.[18] As subsequently related by Revd Thomas Ripley, vicar of Wootton Bassett in Wiltshire, the Earl, whom Scott had already met, had been asked for his comments on a manuscript draft. In return Clarendon had given Scott unexpectedly specific advice about *The Lay*'s opening account of a stag hunt, which, the Earl reported, he had actually found monotonous in its description of an echo (Scott's reply being, wittily, that 'the frequent repetition, namely, of the echo, was characteristic of the mountainous country in which the scene of his Poem had been laid').[19]

Clarendon also told Scott—who was prudently interested in what individual readers would make of his writing—that in the poem's first canto the lines 'The silver light, with quivering glance,/ Played on the water's still expanse' had conveyed to his mind 'an idea which interrupted the calm, and that it would have been more perfect had the light, also, been asleep. This image has been happily expressed by Beattie in a line of the "Minstrel," "The yellow moonlight sleeps upon the halls".'[20] Fortunately, the Earl remained friendly with Scott, and was able in due course to discuss the Waverley Novels with their unacknowledged author—though, graciously, he never pressed Scott on this sensitive question. Ever anxious, however, to convey a useful impression of how texts were actually received by readers, Clarendon duly reported to their creator 'that he perused each work in succession with an equal though varied admiration.'[21] This curious relationship plainly suggests that a reader's capacity for self-examination of his own experiences, and for analysing the responses that particular texts might provoke, could be more than useful even to the most successful authors.

*   *   *

A quite different manner in which the Scottish Enlightenment affected its readers was one of which they might well have been slightly less conscious themselves. This was the ability of certain works to help individuals see the world differently—to view things, as it were, through the eyes of the author. As we noticed in Chapter 2, many books during this period, among the various functions they performed, taught readers literally to *look* at things in a new light. It was in this context that Scottish historiography, poetry and novels, as well as Scottish-oriented travel literature, acquired strong influence over how growing numbers actually perceived Scotland itself—its landscape, its culture, its past and its people. This development was memorably fictionalised in *Mansfield Park*, where Fanny Price refers to *The Lay of the Last Minstrel* so as to encapsulate her own disappointment at finding in a neighbouring chapel 'No signs that a "Scottish monarch sleeps below".'[22] The same habits of mind—applying relevant images drawn from much-loved Scottish texts to their own immediate experiences—were evident also among real English readers.

Samuel Bamford, the Lancashire radical, was one, remarking at Woodstock in Oxfordshire in 1819, on one of his many political pilgrimages to London, that this particular location was actually 'the scene of the tale of Fair Rosamond, which had deeply interested me when a boy.'[23] Bamford, plainly adept at connecting Scott's novels with his own experiences, had also been struck when passing Mavesyn Ridware in Staffordshire by the fact that Malvoisin had been 'one of the heroes of Ivanhoe'—the mere name conjuring up a reference to a favourite book.[24] The same capacity was found in Humphrey Senhouse's father, another Humphrey and M.P., in the later eighteenth century.[25] Himself a correspondent of Pennant's and, as a voracious reader, certainly familiar with much of the recent literature about Scotland's landscape and topography, Senhouse senior compiled his own short manuscript guide to the country, probably written shortly after a visit, which reveals much about the formative impact of his previous reading upon his perceptions and outlook as a traveller.

Some of Senhouse's descriptions bespeak a tendency to read *into* the Scottish landscape the value judgments and cultural references embedded in the contemporary literature with which he was already familiar. When writing about Mull, for instance, it was the Ossianic associations that sprang immediately to this Cumberland gentleman's mind, Morvern becoming explicitly 'the country of Fingal.'[26] Likewise Senhouse followed the tendencies towards the picturesque, the primitive and the dramatic that marked so much of the recent published work on the Highlands. Hence in Sutherland he emphasised the unsophisticated practices still employed, noting that 'The Inhabitants bleed ye Cattle in Spring & Autumn & preserve ye blood to be eaten cold.'[27]

There was a strong sense, too, in which Senhouse's gaze, and what he actually chose to see and to appreciate, was guided by a perceived need to consider those aspects of Scotland to which familiar authors had already directed their own attention. The University of Edinburgh, for example, a near compulsory feature of the English tourist's itinerary and already much discussed in authoritative texts ranging from *Humphry Clinker* to Johnson's *Journey* (and, of course, Boswell's writings), was in Senhouse's phrase (revealingly mouthing Pennant *verbatim*) 'a mean building.'[28] And like many famous visitors before him, Senhouse had also taken in the town of Dundee, a place that, Senhouse noted, once more imitating the statistical obsessions of the professional topographers, 'has about 14,000 inhabitants.'[29]

The sense that, by the closing decades of the century, visitors to Scotland had had not only their itineraries but also their perspectives effectively predetermined by prolonged exposure to travel literature, historiography and creative writing is reinforced by perusal of many documents which, like Senhouse's private journal, find English tourists describing their personal experiences in Scotland. One of Senhouse's neighbours, a member of the Robertson-Walker family from Distington in Cumberland, did so around 1800. Enlightenment categories of analysis clearly informed the writer's description of Islay, laden as it was with assumptions about the island's natural primitiveness—'in the first state of nature & one might without any violence of Imagination suppose it untrodden by the foot of Man.'[30] The picturesque also featured prominently in the interpretation of interactions between landscape and architecture. From Edinburgh Castle, for example, the view was 'enchanting'; the New Town impressed with 'the symmetry of the whole'; and, ultimately, it was possible to declare that 'I have been on the whole much pleased with Edinburgh. I never saw a town I mean of size which from its situation was so picturesque and charming.'[31]

This particular visitor had also acquired from what was obviously a great deal of prior reading a striking ability to locate historical episodes accurately in the Scottish landscape, and especially in those places with romantic or melodramatic resonance. "Mariolatry"—familiar from countless newspaper and periodical references and from a welter of Scottish-focused histories and novels from the 1750s onwards—was very much in the ascendant. At Linlithgow the town was identified as the birth-place of 'the unhappy Mary'; Lochleven Castle, predictably, became the prison of 'the unfortunate Mary' (significantly echoing Pennant's description of the prison of 'the unfortunate Princess'); and the writer also announced himself forcibly struck by the scene of 'the flight of the wretch Bothwell.'[32]

Indeed, Mary's bad luck, a conventional trope of sympathetic historians like Robertson, had become so ingrained a theme among readers that in 1830 Emma Knight of Dodington could write under the heading 'Fate of the Stuarts' that 'the misfortune is hereditary'—adding, her partiality almost palpable, that Mary had been 'driven from her throne, a fugitive in Scotland, and, having languished 18 years in prison, was condemned to die by English judges, and beheaded.'[33] A similar train of thought momentarily preoccupied another female in the late 1770s, probably, if many of the local references in her surviving commonplace book are any guide, in the vicinity of Bristol. She too noted down an epitaph 'On Mary, Queen of Scots,' dedicated to 'the gracious Memory & eternal Hope of Mary . . . ,' acknowledging that she had been 'Eminent for all Accomplishments of Mind & Body,' but that she had succumbed, a victim of 'the Vicissitudes of human Things,' after 'a firm, but alas successless struggle [a]gainst the Calumnies of the Malicious [t]he Suspicions of the Timorous, [a]nd the Snares of the Implacable . . . .'[34]

Much the same re-imagining of the viewed Scottish landscape as that achieved by Senhouse, effected essentially through prior immersion in literature describing Scotland and its richly textured history, also occurred in the case of Thomas Dunne, a Herefordshire doctor who visited in 1807. The drama of nature screams from every page of his journal, almost as if not only following in the famous footsteps but also striving to mimic the specific responses of esteemed predecessors like Pennant, Johnson and the Wordsworths. On entering the Perthshire Highlands, for example, Dunne, implicitly deferring to Pennant who had found this scene 'awefully [sic] magnificent,' wrote that 'the road is exquisitely beautiful—exhibiting a vast variety of the most picturesque scenes that can be imagined—and increases in beauty as we approached nearer to Dunkeld, wch is upon the whole the finest place that I have ever seen.'[35]

But it was once again sensitivity to the misfortunes of the ever-present Mary that produced his most memorable response, jolting Dunne's mood from the merely self-satisfied to the gushingly sentimental. After some 'charming views of the Forth & the town of Edinburgh with the Hills of Pentland, Arthur Seat &c.' there was 'Nothing remarkable till we came near Kinross, when the most beautiful and extensive Loch of Leven was exposed to our view . . . This is however most remarkable for having a small island in it in wch there is now a fine old ruin of a Castle in wch Mary Q. of Scots was for some time confined.'[36] Letitia Napier went even further. A Somerset teenager in the first years of the nineteenth century, she managed to describe physical locations with an imaginative flair which almost suggests that she saw them precisely in the evocative terms in which Robertson and Pennant had painted them: 'In the N.W. Tower of the Palace of Holyrood House in Edinburgh,' Napier wrote, 'is shown the Chamber where Queen Mary sat at supper, when Rizzio was drag'd from her side, and murder'd, and the private staircase by which Ruthven entered with the assassins to perpetrate the ruthless deed.'[37]

Lady Sarah Philips, even if she did not engage in Mrs Sharp's punishing regime of historical reading, did acquire sufficient knowledge to prepare her more than adequately for seeing Scotland in this way. Certainly she was fully alive to the textually derived expectations that increasingly dictated how the literary-aware tourist should respond to their various experiences. As she wrote at one point:

> The evening was too far advanced when we arrived at Edinburgh to allow us to enjoy fully the advantage of the first view & impression of it—Salisbury Crags deep in shadow, rendered more striking by the glowing evening sky behind them, was the principal object we were able to recognise.[38]

Even the lateness of the hour and the unsuitable conditions had not detracted much from Philips's enjoyment of the experience, fully aware, as she was from reading authors like Pennant, of the picturesque prospects that the place ordinarily provided.[39] She had better luck at Craigmillar Castle, just outside the city, picking through the ruins and being able to note (happily, Pennant had again got there well before her) that it had been 'a summer residence of the unfortunate Queen of Scots.'[40]

John Dickenson, a Manchester merchant, felt similarly when he visited in the summer of 1819, his own experiences in Scotland eliciting a series of well-drilled responses with obvious origins in his familiarity with the literature of travel and discovery. At Holyroodhouse, unsurprisingly, it was the luckless princess who sprang automatically to mind: 'we saw the Gallery & poor Queen Mary's apartments.'[41] In Perthshire, it was again the Queen of Scots whose tragedies were most readily conjured up: Dickenson had visited 'Doune Castle one of the favourite hunting residences of the unfortunate Mary.'[42] Most directly, however, Dickenson was able to connect, as if on a detailed mental map, the precise component of his previous reading with the appreciative response that it had prompted. Above Perth, for example, he found that 'The View from the summit of Moncrieffe Hill is as fine as Pennant describes it.'[43] George Gibson, from Monk in Northumberland, made similar links in 1777, alighting as a result upon the stark inhospitability of the land upon which recent published work had harped so obsessively. Along Loch Ness, for example, where Pennant had described land where 'there was no possibility of cultivation,' Gibson willingly affirmed that 'the country at the other side seems to be little plenished and barren.'[44]

Sixty years later Revd Charles Oakley, a Dorset clergyman, found his mind irresistibly drawn to exactly the same textual reference points, supplied by an enthusiastic lifetime of reading about Scotland's history and landscape. 'Four miles of lovely driving through the Park,' he wrote when visiting Contin in Ross-shire,

> brought us to the Lodge Gates and the little village of Contin. Here Queen Mary stopped to refresh her wearied horses as she was travelling to Inverness in the days of her adversity to escape the stern control of the Earls of Angus, Mar and Ruthven. The Stile standing Stone where she dismounted seemed in my eyes a sort of relic of her; whose lovely face I had gazed on in the Gallery at Brahan. . . . [45]

Oakley's journal amounted in effect to a seamless marrying of first-hand experiences with a rich store of information and judgments learned through reading texts like Robertson's histories. Such a capacity for internalising the printed page, and for having one's feelings and responses so profoundly shaped by contact with particular works, was one of the most striking elements in the process of self-fashioning among literate men and women to which the Scottish Enlightenment in particular, and works pertinent to Scotland more generally, was able to contribute.

*   *   *

Because we wish to understand better how English men and women were affected by their encounter with the Scottish Enlightenment, and how their expectations, responses and self-images came to be so markedly altered by what they had read, it may be useful next to consider in greater detail a group of contemporary readers' responses to one key Scottish text in particular. *The Wealth of Nations* is an especially useful example for this purpose. After all, it was an almost compulsory feature of any serious book collection by the 1780s, and a work whose widely acknowledged importance had the happy effect of ensuring that it would attract a huge number of early readers, at least some of whom would be bound to generate enduring evidence of their experiences. One of the most striking results—all the more intriguing for being anonymous—is the account of his encounter with Smith's work preserved by an individual, probably a legally qualified man involved in running a local landed estate, who lived near Kirkby Stephen in Westmorland in the 1790s, which subsequently came into the hands of the Beinecke Library at Yale.[46] This reader was demonstrably preoccupied with a series of immediate practical matters arising out of his own responsibilities, towards which his attitudes may in turn have been influenced by his exposure to Smith's ideas.

At the same time, however, his understanding of *The Wealth of Nations* was also directly affected by his own professional priorities. This is not to suggest that the Westmorland reader (as we can call him) was narrow-minded or philistine. On the contrary, his intellectual tastes were dauntingly eclectic. His commonplace book included, in no particular order, material on geological structures, French regional demography, the boundaries of a local parish, the respective literary merits of Dr Johnson and John Milton, the duration of animal lives according to both Buffon and Linnaeus, the need for parliamentary reform, the nature of bees, the dubious merits of Smollett's *History of England* and the oratorical brilliance of Charles James Fox.[47] Yet it was beyond doubt his immediate concerns about the management of an agricultural estate that primarily influenced his response to what he tellingly called 'that invalueable [sic] political performance, the inquiry of Dr Smith.'[48]

The various techniques used by this reader to record his grappling with *The Wealth of Nations* certainly leave no doubt as to his complete mastery of Smith's work. His command of the text was such that he was quite clearly able to manoeuvre through Smith's complex construction with great dexterity. In particular, he was proficient enough to read selectively rather than sequentially, moving easily and accurately between logically related but physically distinct passages when these seemed germane to his own agenda. As he explained, evidently merging Smith's arguments in two separate passages so as to produce his own summary of the work's claims about the counterproductive effects of price-fixing:

> Corn is the leading Article, which our Rulers have taken under their Care & ordaind that when the Price amounts to a given sum it shall not be exported. This looks very well <u>in the face</u> but its Consequence is, that the farmer finding that he can make a greater Profit by other Articles, than by Corn, sows a smaller Quantity, than he woud do, if left to himself—& consequently in some cases a less Quantity being rais'd, the law which was intended to lower the Price eventually raises it.[49]

The commonplacing practices of the Westmorland reader were also exceptionally adept. They involved not only the seamless interweaving of direct quotation with condensation and paraphrase, but even, as in this same passage, an obvious capacity for intelligent extemporization. In fact, he was able to elaborate points at which Smith had gestured but had not quite managed to make, as well as developing pertinent examples of the same observation that the author had completely failed to consider.

It should be clear from the example just cited that the Westmorland reader's handling of *The Wealth of Nations* was shaped above all by his appreciation of Smith's arguments against the policy of regulating the market price of grain—which is to say, against the so-called "Corn Laws," within which English agricultural producers in the 1790s still operated. This was the intensely polemical strand of Smith's thesis to which, in selecting passages either for extract or for summarisation, he was to return time and time again. Under the heading 'On the Impolicy of granting a Bounty on the Importation of Corn' (this was a rare slip, since Smith's argument is actually against promoting the 'Exportation' of corn), he noted, whilst leaning heavily on the fifth chapter of Book IV, how 'To give a bounty on Corn exported, is, therefore, nothing less than to hire our people to work for foreigners,' since in lowering the price of exported foodstuffs by one-twelfth part, the measure means that 'the nation gives away one part in 12 of all the labour employd in growing this corn and exporting it and of the rents of the land on which it grows.'[50]

Similarly the reader summarised under the heading 'On Arable & Pasture Land, Smith's Wealth [of] Nations' the argument from the eleventh chapter of Book I that land committed to cereal production will yield more food than an equivalent area devoted to livestock: 'A Corn Field of moderate fertility,' he wrote, here copying out Smith's definitive conclusion, 'produces a much greater Quantity of food for Man, than the best pasture of equal Extent.'[51] These words might have been viewed with a certain grim irony by a reader charged with running an estate in the northern Pennines. This was marginal terrain at best, and, as home to some of the remotest communities in England, it was by no means a landscape in which it would have been easy to abandon pastoral use in the way that Smith had counselled.

Yet the Westmorland reader did not simply fillet Smith's text in a rigidly pragmatic manner, hunting for materials bearing only upon his own immediate concerns as an agricultural producer. He was also clearly interested in the wider system of political economy that *The Wealth of Nations* had adumbrated and which provided the rigorous intellectual underpinning for its specific observations about mercantilist practices. At many points he sought to capture the crucial aspects of Smith's broader conceptual framework—aspects not directly connected with grain prices but which, perhaps, had the potential to lend greater philosophical depth to a critique of the "Corn Laws."

At one point the reader noted down a discussion of 'Trade' that skilfully interwove his own summary with a quotation from Smith's Book IV:

> 1st The System of Commerce, which inc[l]udes manufactures & which prevail universally in Europe, affects to enrich the Inhabitants of any nation—as well as to afford them employment by procuring what is call'd a favourable balance of trade, or "by exporting to a greater value than its import; the great object therefore of this System of political œconomy is to diminish as much as possible the importation of foreign goods for home consumption and to increase as much as possible the exportation of the produce of domestic industry.. . . . [52]

This note, of course, indicates that the Westmorland reader had discerned the real significance of Smith's disdain for a policy that at its most simplistic amounted only to the increase of exports and the reduction of imports.

The reader's grasp of the detailed implications of Smith's political economy was further revealed by his continuation of the same note, knitting together elements from Books II and IV so as to provide an account of the psychological dynamics of commercial activity: 'Every individual employed in business,' he observes, now loosely summarising rather than directly quoting Smith, 'naturally endeavours to discover the most beneficial Mode of employing & consequently the most effective Mode of increasing his Capital.' As a result, he continues, here more closely paraphrasing part of Book IV, 'If no particular branches of Industry were encouraged more than others, those woud naturally be prefered which afforded the speediest means of increasing the particular capital of individuals and consequently the general capital of a People.'[53]

The division of labour was another conceptual crux of *The Wealth of Nations* in which the Westmorland reader had become acutely interested. Many of Smith's aphoristic observations on this subject were copied out: where 'foreign produce can be brought to market cheaper than home,' he wrote at one point, on the subject of import restrictions, 'the regulation is pernicious, as generally diminishing the general Capital of a country.'[54]

In fact, Smith had merely described such controls as 'useless,' his reader noticeably sharpening the text's point, in a way of which the author might conceivably have approved, with a more pejorative adjective.

Similarly, the reader appears to have been greatly struck by Smith's love of everyday examples to illustrate the otherwise intangible nature of international specialisation. Thus he paraphrased Smith's discussion in the second chapter of Book IV:

> A Master of a Family never attempts to manufacture at home what it will cost him more to manufacture than to purchase. The tailor will not make the Shoes his Family may wear, but buys them from the Shoemaker. The Shoemaker will not make his own clothes but employs the tailor. Every individual in short, finds it tends more to his advantage & to the increase of his Capital, to buy the different Articles he has occasion for from the cheapest Market.[55]

Now using inverted commas to indicate a quotation (though again the occasional word or syntactical variation was actually slipped in), the reader concluded with another of Smith's characteristic *obiter dicta*: '"What is Prudence in the Conduct of a private Family can scarcely be Folly in a great kingdom. If foreigners can supply us with different Articles at a cheaper rate than our own manufacturers, it is better to purchase at a cheap rate from the former.'[56]

As will be clear, the Westmorland reader's engagement with *The Wealth of Nations*, although shaped by the concerns of a man involved in managing an estate, was nevertheless richly textured. It involved particular interest in Smith's arguments pertaining to the "Corn Laws." But it also entailed broader concerns explicable only by a desire to grasp, at least to his private satisfaction (for, as with most commonplacing, there is no suggestion that these notes were intended for anyone else's eyes), the systematic intellectual framework within which the new political economy was being constructed.

Interestingly, such a practice, alternating continually between the general and the particular, between narrow strands of argument immediately relevant to the reader and supporting material of far wider application, was also seen in another English contemporary's reading of *The Wealth of Nations*. This was our old friend Revd James Gambier, the second of whose commonplace books, begun around 1789, contained intriguing notes on Smith's analysis. The rationale, however, was again essentially personal. For he was, of course, necessarily interested in agricultural questions, being legally entitled, as an Anglican benefice-holder, to a share in the fruits of his Kentish parish as well as to the full output of his own glebe: indeed, these considerations lay behind Gambier's own surviving compositions on the vexed matter of tithes.[57] But the result as far as his reading was concerned was a particular preoccupation with *The Wealth of Nations*—clearly one of the most widely-influential and well-regarded works of the age and also one in which observations directly useful to the landlord and to the farmer were contained.

Like so many others who encountered the Scottish Enlightenment through their reading, Gambier was perfectly capable of viewing a text through more than one prism, depending upon the occasion. His deep familiarity with Smith's book may be illustrated best of all by the use Gambier made of *The Wealth of Nations* not only as a work of political economy but as an exemplary piece of modern literature: it was his complete absorption in the text that stimulated, under the heading 'Obscurity of style,' a reference to 'Smith's W of Nat^s Vol 1 p. 440. 1st sentence'; and it was doubtless also the same detailed knowledge of this particular work that, in a note on 'Eloquence,' led Gambier to observe that 'our judgment conspires with our passions to produce our convictions. See Wealth of Nations 2:400.'[58]

Yet it was undoubtedly as a source of economic arguments pertinent to landownership that Gambier primarily approached Smith's work. Hence, under the heading 'Value,' he composed a lengthy discussion that begins thus:

> Adam Smith observes that there are two kinds of value, viz. a value of sale, & a value of use. Thus, a Diamond, tho of very great value as an Article for Sale, has but little worth as an article of use. The same is true of a multiplicity of other things, on which mankind set a great value, on account of their rarity, or the peculiar skill display'd in their formation, but wch are yet incapable of contributing either to the preservation, or comfort of life. The phrase, the value of use, may be used with some latitude, to denote, not only those things which are necessary for subsistence, or are conducive to comfort; but those also from which any real advantage may be deriv'd . . .[59]

Evidently this was Gambier's own gloss on Smith's handling of the concept of value in Book I, where the text talks of 'value in use' and 'value in exchange' and asserts, by way of illustration, that diamonds have 'scarce any value in use.' Like the Westmorland reader, Gambier accurately captures the burden of Smith's argument, even though the summary is almost entirely his own formulation. Importantly, however, it is an argument identified in the printed text, and recorded during his reading, as a direct result of Gambier's own immediate concerns. For the commonplacing again betrays the distinctive standpoint from which he approached this passage in *The Wealth of Nations*. Beside this discussion he placed in the margin the revealing words 'Rent,' followed by 'Rent of Langley Park & Rumw^d Green 37.'

This is a cross-reference of some significance in explaining Gambier's interest in Smith's discussion of value. Certainly it incorporated a precise piece of navigational commonplacing: at folio 37 (verso) Gambier did indeed add notes summarising the annual rentals for Langley Park and Rumwood Green—two contiguous properties in which the rector had a vested interest—beginning in 1781 and ending in 1828. In other words, Gambier's concern with the theory of economic value was intimately bound up with his practical concerns about the conditions affecting landed proprietorship in Kent at the turn of the nineteenth century.

This connection between Smith's analysis of fundamental concepts and Gambier's own severely practical preoccupations was underlined by the continuation of the same note. Still concerned with explaining Smith's notion of 'value of use,' it runs:

Thus it may include whatever may become a source of gain or profit. Hence in speaking of the value of the rent of a Farm, we may consider the value of use as denoting the profit which the Farmer may reasonably be expected to make of the farm occupied at that rent. Now it seems that this value is what ought to be regarded as the Criterion in determining the magnitude of the rent. This, however, seems to be disregarded; & that which regulates the judgment of the Valuer is really the other kind of value, viz. the value of sale; for, in determining what rent be should [sic] set in the farm, he considers how much he c^d find persons willing to give for it; & not at what rent a Tenant c^d use it, with a reasonable prospect of a fair remuneration. But these two considerations often differ widely . . . [60]

Gambier, in other words, was perplexed by Smith's theoretical distinction between use and exchange in the practical context of rent setting as it actually occurs. As the clergyman knew well from first-hand experience, rents were in reality determined more by what a tenant was willing to pay, and how easy it would be to replace him with someone else, rather than by calculating the productive value of the land as such. This was, of course, an important difficulty. It was also one over which Smith's own exposition, which described rent as 'the price paid for the use of land' and 'the highest which the tenant can afford to pay in the actual circumstances of the land,' had drawn a discreet veil.[61] It was, however, a deficiency that apparently mattered greatly to Gambier as he attempted to relate it to his own circumstances. Accordingly it was a gap that, as he commonplaced, he clearly strove to fill.

If Revd Gambier was inspired by his own experiences to try to drag Smith's political economy rather further in one specific direction than *The Wealth of Nations* had actually gone, then another reader of the same text, William Wyndham Grenville, was even bolder. Like Horace Walpole, Grenville was a prime minister's son; but unlike Walpole, he also enjoyed high office as Baron Grenville. Indeed, he was Speaker of the Commons, then successively Home Secretary, President of the Board of Control, Foreign

Secretary and Prime Minister, playing a leading part in the abolition of the slave trade before political eclipse and eventually a debilitating stroke forced his withdrawal from public life.[62] Grenville's admiration for Smith has long been known, instantiated in an effusive letter to his friend Pitt in October 1800 praising 'the soundness of Adam Smith's principles of political economy,' doctrines to which the premier had apparently also lent his assent at least until, as Grenville sniped, 'Lord Liverpool lured you from our arms into all the mazes of the old system.'[63]

Grenville's commonplace book, however, recently acquired by the Beinecke Library, has hitherto been unknown.[64] It is interesting above all because it confirms his continuing engagement with Smith's writings on political economy, to which the elderly statesman, retired to his Buckinghamshire home by 1822 but actively contributing to controversies over the currency and the sinking fund, was still devoting substantial private study. Smith's articulation of the labour theory of value was examined on the very first page. Like the Kentish parson and the Westmorland reader, Grenville's commonplacing techniques led him to demonstrate his detailed knowledge of *The Wealth of Nations* by summarising in his own words the successive points made on the printed page. Yet it is also obvious that Grenville had come to consider Smith's account in the book's Introduction unclear in important respects, and as dangerously misleading in others.

As a result, the opening précis runs as follows:

> Smith speaks of the <u>annual</u> <u>labour</u> of a nation as being the only source of its' [sic] annual consumption. A mode of speaking which is extremely inaccurate; in as much as it seems to exclude the very important part which <u>past</u> industry, stored and accumulated for the purpose, bears in present production. This however could certainly not be Smith's meaning.

> The consequences of the first of these errors seem to lead in the second Section to the manifest absurdity of excluding Soil & Climate from being numbered among the causes of Plenty. But at the close of the 3[d.] he seems to admit that what he there asserts, as to the effect of labour on abundance of supply, is true only, *caeteris paribus*.[65]

Further underlining Grenville's anxiety about Smith's argument that labour is the source of value, this note was actually preceded by a scored-out paragraph: 'It is remarkable that the first section in Smith's great work should be erroneous. He there asserts labour to be the only source of production. The value of every article of human use is given to it partly by the native produce & powers employed in its production and partly by the industry, whether intellectual or bodily, applied to fit it for human use.' In other words, Grenville appears to have doubted Smith's celebrated claim that 'The annual labour of every nation is the fund which originally supplies it with all the necessaries and conveniences of life which it annually consumes, and which consist always, either in the immediate produce of that labour, or in what is purchased with that produce from other nations.'[66] This doctrine was regarded by most readers as absolutely pivotal. As glossed by another careful reader of *The Wealth of Nations*, William Chute M.P., in the 1790s, the notion that the 'Annual labour of every nation is its fund, which consists in the immediate produce of that labour, or in what is purchased with that produce from other nations' appeared central to Smith's place in the modern development of political economy.[67]

To Grenville, however, the labour theory of value was nothing less than the principal weakness of *The Wealth of Nations*. For, first articulated in the Introduction, it established in his view a basic faultline running throughout the remainder of this most influential of texts. As Grenville's note continued, beside the self-explanatory marginal title 'ss. 3, 4, 5, 6. abundance of supply, its cause erroneously assigned by Smith':

> From the 3[d] to the end of the 6th Section the inaccuracies and error of his language is still more apparent. He there treats of the causes which produce, & govern, <u>abundance</u> of supply. He asserts that <u>this</u> is regulated, partly by the skill, & dexterity, with which labour is applied, & partly by the <u>proportion</u> between the number of labourers, and that of non-labourers: but more by the former than by the latter.

> Now it is self-evident, that the <u>abundance</u> of supply cannot depend <u>at all</u> on this proportion; tho' its <u>adequacy</u> may. The abundance of the supply can depend on nothing but the productiveness of the sources of supply. The source flows neither with more nor fewer waters because few, or many, approach to drink from them in their course.[68]

Grenville's argument, in short, was that *The Wealth of Nations* in fact rested on a systematic misunderstanding, or at least a misunderstood description, of the nature of labour and thus of its true significance in economic activity.

That Grenville believed Smith's whole system had been founded on such a fundamental mistake is clear from his next note. Beside the marginal title 'He confounds Wealth with production,' Grenville argued that Smith had confused, as he put it, '(in the very outset of his work,) two ideas which should be accurately distinguished.'[69] National wealth, which Grenville thought represented the balance between the production and consumption of value by individuals, would

> result manifestly from the comparative <u>number</u> & <u>productiveness</u> of the sources of production on the one hand, and from the <u>extent</u> & <u>value</u> of the consumption on the other, and not at all from any proportion between the <u>number</u> of producers, and that of consumers.[70]

Accordingly, for Grenville it was impossible, as Smith had argued, that 'the real wealth of any Society . . . [was] the same thing with the annual produce of its land and labour.'[71] Nor could the importance of these reservations be minimised. Whilst 'indeed mostly verbal criticisms,' it seemed that 'nothing had more contributed to retard the progress of this Science, than the very loose and inaccurate language in which its doctrines have been delivered by Smith, and others.' The Introduction of *The Wealth of Nations* was therefore especially flawed, having 'no pretension to be considered as a scientific, and logical, distribution of this great subject.' It was, however, 'calculated on the contrary to prepare an intelligent reader for the striking disorder which prevails throughout the work, & is its greatest blemish.'[72]

Having thus despatched the opening pages of *The Wealth of Nations*, and cast aspersions upon the accuracy and coherence of the whole, Grenville turned his attention to Smith's first substantial theoretical analysis—that concerned with the division of labour. Again, it is clear that he understood this as a cornerstone of Smith's political economy because of its relationship with the labour theory of value. Again, however, he found it worryingly deficient. Not least, it suffered once more from imprecision. Smith had been hazy about the meaning of 'labour,' seeming, as Grenville alleged, 'to confine the term to bodily exertion only' when intellectual endeavour should also have been included.[73] Smith had also advanced the incautious claim 'that the increased productiveness of labour, & the greater skill &c. of its application, arise principally from its division.' This too seemed to Grenville 'not very precise or clear.' For 'it supposes labour to be something uniform in character, & capable of being measured by quantity; & it professes to explain why a given quantity of labour, in England for example, is more productive of Cloth, hardware, or Corn, than in Ireland, or in the unsettled parts of N: America.' In Grenville's view Smith's analysis had achieved nothing of the sort. In order to explain this phenomenon more clearly, he considered that it would be necessary, on the contrary, to ask 'Why does the industry of the same number of men directly employed at the loom, the forge, or the plough, obtain greater returns in the civilized, than in the uncivilized, Country.'[74]

The answer to this, according to Grenville, lay in rather more straightforward practical considerations than those concerned exclusively with the division of labour that had so preoccupied Smith. First, 'as natural substances, and their qualities, and powers, bear a large share in the production of all wealth, it must be examined in this comparison whether the supply of these substances, & the facility of calling forth their qualities & powers, are the same in the Countries so compared.'[75] In other words, the widely varying availability of resources such as coal, iron ore and wool would alone go far to explain different levels of productivity. Equally, Grenville insisted that 'Much industry, both intellectual, and bodily, has been previously exerted, & has been as it were stored up, for this purpose.' It was by these means that 'the materials have been produced, & adapted to their object; the tools & implements have been fabricated; the lands fenced & chained; the buildings erected, the roads made, and above all the art & science have successively been raised up, by which all these means and facilities of production are most advantageously employed.'[76] At the same time, it was 'a complete error to suppose that, in any question of production, labour can be measured by the mere computation of the number of those who labour,' since 'The amount of bodily exertion is not the same, the moral qualities & faculties, & intellectual powers, which are brought into action are widely different in all the various states and stages of Society.'[77]

Grenville was plainly perturbed in particular by Smith's insistence upon the labour theory of value and thus his belief that the division of labour accounted for modern levels of productivity and steadily increasing wealth: 'Labour,' claimed Smith in Book I, ' . . . is the real measure of the exchangeable value of all commodities.'[78] For Grenville this was simply wrong-headed. As he concluded,

> In no such article is labour, or industry, the sole valuable ingredient. In none of them therefore is the value of the labour employed in its production the measure of the value of the commodity given in exchange for it. So far from being, as Smith states, the measure of all exchangeable commodities, labour is the measure of value in none.[79]

Indeed, in Grenville's mind this solecism substantially vitiated the intellectual structure of *The Wealth of Nations*. It was nothing less than 'the most considerable, & in its consequences the most extensive, of all the errors in this excellent work.'[80]

Readers were plainly guided by their own circumstances as they set about assigning value and significance to Smith's complex and controversial text. Personal experiences and professional obligations evidently intermingled, providing a context in which the author's words were weighed and imbued with specific meanings and implications. With the Westmorland reader, as with James Gambier, the most pressing concern was simply agricultural land: to the former the "Corn Laws" were of special interest; to the latter it was rentals that mattered, precisely because these were a fact of economic life for a country parson. Yet to both men *The Wealth of Nations* was interrogated not solely for its treatment of these specific topics but for the wider perspectives that Smith's system offered on such problems—though for Gambier there were evidently difficulties in applying his general arguments to a particular practical situation.

More diverse interests, meanwhile, shaped the response of Bertie Greatheed. A squire who lived at Guy's Cliffe in Warwickshire, and who would play a leading role in the development of Leamington Spa around the turn of the nineteenth century, Greatheed was also a noted aesthete, a poet and a moderately successful dramatist, who numbered

Sarah Siddons, Hester Piozzi and, less expectedly, Napoleon Bonaparte (with whom he had travelled) among his wide circle of eminent friends and acquaintances.[81] Pertinently, however, for his experiences with *The Wealth of Nations*, his family also had longstanding interests in the St Kitts sugar plantations. These probably go furthest towards explaining why Greatheed actually sought to reduce Smith's multi-faceted text to a useful list of interesting facts and conclusive judgments derived from the cutting edge of the new economic thinking.

Greatheed's interest in this field was nothing if not eclectic, as befitted the ceaselessly inquiring mind of a larger-than-life polymath. 'The following observations are from Smith's excellent work on the Wealth of Nations,' he wrote as he collated material for his own commonplace book, probably in the early 1780s:

> Man is the only trucking, and tool making animal—Land carriage is to water, in the proportion of 8 men and 1 ship, to 100 men 50 Wagons & 400 horses. Let navigations thus be cut! For whether profitable or not the Companies who undertake them, they must be advantageous to the public—Troye weight so called from the fair of Troyes in Champagne—The value of Gold & silver sunk in the 16 Century to about ½ their value. It is singular that they sunk equally, and shews that the quantities of gold and silver found in the new world bore the same proportion to each other as in the old—Silver is twice the value at Canton that it is in London. Therefore in China the proportion is very different—There was no silver in Rome till the first Punic war, & Copper was always a measure of value there . . . [82]

Such a litany of observations, running to five folio pages and in each case representing Greatheed's summary of Smith's point rather than a direct quotation, demonstrates the lengths to which some readers would go in the attempt to accommodate *The Wealth of Nations* into their own knowledge and understanding of the world.

* * *

The same was true, of course, with William Grenville, though here it was the experiences of a man who had once been responsible for Britain's trade and public finances that had determined the response. For Grenville, unlike Greatheed, and especially unlike the Westmorland reader, had found Smith's relentless polemic against government regulation and commercial policy extremely hard to swallow. Not least this was because it jeopardised much of his own life's work. Accordingly, Grenville had subjected *The Wealth of Nations* to fundamental theoretical criticism, based as it was upon the labour theory of value and the division of labour. Discerning the meaning of one of the Scottish Enlightenment's most eminent publications therefore did not necessarily entail accepting its implications. Nor did it have to mean making one's agreement with the text an integral part of one's own image and identity. Instead, as we shall see more often in the next chapter, it might well involve defining and defending the reader's own position in legitimate opposition to the putative errors of the author.

10 Misreading and Misunderstanding
Encountering Natural Religion and Hume

The Wealth of Nations, as we have seen, served ultimately as pivot around which a whole series of idiosyncratic interpretations, fundamentally self-referential in character, were able to revolve. Similar things, however, can be said for the responses that developed when English readers came across some of those potentially troublesome ideas emanating from Scotland—especially those that appeared to place in doubt the veracity of previously unquestioned theological and ideological principles. More than sufficient evidence survives to allow us to reconstruct these reactions to some of the most characteristic intellectual achievements of the Scottish Enlightenment. Indeed, it actually makes possible a detailed analysis of how these carefully calibrated responses to different forms of scepticism emerged in practice from out of the unique personal circumstances of individual readers.

* * *

Our first protagonist will be Revd Charles Peters, between 1726 and 1774 rector of St Mabyn, which lies adjacent to Bodmin Moor in northern Cornwall.[1] At least as far as his extant notebooks can tell us, Peters was, like virtually all of the Anglican clergymen whom we have met thus far, an avid and an extremely active reader, continually immersed in the writings of various contemporaries. Yet his complete comfort with the business of reading did not in fact prevent him from developing an exceptionally unusual and very revealing interpretation of one of the thought provoking texts of the early Scottish Enlightenment, the work of Thomas Blackwell, professor of Greek and later principal of Marischal College, Aberdeen.

In general terms, Revd Peters' tastes were not all that far removed from those that characterised most of his clerical colleagues. In particular, there was a special fondness, among older Scottish writers, for Gilbert Burnet. There was also an admirable determination to remain abreast of the latest literary news and reputable current criticism through regular inspection of the periodicals—in this instance the *London Magazine* by strong preference. Crucially, however, Peters was an obdurate High Churchman. This definitively conservative stance may have been acquired, and was certainly much strengthened, at Exeter College, Oxford, late in Anne's reign. Long a bastion of theological orthodoxy, Exeter had by Peters' time already produced several leading anti-deists, such as James Edgcumbe and John Conybeare, who published outspoken works denouncing the advances allegedly being made by Enlightenment free-thinking in contemporary society.[2]

Given his formidable Oxford grounding in conservative Anglicanism, we should hardly be surprised by Peters' hostility towards those naturalistic accounts of religion, increasingly popular from the 1720s onwards and widely seen as characteristic of the Enlightenment in the round, that tried to explain Christian beliefs and practices by reference to their adherents' social and cultural circumstances.[3] Yet the unfolding of Peters' personal conflict with the confident exponents of natural religion was in fact far from straightforward. For an important part of it seems to have been a curious encounter, shortly before Christmas 1735, with just one text of Scottish provenance, Blackwell's *Enquiry into the Life and Writings of Homer*.

As Peters' own narrative of his quotidian experiences records for 13 December:

> I have been dipping into a Book lately published entitled an enquiry into Homer's Life &c, and I see that the Author supposes the Religion of the Heathen to have been the Invention of some Wise among the Egyptians, and probably he would infer that all Religion is mere human invention.[4]

Blackwell's work had appeared anonymously in London that March. But Peters' initial response already has some striking implications. First, there appears no doubt that he had correctly deciphered one of the text's overt messages. For the *Enquiry* did indeed venture a sophisticated naturalistic explanation for the theogony of the ancient Greeks. Second, however, Peters had clearly concluded that the *Enquiry* was to be read as a coded attack upon Christianity itself. In short, he judged that its anonymous author, in developing a powerful sociological tool accounting for the historical emergence of Greek mythology, was implying that 'all Religion' must be of strictly human provenance.

Such a problematical analysis by a reader raises all manner of intriguing questions. Not least, we should want to know more about how Peters had actually arrived at this distinctly hostile interpretation of Blackwell's meaning. There are actually several clues that can help us to contextualise as well as to explain his striking early reading of the *Enquiry*. In the first place, Peters' own contemporary notes continue this personal narrative. They give us a better indication of what he understood the text to be saying, in December 1735 and, intriguingly, a year later in December 1736 (the interval implying that Peters, like many habitual commonplacers, regularly reviewed his own notes, on this occasion specifically reigniting his earlier interest in Blackwell's text). At the time of the 1735 encounter, moreover,

Peters had added that 'this author allows that the Reason that put his Wise men upon the invention of Religion, was the necessity of it to Civilize the Barbarous Multitude and keep Mankind in Order.'[5] And he had asked a highly pertinent rhetorical question:

> if there be an absolute necessity of Religion for this purpose, and supposing the author to be no atheist, I would fain ask him, which is most probable? Either that God who saw the necessity of Religion for the government of Mankind, would Reveal the Main Principles and Doctrines of Religion to men from the Beginning, or else put them on a necessity of supplying by their own invention in after Ages, so that the World should all along be governed by a lie?[6]

Blackwell's text, in other words, was most definitely seen by Peters as offering an essentially sociological account of an ancient religion rooted in the pragmatic determination by intelligent rulers to achieve the pacification and obedience of the people that was, as Peters glossed it, 'an absolute necessity' for a stable order. More interestingly still, Peters had decided that the *Enquiry* was grossly impious for implying that God had created mankind without providing initially for this apparent 'necessity,' leaving long-suffering men eventually to realise for themselves the importance of sound religious principles: 'I am apt to think none but an Atheist will be disposed to embrace the latter part of the question,' the Cornish parson acidly concluded.[7]

Peters' reading in December 1736, meanwhile, tells us even more about his understanding of Blackwell's argument and its implications. For when he returned to it a year later, he recalled that the text (he still did not know the author's identity) was 'entitled an enquiry into Homer's Life &c . . . [and] is written with a great deal of spirit in the Polite freethinking way, and seems therefore fitted to do a great deal of mischief.'[8] In other words, Peters' reading of the *Enquiry* appears from the outset to have become inextricably bound up with his wider anxiety about deistic literature— material written, as he dismissively put it, 'in the Polite freethinking way.' By elaborating naturalistic explanations for religious beliefs and sacred practices in general, such works were clearly intended to reveal Christianity also as serving strictly human purposes. As Peters added, 'it Reflects a charge of Atheism upon the wise statesmen of antiquity, and indeed represents Religion in general as no other than a State engine contrived to keep the Multitude in Awe for the common good of Society. . . .'[9]

Much of the explanation for this immediately aggressive response to Blackwell's text, therefore, consists in Peters having assigned it automatically to an existing category of contemporary writing about which he was already deeply suspicious. In effect, Peters had grouped the *Enquiry* with works like Matthew Tindal's very recent *Christianity as Old as the Creation* (1730), a landmark deistical study that had been the subject of a famous refutation by Conybeare, Peters' old Exeter contemporary.[10] But why had he done this? In particular, how had it been possible for Peters to mistake what we know as the scholarly and sophisticated work of an upstanding Scots Presbyterian divine and university teacher for the deliberately subversive polemic of a crypto-atheist?

The most plausible solution lies in the powerful influence of one of the factors that always affects the reception and reading of texts. In Peters' case it is all too obvious that the identification of generic characteristics, on the basis of which a book may be assigned a specific place in relation to continuing discourses and familiar literatures, and comparisons and connections thereby fruitfully initiated, lay at the root of the problem. In most circumstances, indeed, this is an uncomplicated, and to some extent an unconscious, act. Certainly the interrogation of inter-textual relationships by the reader is an integral part of any attempt to construe meanings and so to establish the purpose and significance of a particular text. It is also why, as we have repeatedly seen, those who offered guidance on reading and on book selection so strongly underlined the relationships and compatibilities between otherwise discrete texts.

In his encounter with the *Enquiry*, a newly published work of which he evidently had little or no prior knowledge, Peters had quite simply gone astray during this crucial process. He had been misled, firstly, by his own preoccupation with the defence of orthodoxy against deism; secondly, by over-concentration on one narrow strand of argument in Blackwell's text (since its account of Greek religion's natural origins was but one small part of a very diverse whole); and finally, by a tendency, characteristic of a man who would later engage in a noisy controversy with William Warburton over the Book of Job, to assume that those against whom he had ranged himself intended the most radical and most disturbing conclusions to be drawn from their explicit statements.[11] Peters, in other words, had responded to Blackwell in a way that was largely predetermined by a series of highly specific contingencies that happened to surround and structure that particular encounter. As a direct result, the meanings and significances that this experience of reading constructed were ultimately as singular—and, it transpires, as fundamentally misconceived—as the peculiarly gladiatorial perspective from which Peters had approached this early manifestation of the Scottish Enlightenment.

* * *

Charles Peters was not alone in documenting an early and exceptionally creative encounter with this particularly complex text. His colleague and younger contemporary John Sharp, Archdeacon of Northumberland and canon of Durham, also engaged closely with Blackwell's *Enquiry*.[12] Yet Sharp, crucially for his experience with the same work, was a quite different character. He was a scion of one of the north's leading dynasties of

Anglican ecclesiastics. His grandfather and namesake had become a stoutly Williamite Archbishop of York at the Revolution; his father Thomas a theological writer and an equally reliable prebendary of Durham under George II. Partly because of the grander manner and broader horizons that resulted, John Sharp's reading, in so far as it can be reconstructed from the book collection that he inherited from his father and brother and which today belongs to the University of Durham, also seems to have been far more extensive than Peters.' Like almost all clergymen, he loved Burnet's *Thirty-Nine Articles*, from which he commonplaced freely.[13] But he was also a great admirer of *The Spectator*, and was apparently comfortable with the increasing flow of polite secular literature, some of it daringly speculative, that characterised the first half of the eighteenth century.

Sharp was especially interested, like so many readers in this period, in the question of taste and aesthetic judgment in matters ranging from poetry to gardening: 'Mr Addison observes that there is nothing in this whole Art,' Sharp noted at one point, referring to a well-known discussion in *The Spectator* no. 415, 'that pleases the Imagination, but as it is great, uncommon, or beautiful.'[14] It was in this context, then, that Sharp's own contact with Blackwell's *Enquiry*, which took place some time in the 1740s or 1750s, and after the work had been successfully accommodated into the modern canon, was played out. Accordingly, it was to be in important respects a very different experience from that which had made Charles Peters, one of the *Enquiry*'s first but also most antagonistic readers, such a pointed critic of its author.

Significantly, Sharp's approach, as well as being better informed by accumulated critical opinion, was characterised by a much more careful examination of Blackwell's text. Peters had engaged in précis at a high level of generalisation (with unfortunate consequences for his interpretative acuity): as he said in December 1735, inadvertently hinting at the lack of meticulousness with which he had proceeded, he had been 'dipping' into Blackwell's newly published volume. By contrast, Sharp's commonplacing was clearly dependent upon close and careful reading of the text. He recorded specific page references, enabling easy and accurate future orientation of his own notes in relation to the printed original. Most significantly, however, Sharp's quotations from Blackwell, running to whole passages of the *Enquiry*, were never in fact strictly verbatim.

What he actually appears to have done is to create a subtly different version of Blackwell's own words that nevertheless captures the essence of the printed text. To take just one example, under the heading 'Poetry—Epick,' Sharp's note runs 'For so unaffected & simple were the manners of the early ages, that the folds & windings of the human breast lay open to the eye . . . ': in comparison, Blackwell's original text actually gives us 'For so unaffected & simple were the Manners of those Times, that the Folds and Windings of the human Breast lay open to the Eye . . . .'[15] Clearly the capitalisation has been much altered, though to no material effect. Again, so has some of Blackwell's phraseology—'those Times' had been rendered by Sharp as 'the early ages'—but it is clear that the sense remains unchanged. The essential meaning, in other words, was what Sharp was most concerned to preserve. And in this regard his renditions of the *Enquiry*, as of the other texts he was reading, were invariably flawless.

In addition to Sharp's particular care with the sense of Blackwell's work, it should be underlined that his selection of material was also far more representative of the *Enquiry*'s tenor than the narrow strands on which Charles Peters had chosen to concentrate. The *Enquiry* was, after all, a study in primitivist cultural anthropology, concerned with the origins and function of mythological systems in early Greek society. Such inquiries, moreover, fitted well with Sharp's interests in broader questions of culture, literature and education, providing him with many points and observations to reinforce his own opinions. This is doubtless why it was Blackwell's arguments about epic poetry and about such matters as the formation of customs and habits that Sharp particularly transcribed. At one point, for example, again mildly recasting the typographical presentation of the *Enquiry*, Sharp had noted, under the heading 'Education,' that:

> Young minds are apt to receive such strong impressions from the circumstances of the Country where they are born & bred that they contract a mutual kind of likeness to those circumstances, & bear the marks of that course of life, thro' wch they have pass'd.

This entry continued, actually omitting an intervening sentence in Blackwell's text that seemed less germane:

> The circumstances that may reasonably be thought to have the greatest effect on us, may perhaps be reduc'd to these following.
>
> First, <u>The State of the Country</u> where a person is born & bred, the <u>common manners</u> of the inhabitants, their constitution civil & religious with its causes & consequences
>
> 2dly The <u>manners</u> of the <u>Times,</u> or the prevalent Humours or Professions in vogue
>
> Private Education
>
> The <u>particular way of life</u> we chuse & pursue, with our fortunes in it.

Two further sentences from the *Enquiry* were then skipped before Sharp's note, reinforcing the real thrust of Blackwell's analysis here, concluded simply:

We must consider these as the moulds that form us into those Habits &
dispositions, which sway our conduct & distinguish our actions. vide
Life of Homer p. 11 & 12.[16]

Evidently Sharp's effectiveness as a commonplacer was, if anything, only
increased by his skill in stripping out extraneous material. In effect, this
process of editing and recasting, reminiscent of the techniques of the Westmorland reader and Revd Gambier with *The Wealth of Nations*, allowed
him to produce an even more forceful and economical rendition of the text,
saying the same thing in fewer words. The result was that the *Enquiry*
was transformed by Sharp, who appreciated its capacity for buttressing
those interests which he shared with Blackwell, into something far different from the cynical attempt to bend natural religion to the seditious cause
of atheism that Revd Peters had perceived. Rather it had been reimagined
as a safe point of reference for mainstream Enlightenment inquiries, and as
a valuable reservoir of epigrammatic truisms on questions of literary and
cultural development.

*   *   *

Hume's *History* has justifiably brooked large in our own discussion. It is
the sheer pervasiveness of this author's influence as a historian, together
with the urgency with which readers of all descriptions scrambled to engage
with his most accessible text, that makes it such a touchstone example to
which to return. There was, after all, a very real sense in which no-one
from the 1760s onwards could be considered a truly accomplished reader,
or fully acquainted with the modern canon—or even, perhaps, properly
politically aware—unless he or she knew the *History* well, and so could
pronounce intelligently and plausibly on its various strengths and weak-
nesses. Whether agreeing with a critic in the *Monthly Ledger* in 1775 that
Hume's work granted one 'a full expectation of being highly entertained'
or instead feeling that the *Monthly Review* had been right in 1757 when
assessing another of Hume's publications—'few of any just discernment,
we apprehend, will envy him any honours his acuteness, or elegance, can
possibly obtain, when they are only employed in filling the mind with the
uncomfortable fluctuations of scepticism, and the gloom of infidelity'—
readers were unable to ignore his intellectual power, his persuasiveness and
his elegance as a writer.[17]

Witness, for example, the imprecations from Mrs Sharp to Lady Philips
or from Mary Cornwallis to her daughters, both of them self-consciously
respectable ladies anxious to encourage the study of Hume's writings,
although equally alive, as so many critics had advised, to the need for caution and the exercise of critical discretion. Witness also Hume's place of
honour in the characteristically earnest reading regimes followed by emerging early nineteenth-century working-class autodidacts like John Thelwall

and James Malton (the latter having encountered the *History* when in Coldbath Fields prison and, as he later reflected, reading it 'with deep interest and much profit').[18] It is therefore unsurprising, and nor is it unhelpful for our own purposes, that readers' experiences with Hume's masterwork sometimes came to be documented at considerable length. This is what allows us to explore in unrivalled detail the process by which a single text, indelibly associated with the Scottish Enlightenment, came to mean quite different things—indeed, in some cases was able to appear diametrically *opposing* things—to different individuals.

William Constable is an exceptionally fine example of a man whose response to Hume was not only private but also, in an important sense, intensely personal. Fellow of the Royal Society, antiquarian and aesthete, Constable, who had inherited Burton Constable in the East Riding of Yorkshire in 1747, was by any standards a learned and sophisticated mid-Georgian gentleman.[19] Despite his obvious connections with the cultural establishment, however, Constable, who once remarked that his principal interests in life were 'Reading and Reflection,' remained in an important sense an outsider.[20] He was a member of one of northern England's leading Catholic families, a long and distinguished line of recusant gentry whose religion had barred them from office and formal political influence for many generations past. These unpromising personal circumstances ensured that Constable would be able to perform what we might wish to think of as the Catholic reading of Hume—a distinctive analysis of the *History* that he recorded with typical assiduity in a document called simply the 'Notebook of Extracts from Works of David Hume.' Compiled around 1758, this detailed his thoughts on Hume's writings, but above all on the *History*. There was the near-obligatory list of historical facts and observations that, as we have seen, was a desideratum for so many of Hume's contemporary readers: in this case, the population of London in 1603, Shakespeare's death aged fifty-three, the various battles of the 1640s, and so forth.[21] But the analytical content went much further. It included a series of quotations that can only have been specifically designed to co-opt Hume's authority as an historian for the validation of Constable's own outlook and identity.

Constable was particularly concerned with those passages that touched upon ecclesiastical history and, above all, the Reformation. This was not in itself unusual. As we have seen, most people were immediately aware, not least courtesy of Hume's very public mauling by the critics, that his handling of religious questions was highly questionable. Accordingly we should not be surprised that readers so often devoted their enthralled attention to this aspect of his work. But Constable's interest was evidently rather more personal. For if the extracts indicate where his eye had fallen most keenly on Hume's text, he was attracted above all by those comments that cast the Protestant reformers and their motives in a thoroughly dubious light. Royal support for the break with Rome elicited Constable's particular curiosity: 'Tho' the prospect of sharing the plunder of the Church had engag'd some princes to embrace the Reformation,' he noted, quoting Hume exactly, 'it may be affirm'd, that the Romish System remain'd still the favourite religion of sovereigns . . . it reconciles the penitent to his offended Duty.'[22]

Constable was clearly seduced by Hume's deliciously ironic remarks on avaricious royal policy and the intrinsic attractions of the old faith. But details like the *History*'s treatment of Archbishop Laud's exact relationship with Catholicism—a bone of contention ever since the unfortunate prelate's execution—also interested him. Here too Hume's words were extracted because they were discernibly sympathetic to the tenor of Catholicism: 'though Laud deserved not the appellation of papist, the genius of his religion was, though to a lesser degree, the same with that of the Romish: The same profound respect was exacted to the sacerdotal character, the same submission required to the creeds and decrees of synods and councils, the same pomp and ceremony was affected in worship, and the same superstitious regard to days, postures, meats, and vestments.'[23]

Constable, however, was not immune to English patriotism, despite the distaste for militant Protestantism—one of its eighteenth-century cornerstones—that he shared with the iconoclastic Hume. Indeed, his Catholicism was ultimately no barrier to a confidence in the reality of England's liberties that, in the loosest sense, might meaningfully be described as "Whiggish." Thus where Hume praised England's constitutional traditions (presumably massaging the egos of his paying public), Constable recited the remarks with no obvious discomfort. He quoted approvingly, for example, the *History*'s comment—the latter part probably intended ironically—about the bill against monopolies passed in 1624:

> It was there supposed, that every subject of England had entire power to dispose of his own actions, provided he did no injury to any of his fellow subjects; and that no prerogative of the king, no power of any magistrate, nothing but the authority alone of laws, could restrain that unlimited freedom. The full prosecution of this noble principle into all its natural consequences, has at last, through many contests, produced that singular and happy government, which we enjoy at present.[24]

Yet Constable's familial attachments prevented his complete absorption in the conventional Protestant-grounded patriotism of his own day. This was particularly true when it came to the pantheon of moderate Parliamentarians from the 1640s, much admired by Constable's Whiggish contemporaries but viewed with significant scepticism by Hume.

About these men Constable again simply copied out the *History*'s sobering judgment:

> Some persons, partial to the patriots of this age, have ventured to put them in a balance with the most illustrious characters of antiquity; and mentioned the names of Pym, Hambden, Vane, as a just parallel to

those of Cato, Brutus, Cassius. Profound capacity, indeed, undaunted courage, extensive enterprise; in these particulars, perhaps the Roman do not much surpass the English worthies: But what a difference, when the discourse, conduct, conversation, and private as well as public behaviour, of both are inspected![25]

Constable, in other words, was especially struck by Hume's demotion of some of Charles I's most prominent opponents, and wished to preserve this useful piece of revisionism in his own notebook. Again, it is not difficult to imagine why this should have been so. For as a man whose ancestors had fought against the Parliamentarians, he was unwilling—as was Hume on quite different grounds—to accept this key element in the Whiggish mythology of English patriotism.

Hume's *History*, however, also received entirely the opposite treatment from certain readers. Such a response was especially likely among those who lacked William Constable's peculiar affiliations and outlook. Horace Walpole, for example, a man with Whiggism in his blood, positively loathed Hume's mischievous treatment of Hanoverian sacred cows. Walpole noted darkly in one of his many notebooks in 1760, *apropos* any history of England, that 'if written with any view, [it] shd be for liberty' but that too often it had been 'written by a Jacobite, whose chief view, as Hume's & Smollett's, is to decry Q. Eliz. To exalt the Stuarts, that despicable race . . . The Papists, the Jacobites, the Enthusiastic Admirers of Slavery, blame Q. Eliz. for executing the Q. of Scots, & take great pains to expose all the arts & subterfuges she used to colour her proceedings . . . .'[26] This characterisation of Hume's historical work as a crypto-Jacobite assault upon the constitution that formed part of a wider Scottish subversion of England's ancient liberties seems to have been especially popular in Whiggish circles, above all in the 1760s and early 1770s, as they first laboured under the yoke of the Earl of Bute and then perceived George III's government falling under the influence of Scottish politicians.[27]

The metropolitan radical John Horne Tooke, for example, who loved and repeatedly returned to Hume's *Essays*, was nevertheless deeply suspicious of the *History*. As he observed at one point, in a memorable put-down that exploited the fact that it had not been composed in chronological order, it had been 'written as witches say their prayers, backwards.'[28] A no less vociferous exponent of this jaundiced Whiggish view of Hume's purpose was Charles Lee, anti-hero of the American Revolution. A British officer during the Seven Years' War who subsequently had the unusual pleasure of travelling with the Polish embassy to the Ottoman empire in 1766, he later sided with the American revolutionaries, serving under Washington and eventually facing trial and disgrace as a supposed British agent.[29]

Lee was by any standards a devout Whig, as his attraction to the American cause, and ultimately his willingness to fight for it, pointedly affirms. Furthermore, his notes and correspondence, much of which survives, reveals from an early stage a loathing of authoritarian government that he associated instinctively with ideological Toryism. Lee certainly contracted an early and enduring dislike of Hume, whom, just as Walpole had done, he viewed as one of the principal apologists for absolutism. Writing to the Irish politician James Caulfield, 4th Earl of Charlemont, from Warsaw in June 1765, Lee condemned the unthinking hierarchicalism among the Polish elite, but he did so in the following striking terms: 'I would to God that our Tory writers, with David Hume at their head, and the favourers of our damnable administration, were to join this noble community, that they might reap the fruits which their blessed labors entitle them to, and that the effects might not fall on harmless posterity.'[30] Yet as if this were not enough, Lee's identification of Hume as the antithesis of his own libertarianism—a vicious reactionary against which to define his own progressive virtues—only hardened as his diplomatic mission advanced.

As he wrote to his sister Miss Sidney Lee from Constantinople in March 1766, his present immersion in a profoundly authoritarian society was making him ponder even more carefully his previous reservations about the *History*:

> On my journey I cou'd not help reflecting upon the vast obligations our Country has to Mr. David Hume and other Monarchical Writers who wou'd entail upon us their favourite absolute Government; at least we must imagine these to be their intentions when they wou'd weaken our jealousy which is the preservative of liberty, and lessen the horrors of despotism. Here they wou'd see their beloved scheme come to perfection; the finest provinces of Europe upon which Nature has pour'd a profusion of her gifts, one continued desert; the few Inhabitants who survive the oppression of Their Tyrants presenting famine and apprehensions of still greater misery on their countenances, to each trifling village burying places of so prodigious extent, as to denote the once existence of a considerable Town, in short every species of wretchedness I most sincerely wish that Mr. Hume and his fellow laborers were to join this happy community that they might enjoy the just fruits of their labours and not entail 'em on innocent posterity.'[31]

Lee's hostile impression of eastern Europe doubtless contains much chauvinism and not a little exaggeration. It certainly comprises an exceptionally powerful series of images. It also reveals, however, a remarkable capacity for imaginatively linking the alien landscapes and culture of the Ottoman world around him with his own deeply unsympathetic reading of one of the major works of the Scottish Enlightenment.

Lee clearly objected so strongly to the *History* because he saw it as jeopardising the English people's enjoyment of their hard-won liberties. Writing in July 1771 to John Hall-Stevenson, an associate of Wilkes and

Walpole, Lee appeared still preoccupied with Hume's malign presence in modern literature, as he described to his friend a projected history of Claudius and Nero that he was then sketching out. It had been conceived, Lee claimed, 'professedly in imitation of Mr David Hume's history of the house of Stewarts [sic], wherein I pretend to moderate the decent soften-ing and coloring the ill humour and prejudice of mankind with regard to those injur'd characters—it is likewise dedicated to the same Mr Hume—but I will send you the dedication by which you will judge of the scheme.'[32] There then followed from Lee's hand 'An Epistle to David Hume, Esq.,' in which the Scotland's foremost historian was sarcastically praised:

> No task can be equally laudable in a philosopher, an historian, and a gentleman, as to endeavour, to eradicate from the minds of our youth all prejudices and prepossessions against the memory of deceased, and the character of living princes; and by obviating the cavils and malice of republican writers, to inspire mankind with more candour in judging of the actions of governments and sovereigns . . . [33]

Nothing in fact came of the proposed historical work, probably because Lee was soon thereafter fully occupied in America.[34] Yet even then his fixation with Hume's *History* did not abate. From his friend Walter Pat-terson, Governor of Nova Scotia, there came a letter in November 1772 in which Lee was chided for his almost pathological obsession: 'Come Lee,' pleaded Patterson, 'and leave Hume to cramb his history down the throats of his countrymen, for few others read it.'[35] Neither Patterson nor Lee may have been much reassured; and we can certainly dismiss this claim because of what know about the unrestrained enthusiasm with which English contemporaries were actually devouring Hume's work.

Even when on active service, Lee remained not only keen to reflect upon the political implications of Hume's text but also to argue about it with others. There survives in his papers an 'Account of a Conversa-tion, Chiefly Relative to the Army' that preserves a remarkable exchange between Lee and some of his brother-officers. For they talked 'upon the history of England'—presumably the subject rather than Hume's book—as well as upon 'the respective merits of the different historians':

> A young subaltern, who seemed to have great fire and sentiment, and with more reading than young subalterns are generally masters of, was extremely bitter of Mr Hume: he loaded him with a thousand opprobriums; he styled him a sophist, a Jesuit, a theistical champion of despotism, who had dethroned the God of Heaven, and deified the sceptered monsters of the earth. The young man was taken up by a grey-haired field officer, who was so warm a partisan of Mr. Hume's, that he leaned not only towards absolute (or in his favourite author's terms) pure unmixed monarchy, but visibly towards jacobitism . . . [36]

Just what had provoked the argument is unclear. We may suspect, however, that it was probably the presence of Lee himself that had triggered such a heated campground discussion of English history and David Hume's contributions to it.

Lee also composed during in the 1770s "A Political Essay" that, perhaps predictably, allowed him further to vent his spleen with regard to Hume's historical writing. Now, however, it was the contrast between the Scot's treacherous political analysis and the far superior multi-volume *History of England* (1763–83) that was in the process of appearing from the more liberal pen of Catherine Macaulay that was the focus of Lee's concerns about appropriate reading. As he opined:

> a more effectual antidote to the poison of Hume's history cannot be desired than Mrs M'Caulay's, if they are but read and compared together with their respective authorities; but the misfortune is, the perusal and comparing of two so bulky writers cannot be expected from the laziness of modern readers; and it is on the notions and principles of the lazy class of readers that the present welfare of our country and the fate of posterity, in a great measure, depend . . . [37]

Lee's criticism of modern readers, of course, coheres with the increasing despondency among critics about the tastes and capacities of those who now comprised the literate public. If it was not a sapping obsession with vacuous prose fiction, it was an unwillingness to tackle a sufficiently wide range of serious scholarly works that supposedly characterised this new breed of book-buyers and literary consumers.

Yet Lee's pessimism about English reading tastes was also a reflection of his deepening gloom about the prospects for English political liberties—a prognosis that would soon catapult him spectacularly towards the Patriot cause. As he continued:

> For these reasons, I think that some work so compendious as not to terrify by its bulk, confined simply, and bearing the import of such in its title, to a refutation of Hume's tenets, and demonstration of his partial and pernicious principles, would be more beneficial than a full complete body of history, digested methodically, supported by the best authority, and animated by the noblest sentiments.[38]

Lee's hopes for a concise work of political education based around a demolition of Hume's *History* were to be dashed. But they are a powerful indication of the extent to which Hume's work, fully capable of being characterised by unsympathetic Whig readers as a brazen re-assertion of absolutist principles, came in the minds of some to represent everything that was wrong with the state of modern Britain. In these circumstances, and from one political perspective, Hume was a sure symptom of the malady of the age. At the same time, as Lee's regular tussles with the supposed implications of the *History* make only too clear, responses to Hume also provided a reliable measure against which the political health and vitality of each individual reader could be accurately and reassuringly calibrated.

* * *

A similar attitude towards the *History*—though one arguably even more crowded round with expectations and interpretations of the text that made an appreciative response all but impossible—came from Revd Gambier, who used the *History* to test and re-assert his own potentially contradictory identity as both a reasonably orthodox religious minister and a sophisticated and progressively inclined reader. On matters of religion, Gambier's difficulty with Hume was no surprise. He was irritated, for example, by Hume's treatment of it in the *Natural History of Religion* (1757). As the parson complained, highlighting doubts as to the veracity of that work's claims:

> Hume asserts that the farther we descend into Antiquity the more we find Mankind plunged into idolatry. But the truth of this is disputed. The primeval Religion of Mankind was not discovered by Reason but was taught by Revelation. It convinced in the following points viz. One perfect God the Creator, & Govr of the World, the O^{b}g^t of y^r Worship & obedience; the institution of the Sabbath in memory of the Creation; an intimation of the redemption of the World (Gen 3:15) . . . [39]

But it was not in fact Hume's quasi-sociological attack upon religious belief in the *Natural History* that troubled Gambier most. It was the *History of England*'s equally contentious and much disputed account of the nation's history. For Gambier made extensive notes 'On Hume's Hist^y of Engl^d' in which, rather than transcribing from the text itself, he collected a series of well-known contemporary criticisms, almost as if seeking to vindicate his own negative judgment by reference to the helpful observations of authoritative critical arbiters.

Gambier was particularly interested in the comments of Richard Hurd, Bishop of Worcester. Hurd was a vigorous and versatile controversialist, famous as a literary critic and in particular for his published riposte to Hume's *Natural History*.[40] Yet it was to Hurd's *Moral and Political Dialogues* (1759) that Gambier turned for solace on the troubling matter of the *History of England*. Gambier was only too aware that the latter was an exceptionally stylish literary performance that presented itself to the unsuspecting reader as an entirely trustworthy narrative. Indeed, he had already cited the *History* in his commonplace book, along with the earlier work of Rapin, as an illustration of how to avoid 'Obscurity of Style,' adding that 'Perspicuity is greatly promoted by marginal notes, which contain the Substance of each Section.'[41]

It followed, however, that such masterly authorship could only be countered with the assistance of the most authoritative critics, of whom Hurd was among the very greatest. Thus Gambier began his note on the *History* with the reassuring finding that Hurd had considered at least part of it perfectly acceptable:

> From Bp Hurd's Dialˢ Vol2 p.326. Hurd says in the Text, that "Eng. Liberty was inclosed in the ancient trunk of the Feudal Law, & was propagated from it": On this passage he gives the followᵍ Notes viz. "This appears even from Mr Hume's own accᵗ of the feudal times; incomparably the best part of his Hʸ of Engᵈ. . . . [42]

Gambier's doubts about Hume's work—scarcely moderated by Hurd's deliberate choice of the word 'even'—were nevertheless reinforced by the less restrained criticisms of other authorities.

From the writings of Francis Wrangham, for example, a like-minded Yorkshire clergyman with whom he cannot have known that he shared, amongst other things, a fondness for the *Edinburgh Review*, Gambier seems to have drawn particular intellectual sustenance.[43] Archdeacon of Cleveland and later of the East Riding, Fellow of the Royal Society and a noted classicist and literary patron in his own right, Wrangham was the author of *The British Plutarch* (1816), in which he too had offered some stinging rebukes to Hume's *History*. Unsurprisingly, given the contemporary obsession with all things Marian, Wrangham's comments on Hume's handling of Mary, Queen of Scots, offered amid a densely argued literary biography of John Knox, especially caught Gambier's eye. The *History* was not only unfair, Wrangham had claimed, in a rapier thrust that Gambier transcribed into his own commonplace book: Hume's deliberate 'misrepresenting the conduct of the Reformers toward her,' by obscuring Mary's aim of restoring Catholicism, had also made his treatment of her little more than 'an overcharged satire.'[44] Similar reservations about Hume had been posted by Thomas Jefferson, and, demonstrating his wide reading on this question, the American too was copied out by Gambier: 'Thos Jefferson,' he wrote, 'speaking of Hume's Histʸ', says "Baxter has performᵈ a good operation on it. . . ."[45]

This was, as it happens, a particularly illuminating borrowing for Gambier, since Jefferson had actually homed in upon the neutralisation of some of Hume's most egregious ideologically motivated manipulations of the English past in John Baxter's *A New and Impartial History of England* (1796). As the American had noted:

> He has taken the text of Hume as his ground work, abridging it by the omission of some details of little interest, and wherever he has found him endeavouring to mislead, by either the suppression of a truth or by giving it a false coloring, he has changed the text to what it should be, so that we may properly call it Hume's history republicanised . . . [46]

In other words, Gambier had alighted upon another sensitive reading of Hume's *History*, evidently made familiar to him from his own knowledge of Jefferson's correspondence, that had successfully identified the peculiar problems in that most difficult of modern texts.

Unease about the implications of Hume's literary finesse and about his abilities as an entertainer, rooted firmly in alarm at what many supposed were actually the sinister motives lying behind the *History* in particular, also coloured the response of the Westmorland reader. His considered assessment of Hume—as ever, informed by a strong sense that a proficient reader was required to exhibit clear and discriminating judgment, but also that this should be achieved with explicit reference to a wider community of readers—was pointed in the extreme:

> Hume as an historian has long enjoy'd an extraordinary Share of Popularity & his performance seems to be considered by the Majority of Readers, as the best Account of the Affairs of this Nation. His Abilities were competent to the production of an History, which might have surpass'd all the Efforts of his British Predecessors, and if his talents had been exerted with a just regard to Candour & Impartiality & with the sole View of exhibiting a fair & accurate Delineation of the transactions of former Days, his historic Fame would have rested on a more solid basis than that which now supports it. The Spirit of Philosophy which animates his Work gives it a manifest Superiority over most of the English Histories by which it is preceeded [sic]. His Style is elegant without affectation, & nervous without an appearance of labour. His Arguments in defence of a favourite Hypothesis possess all the acuteness of Sophistry, though their force is disarm'd by the Application of sound logic & the adduction of undistorted Facts. Under the Pretext of exposing the delusions of fanaticism, the Weakness of Bigotry, & the Arts of selfish & designing Ecclesiasticks, he indirectly endeavours to sap the Fabrick of religion itself & undermine the dearest Interests of Society. His political Principles are adverse to the Claims of Freedom and, under the cloak of impartial discussion, he vilifies the exertions of the patriot and depresses the generous flame of Liberty.[47]

Such a balanced judgment of Hume was commonly considered, as this particular individual appreciated only too well, the mark of a sophisticated and proficient reader.

A basic uncertainty about Hume's qualities, arising out of an ability to discriminate between his dubious motives and his consummate skill, seems to have been quite widely found among contemporary English readers. James Smith, a prominent Unitarian wool merchant in Norwich, was, as we have seen, a great admirer of William Robertson. But he was much less certain about Hume, inserting into his commonplace book an assessment of the *History*, which he had read in 1766, that was both highly equivocal and intriguingly detached:

> Hume's abilities as a writer, made his history of England read with great expectation & it answers well to the ingenious character of the Author, his remarks & reflections are extremely judicious & Philosophical, almost always where they are upon the nature dispositions and circumstances of Mankind & Government in general, but when they relate to particular parties, opinions & sects, & even to Nations he is not devoid of prejudice & partiality, which often betrays him into self contradictions, & makes it much to be lamented that it is so difficult for Men of the finest Understandings and the most extensive geniuses, capacities to become true Philosophers & to make themselves masters of their principles & way of thinking . . . [48]

Smith later returned to his analysis, focusing now upon what he took to be Hume's political orientation:

> Shew Mr Hume to be an uncandid partial Historian a great favourer of arbitrary principles and measures & an enemy to or detractor of every Genius that wrote in favour of Liberty. What every unprejudiced reader of his History must discover, is also that he always endeavoured to lessen the Character & exploits of the English.[49]

Even to someone who was not immune to his considerable charms, Hume was plainly still a menace to respectable society. He was a threat because he sought to undermine the foundations of freedom, not only by so eloquently advancing the case for absolutism but also by violently assaulting those rival authors who laboured manfully to defend liberty. Above all, however, Hume appeared dangerous because he was a Scottish polemicist whose intention, beneath a beguilingly polite and polished manner, was nothing less than to diminish in the minds of English men and women the unrivalled political heritage of their own people.

*   *   *

If James Smith's conclusions are any guide, and if the bitterly worded suspicions of readers like Walpole and Lee are also weighed in the balance, it was more than possible for a palpable feeling of injured and affronted Englishness—which is to say, a highly specific identification with a nation and a people—to be a direct consequence of an individual's protracted and thoughtful engagement with Hume's *History*. The notion that Hume represented a threat not merely to piety and decency, nor even just to liberty, but actually to a sense of English nationhood itself, is in many ways a remarkable one. It is also curious, to say the least, in a man like Smith, who, just a few years later, would despatch his own son, the future botanist Sir James Edward Smith, not to Oxford or Cambridge but to Edinburgh, where he would study medicine under Dr John Hope, presumably in the firm paternal expectation that he would benefit from, rather than be injured by, that experience. If nothing else, these responses suggest a complicated—in truth, a confused—attitude towards Scottish learning, as well as a degree of ambivalence about its prominent contribution to the moulding and shaping of the mainly English audiences who were increasingly exposed to it. The resulting shifts in identity and self-image are, however, something to which we must return as we try to assess how the experiences of readers with Scottish texts ultimately impacted upon literate English society as a whole.

Part V
Consequences

11 The Making of British Culture
Reading Identities in the Social History of Ideas

English men and women, as we have repeatedly seen, were inveterate consumers of the much-talked-about literature of an enlightened age. More than this, and crucially for our own inquiries, they were also widely acquainted—sometimes obsessively so—with the published output of their Scottish contemporaries. Accordingly, it is clear that even if they would not have recognised the label, and even though they would certainly have had divergent opinions about which texts and authors it might connote as well as in relation to what was singularly *enlightened* or definitively *Scottish* about it, English readers would often have acknowledged, as recent historians have largely been content to do, the reality of a Scottish Enlightenment.[1] The myriad individual encounters between English consumers and Scottish books upon which this increasing intimacy at the developing heart of a new British culture was founded, however, were demonstrably diverse. Indeed, from the disparate evidence at which we have now looked, the experience of reading clearly took a great many forms, differing widely from person to person and from occasion to occasion.

Nevertheless, a common feature of all acts of reading was that the meaning and significance of texts was always ultimately a matter for resolution by readers themselves. It will be evident, moreover, that individuals performed these exercises not in isolation—for however physically alone he or she might appear to be, no reader is ever truly an island, entire of itself—but under the powerfully formative influence of a number of other agencies. Most obviously, the processes by which sense was made of a text, and its implications construed, were affected by an author's decisions, intentional or otherwise, even before the deliberate (and not always benevolent) interventions of publishers, editors, critics and other commentators. A not much less influential role was often played, prior to as well as during a text's reception, by the reader's friends, colleagues, neighbours and family members, whether consciously or unconsciously, and whether acting autonomously or else as members of wider interpretative communities of various descriptions.

Yet if such a contingent phenomenon was really so widespread and so utterly central to the cultural lives of Georgian men and women, and in particular to the meanings that the texts that they encountered ultimately came to bear, what does this intriguing window on the history of reading reveal about the set of larger historical problems with which we first set out? What might be the implications of the social determination of meaning for our understanding of the function of the Scottish Enlightenment in contemporary England? How did the continual endeavour by readers to make sense of texts—whether or not influenced by those who sought to guide them—affect the project of defining a coherent national civilization in Great Britain? Might a culture in which innumerable reading experiences played such an important constitutive role have had consequences in turn for the creation and distribution of new identities in eighteenth- and early nineteenth-century England? And given the priority that the foregoing interpretation has unapologetically conceded to the substantially anonymous mass of people who read books rather than to the small community of relatively well-known individuals who wrote and manufactured them, might we also need to consider the phenomenon of the Enlightenment itself, and the methodology of the 'social history of ideas' through which it has lately come to be approached, in rather different ways from those to which we have hitherto been accustomed?[2]

*   *   *

Fundamental to the interpretation of how the Scottish Enlightenment was read that has been developed in the present study is, of course, the notion of appropriation. By this has been meant simply readers' ability to stake a claim at least to part-ownership, or to a share in control, of the specific operations of printed texts, and above all in the generation of meaning. This is why Michel de Certeau, somewhat mischievously but with serious intentions, has likened reading to poaching—an activity that, precisely because it contests proprietorship, is at once both illicit and subversive.[3] It is true that appropriation is ordinarily not a difficult (or even necessarily a fully conscious) enactment, at least for proficient readers. In fact, it is intrinsic to the nature of a text that it should have the capacity to initiate in its recipients, however aware of this fact they may or may not be, an attempt to construe meaning and significance. In other words, it is integral to its very textuality that *The Wealth of Nations*, for example, should have been able to stimulate the Westmorland reader to ponder questions concerned with such matters as labour specialisation and the optimal use of agricultural land; but at the same time, it is no less a function of its textuality that the same work could lead Revd James Gambier to speculate about the methods for determining rent levels, or, for that matter, George Grenville to question the true basis of value.

Yet if the reader's irresistible urge to appropriation is inseparable from textuality itself, then acts of construal—with individuals attempting to associate certain pieces of text with a specific register of meanings that are intelligible to themselves—are also an intrinsic feature of what we call 'reading.' As Adrian Johns has recently argued, the latter phenomenon, considered as the subject of historical study, amounts in its rudiments to the 'different practices' by which individuals 'attribute meanings to objects of their reading.'[4] To put this another way, a hypothetical encounter with a body of verbiage that failed to generate any meanings at all in the mind of a literate person would not only call into question its object's status as text. Whatever else we might wish to describe it as, that person's performance, although we should still be at liberty to think of it as some form of reception, would have excluded the possibility of its also being properly recognisable as reading. Hence both texts as objects and readings as performances by those who encounter them are inextricably bound up with the attribution of potential and actual meaning.

Appropriation, by extension, is merely the set of processes by which the reader-as-recipient actualises or, to return once again to Wolfgang Iser's term, 'realises,' some of those meanings that are potentially viable in relation to a given text. A text, according to Iser, is simply 'a structured indicator to guide the imagination of the reader.'[5] In Roger Chartier's not-dissimilar account, although articulated with the concerns of the historian of reading more obviously in mind, 'the process of the appropriation of texts' might be viewed as one that 'designates the "effectuation" or "actualisation" of the semantic possibilities of the text' and thus 'sees interpretation of the text as a mediation that enables the reader to reach self-comprehension and construct "reality".'[6] As we have frequently noticed, moreover, these processes are shaped by a number of interacting influences, ensuring, amongst other things, that whilst, as one recent writer has claimed, 'reading is an anarchic act,' it is neither inexplicable nor remotely random in its consequences.[7] The author's intentions, which first embodied the text and dictate (or at least have conventionally been understood to dictate) its shape and form, are by no means least among these controlling factors. This is the reason why, for example, Archdeacon John Sharp came to consider Thomas Blackwell's *Enquiry*—and perfectly reasonably, one might want to add—an interesting-looking work of cultural anthropology.

Yet other influences serve to clarify, though sometimes also to confuse, such acts of appropriation. Criticism and other cultural authorities, as we have seen, deliberately seek to exert influence. Thus they told the Georgian readers of David Hume's *History of England*, for example, to be fully appreciative of its author's consummate literary polish and entertaining narrative whilst remaining suitably cautious about the text's unsettling religious and political implications. Forming the recipient's expectations and imbuing them with assumptions, other previous acts of reading are also important: we might recall here, for example, how prior exposure to recalcitrant High Church Anglicanism, and then, by contrast, to the troubling literature of deism, prepared Revd Charles Peters to think that Blackwell's *Enquiry* was really, beneath its beguiling academic façade, just another thinly disguised and glibly fashionable attack upon Christianity—a theoretically tenable but highly idiosyncratic reading of this text which, with our superior knowledge of its anonymous author and our more dispassionate perspective on the early eighteenth-century controversy over natural religion, we would clearly be justified in regarding with extreme scepticism. Ultimately, the purposes for which reading occurs, and a text's contingent relationship with individual recipients, are also determinative. Hence William Constable's recusant background, for example, cannot be left out of an explanation of his approval for Hume's *History* as a powerful critique of royal motives in embracing the Reformation. Nor should we neglect Charles Lee's militant Whiggism when seeking to make sense of his angry rejection of the same work as a shameless apology for monarchical authoritarianism.

This account of the processes by which textual meanings have historically been constructed obviously has certain affinities not only with recent literary theory but also with current methodological concerns in the history of ideas. Led by Quentin Skinner and other exponents of what, fairly or not, has sometimes been called the "Cambridge paradigm," great emphasis has been placed upon the study of words and ideas in their immediate context.[8] If we wish to understand them, we have been implored to locate the great texts not in the perspective of their later admirers but in their original historical environment—*Il Principe*, for example, in early sixteenth-century Florentine politics, *Leviathan* in an England and a Europe beset by political discord and religious turmoil, the *Two Treatises of Government* amid the struggle between obdurate Stuart absolutism and its emergent Whig antithesis, and so forth. At the same time, building on the speech-act theory of the linguistic philosopher J.L. Austin, it has been emphasised that a text can be viewed, in one of its manifestations, as an 'illocutionary act'—as an action, in other words, that is a kind of event or performance which by its nature involves something actually *happening*.

As a result, we are enjoined to inquire of individual authors, as Skinner famously asks (with pointed emphasis) before commencing his seminal study of the major texts of pre-modern political thought, what they 'were *doing* in writing them.'[9] The practical implications of such an approach are evidently that texts need to be recognised by the historian as 'utterances' by their author that belong precisely to one particular place and time. A comprehensive understanding of a text therefore requires us to study the language in which, like the other contributions to the same conversation, it was cast; the specific institutional and intellectual conditions in which that text, as a performance, was enacted; and the purposes or intentions with which the author, as the single most important agent in its realisation, might be said to have carried it out.

Yet there is in fact more than one available route running from linguistic philosophy to the better understanding of meaning that also happens to take us by way of a proper emphasis upon contextualisation. This is not, of course, to deny the validity of utilising these same insights so as to sharpen the historian's focus upon the author and the initial setting in which a text's composition occurred. Indeed, it has been argued, cogently if not wholly convincingly, that the elucidation of the historical conditions of authorship is the principal obligation of the historian of ideas.[10] It is equally possible, however, and obviously much more useful for the purposes of the history of reading in particular, to build some of these same emphases into a rather different account of the role of context in the creation of meaning. In fact, Iser himself has made much use of speech-act theory in developing his influential analysis of reading as a crucible in which textual meanings are wrought, and he has also ventured a number of observations on the usefulness of Austin's philosophical insights; whilst, significantly, John Pocock, for his part, has conceded, with critical consequences for an understanding of how texts function historically, that, in the necessary search for their meaning, 'we cannot absolutely distinguish the author's performance from the reader's response.'[11] Stanley Fish, meanwhile, has gone further, arguing that texts need to be recognised as 'events,' and treated as such for analytical purposes. Each constituent sentence is, he insists, 'something that *happens* to, and with the participation of, the reader. And it is this event, this happening—all of it and not anything that could be said about it or any information one might take away from it—that is, I would argue, the *meaning* of the sentence.'[12]

The crucial point here is that the justifiable emphasis upon context in the mind of the historian now becomes less an argument for investigating the original performance of the text's creator and much more a matter of directing our attention to the peculiar circumstances in which individual acts of reading, themselves conceived as performative actions which generate meaning, subsequently occurred. Nor is it clear that the implications of this approach, which the present study has attempted to pursue in relation only to one significant problem in the history of British culture, are necessarily restricted to the history of reading. For in revealing the conditions prevailing among those who receive, consume and reflect upon texts—which is to say, among real people like Matthew Flinders, William Chute and Ann Bletchley—what is offered is surely no less germane to the history of ideas, and, more particularly, to the *social* history of ideas. In other words, the study of the construction of textual meaning through reading must also benefit those wider historical projects which concern themselves with recovering the conditions in which certain ideas came to be encountered and embraced—we might now even want to say appropriated—by specific individuals and communities. This is an important deduction from our own inquiry, with potentially far-reaching consequences for our understanding of processes like the Enlightenment, as well as for our approach to cultural and intellectual history in general. It is therefore one to which we ought to return in a moment, after considering another of the implications of this study of English readers' encounters with the Scottish Enlightenment.

*   *   *

The creation of meaning, as we have also seen, is at all times fundamental to the business of reading. Texts, however, whether from the Scottish Enlightenment in the narrowest sense or from other types of Scottish authorship that were current in the eighteenth and early nineteenth centuries, were not the only things whose meanings were being constructed afresh whenever acts of reading were performed. For Georgian readers themselves, as we have seen over and over again, were simultaneously the subject of construction. In particular, the essential characteristics of individuals' personal identities, both as they understood them themselves and as they hoped they would be perceived and appreciated by others, were continually reinforced and redefined through the subtle processes of 'self-fashioning' that occurred whenever reading took place. To employ the terms used in one recent study of nineteenth-century identities, 'the identity of the reader' is 'not the unity often imagined' but rather 'the product of a complex set of negotiations and exchanges between historically informed discursive practices and the individuals and communities with whom they come into contact.'[13]

   In their fruitful experiences with the Scottish Enlightenment, we have seen convincing evidence that reading—plainly an open-ended negotiation and a continuous exchange rather than a one-way street carrying meaning ineluctably from articulate author to mute recipient—was central to the construction of the personalities of many ordinary men and women. Indeed, we might now want to agree with Greenblatt's claims for the early-modern period as a whole, that there was 'an increased self-consciousness about the fashioning of human identity as a manipulable, artful process.'[14] Virtue, truth, orthodoxy, decency, rationality, humanity—to list just a few of the values that meant a great deal (though in myriad different ways) to Georgian people—were among the elemental qualities with which, by responding appropriately to particular passages and works, and not least by documenting those responses through marginalia, commonplacing and other forms of instantiation, it was assumed by readers that they would be able to validate and reinforce their own alignments. As that most perplexing of the Enlightenment's theorists of personal identity, Rousseau, made this point in relation to his own formation, 'I don't know how I learned to read; I only remember my first readings and their effect on me: it is from that time that I date without interruption my consciousness of myself.'[15]

   Ultimately it was for something like this reason that Thomas Binns and Hester Piozzi gloried in *The Minstrel*. It was also why John Tompkins on the Sussex coast and Elizabeth Carpenter at Barnard Castle so readily embraced different passages in *The Seasons*. For engagement with these poems in each case had significant implications for a reader's identity and sense of self. Partly this was a matter of general identification with iconic poems with which close acquaintance provided useful outward confirmation of polite respectability. More importantly, however, it was about identification with the specific meanings and significances associated with those particular texts—widely taken to include such desiderata, variously attractive to individual readers, as a sincere sympathy for the life of simple virtue, an instinctive preference for uncomplicated piety, and a capacity for appreciating the design and sublimity of divinely created Nature.

In short, reading aided the construction (or, perhaps, the necessary routine maintenance and reaffirmation) of some of those different social identities that collectively constituted their personality—a fact that further underlines the merit in the cultural anthropologist Clifford Geertz's observation in *The Interpretation of Cultures* (1973) that humans might themselves be thought of as 'cultural artefacts,' essentially meaningless when marooned in hypothetical isolation from culture and its expressions.[16] As we have seen, the experience of reading helped define who and what its exponents were by allowing them, as Alison Scott has said, 'to establish private and social identities.'[17] It did so, furthermore, by affording them what they recognised—in fact, were positively encouraged by authors, by critics, and by the ingrained cultural practices of reading, to recognise—as a fitting and reassuring reflection of themselves.

If reading is therefore heavily implicated in the formation and upkeep of its participants' multiple self-images within a social environment—if, as Patricia Meyer Spacks puts it more succinctly, 'The experience of reading unites the private and the communal'—then there are clearly some potentially important consequences here for our understanding of the relationship between English culture and English politics and society in the Georgian period.[18] After all, it has lately become something of a historiographical commonplace that certain kinds of self-image, and specifically collective identities and a sense of belonging to a wider national community, were in flux at precisely this juncture. In particular, it has been argued, notably by Linda Colley in her study *Britons* (1992), that Britain and the accompanying sense of Britishness were themselves substantially constructed in the period framed by the Anglo-Scottish Treaty of Union and the accession of Queen Victoria.[19]

To some extent, of course, this assertion is simply an uncontroversial description of tangible developments. It relates closely to the familiar narrative of a new British Parliament (with Ireland added two-thirds of the way through the period), an expanding British economy (further energised by industrialisation from mid-century onwards) and an ever-widening British empire (notwithstanding the crises which led to the shift perforce from an Atlantic to an Asian-oriented *imperium*). Yet simultaneously Colley's plea is that we consider Britain as an 'imagined community,' to employ Benedict Anderson's much-used phrase, and as a focus for new loyalties that were being actively fashioned after 1707 by the necessarily reorienting experiences of state-building, warfare, colonialism and social and economic inter-penetration between Scotland, Ireland and England.[20]

This argument, it is true, is also usually reinforced, particularly in respect of Anglo-Scottish relations, by reference to the continuing impact of one important pre-existing shared identity. For the two peoples of Great Britain, despite their ancestral antagonism, were also united by a common Protestantism that frequently had cause to feel both embattled and justified amid the Hanoverian state's continuing, and largely successful, struggles with the Catholic kingdoms of the Continent.[21] The result, we are told, was a powerful and widespread notion of Britishness—perceived, to be sure, in a multitude of different ways by different groups at different times, and never without its contradictions and its problematics. But a nation, and an identity, had been born.

This interpretation of Georgian British history is obviously most cogent in drawing our attention to a series of major factors, some institutional, others ideological, and a few merely circumstantial, by which people were brought increasingly to recognise the emergence—the 'forging,' in Colley's preferred idiom—of a new sense of nationhood. It has an important weakness, however. For this thesis, at least as initially presented, paid insufficient attention to the problems involved in the dissemination, transmission and articulation of identities among and between the individual members of society. As a consequence, it worked better as an explanation for the growing cohesion within a relatively narrow and often downright incestuous elite than as an account of gradual modifications in attitudes among the public at large. It also exhibited a tin ear for some of the distinctive sounds generated by the peculiarly Scottish narrative of national identity, in which emphatically different and generally mutually antagonistic forms of Protestantism loudly contested the public space, actually providing a decidedly uncertain basis for a sense of either Scottish or British nationhood deep into the modern period.[22]

These lacunae have to some extent begun to be filled in the past decade by studies emphasising the importance of print culture not only as a vehicle for the distribution of information and opinion in eighteenth-century England but also as an instrument in the construction of different kinds of identities. The newspapers and their growing readership evidently played an especially significant role. Hannah Barker, for example, has written convincingly of the impact of the press upon the formation of something recognisable as public opinion.[23] Kathleen Wilson, too, in an important study of the relationship between culture and imperialism, has emphasised the power of journalism and publishing in engaging the populace in the projects envisioned by statesmen and politicians.[24] This has underlined that public discourse in Hanoverian England was facilitated and articulated by a large, complex and dynamic media network whose tentacles increasingly reached far and wide into the homes and the everyday lives of ordinary men and women. Here it was able to influence—though never rigidly to dictate—how individuals acted, how they thought and spoke, and even how they now saw themselves.

Literature as a cultural construct has also been the focus of recent work that has not only tested but also elaborated and modified Colley's thesis in interesting ways, again with special emphasis upon Anglo-Scottish relations. Most notably, perhaps, Howard Weinbrot, in *Britannia's Issue: The Rise of British Literature from Dryden to Ossian* (1995), has charted the emergence of a British literary culture by the 1760s, a process of amalgamation *e pluribus unum* in which disparate elements—Hebrew, Christian, Classical, Celtic, Gothic—adhered to become 'part of the nation's religious and emotional consciousness,' the constituents of 'a polyglot synthetic culture.'[25] A comparable exercise, although also contesting what she sees as Weinbrot's and Colley's excessive faith in the success of these attempts at cultural integration, is performed by Leith Davis in her *Acts of Union: Scotland and the Literary Negotiation of the British Nation 1707–1830* (1998). Here the interpretative burden is borne by a narrower line of major contributors, significantly confined to Scotland and England, running from Lord Belhaven and Daniel Defoe through Fielding, Smollett and Macpherson and on to Burns, Wordsworth and Scott. Her conclusion is that 'conflicted articulations of national identity by Scots and English writers combined to create a British identity, but one that was intrinsically unstable, demanding constant renegotiation.'[26]

It is not necessary for us to deny the value of such studies for an understanding of one of the more problematical contexts in which both English and Scottish authorship existed after 1707. Nor is it to be doubted that many authors were engaged in a project—*pace* Davis, the negotiation of Britishness—with profound cultural and ideological significance for contemporaries. Yet we have already seen more than enough about how particular Scottish texts were responded to in Georgian England to suspect that there must be a fundamental difficulty with any account in which the acts of writing undertaken by the few, rather than the acts of reading performed by the many, dominates thinking about the formation of identities within Great Britain. By their nature, self-images of all descriptions had—and continue to have—functions at once social and public in their operation. At the very least, therefore, we should need to bring into clearer focus how different audiences may have received, experienced and appropriated the meanings and significances of the relevant texts for themselves.

To some extent this requirement can be satisfied by specific reference to the processes by which, as we saw in Chapter 2, canons were now being formed, confirmed and reconstructed. It is unlikely, for example, that authoritative works like Kincaid's *The British Poets* and Bell's *The Poets of Great Britain*, which proffered a seductive vision of a coherent British literary culture, would have been so successful if their principal premise had been deemed either implausible or unattractive by a reading public at large which for the most part comprised English men and women. Indeed, the whole idea of a British national culture underpinned by a reasonably well-defined (though endlessly argued-over) canon of British texts became increasingly endemic. This is why Gustavus Gale, for example, in early nineteenth-century Carlisle, could without pausing for breath hail Addison not as a valuable English writer but simply (and fairly, as we know) as 'a standard author of the British nation.'[27]

Equally, the Scots' high profile in the burgeoning new activities of criticism, literary commentary, and, in due course, the academic study of literature, can only have helped Scottish work—sometimes by accident, often by design—play an important part in the acceptance among the reading public of a wider British canon. Hence by 1800 it was commonplace, as we have seen, to consider Blair a paragon among polite modern sermonisers and *The Seasons* a model of the humane poetic sensibility. It was also normal, however (though not, as we shall shortly see, invariable), to do so in a manner that no longer even drew any real distinctions within British literature as a whole between contributions hailing from north and south of the Border. Meanwhile, the central role of Scottish academic texts, Scottish curricula, the Scottish universities and Scottish professors like Blair, Gerard and Campbell in the formation of an institutionalised literature syllabus by the mid-nineteenth century, much discussed by recent scholars, only further entrenched such inclusive and panoptic perspectives on British culture across literate anglophone society.[28]

Even at a superficial level, the increasing viability of Britishness as a specific cultural identifier is also evinced by the appearance of a succession of works that confidently attached themselves to its coattails. From Sir John Oldmixon's *The British Empire in North America*, a book with a famously precocious title that was published in the year after the Union had transformed a formally English into an explicitly British enterprise, to significantly-labeled contributions of the mid-century Scottish Enlightenment—such as Dalrymple's *Memoirs of Great Britain and Ireland*, Hume's title (at least initially) *The History of Great Britain*, and Henry's permanent use of the same moniker for his popular multi-volume study—it is clear that Britishness was assumed to be meaningful, as well as having generally positive connotations, to an audience that was in practice still, of course, preponderantly English.

Moreover, that authors and booksellers were broadly correct in their estimation of English readers' likely responsiveness to the beckoning call of Britain is also plain from the prominence achieved by many of these most explicitly British of texts in the libraries and book collections of the Georgian era. Indeed, the lasting success of the *Encyclopaedia Britannica* above all from 1768 onwards, emblematically representing but also powerfully legitimising the notion of a definitively *British* presentation of knowledge and understanding, is hard to imagine without the widespread acceptance of this same set of altered assumptions about their own national culture among English readers in particular.

We have also seen how a generally agreeable familiarity with Scotland on the part of English readers grew exponentially as the century progressed.

This was made possible by the normal operations of a shared anglophone print culture throughout Great Britain of which Edinburgh and other Scottish centres were a fully integrated part as well as making in certain respects a disproportionate and highly visible contribution to its vitality. Magazines and newspapers provided regular coverage from both sides of the Border. At the same time, vehicles such as the *Scots Magazine*, and, especially, the *Edinburgh Review*, declared their Scottish provenance even as they were accommodated without perceptible discomfort into the lives, as well as the growing library collections, of English readers.

There were even, of course, deliberate attempts by certain texts, and most famously by those published successively by Pennant, Johnson and Boswell, to educate their English readers about Scotland. The intention here was usually to instil both a genuine curiosity and a profound sympathy for their fellow Britons that would override the demeaning mixture of extreme ignorance and instinctive hostility that had characterised the responses of many previous English observers. Individuals like Humphrey Senhouse, a West Cumberland squire, and Thomas Dunne, a Hereford doctor, as we saw in Chapter 9, were as one in finding in such works a beguiling vision that literally prescribed how they would now see and respond—positively, fondly, inquisitively—to Scotland and its culture.

Attitudes of this kind, inculcated by the raging torrent of didactic literature that swept all before it after mid-century, had become widespread—though, it should be added, not universal—even before the end of the eighteenth century. They were expressed, for example, by a contributor to the *St. James's Chronicle* in October 1767, under the significant pseudonym 'Britannicus.' This English correspondent reported upon his own enjoyable experiences in the north, where warm feelings of admiration for Scotland, and particularly for the advantages wrought for both countries by the Union, had quickly been kindled:

> I have been lately making a Tour through Scotland, where I was equally delighted with the ingenuous Hospitality of the People in general, and with the Spirit of Improvement daily growing in that Country, especially in and about the Metropolis. The Communication opened between the Nations since the Union of the Kingdoms has served many Purposes valuable to both. Trade and Science have been reciprocally promoted; and the Prejudices which so long kept even the Subjects of one Sovereign either hostile or shy to each other, are happily become Prepossessions in each other's Favour. London and Edinburgh are gloriously exchanging Improvements: One disdains not to borrow the Matter, and the Manner of new-paving her Streets; the other is proud to adopt the Plan and Propriety of her Sister's Buildings. While both Capitals cultivate the Sciences and Arts, Edinburgh goes to London for Purity of Language, and London to Edinburgh for the Study of Physic . . . [29]

Gushing responses of this sort, instilled by exposure to text after text and authority after authority, further encouraged—perhaps even obliged—English readers to identify increasingly closely and favourably with Scottish culture and Scottish life.

For some, not surprisingly, a certain hesitancy about the precise nature of the composite identities that were emerging was hard to avoid. E.D., for example, the anonymous Dovedale commonplacer in the early 1750s, noted down a list of books to read whose heading encapsulated this ambiguity in a nutshell. They were 'on the Subject of an ENGLISH, or BRITISH EDUCATION in particular.'[30] But even such imprecision did not preclude an English reader's growing receptiveness to the notion that Scotland was part of a common culture—and of a nation with a single identity—that was now shared in by the two close neighbours and partners. After all, E.D.'s list in practice included much unmistakably Scottish scholarship, not just Burnet but the definitive Presbyterian historians Knox and Calderwood, alongside most of the older staples of the narrowly English canon.

Similarly, it was possible for readers to share the perception of many of the critics that the Scottish Enlightenment reflected glory and honour upon an anglophone culture in which both Scots and English properly shared. Like Robertson's *Historical Disquisition of the Knowledge Which the Ancients Had of India* (1791), in which the *Monthly Review* on its first publication hailed 'the same discernment in arranging them, the same perspicuity of narrative, and the same power of illustration, which so eminently distinguish his other writings, and which have long rendered them the delight of the English reader at home, and an honour to English literature abroad,' it was increasingly normal for the literate to see in Scottish texts only a beneficial additional contribution to the steadily growing sum of British civilization as a whole.[31]

The popularity of Scottish literature, song and music, and the sheer eagerness with which it was disseminated in the mass-circulation periodicals, was, of course, another facet of the same process of acculturation. By the early nineteenth century there were large numbers of English readers for whom Scotland had wholly positive associations—a seductive land of ballad, history and myth. A good example is the elderly Gloucestershire gentleman John Nourse, who lived at Newent near Ross-on-Wye and who made the following welcome addition to his own commonplace book—probably, the layout suggests, from an item printed in a newspaper:

A favourite SCOTCH SONG, Sung at VAUXHALL by Mrs. WEICHSELL Set to Music by Mr. HERON.

I.   ALL on the pleasant banks of Tweed,
Young Jockey won my heart;
None tun'd so sweet his oaten reed,
None sung with so much art:

His skilful tale
Did soon prevail
To make me fondly love him;
But now he hies,
Nor hears my cries,
I wou'd I ne'er had seen him . . .[32]

Nourse may simply have been one among very many English people who by this time associated Scotland primarily with a distinctive literary culture of which songs and ballads—often Jacobite in origin, frequently concerned with romantic love and loss—appeared to be one of the most characteristic and attractive expressions.[33]

As we have also seen, however, the increasingly close encounter with Scottish authorship that was palpably taking place in Georgian England was by no means always quite so meekly accepted. In fact, the formation of new identities, indeed their very possibility, was perfectly capable of being contested by those who were more sensitive even than E.D. to what Davis insists were the 'inherent contradictions' within the entity now known as Great Britain.[34] Such reservations had a solidly political, even a constitutional, foundation, typically expressed in an address "To the Free Electors of England" on the vexed subject of the Scots' 'strong propensity to Encroachment' which had been printed in the pages of the *St. James's Chronicle* just two months before the appearance of the breezy encomium on Scotland's modern apotheosis penned by the pseudonymous 'Britannicus': 'How can you expect but Scots Interests and Scots Measures must prevail, and your own be neglected,' railed this much less contented Englishman, 'if you choose Scotsmen to represent you?.'[35] Anxieties about the implications of Anglo-Scottish integration also had a specifically cultural and literary dimension. This took the form of an accusation, frequently heard by mid-century, that Scottish authors and critics retained—though they might well try hard to disguise it within the new British dispensation—a fundamental partiality and self-interest on behalf of their own nation.

In some contexts this critique of the new cultural order articulated a deep sense of embitterment. It did so in March 1772 for Charles Lee, still at this stage an English Whig rather than an American revolutionary. For in a letter sent to his sister from Lyons, he alleged that budding English authors faced unfair treatment at the hands of a cabal of biased Scottish literary arbiters bent on using their excessive influence within British print culture so as to advance their own interests at England's expense. Indeed, Lee's own manuscript commentary on Hume's *History*, he reflected ruefully, was 'a very bulky work which will afford fruitful subject of criticism to my Lords the Scotch reviewers . . . .'[36] A later and more famous Whiggish observer was more publicly vituperative. For Byron, in *English Bards and Scotch Reviewers* (1809), it seemed apposite to denounce the 'Northern wolves' of the *Edinburgh Review*. A 'coward brood' who 'o'er politics and poesy preside,' they were determined to ensure that, as Byron claimed—not wholly unrealistically in view of the *Edinburgh*'s immense influence over British readers' responses (though many of its critics, like Wordsworth and Southey, were palpably more English than Byron himself)—'Scottish taste decides on English wit.'[37]

Horace Walpole favoured an even more overtly ideological reading of the putatively common culture with which the put upon inhabitants of the southern parts of Great Britain (as he loved to portray them) were increasingly being bullied into identifying. In this analysis, especially characteristic of the period following Lord Bute's unpopular premiership and the long-drawn-out saga of John Wilkes's legal battles, cultural identities tended if anything to become even more sharply defined as a result of Whig suspicions that the Scots as a nation were fanatical Tories committed to the imposition of authoritarian government upon freedom-loving Englishmen. Walpole's newspaper cuttings, for example, provided him with a carefully chosen and continuous commentary upon the allegedly subversive aims of Scotland's authors, usually portrayed as acting in concert with those London-domiciled Scottish politicians who were believed to be intent on undermining English interests, English honour and English liberties.

Sir John Dalrymple, said the *Middlesex Journal* in one satirical piece printed in January 1774 but still referring back bitterly to that author's *Memoirs*, had 'lately been—Apprehended and capitally convicted of publishing as true a variety of letters, knowing them to be forged.'[38] Another piece that Walpole specifically preserved in his clippings collection again captured the ripe flavour of this most un-British of discourses: 'the Scots still keep their old enmity alive,' it reported, 'and will never rest till they have made us as complete slaves to power as themselves.'[39] That such barbed sentiments reflected their owner's suspicions about the Scots' hold over public opinion throughout Great Britain, and not least its English portion, is clear. As Walpole wrote either in or shortly after 1760 in one of the notebooks in which he tried to accumulate gleanings from his own reading: 'It is not surprising that the Scotch sh^d defend the Stuarts—if ever the line of Brunswick sh^d be expelled, I don't doubt but the Hanoverians will affirm that Q. Eliz. was more parsimonious than some frugal king of that House.'[40]

It was precisely doubts of this kind about the ulterior motives of Scottish authors who seemed increasingly to dictate English readers' perceptions of their own past, and so of their very identities, that frequently determined the selection of the press clippings and extracts that Walpole hoarded at Strawberry Hill. A particularly revealing one that almost certainly crystallised his own reservations about the Scots' stranglehold on the public's imagination came from the *Public Advertiser* of March 1773. Here the threat posed to England's identity by Scottish manipulation of readers' understanding of their own history as a people was pointedly articulated:

I have long, with great regret, seen the encouragement given to Scotch writers, as if it was not enough for them to have engrossed to themselves all the good places, but they must likewise have the presumption to write more books than we do, and to pretend to write our language better than we do.

Not content with sending up a David Hume to corrupt our manners with his infidel-like philosophy, and set us asleep with his tedious History of England, in six volumes, they also send us a Doctor Robertson, with the dullest of all histories, the History of Charles the Fifth; and after him comes a pert Baronet [ie. Dalrymple], with a set of lies from France, blaspheming, if I may so, the name of Algernon Sydney, and those heroes who saved their country at the expense of their blood. But what raises my choler the most, and ought to raise the wrath of every Englishman, is, that a Scotchman (Mr. Macpherson), lately arrived from the wildest part of the northern mountains, presumes to attempt to translate Homer after our immortal Pope.

I have not read him; I will not read him; I am determined not to read him, and I hope no Englishman will read his translation; and my reason is, that it is the encouragement given by foolish English readers, that makes Scotch writers so numerous in this country . . . [41]

Such a cynical view of recent publishing history, and of the disastrous implications of English men and women being prepared enthusiastically to embrace texts of Scottish authorship (and, indeed, we have seen ample evidence that they were doing so), plainly appealed to some in England specifically because it warned contemporaries about the problematical fault-lines rather than the potential unities in modern Britain's emerging cultural identity.

Indications of a capacity for resistance to the increasing accommodation of Scottish with English culture, or at best for complete indifference to a process of forced integration (or, as some saw it, brutal takeover) that was being unthinkingly welcomed (or, again, spinelessly colluded in) by most other English readers, can also be seen in the idiosyncratic patterns of book buying and reading maintained by certain individuals. John Ives, for example, Suffolk Herald Extraordinary and, before he died at the tender age of just twenty-five, one of the mid-century's most acquisitive young English bibliophiles, appears to have been remarkably untouched by the growing fashion for collecting and reading the works that had recently flowed from talented Scottish pens. When his personal library was sold in Covent Garden in March 1777, it numbered as many as 1,256 lots, and included most of the expected major works of the English Enlightenment, including texts by Mandeville, Voltaire, Shaftesbury and Locke. Remarkably, however, for a man so interested in the British past, it contained nothing by Hume. Nor was there anything by Smith or Robertson; and there was also nothing by Kames, Ferguson, Hutcheson, Beattie or Reid. In fact, apart from Sir John Pringle's *A Discourse on the Different Kinds of Air* (1774) and *A Discourse on the Torpedo* (1775), Smollett's *History* and Thomson's *The Seasons* (all of them, interestingly, the work of Scots who had moved to London and become substantially anglicised), there was not a single modern Scottish text anywhere to be found in this otherwise ample collection—a striking fact that would surely have pleased the *Public Advertiser*'s critic.[42]

The direct evidence of Ives's actual reading is similarly intriguing. His surviving letters reveal, as we would expect, an obsessive interest in antiquities and historical anecdotes. But, whilst replete with textual references to writers like J. Morgan (author of *Phoenix Britannicus* (1732)), they are entirely devoid of allusions to the contemporary Scottish authors, so much involved in antiquarianism and historiography, that bibliophiles like Topham Beauclerk, as we saw in Chapter 5, had unhesitatingly embraced.[43] The same peculiarity marks out another man with deep Suffolk roots, Samuel Lindsey, an officer in the 14th Regiment with which he participated in Byng's lethal failure at Minorca in 1757. Although a keen reader, Lindsay seems utterly to have neglected, or perhaps even to have spurned, the opportunities for the book lover ordinarily presented by the Scottish Enlightenment.

Thus his commonplace book, which survives for the period up to 1767, contains a rich mixture of copied material, ancient and modern—Pliny and Horace jostling for elbowroom beside Akenside and Pope. It contains, however, nothing remotely Scottish at all, and suggests rather a dogged determination on Lindsey's part to hold on to an older notion of the canon, exclusively comprising a well-established amalgam of England's own literary luminaries and the major works of classical antiquity.[44] Even later, yet another Suffolk reader, the young John Barber Scott, a tanner's son from Bungay, was equally oblivious to the attractions of modern literature, Scottish or otherwise. Drawing up what he called a 'Rough list of books and plays, 1807' containing everything that he either already owned or wished to acquire, it became a litany of familiar ancient texts such as Xenophon's *Cyropaedia*, the *Iliad*, Demosthenes's *Orations*, Tacitus's *Annals*, Horace's *Ars Poetica*, the Greek New Testament and the plays of Sophocles.[45]

Pride in the successful formation of a properly Anglo-Scottish culture, and the desire that often accompanied it to brandish and burnish a newly minted sense of Britishness, was therefore by no means the only response that a genuine love of books, and a sound knowledge of recent literature, could stimulate in the English reader. For a great many, certainly, it was easiest to embrace at least those Scottish texts that seemed very largely straightforward in their implications. Thus the poetry of Thomson, Burns and Scott—each capable, as we have seen, of being made directly relevant by readers to their own concerns and anxieties—entered the canon not only smoothly but, as things turned out, enduringly. So too, in due course, did Scott's novels, for they likewise did little to challenge or to unsettle, and a great deal to stimulate and to enthuse, their readers.

Indeed, the deeply satisfied reaction of the poet Felicia Hemans in February 1820 may have been typical of many English people's happy experiences with Scott's prose fiction, since, evidently still unaware of the anonymous author's identity, she wrote to a friend describing

> the pleasure of reading "Ivanhoe" with which I am more delighted than with any of its Author's Works, not excepting "Waverley"— How completely the whole Spirit of the Age if portrays, is embodied in the Work! Nothing ever gave me so complete an idea of "Merry England" in those chivalrous, but lawless days, when knights roamed about to <u>redress</u> and <u>commit</u> injuries, and every Englishman's house was literally "a Castle," because nothing else could protect him from the depredations of his neighbours of the "poor Greenwood."—not one characteristic of the age is omitted, and Minstrels, Monks, Archers, Templars, Knights and Dames, seem to pass before one as <u>large as life</u>, and make so vivid an impression, that we can hardly persuade ourselves it is a work of fiction, and not really written by some old Chronicler, like Froissart, who lived among the beings he describes with so much <u>bonhommie</u>.[46]

For a reader like Hemans, clearly, it was possible to share in the experience of Mary Archbald, who left Glasgow for the United States in the second half of the eighteenth century. Like large numbers of her English contemporaries, Archbald not only read and enjoyed work by authors like Scott but to a degree actually had her identities constructed by her sympathetic engagement with it. As the fruitful personal consequences of her immersion in the Waverley Novels have recently been described, 'she read these books nostalgically and critically and used this reading to keep the country and the circumstances of her youth and early womanhood clear in her imagination and memory.'[47]

At the opposite end of the spectrum, however, it was predictably texts like Hume's *History* and Dalrymple's *Memoirs* that tended most to be associated with a quite different and much less tolerant reaction. Overtly revisionist as well as unmistakably confrontational in intent, such works were inherently more likely to elicit suspicion as to their implications. More particularly, they were liable to generate an uneasy feeling that for some readers immediately became entangled with their own anxieties about the problems inherent in the fashionable notion of Britishness. These works did not, of course, fail to penetrate the canon. Indeed, their enthusiastic acceptance by some, but also the antagonism that they provoked from others (all publicity, as ever, being good publicity), naturally made them important for many proficient readers. There is no doubt, however, that it was their specifically Scottish provenance that had made them objectionable, and which in turn provided a ready focus for plausible insinuation by the determinedly unimpressed.

Acts of reading and reflecting upon certain Scottish texts do seem in many cases to have allowed notions of common Britishness to flourish. They did so, moreover, among many, perhaps most, of those whose personal habits and specific responses as readers can now be reconstructed. Exactly the same experiences, however, particularly when focused upon certain works of Scottish provenance that were either contentious in character or otherwise difficult to appropriate, also created opportunities for some readers to react in a quite different manner. As a result, they responded, it would seem, in ways that tended not to dissolve but instead to reinforce their own essentially English identities—and thus in direct and deliberate opposition to the supposedly integrated national culture in Great Britain with whose making they were increasingly confronted.

*   *   *

The consequences of eighteenth-century readers' encounters with contemporary texts, claims Robert Darnton in his seminal study of the destabilising effects of the illegal literature circulating in pre-Revolutionary France, 'though varied, tended to be strong'; and this was because 'books aroused emotions and stirred thoughts with a power we can barely imagine today.'[48] Yet if, as we have seen, the experience of reading was truly central to the processes involved in generating not merely textual meanings but also the shifting identities and multiple self-images of individual readers, there are clearly important implications for our understanding of eighteenth- and early nineteenth-century British culture. In fact, we may need to be prepared to begin conceptualising the Enlightenment as a whole in a quite different way, as the aggregation of the countless personal responses of largely anonymous men and women to what they read—rather than, as has been customary, as a clearly-defined set of ideas, agendas and vocabularies, let alone as a single all-encompassing philosophical or ideological project, formulated exclusively by the authors of the age.

There has, of course, long been a tendency to describe the Enlightenment, Scottish or otherwise, almost as a litany of canonical writers and printed works. It is for this reason that it has often appeared to be a reasonably neatly defined cultural programme above all marked by the shared commitment of certain well-known participants to a series of common outcomes. Peter Gay's *The Enlightenment* (1966–9) in many ways embodied, and still embodies, this conception at its most elegant, with its unapologetic concentration—in parts verging on the hagiographical—upon individuals such as Voltaire, Diderot and Rousseau, towering figures in the history of Western culture who were bent on nothing less than the comprehensive de-sacralisation of thought and the rationalisation (in several related senses) of modern society.[49] For the Scottish Enlightenment something of the same understanding has always underlain the most important contributions, ranging from H.G. Graham's late-Victorian masterpiece *Scottish Men of Letters in the Eighteenth Century* (1901), through Gladys Bryson's and Charles Camic's studies of the leading Scottish social theorists, to Richard Sher's exploration of the Moderate clergy of Edinburgh and Alexander Broadie's more recent anthological approach that has again foregrounded a number of major writers and their texts as the prime focus of attention.[50] So easy has it been to think of it as a publishing phenomenon *par excellence* that it appears the Scottish Enlightenment—virtually always defined as a select group of cultural producers—has almost invited historians to conceive it as the highly-structured outcome of specific processes of authorship, printing and bookselling.

Yet the evident importance of reading not merely in relaying but in enabling and constructing the meaning of texts surely demands that we reconsider how we approach the Enlightenment as an historical episode, as well as how we might hereafter set about studying it. For the significance of the processes of appropriation, of self-fashioning and of the contextual determination of specific meanings in the experience that English men and women clearly had with the Scottish Enlightenment implies that reading needs to be viewed as an intensely active rather than as a passive process, and as a performance *by* and *for* the reader rather than an action of the author and the text done *to* or performed *upon* the reader. On this understanding, the Enlightenment itself was no neatly-packaged product, created by a group of exceptional intellects—Gay's 'little flock of *philosophes*'—and sent out into the world through the good offices and entrepreneurial talent of the booksellers, there to be received and absorbed by an appreciative and largely compliant audience. Rather it was characterised by an unending sequence of acts of creation, reception and responding in which substantial populations of now-unknown individuals, and not just the famous thinkers and best-selling authors, were all implicated, as its meaning and significance were constantly confronted, contested and renegotiated.

The Enlightenment, in other words, was about consumption at least as much as it was about production. It was a protracted cultural event that took place, and only made sense, in an extended social arena. It was a phenomenon, moreover, whose ultimate meaning remained always contingent, always undetermined, and consequently always beyond the capacity of individual contemporaries properly to know. This in turn suggests, perhaps, that the celebrated and much-repeated question that Kant set himself to explore—'Was ist Aufklärung?'—had, and still has, no coherent or straightforward answer.[51] In a fundamental respect, whether we are dealing with its Scottish manifestation or otherwise, Enlightenment in its own time (leaving aside for the moment the nice problem of whether or not the historian should insist upon the insertion of a definite article) was nothing more than whatever a man or woman reading, say, Beattie's *Essay on Truth* or Reid's *Inquiry* at that point actually construed it as being.

Given what increasingly seems the absolute centrality of the performance of reading to an understanding of the Scottish Enlightenment in particular, there may thus be an opportunity for us also to begin to connect the specific concerns of intellectual history—the study of the authorship of Hume, Smith, Robertson and the rest—much more convincingly with the broader social and cultural history of Britain during this period. A renewed emphasis upon the consumers rather than the producers of texts would clearly effect a transformation in the relationship between the Enlightenment *sensu strictu* and other significant aspects of contemporary life. This in turn would potentially render it less peripheral and much more mainstream than it has sometimes been made to appear. It was, after all, the commercialisation of culture, and the growing tendency to think of culture as a marketable commodity, as John Brewer has suggested, that so characterised the eighteenth century, in England at least as much as anywhere else.[52] This was what lay behind, for example, the new fashions of shopping and promenading, the rejuvenation of dancing, concertgoing and the stage. In sum, it was public absorption, in large and increasing numbers, in cultural consumption, rather than simply new and expanded forms of cultural production occurring for their own sake, that was the principal engine behind the age's extraordinary creativity.[53]

In this context the 'relish for reading,' which at its most basic entailed mass involvement in making sense of *The Seasons* or the Kilmarnock Edition, the *History of England* or the *Lectures on Rhetoric and Belles Lettres*, may be viewed as yet another symptom of the same impulse, if not genuinely towards the full democratisation of culture then at least in the direction of steadily greater levels of unimpeded participation. Authorship and printing, needless to say, were far from new. In making possible Johnson's 'age of authors,' however, they were responding to the growing audience for texts, and the increasing demand for opportunities to read from those who had come to appreciate its fundamental importance. In this context, the great achievement of contemporary Scottish authorship, and of the Scottish Enlightenment, if that is still how we wish to describe it, was actually to serve as a disproportionately important source of supply in the widening market-place for reading materials, a role facilitated by the Scots' competitive advantages in the post-Union printing industry in Britain and also underpinned by deep native traditions of scholarship and writing which happened—conveniently, lucratively, gloriously—to reach their apogee in the age of Hume and Smith.

The dominant place of reading in structuring and giving meaning to the English experience of what we have more recently grown accustomed to thinking of as the Scottish Enlightenment also suggests that we may need to reconsider how we conceptualise intellectual and literary culture not only as a feature of Georgian society in Great Britain but also as the focus of concerted historical study. After all, it was less than twenty years ago that, reiterating a point first made in 1971, Robert Darnton reported that 'the social history of ideas' was still 'searching for a methodology.'[54] Darnton also argued credibly, by way of a measured but devastating critique of Gay's *The Enlightenment*, that the study of the great texts of eighteenth-century Europe was itself an insufficient basis even for that relatively narrow understanding of the history of ideas which amounts merely to 'the social history of the intellectual elite': the 'finances, milieux, and readership of the *philosophes*,' Darnton warned, 'can only be known by grubbing in the archives.'[55]

Our own inquiries have taken us very far in this particular direction, from Portsmouth to Ponteland, from the high Kentish Weald to the remote west coasts of Cornwall and Cumberland. In the process, we have considered a large body of archival material that sheds unprecedented light upon the contemporary readership of the Scottish philosophers, as well as the Scottish poets, novelists, historians, theologians, natural scientists and political economists. We have been able to see beyond doubt that the reading of individuals was at all times guided and influenced by others; to discover how and where they were likely to come across many of the books now ordinarily ascribed to a Scottish Enlightenment; and to begin to understand how, in a great number of different ways, their experiences as readers subsequently unfolded, as they encountered, for good or ill, what were by any standards some of the most popular and most stimulating works of the age. As Hazlitt argued in 1826—though he did not have Scottish authorship specifically in mind—this kind of familiarity with certain favourite texts was important because collectively they are 'links in the chain of our conscious being. They bind together the different scattered divisions of our personal identity . . . .'[56]

For its part, the present study has also shown just how integral to the social, cultural and moral identities of contemporaries the experience of reading really could be. To those who read or who even aspired to do so, the consumption of texts, precisely because of its function, as Hazlitt suggested, in the construction of meanings and the continual refashioning of the self, carried an inter-linked personal and public significance that today, in a much-altered environment with a very different value system, and with many more routes to diversion, to identity and to enlightenment (with or without a capital letter), we can scarcely even begin to imagine. It may also have been this sense, more than anything else, that allowed the English to make themselves, as Johnson proudly suggested in 1781, 'a nation of readers.'[57]

A few years later, in the burgeoning industrial centre that was Sunderland in County Durham, the founders of the town's first subscription library also seem fully to have shared in these far-reaching assumptions. Certainly they took it for granted that their proposed activities would play a central role both in the formation and dissemination of public culture and in the successful promotion of appropriate attitudes and behaviour amongst themselves. In enabling wider and deeper reading, they claimed in 1795, with almost audible faith in the genuinely metamorphic power of what they were setting out to do, this new institution would 'furnish the ready means of useful information to many who could not otherwise obtain it, and, by diffusing instruction, equally serve to improve their manners and their taste.'[58] If their experiences as readers were indeed as varied, as exciting, as rewarding and, ultimately, as transformative as those of many of their contemporaries whom we have met—eager English readers whose active engagement with Scottish texts, amongst other things, was even then help-ing to construct, as it were *from below*, a meaningfully British culture—it would be a stony-hearted historian who would think that such confidence was entirely misplaced.

Notes

NOTES TO CHAPTER 1

1. William Smellie, *Literary and Characteristical Lives of John Gregory, Lord Kames, David Hume and Adam Smith* (Edinburgh, 1800), p. 1612.
2. Tobias Smollett, *The Expedition of Humphry Clinker*, (ed.) L.M. Knapp (London, 1966), p. 233.
3. Quoted in Paul Langford, *Public Life and the Propertied Englishman, 1689–1798* (Oxford, 1989), p. 84.
4. D.B. Horn, *A Short History of the University of Edinburgh, 1556–1889* (Edinburgh, 1967), p. 64.
5. Carlo Denina, *An Essay on the Revolutions of Literature* (ed.) and (trans.) J. Murdoch (London, 1771), p. 276.
6. Voltaire, *Philosophical Letters*, (trans.) E. Dilworth (Indianapolis, IN, 1961), p. 25.
7. David Allan, 'The Age of Pericles in the Modern Athens: Greek History, Scottish Politics and the Fading of Enlightenment,' *Historical Journal*, 44 (2001), 391–417; J.S. Gibson, 'How did the Enlightenment Seem to the Edinburgh Enlightened?,' *British Journal of Eighteenth-Century Studies*, 1 (1978), 46–50.
8. Roy Porter, *Enlightenment: Britain and the Creation of the Modern World* (London, 2000), esp. cap. 1; idem., 'The Enlightenment in England,' in his and M. Teich, (eds.), *The Enlightenment in National Context* (Cambridge, 1981), pp. 1–18.
9. Porter adopted this position in particular in *Enlightenment*, though his highly suggestive comments that the Scottish and English Enlightenments were 'in constant dialogue,' and that 'the traditions fed off each other' (p. 243), were not fully explored.
10. Roy Porter, 'Science, Provincial Culture and Public Opinion in Enlightenment England,' in Peter Borsay, (ed.), *The Eighteenth-Century Town: A Reader in English Urban History, 1688–1820* (London and New York, 1990), p. 251.
11. The historiography of the Scottish Enlightenment is immense, though there have been a number of attempts at bibliographical guidance. See, for example, Richard B. Sher, *Church and University in the Scottish Enlightenment* (Princeton, NJ, and Edinburgh, 1985) and my own *Virtue, Learning and the Scottish Enlightenment: Ideas of Scholarship in Early Modern History* (Edinburgh, 1993), cap. 1.
12. I. Hont and M. Ignatieff, (eds.), *Wealth and Virtue: The Shaping of Political Economy in the Scottish Enlightenment* (Cambridge, 1983).

13. Nicholas Phillipson, 'Politics, Politeness and Anglicisation in Early Eighteenth-Century Scottish Culture,' in R.A. Mason, (ed.), *Scotland and England, 1286–1815* (Edinburgh, 1987), pp. 226–46.
14. Ian McBride, 'The School of Virtue: Francis Hutcheson, Irish Presbyterians and the Scottish Enlightenment,' in D. George Boyce, Robert Eccleshall and Vincent Geoghan, (eds.), *Political Thought in Ireland Since the Seventeenth Century* (London, 1993), pp. 73–99.
15. Roger L. Emerson, 'Sir Robert Sibbald, Kt., the Royal Society of Scotland and the Origins of the Scottish Enlightenment,' *Annals of Science*, 45 (1988), 41–72; Gordon Donaldson, 'Stair's Scotland: The Intellectual Heritage,' *Juridical Review* (1981), 128–45.
16. Peter Gay, *The Enlightenment*, 2 vols (New York, 1966–9).
17. David Kettler, *The Social and Political Thought of Adam Ferguson* (Columbus, OH, 1965); Knud Haakonssen, *The Science of a Legislator: The Natural Jurisprudence of David Hume and Adam Smith* (Cambridge, 1981); Trevor Palmer, *Perilous Planet Earth* (Cambridge, 2003), pp. 16–22.
18. Hugh Trevor-Roper, 'The Scottish Enlightenment,' *Studies on Voltaire and the Eighteenth Century*, 58 (1967), 1635–58 (p. 1639).
19. John Lough, 'Reflections on Enlightenment and *Lumières*,' *British Journal of Eighteenth-Century Studies*, 8 (1985), 1–15 (p. 9).
20. J.J. Carter and J. H. Pittock, (eds.), *Aberdeen and the Enlightenment* (Aberdeen, 1987); R. Sher and A. Hook, (eds.), *Glasgow and the Enlightenment* (East Linton, 1995). See also Bob Morris's shrewd observation that Edinburgh 'had characteristics of both a metropolitan and provincial urban centre': 'Voluntary Societies and British Urban Élites, 1780–1850: An Analysis,' in Borsay, (ed.), *Eighteenth-Century Town*, pp. 336–66 (p. 341n).
21. Rare exceptions include K. Holcomb, 'A Dance in the Mind: the Provincial Scottish Philosophical Societies,' *Studies in Eighteenth-Century Culture*, 21 (1991), 89–100 and my own 'The Scottish Enlightenment and the Politics of Provincial Culture: The Perth Literary and Antiquarian Society, c.1784–1790,' *Eighteenth-Century Life*, 27 (2003), 1–31.
22. On English provincial readership, see *infra*, note 56. For Scotland, see W.R. Aitken, *A History of the Public Library Movement in Scotland to 1955* (Glasgow, 1971); Paul Kaufman, 'Innerpeffray: Reading for All the People,' in his *Libraries and Their Users* (1969), pp. 153–62; J. Crawford, 'Reading and Book Use in Eighteenth-Century Scotland,' *The Bibliotheck*, 19 (1994), 23–43; David Allan, 'Provincial Readers and Book Culture in the Scottish Enlightenment: The Perth Library, 1784–c.1800,' *The Library*, 4 (2002), 367–89. In relation to the Enlightenment, however, the emphasis has principally been upon studies of publishing and bookselling, as in Richard B. Sher, *The Enlightenment and the Book: Scottish Authors and Their Publishers in Eighteenth-Century Britain, Ireland and America* (Chicago, IL, and London, 2007) and William Zachs, *The First John Murray and the Late Eighteenth-Century Book Trade* (Oxford, 1998).
23. Richard Sher, 'Science and Medicine in the Scottish Enlightenment: The Lessons of Book History,' in Paul Wood, (ed.), *The Scottish Enlightenment: Essays in Reinterpretation* (Rochester, NY, 2000), p. 113.
24. *Early Responses to Hume*, (ed.), James Feiser, 10 vols (Bristol, 1999); *On The Wealth of Nations: Contemporary Responses to Adam Smith*, (ed.), Ian S. Ross (Bristol, 1998); R.F. Teichgraeber, '"Less Abused Than I Had Reason to Expect": The Reception of *The Wealth of Nations* in Britain,' *Historical Journal*, 30 (1987), 337–366; *Adam Smith: Critical Responses*, (ed.), Hiroshi Mizuta, 6 vols (London, 2000).

25. Kenneth E. Carpenter, *The Dissemination of* The Wealth of Nations *in French and in France, 1776–1843* (New York, 2002); Richard Whatmore, 'Adam Smith's Role in the French Revolution,' *Past and Present*, 175 (2002), 65–89; Samuel Fleischacker, 'Adam Smith's Reception Among the American Founders 1776–1790,' *William and Mary Quarterly*, 3rd series, 19 (2002), 897–924.

26. James McCosh, *The Scottish Philosophy: Biographical, Expository, Critical, From Hutcheson to Hamilton* (London, 1875); Mark G. Spencer, *David Hume in Eighteenth-Century America* (Rochester, NY, and Woodbridge, 2005).

27. D.S. Sloan, *The Scottish Enlightenment and the American College Ideal* (New York, 1971); J.D. Hoeveler, *James McCosh and the Scottish Intellectual Tradition* (Princeton, NJ, 1981).

28. David Daiches, 'Style Périodique and Style Coupé: Hugh Blair and the Scottish Rhetoric of American Independence,' in R. Sher and J.R. Smitten, (eds.), *Scotland and America in the Age of the Enlightenment* (Edinburgh, 1990), pp. 209–26; D.W. Howe, 'Why the Scottish Enlightenment Was Useful to the Framers of the American Constitution,' *Comparative Studies in Society and History*, 31 (1989), 572–87.

29. Ann Matheson, *Theories of Rhetoric in the Eighteenth-Century Scottish Sermon* (Lewiston, NY, and Lampeter, 1995); Lynee Lewis Gaillet, (ed.), *Scottish Rhetoric and Its Influences* (Mahwah, NJ, 1998).

30. A rare study directly focusing upon the complex problem of textual transmission is Warren McDougall, 'Scottish Books for America in the Mid-Eighteenth Century,' in R. Myers and M. Harris, (eds.), *Spreading the Word: The Distribution Networks of Print, 1550–1800* (Winchester, 1990), pp. 21–46.

31. Norbert Waszek, *The Scottish Enlightenment and Hegel's Account of "Civil Society"* (Dordrecht, 1988); M. Kuehn, *Scottish Common Sense in Germany, 1768–1800: A Contribution to the History of Critical Philosophy* (Kingston, Ont., 1987). See also *The Reception of the Scottish Enlightenment in Germany: Six Significant Translations, 1755–1782*, (ed.), Heiner F. Klemme, 7 vols (Bristol, 2000).

32. Fania Oz-Salzberger, *Translating the Enlightenment: Scottish Civic Discourse in Eighteenth-Century Germany* (Oxford, 1995); David Allan, *Adam Ferguson* (Aberdeen, 2007), cap. 6; Hans Eric Bödeker, 'Staatswissenschaften and Political Economy at the University of Göttingen: The Scottish Influence,' *Studies on Voltaire and the Eighteenth Century*, 305 (1992), 1881–4; Dushan Breski, 'Schiller's Debt to Montesquieu and Adam Ferguson,' *Comparative Literature*, 13 (1961), 239–53; Roy Pascal, 'Herder and the Scottish Historical School,' *Publications of the English Goethe Society*, 14 (1938–9), 23–42; László Kontler, 'William Robertson and His German Audience on European and Non-European Civilisations,' *Scottish Historical Review*, 80 (2001), 63–89.

33. Daniel Gordon, 'Sociability and Universal History: Jean-Baptiste Suard and the Scottish Enlightenment in France,' in his *Citizens Without Sovereignty* (Princeton, NJ, 1994), pp. 129–176; John Renwick, 'The Reception of William Robertson's Historical Writings in Eighteenth-Century France,' in S.J. Brown, (ed.), *William Robertson and the Expansion of Empire* (Cambridge, 1997), pp. 145–63; Franco Venturi, 'Scottish Echoes in Eighteenth-Century Italy,' in Hont and Ignatieff, (eds.), *Wealth and Virtue*, pp. 345–62; and several of the essays in Deirdre Dawson and Pierre Morere, (eds.), *Scotland and France in the Enlightenment* (Lewisburg, PA, and London, 2004).

34. Oz-Salzberger, *Translating the Enlightenment*, pp. 77–85. See also Bernhard Fabian, 'English Books and Their Eighteenth-Century German Readers,' in Paul J. Korshin, (ed.), *The Widening Circle: Essays on the Circulation of Literature in Eighteenth-Century Europe* (Philadelphia, PA, 1976), pp. 119–75.
35. Howard Gaskill, (ed.), *Ossian Revisited* (Edinburgh, 1991); F.J. Stafford, *The Sublime Savage: A Study of James Macpherson and the Poems of Ossian* (Edinburgh, 1988); Richard Sher, '"Those Scotch Impostors and Their Cabal": Ossian and the Scottish Enlightenment,' in R.L. Emerson, G. Girard and R. Runte, (eds.), *Man and Nature: Proceedings of the Canadian Society for Eighteenth-Century Studies*, vol I (London, Ont., 1982), 55–63.
36. J.G.A. Pocock, *Barbarism and Religion—Volume Two: Narratives of Civil Government*, (Cambridge, 1999); Isabel Rivers, 'Responses to Hume on Religion by Anglicans and Dissenters,' *Journal of Ecclesiastical History*, 52 (2001), 675–95.
37. Anand Chitnis, *The Scottish Enlightment and Early Victorian English Society* (London, 1986). Biancamaria Fontana, *Rethinking the Politics of Commercial Society: The Edinburgh Review, 1802–1832* (Cambridge, 1985), J.O. Hayden, (ed.), *Scott: the Critical Heritage* (London, 1970). See also, covering different angles entirely, J.B. Morrell's 'Science in Manchester and the University of Edinburgh, 1760–1840,' in D.S.L. Carswell, (ed.), *Artisan to Graduate: Essays to Commemorate the Foundation in 1824 of the Manchester Mechanics' Institution . . .* (Manchester, 1974), pp. 39–54, and Robert Crawford, *The Scottish Invention of English Literature* (Cambridge and New York, 1998).
38. A. Everitt, 'Social Mobility in Early Modern England,' *Past and Present*, 33 (1966), 56–73.
39. C. Wilson, *England's Apprenticeship, 1603–1763* (London, 1967); D.C. Coleman, *The Economy of England, 1450–1750* (London, 1977); Peter Mathias, *The First Industrial Nation: An Economic History of Britain, 1700–1914* (London, 1969).
40. John Brewer, *The Pleasures of the Imagination: English Culture in the Eighteenth Century* (London, 1997), p. 665.
41. Ibid., pp. 28–55.
42. E.A. Wrigley, 'Urban Growth and Agricultural Change: England and the Continent in the Early Modern Period,' Borsay, (ed.), *Eighteenth-Century Town*, p. 42.
43. Peter Borsay, *The English Urban Renaissance: Culture and Society in the Provincial Town, 1660–1770* (Oxford, 1989); Peter Clark, (ed.), *The Early Modern Town* (London, 1976).
44. Borsay, *Urban Renaissance*, esp. pp. 41–196.
45. Ibid., pp. 31–4; J. Barrett, 'Spas and Seaside Resorts, 1660–1780,' in J. Stevenson et al., (eds.), *The Rise of the New Urban Society* (Milton Keynes, 1977), pp. 37–70.
46. J.H. Plumb, *The Commercialisation of Leisure in Eighteenth-Century England* (Reading, 1973); Ann Bermingham and John Brewer, (eds.), *The Consumption of Culture, 1600–1800. Image, Object, Text* (London and New York, 1995).
47. Borsay, *Urban Renaissance*, pp. 180–96; Brewer, *Pleasures*, esp. pp. 630–41, 652–60.
48. C. Brookes, *English Cricket: The Game and its Players through the Ages* (Newton Abbot, 1978), pp. 9–66; S. Rosenfeld, *Strolling Players and Drama in the Provinces, 1660–1765* (Cambridge, 1939); M. Tilmouth, 'The Beginnings of Provincial Concert Life in England,' in C. Hogwood and R. Luckett, (eds.), *Music in Eighteenth-Century England* (Cambridge, 1983), pp. 1–17.

49. Lorna Mui and Hoh-cheung Mui, *Shops and Shopping in Eighteenth-Century England* (Montreal, 1989); Neil McKendrick, John Brewer and J.H. Plumb, *The Birth of a Consumer Society: The Commercialization of Eighteenth-Century England* (London, 1983).
50. Brewer, *Pleasures*, esp. pp. 98–112; Lawrence Klein, *Shaftesbury and the Culture of Politeness: Moral Discourse and Cultural Politics in Early Eighteenth-Century England* (Cambridge, 1994).
51. Michael Ketcham, *Transparent Designs: Reading, Performance and Form in The Spectator Papers* (Athens, GA, 1985).
52. *The Spectator*, 12 March 1711.
53. *Rules and Orders to be Observed by the Historical Society for the Cultivation of Useful Knowledge . . .* (Canterbury, 1816), p. 3.
54. Peter Clark, *British Clubs and Societies, 1580–1800: The Origins of an Associational World* (Oxford, 2000). See also R.J. Morris, 'Voluntary Societies and British Urban Elites, 1780–1850,' *Historical Journal*, 26 (1983), 95–118.
55. *A Catalogue of the Present Collection of Books in the Liverpool Library. . . .* (n.p., n.d.), p. 3.
56. The definitive survey is Paul Kaufman, 'The Community Library: A Chapter in English Social History,' *Transactions of the American Philosophical Society*, 57 (1967), Pt. 7, 3–67. See also my own *"A Nation of Readers": The Lending Library in Georgian England, c.1720–c.1830* (London, 2008), caps. 2 and 3, which offers a full historiographical overview, and, for a case study, idem., 'Eighteenth-Century Private Subscription Libraries and Provincial Urban Culture: the Amicable Society of Lancaster, 1769–c.1820,' *Library History*, 19 (2001), 57–76. Alston represents the obvious way into this subject in the future.
57. Allan, *"Nation of Readers,"* cap. 4; Kaufman, 'Community Library'; D.P. Varma, *The Evergreen Tree of Diabolical Knowledge* (Washington, DC, 1972); Charlotte A. Stewart-Murphy, *A History of the British Circulating Libraries: The Book Labels and Ephemera of the Papantonio Collection* (Newtown, PA, 1992).
58. *MM*, 11 (1801), 238.
59. Richard D. Altick, *The English Common Reader: A Social History of the Mass Reading Public, 1800–1900* (Chicago, IL, 1957); Isabel Rivers, (ed.), *Books and their Readers in Eighteenth-Century England* (Leicester, 1982); idem. *Books and Their Readers in Eighteenth-Century England: New Essays* (Leicester, 2001); Jonathan Rose, *The Intellectual Life of the British Working Classes* (New Haven, CT, 2001); Stephen Colclough, *Consuming Texts: Readers and Reading Communities, 1695–1870* (Houndmills and New York, 2007), the latter appearing so late that it has not been possible properly to assimilate it in my own analysis. Another notable recent contribution to this exciting and desperately under-researched subject is James Raven, Helen Small and Naomi Tadmor, (eds.), *The Practice and Representation of Reading in England* (Cambridge, 1996): see, especially, the essays by Raven, Tadmor, John Brewer and Jan Fergus. Also useful are Fergus's 'Eighteenth-Century Readers in Provincial England: The Customers of Samuel Clay's Circulating Library and Bookshop in Warwick, 1770–72,' *Papers of the Bibliographical Society of America*, 78 (1984), 155–213; Fergus, Jan, *Provincial Readers in Eighteenth-Century England* (Oxford, 2006); Paul Kaufman, *Reading Vogues at English Cathedral Libraries of the Eighteenth Century* (New York, 1964); Jacqueline Pearson, *Women's Reading in Britain 1750–1835: A Dangerous Recreation* (Cambridge, 1999).

60. David Allan, 'Some Notes and Problems in the History of Reading: Georgian England and the Scottish Enlightenment,' *The Journal of the Historical Society*, 3 (2003), 91–124.
61. William G. Rowland, *Literature and the Marketplace: Romantic Writers and Their Audiences in Great Britain and the United States* (Lincoln, NE, 1996), p. ix.
62. St Clair, pp. 9–10.
63. For a preliminary case study, see my own 'The Scottish Enlightenment and the Readers of Late Georgian Lancaster: "Light in the North",' *Northern History*, 36 (2000), 267–81.
64. H.R. Jauss, *Aesthetic Experience and Literary Hermeneutics*, (trans.), M. Shaw (Minneapolis, MN, 1982); idem. *Towards an Aesthetic of Reception*, (trans.), T. Bahti (Minneapolis, MN, 1982); W. Iser, *The Implied Reader: Patterns of Communication in Prose Fiction from Bunyan to Beckett* (Baltimore, MD, and London, 1974); idem., *The Act of Reading: A Theory of Aesthetic Response* (Baltimore, MD, and London, 1978); S. Fish, *Is There a Text in This Class? The Authority of Interpretive Communities* (Cambridge, MA, 1980).
65. Jacques Derrida, *Of Grammatology*, (trans.) G. Chakravorty Spivak (Baltimore, MD, 1976), p. 158; Roland Barthes, 'The Death of the Author,' in David Lodge, (ed.), *Modern Criticism and Theory: A Reader* (London, 1988), p. 172.
66. Ibid., p. 150.
67. Recent calls for an overdue historicisation of the study of reading, and for attempts to test theoretical claims against specific historical examples of textual reception by audiences, have included Jonathan Rose, 'Rereading the English Common Reader: A Preface to the History of Audiences,' *Journal of the History of Ideas*, 53 (1992), 47–70; idem., 'Arriving at a History of Reading,' *Historically Speaking*, (Jan. 2004), 36–9; and Robert D. Hume, 'Texts Within Contexts: Notes Towards a Historical Method,' *Philological Quarterly*, 71 (1992), 69–100. The problem of relating theories of reading to a history of reading, and so, potentially, on to other histories, is also embedded in much of the recent literature on that part of book history which seeks to study audiences. For example, Robert Darnton, 'What is the History of Books?,' *Daedalus*, 111 (1982), 65–83; David D. Hall, 'The History of the Book: New Questions? New Answers?,' *Journal of Library History*, 21 (1986), 27–38; Roger Chartier, *The Order of Books: Readers, Authors, and Libraries in Europe between the Fourteenth and Eighteenth Centuries*, (trans.) Lydia G. Cochrane (Cambridge, 1994); Guglielmo Cavallo and Roger Chartier, (eds.), *The History of Reading in the West*, (trans.) Lydia G. Cochrane (Cambridge, 1999), first published as *Histoire de la Lecture Dans le Monde Occidental* (Rome, 1995).
68. Duncan Forbes, *Hume's Philosophical Politics* (Cambridge, 1975); Nicholas Phillipson, *Hume* (London, 1989).
69. Fish, *Is There a Text?*, p. 14.
70. Iser, *Act of Reading*, p. 34; idem., *Implied Reader*, p. xii.
71. Robert C. Holub, *Reception Theory: A Critical Introduction* (London and New York, 1984), esp. pp. 58–63.
72. For a bold and illuminating excursion across hotly contested scholarly terrain, where both its exact chronology and its specific contents are placed in more than usual doubt, see John Robertson, *The Case for the Enlightenment: Scotland and Naples, 1680–1750* (Cambridge, 2005), cap. 1. A pragmatic approach similar to my own informs the most recent attempt to present the

Scottish Enlightenment as an identifiable body of literature: see Sher, esp. pp. 77–81.

NOTES TO CHAPTER 2

1. David Vincent, *Literacy and Popular Culture: England, 1750–1914* (Cambridge, 1989); R.A. Houston, *Literacy in Early Modern Europe: Culture and Education, 1500–1800* (London, 1988), esp. pp. 116–54.
2. Altick, p. 49.
3. Ibid., p. 170.
4. J. Paul Hunter, *Before Novels: The Cultural Contexts of Eighteenth-Century English Fiction* (New York and London, 1990), pp. 62–6.
5. Samuel Johnson, *The Idler and Adventurer*, (eds.), W.J. Bate, J.M. Bullitt and L.F. Powell (New Haven, CT, 1963), p. 457.
6. Lucy Newlyn, *Reading, Writing, and Romanticism: The Anxiety of Reception* (Oxford, 2000), p. 3.
7. Frank Donoghue, *The Fame Machine: Book Reviewing and Eighteenth-Century Literary Careers* (Palo Alto, CA, 1996); Jon Klancher, *The Making of English Reading Audiences, 1790–1832* (Madison, WI, 1987); James Engell, *Forming the Critical Mind: Dryden to Coleridge* (Cambridge, MA, and London, 1989).
8. Quoted in Porter, *Enlightenment*, p. 84.
9. Ernest C. Mossner, *The Life of David Hume* (Oxford, 1954), p. 10. Poets, claimed Goldsmith in similar vein, 'have now no other patrons but the public, and the public, collectively considered, is a good and generous master': *Goldsmith: Selected Essays*, (ed.), J.H. Lobban (Cambridge, 1910), p. 65. Cf. Sher, esp. pp. 203–09.
10. Donoghue, *Fame Machine*, pp. 1–2.
11. Robert L. Patten, 'Dickens as Serial Author: The Case of Multiple Identities,' in Laurel Brake, Bill Bell, and David Finkelstein, (eds.), *Nineteenth-Century Media and the Construction of Identities* (Basingstoke, 2000), p. 148.
12. Walter J. Graham, *The Beginnings of English Literary Periodicals: A Study of Periodical Literature, 1665–1715* (New York, 1926); R.D. Spector, *English Literary Periodicals and the Climate of Opinion During the Seven Years' War* (The Hague, 1966).
13. James G. Basker, *Tobias Smollett: Critic and Journalist* (Newark, NJ, 1988).
14. Pearson, esp. pp. 1–21.
15. *ML*, i (1773–4), 4.
16. Ibid., i (1773–4), 671.
17. Spector, *English Literary Periodicals*, p. 244.
18. Vicesimus Knox, *Essays Moral and Literary*, 12th edition, 2 vols (London, 1788), II, 366.
19. *MR*, v (1751), 10.
20. *Remarks on the Behaviour of Sectaries; occasioned by "The York Select Subscription Library," addressed to the Friends of the Established Church: by a Churchman* (York, 1819), p. 4.
21. Spector, *English Literary Periodicals*, p. 244; J.T. Taylor, *Early Opposition to the English Novel: The Popular Reaction from 1780 to 1830* (New York, 1943).
22. Hugh Blair, *Lectures on Rhetoric and Belles Lettres*, 14th edition (London, 1825), p. 24.

23. *The World* (1753), p. 191; Laurence Sterne, *The Life and Opinions of Tristram Shandy, Gentleman*, (eds.) M. and J. New (Harmondsworth, 2003), p. 75.
24. Ibid., p. xii.
25. [George Colman], *Polly Honeycombe* . . . (London, 1760), p. vi.
26. *The Spectator*, 12 March 1711.
27. *A Catalogue of the Present Collection of Books in the Manchester Circulating Library* . . . (Manchester, 1766), p. 21.
28. Woking: Surrey History Centre: 2346/1, Pulborough Reading Society book, 1807- , fo. 2r.
29. Kendal: Cumbria RO: WD/K/189, 'Minutebook of the Kendal Coffee Room 1779–1879,' passim.
30. Marilyn Butler, 'Culture's Medium: The Role of the Review,' in Stuart Curran, (ed.), *Cambridge Companion to British Romanticism* (Cambridge, 1993), pp. 120–147 (at p. 136).
31. *Rules for the Regulation of the Carlisle Library* (Carlisle, 1819), pp. iii, xiii; Carlisle: Carlisle PL: L33, 'Carlisle Library: Minute Book 1804–1828,' fo. 1r.
32. *A Catalogue of the Books Belonging to the Coventry Library* . . . (Coventry, 1812), p. 2.
33. *Catalogue of the Worcester Library* (Worcester, 1818), p. 85.
34. *Laws of the Lichfield Permanent Library* (Lichfield, 1808), p. 7; Bradford: West Yorkshire AS: DB17/C37, 'Pontefract Library and News Room Minute Book 1783–1854,' fo. 2r.
35. BL Add. MSS 27617, 'Commonplace book of J.H. Ott, rector of Bexhill,' fos. 11r, 12r, 14r, 17r.
36. Altick, p. 38.
37. *The Diary of Thomas Turner 1754–1765*, (ed.), David Vaisey (Oxford, 1984), p. 3.
38. Trowbridge: Wiltshire and Swindon RO: 1461/1352, Memorandum book of Charles Morgan, 1748–52, eg. fos. 10v-27r, 29r, 53r. Addison's discussion had begun in *The Spectator*, 31 December 1711, and continued thereafter in the Saturday issues until 3 May 1712.
39. Truro: Cornwall RO: DD.CY/1712, 'Will of Elizabeth Goodall of Fowey, spinster.'
40. Lincoln, Lincolnshire Archives: FLINDERS 1, 'Diary and Account Book of Mathew Flinders of Donington, 1775–85,' fo. 57v.
41. FLINDERS 2, '. . . . , 1785–1802,' fo. 11v.
42. *CR*, xiii (1762), 427.
43. Maidstone: Centre for Kentish Studies: U194 F9/1, Commonplace Book of Revd J.E. Gambier, 1780- , eg., fos. 3r, 4r, 6r, 7r, and U194 F9/2, 1789-, e.g. fos. 4r, 52v.
44. Bury St Edmunds: Suffolk RO: E2/34, 'Memoranda Quaedam, Sir John Cullum F.R.S.—F.S.A.,' passim; *Comp. Bar.*, III, 43.
45. Matlock: Derbyshire RO: Gell of Hopton, D258/14/11/1, 'Extracts No. 1: Jany. 1803,' eg., pp. 14, 16.
46. Stephen Colclough, 'Procuring Books and Consuming Texts: The Reading Experience of a Sheffield Apprentice, 1798,' *Book History*, 3 (2000), 21–44 (esp. 32–3, 35).
47. Bury St Edmunds: Suffolk RO: P504, 'A Catalogue of the Books belonging to the Revd George Burton. . . . Nov[r] 27th 1753.'
48. Halifax: West Yorkshire AS: MISC 509/10, 'Commonplace Book of the Reverend James Franks . . . ,' passim.
49. Gosforth: Northumberland RO: ZBK/C/1/A12/7, Notebook diary of the Revd James Snowdon, 14 Dec. 1763; /9, 17 May 1768; /18, 30 Jan. 1778.

50. Engell, *Forming the Critical Mind*, p. 3.
51. Iser, *Act of Reading*, p. 34.
52. *TCM*, viii (1776), 380.
53. Ibid., viii (1776), 462.
54. *CR*, xxiii (1767), 186.
55. *MR*, xxxvi (1767), 352.
56. *MM*, 49 (1820), 344–5.
57. *LM*, 38 (1769), 156.
58. *MR*, v (n.s.) (1791), 214.
59. C.H. Hinnant, *"Steel for the Mind": Samuel Johnson and Critical Discourse* (Newark, NJ, and London, 1994); J.H. Pittock, *The Ascendancy of Taste: The Achievement of Joseph and Thomas Warton* (London, 1973).
60. Michael Dobson, *The Making of the National Poet: Shakespeare, Adaptation and Authorship, 1660–1769* (Oxford, 1992).
61. J.B. Kramnick, *Making the English Canon: Print-Capitalism and the Cultural Past, 1700–1770* (Cambridge, 1998); Trevor Ross, *The Making of the English Literary Canon: From the Middle Ages to the Late Eighteenth Century* (Kingston, Ont. and Montreal, 1998).
62. Sher, esp. pp. 25–8, 288–9, 313–16, 414–15.
63. Richard Terry, *Poetry and the Making of the English Literary Past* (Oxford, 2001); St Clair, esp. cap. 7.
64. Thomas F. Bonnell, 'Bookselling and Canon-Making: The Trade Rivalry over the English Poets, 1776–1783,' *Studies in Eighteenth-Century Culture*, 19 (1989), 53–69; Sher, p. 355.
65. Thomas F. Bonnell, 'John Bell's *Poets of Great Britain*: The "Little Trifling Edition" Revisited,' *Modern Philology*, 85 (1987), 128–52.
66. Walpole: 'Commonplace Book of William Chute Esq. of The Vine in Hampshire,' p. 18; Add. MSS 61842, 'Eighteenth Century Verse,' fo. 125v–126r; *Johnson's Lives of the English Poets*, (ed.) G. Birkbeck Hill, 3 vols (Oxford, 1905), III, 299.
67. 'Commonplace Book of Revd J.E. Gambier, 1780- ', fo. 114v; 'Commonplace Book of the Reverend James Franks,' fos 59v–60r; *Johnson's Lives*, III, 247.
68. Beinecke: Osborn Shelves c.83/1, 'Commonplace book compiled by William Warren Porter (1776–1804),' p. 2044.
69. Winchester: Hampshire RO: 84M95/2, Commonplace book of Robert Bristow of Micheldever, 1793, fo. 14r; Matlock: Derbyshire RO: D239M/F10224, 'Commonplace Book of Sir William Fitzherbert, c.1770–1790,' p. 4; Samuel Johnson, *Life of Savage*, (ed.), Clarence Tracy (Oxford, 1971), p. 4.
70. New York: Pierpont Morgan Library: MA4960, George Hibbert, commonplace book, 1785–1820, fos. 1r-2r. See *LJ*, p. 122; *HP(3)*, IV, 193–4.
71. BL: Egerton MSS: 3700B, 'B. Barrett Collection, Vol. XIII, Literary papers etc.,' fo. 1r; *LJ*, p. 414.
72. 'B. Barrett Collection, Vol. XIII, Literary papers etc.,' fo. 102v; *LJ*, p. 202.
73. Lewes: East Sussex RO: SHR 1349, Notes and memoranda mostly by George Shiffner, passim; *LJ*, p. 532.
74. Christopher Thomson, *The Autobiography of an Artisan* (London, 1847), p. 67.
75. Leicester: Record Office for Leicestershire, Leicester and Rutland: 18D35/1, Minutes of the Leicester Permanent Library 1800- , fos. 26v, 27r, 34v.
76. Carlisle: Cumbria RO: D/LONSW20/5/1, Minute Book of the Whitehaven Library, 1823–36, 22 Aug. 1826.
77. Thomas Warton, *The History of English Poetry* (London, 1870), p. 491.
78. BL: Add. MSS. 61842, 'Eighteenth Century Verse,' fos. 116v–117v, 121v–124r, 146r–147v.

79. Bristol: Bristol RO: 41213/L/1/1, Thomas Eagles, Commonplace Book 1781–1802, fos. 1r–23r.
80. Cumbria RO (Carlisle): In D/SEN/10/Box 197, Early nineteenth-century commonplace book, pp. 36–7; *Catalogue of the Books Belonging to the Whitehaven Library* . . . (Whitehaven, 1808), p. iii; Thomas Warton, *The History of English Poetry*, 3 vols (London, 1840), III, 179–80.
81. 'Memoranda Quaedam . . . ,' fo. 46v; Warton, *History*, II, 1–15.
82. BL: Add. MSS 22667: 'Liber memorandorum et referentiarum . . . ,' fo. 35v; Joseph Warton, *An Essay on the Writings and Genius of Pope*, 2 vols (London, 1756–82), II, 186.
83. Carlisle: Carlisle PL: M1312, 'Common-Place Book After Locke's Method. By Gustavus Gale,' pp. 88, 358.
84. Ronald Paulson, *Breaking and Remaking: Aesthetic Practice in England, 1700–1820* (New Brunswick, NJ, and London, 1989).
85. Alexander Pope, *An Essay on Criticism* (London, 1713), p. 6.
86. Engell, *Critical Mind*, p. 195.
87. Patrick Parrinder, *Authors and Authority: English and American Criticism 1750–1990* (Basingstoke, 1991), p. 8.
88. 'Commonplace Book of Revd J.E. Gambier, 1780–,' fos. 55r, 59v, 60r.
89. D.B. Paxman, 'The Genius of English: Eighteenth-Century Language Study and English Poetry,' *Philological Quarterly*, 70 (1991), 27–46.
90. Phillipson, 'Politics'; Klein, *Shaftesbury*.
91. Norfolk RO: MF/RO334/1, 3, 'Commonplace book begun in 1750 . . . ,' fos. 7v, 48r.
92. I. Duncan, 'Adam Smith, Samuel Johnson and the Institution of English,' in R. Crawford, (ed.), *The Scottish Invention of English Literature* (Cambridge and New York, 1998), pp. 37–54.
93. Paul G. Bator, 'Robert Watson,' in Moran, (ed.) *Eighteenth-Century British and American Rhetorics*, pp. 244–59; J.M. Suderman, 'The Context of George Campbell's *Philosophy of Rhetoric*: A New Perspective,' *Eighteenth-Century Scotland*, 9 (1995), 9–11.
94. *CR*, xlii (1776), 1.
95. *AR*, xxvi (1783), 125–53.
96. *GM*, liii (1783), 684.
97. Carlisle: Carlisle PL: M822, 'Essays on Various Subjects,' p. 15. This was published in Gale, *Miscellanies in Prose and Verse* (London, 1794).
98. Norfolk RO: MS4379, T138C, 'A Catalogue of Title Pages of Books Read . . . 1762–1786,' fo. 1r; *ODNB*; Trevor Fawcett, 'An Eighteenth-Century Book Club at Norwich,' *The Library*, 23 (1968), 47–50.
99. Bury: Bury AS: A.87.4 BUR, Bury Library, Minutes 1825–1848, p. 22.
100. James Raven, 'From Promotion to Proscription: Arrangements for Reading and Eighteenth-Century Libraries,' in his, Small and Tadmor, (eds.), *Practice and Representation of Reading*, pp. 191–2.
101. Edward Mangin, *Essays on the Sources of the Pleasures Received from Literary Compositions* (London and Edinburgh, 1813), pp. 1, 45–7, 48–52; Alexander Gerard, *An Essay on Taste* (London, 1759), pp. 13–30; Lord Kames, *Elements of Criticism* (Honolulu, HI, 2002), pp. 89–90.
102. Mangin, *Essays*, pp. 53, 73; Blair, *Lectures*, pp. 29–50.
103. Mangin, *Essays*, p. 9.
104. Ibid., pp. 32, 25, 76–8, 89–90.
105. Ibid., pp. 4–5; *Lives*, III, 299: 'The reader of *The Seasons* wonders that he never saw before what Thomson shews him, and that he never yet has felt what Thomson impresses.'

106. *Letters on the Improvement of the Mind: Addressed to a Lady. By Mrs Chapone. And a Father's Legacy to His Daughters. By Dr Gregory* (London, 1808), p. vii; Pearson, pp. 46–9.
107. J. Aikin, *Letters from a Father to his Son on Various Topics Relative to Literature and the Conduct of Life*, 2 vols (London, 1806), I, 289; Pearson, p. 47.
108. Aikin, *Letters*, II, 321.
109. Raven, 'Promotion to Proscription,' pp. 191–2.
110. *Directions for a Proper Choice of Authors to Form a Library* ... (London, 1766), p. 1.
111. Ibid., p. 2.
112. *Directions*, p. 12.
113. Ibid., p. 12.
114. Ibid., p. 14.
115. Ibid., pp. 41–2.
116. 'NB. All the Books mentioned in the foregoing list, may be had of John Whiston, Bookseller in Fleet-street,' the guide concluded, lest any reader still think it purely an altruistic and disinterested service to literature: Ibid., p. 44.
117. *The Oeconomist; or Englishman's Magazine*, 2 (1799), 149–54, 169–72.
118. Ibid., 350–7.
119. Ibid., 325–9.
120. William Goodhugh, *The English Gentleman's Library Manual* ... (London, 1827), p. 22; *LJ*, p. 557.
121. Ibid., pp. 34, 40, 44.
122. Penzance: Morrab Library: MOR/LIB/1a, Minutes of Penzance Library, fos. 3r–3v.
123. Truro: Cornwall Record Office: DDX 15/1, 'Minute book, County Library Committee 1792–1849,' p. 5; *CR*, xli (1776), 193; *MR*, lv (1776), 81; *Monthly Miscellany*, iv (1776), 316.
124. *Catalogue of Books Belonging to the Wolverhampton Library* ... (Wolverhampton, 1835), p. 60; *TCM*, viii (1776), 460; *MR*, xiv (1756), 309.
125. *Catalogue of Books*, p. 92; *AR*, xxxiii (1791), 168.
126. Lord Shaftesbury, *Characteristicks of Men, Manners, Opinions, Times*, 3 vols (Indianapolis, IN, 2001), III, 149.

NOTES TO CHAPTER 3

1. *LM*, 36 (1767), 14–15, 30, 129, 204, 345, 409–15, 434, 437–8, 411–12, 618–20; Karen O'Brien, *Narratives of Enlightenment: Cosmopolitan History from Voltaire to Gibbon* (Cambridge, 1997), pp. 114–22; *New Lady's Magazine*, vi (1791), 70–4.
2. *LM*, 24 (1755), 450–1, 500.
3. Ibid., 28 (1759), 78–80, 109.
4. *Western County Magazine*, 4 (1790), 17, 68, 138–9.
5. Ibid., 6 (1792), 230, 283–4.
6. *St. James's Chronicle*, (1767), nos. 947, 952, 961.
7. Ibid., nos. 944, 956, 964.
8. Warwick: Warwickshire County RO: CR223/2, Commonplace book of John Smith, Admington, Gloucestershire, 1764- , passim; Bodl.: MS.Eng.poet.c.51, Scrapbook of Mary Madan, pp. 40, 49, 59, 73, 75.
9. Chester: Cheshire and Chester Archives and LS: DAR/J/10, Commonplace Book of John Arden, p. 63.

10. Beinecke: Speck Yc M1 760.
11. *MR*, v (n.s.) (1791), 404.
12. *LM*, 36 (1767), 646–7.
13. *St. James's Chronicle* (1767), no. 1061.
14. *LM*, 36 (1767), 129.
15. R. Trench, 'The Discovery of Scotland,' in his *Travellers in Britain* (London, 1990), pp. 165–90; Katherine Haldane Grenier, *Tourism and Identity in Scotland, 1770–1914: Creating Caledonia* (Aldershot, 2005), esp. cap. 1.
16. Jean Viviès, *English Travel Narratives in the Eighteenth Century: Exploring Genres*, trans. Claire Davidson (Aldershot, 2002).
17. *The Literary Life of the Late Thomas Pennant, Esq., By Himself* (London, 1793), p. 13.
18. Thomas Pennant, *A Tour of Scotland in 1769*, 3rd edition (Warrington, 1774; repr. Perth, 1979), pp. 52, 56–7, 123–4, 125–7, 155, 232.
19. *Monthly Miscellany*, ii (1774), 93.
20. *CR*, xli (1776), 416. Subsequent extracts are at *CR*, xlii (1776), 54, 93, 170, 248 and 345. For Pennant's first volume, see ibid. xxxiii (1772), 14, and xxxviii (1774), 17.
21. MS Eng 767, Felicia Dorothea (Browne) Hemans, Commonplace book, courtesy of Houghton Library, Harvard College Library, fo. 85v; Thomas Pennant, *A Tour in Scotland and Voyage to the Hebrides* (Chester, 1774), p. 346.
22. 'Commonplace Book of the Reverend James Franks . . . ,' fo. 29v; Pennant, *Voyage to the Hebrides*, 2 vols, 2nd edition (London, 1776), I, 10–11.
23. 'Liber memorandorum et referentiarum . . . ,' fo. 23v; Pennant, *Tour*, p. 98.
24. *A Catalogue of the Books Belonging to the Portico-Library, Mosley-Street, Manchester* (Manchester, 1810), p. 53.
25. Bradford: West Yorkshire AS: 42D81/1/2/1/3, 'Minutes of Meetings of the Subscribers,' fo. 10v.
26. Samuel Johnson and James Boswell, *A Journey to the Western Islands of Scotland and The Journal of a Tour to the Hebrides*, (ed.), Peter Levi (Harmondsworth, 1984), p. 166.
27. Ibid., p. 42.
28. Ibid., pp. 37–9, 42–4.
29. Ibid., p. 35.
30. 'Liber memorandorum et referentiarum . . . ,' fos. 23v, 53r.
31. Johnson and Boswell, *Journey* and *Journal*, p. 151.
32. Ibid., pp. 170–1, 172–5, 176–8, 198–200, 400–1, 407.
33. Preston: Lancashire Record Office: DDX 274/7, Memorandum Book of John Dickenson, fos. 4r–4v; Johnson and Boswell, *Journey* and *Journal*, p. 162n.
34. SUL: MS. 017, Anonymous commonplace book, 1751–1822, fos. 1r–1v.
35. David Nokes, *Jane Austen: A Life* (London, 1998), pp. 184–5.
36. *CR*, xlii (1776), 87.
37. *Monthly Miscellany*, iii (1775), 67.
38. Leith Davis, *Acts of Union: Scotland and the Literary Negotiation of the British Nation 1707–1830* (Palo Alto, CA, 1998), p. 15.
39. Tobias Smollett, *The Expedition of Humphry Clinker*, (ed.) P. Miles (London, 1993), pp. 237–40.
40. *AR*, xxxiii (1791), 182.
41. *TCM*, iii (1771), 317.
42. *CR*, xxxii (1771), 88.
43. *ML*, ii (1774–5), 262–1 (quotation at 261); Sher, pp. 363–5.
44. Christine Ferdinand, 'Constructing the Frameworks of Desire: How Newspapers Sold Books in the Seventeenth and Eighteenth Centuries,' in Joad

Raymond, (ed.), *News, Newspapers, and Society in Early Modern Britain* (London and Portland, OR, 1999), pp. 157–75.

45. Sher, p. 363.
46. Ibid., pp. 380–1.
47. *Catalogue of Standard Books on Sale . . . at the Shop of Richardson and Handford . . . Market-Place, Derby* (Derby, 1823), pp. 5, 10, 23, 24, 26.
48. John Feather, *The Provincial Book Trade in Eighteenth-Century England* (Cambridge, 1985), p. 77.
49. *The Spectator*, 15 June 1711.
50. Carlisle: Cumbria RO: In D/SEN/10/Box197, Early nineteenth-century commonplace book, pp. 108, 172, 182.
51. Leeds: Brotherton Library, University of Leeds: MS. 76, 'Diary of Isaac Stockton Clark,' fo. 5v.
52. Lowestoft: Suffolk RO: ES 185/3/3, 'Rough list of books and plays, 1807.'
53. Hertford: Hertfordshire Archives and LS: D/EB650/F3, 'Book Containing daily Occurrences. 12th of Octr 1819,' fo. 6v.
54. Walpole: 'Walpole's Newspaper Cuttings,' p. 1.
55. Beinecke: Uncat. MS Vault 757, anonymous (E.D.), 'The Last Memorandum Book' (1754–55), pp. 16, 55, 98.
56. Whitehaven: Cumbria RO: In D/CU/1/18, Charles Curwen, 'Copy Books of Poetry and Prose in French and English.'
57. Leicester: RO for Leicestershire, Leicester and Rutland: P40.
58. Altick, p. 58.
59. Kendal: Cumbria RO: WDB/63/3a, 'Day Book of Abraham Dent,' p. 16; T.S. Willan, *An Eighteenth-Century Shopkeeper: Abraham Dent of Kirkby Stephen* (Manchester, 1969).

NOTES TO CHAPTER 4

1. Allan, *"Nation of Readers,"* cap 2.
2. Pulborough Reading Society book, 1807- , fo. 1r.
3. Oxford: Oxfordshire RO: Budd. XIV/2, 'Rules of the Woodstock Book Society.'
4. Beinecke: Osborn Shelves c.173, 'Botesdale Book Society, list of members, books, borrowings etc. (1778–89),' fo. 1r; Durham: Durham County RO: D/HH/10/2/1, Barnard Castle Book Society: Account Book and Subscription Book 1819–1831, fo. 1r.
5. C. Frederick Lawrence, 'Early Cheshire Book Clubs,' *Cheshire Notes and Queries*, no. 24 (1899), 83.
6. *An Alphabetical And a Classed Catalogue of the Subscription Library, York . . .* (York, 1823), pp. xviii–xxv.
7. *A Catalogue of the Books Belonging to the Society of the Norwich Public Library* (Norwich, 1792), pp. 13–20.
8. *A Catalogue of the Present Collection of Books in the Liverpool Library*, pp. 12–15; St Clair, p. 667; *A Catalogue of the Library of The Athenaeum, Liverpool* (Liverpool, 1820).
9. *Laws and Regulations of a Subscription Library, at Whitby . . .* (Whitby, 1789), pp. 16, 18.
10. Matlock: Derbyshire RO: D307/A11, 'Hartington Union Book Society: Account Book 1787–1805.'
11. Leicester: RO for Leicestershire, Leicester and Rutland: DE3077/1, Records of Kibworth and Harborough Book Society, 1772- . fos. 30v, 35v.

12. Sheffield: Sheffield Archives, MD2221/1, Sheffield Book Society records, fos. 12r, 14v, 24v, 26v, 30r, 32v.
13. Penzance: Morrab Library: MOR/PEN/23, Penzance Ladies' Book Club, rules and minutes, 1770- , fos. 1v-2r.
14. *Jane Austen's Letters to Her Sister Cassandra and Others*, (ed.), R.W. Chapman, 2nd edition (London, 1969), pp. 294, 304.
15. *Catalogue of the Books Belonging to the Permanent Library, Lichfield* (Lichfield, 1815), pp. iii–iv.
16. *Catalogue of the Books Belonging to the Lewes Library Society . . .* (Lewes, 1827), p. iv and endpaper; Pearson, pp. 160–2.
17. *A Catalogue of the Books Belonging to the Nottingham Artisans' Library . . .* (Nottingham, 1824); *Catalogue of Books in the Subscription Library, Instituted in Blackburn, March 12th 1770 . . .* (Blackburn, 1825), p. xi.
18. *An Account of the Liverpool Mechanics and Apprentices' Library . . .* (Liverpool, 1824), p. 24; Mabel Tylecote, *The Mechanics Institutes of Lancashire and Yorkshire before 1851* (Manchester, 1957), esp. pp. 31–2, 53–6, 226; Steven Shapin and Barry Barnes, 'Science, Nature and Control: Interpreting Mechanics' Institutes,' *Social Studies of Science*, 7 (1977), 31–74.
19. William Heaton, *The Old Soldier, The Wandering Lover; and Other Poems . . .* (London, 1857), p. xviii–xix.
20. Newcastle upon Tyne: Robinson Library, University of Newcastle upon Tyne: Hospital Archives 16, 'Medical Society, minutes 1795–1800,' Rules 1, 2 and 8.
21. *Rules of the Nottingham Medical Book Society . . .* (Nottingham, 1828), pp. 3–6.
22. Ibid., p. 9.
23. *Catalogue of the Sunderland Medical Library . . .* (Sunderland, 1820), pp. 11, 12, 13.
24. Nottingham: Nottinghamshire Archives: D463/22, 'Newark Book Society: Rules and Orders, Catalogues of Books, 1779–89,' fos. 49v, 50v.
25. Ibid., fos. 51v, 68v.
26. Lancaster: Lancaster PL: MS. 144, 'Minutes of the Amicable Society, Lancaster, 1769–1785,' 26 Jun. 1771, 16 Jan. 1774; Allan, 'Private Subscription Libraries,' 61–3.
27. Elizabeth Sparrow and Maurice Smelt, eds, *The Penzance Library: Celebration Essays . . .* (Penzance, 1988) , p. 5.
28. Altick, p. 60.
29. *Rules for the Regulation of the Carlisle Library*, p. iii.
30. Alston.
31. *Catalogue of Books belonging to the Subscription Library in Shrewsbury . . .* (Shrewsbury, 1812), p. 13; *Rules and Regulations of the Hereford Permanent Library . . .* (Hereford, 1815), p. 6.
32. Peter Hoare, 'Nottingham Subscription Library: Its Origins, its Collection and its Management over 175 Years,' in Rosalys T. Coope and Jane Y. Corbett, (eds.), *Bromley House 1752–1991: Four Essays Celebrating the 175th Anniversary of the Formation of the Nottingham Subscription Library* (Nottingham, 1991), p. 11.
33. Lincoln, Lincolnshire Archives, DAUB II/5: *Rules and Orders of the Book-Club Society, at Market-Rasen* (n.p., n.d.).
34. Lord Shaftesbury, *Characteristicks of Men, Manners, Opinions, Times*, 2 vols (Oxford, 1999), I, 39.
35. Matlock: Derbyshire RO: D5047/1, 'Journal of the Literary and Philosophical Society of Derby, 1808- ,' p. 3; *Rules and Catalogue of the Library*

Belonging to the Derby Philosophical Society (Derby, 1835); Sturges, 'Context for Library History.'

36. 'Journal,' p. 15.
37. *Account*, pp. 3–4.
38. *Arranged Catalogue of the Library of the Literary and Philosophical Society of Newcastle Upon Tyne* . . . (Newcastle, 1819), pp. vii, 177–82.
39. *Laws of the Society for Promoting Useful Knowledge* . . . (Cambridge, 1813), p. 7.
40. 'Minutes, 1769–1785,' 3 Dec. 1772; Allan, 'Private Subscription Libraries,' 60.
41. Lincoln: Lincolnshire Archives: MISC DON 315/2, 'Boston Literary Society. Rules,' fos. 1r–2r.
42. Hackney: Hackney Archives Department, D/S/36/1, Hackney Literary Institution and Subscription Library, 'Minutes of the Proceedings of the Committee, Monthly, & Anniversary Meetings,' 1815–17, fos 1r, 4r, 6r.
43. Ibid., fo. 13r.
44. Ibid., fos. 31v-32r.
45. *Questions proposed by a Society established in 1810* (Sheffield, 1820), pp. 6, 7, 8, 11.
46. Allan, *"Nation of Readers,"* cap. 5; *The Parochial Libraries of the Church of England* . . . [(ed.) Neil Ker] (London, 1959).
47. Norwich: Millenium Library: FAK 017.2.
48. Lichfield: Staffordshire and Stoke-on-Trent AS: B/A/22/7, 'Catalogue of the Parochial Library at Stone, Co. Stafford, 21 Oct 1765.'
49. Paul Kaufman, 'Coleridge's Use of Cathedral Libraries,' *Modern Language Notes*, 75 (1960), 395–9; Elizabeth Brunskill, *Eighteenth-Century Reading* . . . (York, 1950), pp. 14–20; Paul Kaufman, 'Readers and Their Reading in Eighteenth-Century Lichfield,' *The Library*, 28 (1973), 108–15.
50. *Catalogue of Books from Parochial Libraries in Shropshire* (London, 1971); *Suffolk Parochial Libraries: A Catalogue* (London, 1977).
51. *Catalogue of Books in the Library of the Parish Church of St Owen, Bromham, Bedfordshire* (n.p., 1959), p. 2.
52. Paul Kaufman, 'New Light from Parochial Libraries,' in his *Libraries and Their Users* (London, 1969), pp. 93–101 (quotation at p. 94).
53. *Parochial Libraries*, p. 17.
54. *Bibliothecae Ecclesiae Cirestrensis Librorum* . . . (Cicestriae, MDCCCLXXI); Chichester: West Sussex RO: Cap. I/51/17, Photocopy of Catalogue of Chichester Cathedral Library, fo. 53r et seq.
55. Kaufman, 'Community Library,' 35, 38–40; Phillip G. Lindley, *The Town Library of Leicester* (Upton, 1975); *Parochial Libraries*, p. 16; Alston.
56. Gwendolen Woodward and R.A. Christophers, *The Chained Library of the Royal Grammar School, Guildford: Catalogue* . . . (Guildford, 1972), Preface; *Bibliothecae Colfanae Catalogus* . . . (Lewisham, 1831), p. xxxv.
57. *The Old Church and School Libraries of Lancashire*, ed. by Richard Copley Christie (Manchester, 1885), pp. 167–8.
58. *Parochial Libraries*, pp. 8–24.
59. Alston.
60. *A Catalogue of the Standfast Library* (Nottingham, 1817), pp. iii–v.
61. *A Catalogue of the Library Belonging to the Norfolk and Norwich Clerical Society* . . . (Norwich, 1838).
62. *A Catalogue of the Ashbourne Moral and Religious Permanent Library* (Derby, 1823), p. iii.
63. *Catalogue of Books Belonging to the Church and King Library at Bolton* . . . (Bolton, 1837), pp. 17, 35, 53.

64. Lewes: East Sussex RO: AMS 6034/1, 'Northiam Unitarian Chapel Church Book,' passim.
65. East Sussex RO: NU1 6/1: Westgate Unitarian Chapel, 'Vestry Library, minute book, 1808–1818'; *Catalogue of the Congregational Library at the Unitarian Chapel, Portsmouth* (n.p., 1823).
66. *Norwich: Octagon Chapel—Catalogue of Vestry Library* (Norwich, 1825), p. 3.
67. E.g. Aylesbury: Centre for Buckinghamshire Studies: NQ2/22/2, 'An Account of Books belonging to the Monthly Meeting of Friends of the Upperside in the County of Bucks, 1799.'
68. *A Catalogue of Books Belonging to the Methodist Subscription Library* (Yarmouth, 1832).
69. Bristol: Bristol RO: 30251/Bd/51, Broadmead Vestry Library records 1820–7, fo. 1r.
70. *Rules and Catalogue of the Subscription Library, Established at the Independent Chapel, Blackburn* . . . (Blackburn, 1827), p. 3.
71. *A Catalogue of the Books belonging to the Library of the New Jerusalem Temple, Percy Street, Newcastle* . . . (Newcastle, 1836), p. 2.
72. Altick, pp. 213–4.
73. Herbert E. Reynolds, 'Our Cathedral Libraries: Their History, Contents and Uses,' *Transactions and Proceedings of the First Annual Meeting of the Library Association. . . . 1878* (London, 1879), p. 38.
74. *Parochial Libraries*, p. 13.
75. *Bibliothecae Ecclesiae Cirestrensis*, p. 76.
76. *An Alphabetical Catalogue of the Books in the Town Library Under the Public Grammar School, Ipswich* . . . ([Ipswich], 1799), passim; *Old Church and School Libraries of Lancashire*, pp. 167–8; Woodward and Christophers, *Chained Library*, p. 4; *A Catalogue of the Books Preserved in the Library of the Free Grammar School, of Elizabeth, Queen of England, In Faversham* (Faversham, 1865), p. 18; *Catalogue of Books in the Library of the Free Grammar School, Leeds* (Leeds, 1840), p. 11.
77. Kaufman, *Reading Vogues*, pp. 57, 58, 59, 61.
78. *Parochial Libraries in Shropshire*, passim.
79. Ibid.
80. Beinecke: Osborn Shelves c.514, 'A Catalogue of Books Left at Norbury,' fo. 14r.
81. *Catalogue of . . . the Methodist Subscription Library*, pp. 8–9.
82. *Catalogue of Brunswick Library* . . . (Liverpool, 1805), pp. 27, 39.
83. Newcastle upon Tyne: Tyne and Wear AS: 1041/6, Brunswick Chapel Library, minute book 1808- , pp. 4, 6, 7, 17.
84. *Catalogue of . . . Unitarian Chapel, Portsmouth*, pp. 2, 46–8, 62, 84, 85, 111–12.
85. Alston.
86. John A. Leatherland, *Essays and Poems* (London, 1862), pp. 9–16.
87. *MM*, 11 (1801), 238.
88. *Catalogue of Books Belonging to Edward Banks's Circulating Library, Cockermouth* (n.p., n.d); *Catalogue of Brown's Circulating Library* . . . (Wigan, 1821).
89. *Catalogue of the Books in Marriott's Subscription Library* . . . (Stafford, 1795).
90. Altick, p. 62; Kaufman, 'Community Library,' p. 11.
91. *The Shaftesbury Subscription Library for Circulation and Reference* . . . (Shaftesbury, 1827), fos. 1r-1v.
92. *A Catalogue of Lansdown's Circulating-Library. . . .* (Bristol, 1807), p. 3.

93. Alston; St Clair, pp. 349–50.
94. *Wallis's Royal Edition, Patronized by the Queen. Brighton As It Is . . .* (Brighton, n.d.), p. 41.
95. Ibid., pp. 41–2.
96. Ibid., p. 43.
97. Ibid., p. 43.
98. *Moore's Subscription Library and Newsroom* (Buxton, 1826), eg. pp. 7, 8, 10, 11, 20, 28, 31.
99. *A Catalogue of Books in the Library of the Assembly News Rooms in Newcastle* (Newcastle, 1842), pp. 4, 6.
100. Richard Sheridan, *The Rivals*, (ed.), Elizabeth Duthie (London, 1979), p. 26.
101. Bath: Bath Central Library: B027.3, 'Marshall's Library, List of Subscribers, 1793–9.'
102. Cheltenham: Cheltenham Library: 639027.5, 'Subscription Book to Williams's Library for One Lady or Gentleman,' fos. 13v, 28r, 31v.
103. Kaufman, 'Community Library,' 20–1, 62; Pearson, pp. 162–9.
104. Surrey History Centre: 1534/6, 'Inventory of the Stock in Trade, Working Tools, &c. of the Late Mr Samuel Russell, taken May 12th 1829.'
105. Fergus, 'Eighteenth-Century Readers'; idem., *Provincial Readers.*
106. Stewart-Murphy, *British Circulating Libraries*, esp. p. 20; Kaufman, 'Community Library,' passim; Allan, "Nation of Readers," cap. 4.
107. *Catalogue of J. & S. Waters' Circulating Library . . .* (Kettering, 1813), pp. 6, 10.
108. *Catalogue of Collinson's Circulating Library . . .* (Wirksworth, 1805), pp. 18, 21.
109. *Shaftesbury Subscription Library*, fo. 1r.
110. *Catalogue of C.N. Wright's New Circulating Library . . .* (Nottingham, [1821]), pp. 19, 22.
111. Feather, *Provincial Book Trade*, p. 41.
112. *Catalogue of Brown's Circulating Library . . .* pp. 8, 9.
113. Frank Beckwith, 'The Eighteenth-Century Proprietary Library in England,' *Journal of Documentation*, 3 (1947–8), 81–98 (at 82n).

NOTES TO CHAPTER 5

1. *LJ*, p. 805; *Horace Walpole's Correspondence: Volume 33*, (ed.), W.S. Lewis (London, 1965), p. 136.
2. *Bibliotheca Beauclerkiana. A Catalogue of the Large and Valuable Library of the Late Honourable Topham Beauclerk. . .* (London, [1781]).
3. ODNB.
4. Malcolm Warner, Julia Marciari Alexander and Patrick McCaughey, *This Other Eden: Paintings from the Yale Center for British Art* (New Haven, CT, 1998), p. 106.
5. *Bibliotheca Beauclerkiana*, (Part I): pp. 110, 181–2; (Part II): pp. 81, 84.
6. Ibid., (Part I): p. 217; (Part II): p. 123.
7. Ibid., (Part I): p. 117; (Part II): pp. 6, 97, 106–7, 121–3, 134.
8. Ibid., (Part II): pp. 48, 79, 122.
9. *MR*, v (n.s.) (1791), 403.
10. *Bibliotheca Beauclerkiana*, (Part II): p. 123. Other individuals who possessed Arnot's work included William Orde-Powlett, 2nd Baron Bolton, who lived at Hackwood in Hampshire, and Revd Michael Lort, chaplain to the Archbishop of Canterbury: see Winchester: Hampshire RO: 1/M49/208,

Hackwood Library Catalogue, 1828, p. 26; *A Catalogue of the Entire and Valuable Library of the Late Rev. Michael Lort. . .* (London, 1791), p. 36.

11. Johnson and Boswell, *Journey* and *Journal*, p. 217.
12. *Bibliotheca Beauclerkiana*, (Part I): pp. 186–7, 201, 203.
13. *MR*, v (n.s.) (1791), 181.
14. Arnold Hunt, 'The Sale of Richard Heber's Library,' in Robin Myers, Michael Harris and Giles Mandelbrote, (eds.), *Under the Hammer: Book Auctions Since the Seventeenth Century* (New Castle DE, and London, 2001), pp. 143–172.
15. *Catalogue of the Curious and Distinguished Library of the Late Reverend and Learned Thomas Crofts. . .* (London, 1783); *Catalogue of a Valuable and Curious Collection of. . . the Late Rev. Thomas Clarke, D.D. . .* (York, 1798);
16. Ibid., pp. 91, 114.
17. *Catalogue of Mr E. Rhodes' Valuable Library. . .* (Sheffield, 1828), pp. 6–7.
18. *Catalogue of. . . the Late Rev. Francis Gisborne. . .* (Chesterfield, 1822), pp. 9, 14.
19. *Catalogue of the Valuable. . . Property of W.B. Thomas Esq.. . .* (Chesterfield, 1826), pp. 34, 36.
20. *Catalogue of [an] Extensive Sale. . . on the Premises of John Longden, Esq., Ashbourne. . .* (Ashbourne, 1827), pp. 50, 53, 55.
21. Henry Fielding, *Tom Jones*, (ed.), R.P.C. Mutter (Harmondsworth, 1987), p. 148.
22. Huntingdon: Cambridgeshire RO: 1876/28/1, 'Catalogue of Books Belonging to Mr C. Beauchamp. 1793,' passim. One book that actually belonged to Beauchamp, still bearing his characteristic bookplate, is in the British Library. With pressmark BL 1164.l.4 (1–2), it is a miscellaneous volume titled simply *Poetical Works* (London, 1793–4), and, coincidentally, includes the only published compositions of another provincial reader whom we know, Gustavus Gale of Carlisle.
23. Simon Jervis, 'The English Country House Library: An Architectural History,' *Library History*, 18 (2002), 175–90.
24. Beinecke: Osborn Shelves c.131, 'Mentor, or the True Guide to Wisdom. . . by the Revd Jas. Ashton. . . ', p. 62. See also Henry Petroski, *The Book on the Book Shelf* (New York, 1999) and David McKitterick, 'Bibliography, Bibliophily, and the Organization of Knowledge,' in David Vaisey and his (eds.), *The Foundations of Scholarship: Libraries and Collecting, 1650–1750* (Los Angeles, 1992), pp. 29–61.
25. *HP(2)*, II, 438.
26. Kendal: Cumbria AS: WD/Ry Box 5, 'Catalogue of Books in the Drawing Room,' fos. 1r-1v; *GM*, xl (1777), 497.
27. *CR*, lxiv (1777), 280.
28. Warwickshire RO: CR895/49, 'Inventory of the Furniture and Effects at Grove Park Bequeathed as Heir Looms by The Rt. Hon. Charles Lord Dormer, 1819,' fo. 17r.
29. 'Inventory. . . at Grove Park,' fos. 25r, 25v, 26r.
30. Hackwood Library Catalogue, 1828, pp. 58, 65, 66.
31. *HP(2)*, II, 635.
32. Chelmsford: Essex RO: D/DQs40, 'Catalogue of the Library of Filmer Honywood Esqr. . . ', pp. 1, 11, 13, 18, 21.
33. *Comp. Bar.*, III, 32.
34. Northampton: Northamptonshire RO: L(C) 1444, 'Catalogue of Library at Cottesbrooke Hall, 1791,' fos. 1r, 14r, 14v, 50r, 53r.
35. *GM*, liii (1783), 418.

36. James Raven, *Judging New Wealth: Popular Publishing and Responses to Commerce in England 1750–1800* (Oxford, 1992), pp. 57–8.
37. Leeds: Brotherton Library, University of Leeds: MS. 500, 'A Commonplace Book of Mary Cowgill. . . . ,' *passim*.
38. Oxford: Oxfordshire RO: Parrott II/114, 'An Inventory of. . . Mrs Sarah Long.. . . March 1797,' p. 20.
39. Chelmsford: Essex RO: D/DU 676/1, Journal of William Barnard of Harlow Bury Farm, 1807–1823, inside back cover; Brewer, *Pleasures*, pp. 169–70.
40. William Dodd, *The Factory System Illustrated*. . . (London, 1842), p. 288.
41. Walpole Library: shelfmarks 49 3185 and 4to 813 753B; *Comp. Peer.*, III, 195, 283.
42. Walpole: 'Catalogue of the Library of the Right Honble. Earl of Chesterfield. . . taken in June 1778'; *Comp. Peer.*, III, 182–5.
43. Whitehaven: Cumbria RO: In D/DA/35.
44. Nottinghamshire Archives: DD/CH/24/22, Will of John Randle of Breaston.
45. Centre for Buckinghamshire Studies: D138/16/5/1, Commonplace and letter book of the Russell family, 1715–1751, fos. 7r, 15r.
46. Hertford: Hertfordshire Archives and LS: In D/EGd E9, lists of books.
47. Bristol RO: Commonplace books of Lieut. Hopper, 89th Regt: 12453(1), fo. 21v; 12453(3), fos. 26r-27r; 12453(6), fos. 8v-9v.
48. Sheffield Archives: Wh.M. 135/3, 'Catalogue of Lady Mary Wortley's Books Packed Up to be Sent Abroad, July 1739,' pp. 2–3; Robert Halsband, *The Life of Mary Wortley Montagu* (Oxford, 1956).
49. Gloucester: Gloucestershire RO: In D45/F39, 'Catalogue of Mr Whitmore's Books, 1st of Jany 1786,' fos. 6v, 7r, 8r, 8v, 13r.
50. Amy Cruse, *The Englishman and His Books in the Early Nineteenth Century* (London, 1930), pp. 14–15; William Makepeace Thackeray, *The Newcomes* (ed.), Arthur Pendennis, 2 vols (London, 1911), I, 51.
51. Purcell, 'Country House Library,' 161.
52. Beinecke: Osborn MSS file 433, Dr John Ash to Sir Joseph Banks, undated, but after 1787.
53. Beinecke: Osborn MSS file 17945, Charles Burney to J.W. Callcott, 30 Oct. 1799.
54. David Vincent, *Bread, Knowledge and Freedom: A Study of Nineteenth-Century Working Class Autobiography* (London, 1981), p. 117; Brewer, *Pleasures*, pp. 186–7.
55. *A Narrative of the Life and Adventures of William Brown*. . . (York, 1829), p. 140.
56. Robert Southey, *Attempts in Verse, By John Jones, An Old Servant* (London, 1831), p. 173.
57. Chester L. Shaver and Alice C. Shaver, eds, *Wordsworth's Library: A Catalogue* (New York and London, 1979), pp. xxiii–xxv.
58. Beverley: East Riding of Yorkshire RO: DDCC/150/58, 'List of Books Lent to Mr de Villedeuil by Mr Constable.'
59. Hertford: Hertfordshire Archives and LS: D/EB650/F3, 'Book containing daily Occurrences. 12th of Octr 1819,' fo. 8r.
60. Naomi Tadmor, 'In the Even My Wife Read to Me: Women, Reading and Household Life in the Eighteenth Century,' in Raven, Small and her (eds.), *Practice and Representation*, pp. 162–74 (at p. 165); Pearson, pp. 170–5.
61. Jane Austen, *Mansfield Park*, (ed.), Kathryn Sutherland (Harmondsworth, 2003), p. 314. The author herself, according to her brother Henry, was an enthusiastic and accomplished practitioner of reading aloud to family and friends, 'with very great taste and effect': Jane Austen, *Northanger Abbey*, (ed.), Anne Ehrenpreis (Harmondsworth, 1985), p. 32.

62. Beinecke: Osborn MSS File 17834, AL of Henrietta Maria Bowdler to Mrs Pares, 5 Sept. 1812, fo. 1v.
63. Mary Wollstonecraft, *The Female Reader* (London, 1789), p. v; Cruse, *Englishman and His Books*, p. 116.
64. Lancaster PL: MS. 8752-3, Mary Chorley's diaries, 1778, passim.
65. Ibid., passim; Amanda Vickery, *The Gentleman's Daughter: Women's Lives in Georgian England* (New Haven, CT, 2003), p. 378.
66. *Comp. Bar.*, V, 139.
67. Reading: Berkshire RO: D/EX 1306/1, Diary of Lady East, 1791-2, passim.
68. *CR*, lxiv (1777), 101.
69. Tadmor, 'In the Even My Wife Read to Me,' esp. pp. 165-7; *The Commonplace Book of William Byrd II of Westover*, (ed.), Kevin Berland, Jan Kirsten Gilliam and Kenneth A. Lockridge (Chapel Hill, NC, and London, 2001), p. 5n. Tillotson was the very embodiment of the uplifting and uncontentious Anglican sermoniser: the point is transformed into humour by Fielding who has Square relate to Thwackum that there had been 'a very devout woman, who out of pure regard to religion, stole Tillotson's Sermons from a lady of her acquaintance': *Tom Jones*, p. 145.
70. Alison M. Scott, '"This Cultivated Mind": Reading and Identity in a Nineteenth-Century Reader,' in Barbara Ryan and Amy M. Thomas, (eds.), *Reading Acts: United States Readers' Interactions with Literature, 1800-1950* (Knoxville, TN, 2002), pp. 29-52 (quotation at p. 32).
71. Mary Chorley's diaries, 1776-8, passim.
72. Berkshire RO: D/Enm2 C5, AL from Elizabeth Montagu to Matthew Montagu, 20 July 1803; *HP(2)*, III, 157.
73. Cruse, *Englishman and His Books*, pp. 31-2
74. Ibid. p. 75.
75. John Ruskin, *Praeterita* (Oxford, 1978), pp. 52-3.
76. Liverpool: Sydney Jones Library, University of Liverpool: MS.3.62, Liverpool Literary and Philosophical Society: bound unpublished papers read before the Society [1812-27], no. 4, pp. 1-2.
77. Ibid., no. 5, pp. 1-2, 4, 10-11, 13.
78. Altick, p. 252.
79. George Spater, *William Cobbett: The Poor Man's Friend* (London, 1982), p. 18.
80. *The Life of John Strickland*. . . 2nd edition (London, n.d.), p. 19.
81. Dodd, *Factory System*, p. 289.
82. Warwickshire County RO: CR464/145/2, Notebook belonging to Letitia Napier, 1798- , fo. 14r; *Landed Gentry of Great Britain*, (ed.), Sir Bernard Burke (London, 1914), p. 1381.
83. Hertfordshire Archives and LS: D/EHx/F33, 'Continuation of the Extracts from the Encyclopaedia Britannica, vol. xvii part1,' passim.
84. BL: shelfmark 1609/3963.
85. *LJ*, p. 917.
86. William Godwin, *The Enquirer. Reflections on Education, Manners and Literature*. . . (Philadelphia, 1797), p. 116.

NOTES TO CHAPTER 6

1. Anthony Grafton, *Joseph Scaliger: A Study in the History of Classical Scholarship. Vol. I: Textual Criticism and Exegesis* (Oxford, 1983); idem., 'Is the History of Reading a Marginal Enterprise?: Guillaume Budé and His Books,' *Papers of the Bibliographical Society of America*, 91 (1997), 139-57.

2. Anthony Grafton and Lisa Jardine, '"Studied for Action": How Gabriel Harvey Read His Livy,' *Past and Present*, 129 (1990), 30–78.
3. Robert C. Evans, *Jonson, Lipsius and the Politics of Renaissance Stoicism* (Durango, CO, 1992); William H. Sherman, *John Dee: The Politics of Reading and Writing in the Renaissance* (Amherst, MA, 1995); Kevin Sharpe, *Reading Revolutions: The Politics of Reading in Early Modern England* (New Haven, CT, 2000).
4. *Collected Works of Samuel Taylor Coleridge: Marginalia I: Abbt to Byfield*, (ed.), George Whalley (Princeton, NJ, and London, 1980), p. lvii.
5. *Thraliana: The Diary of Mrs Hester Lynch Thrale (Later Mrs Piozzi)*, 2 vols, (ed.), K.C. Balderstone (Oxford, 1942), p. 780.
6. *Piozzi Marginalia: Comprising Some Extracts from Manuscripts of Hester Lynch Piozzi and Annotations from Her Books*, (ed.), E.P. Merritt (Cambridge, MA, 1925); Hester Piozzi, *The Life of Samuel Johnson, LL.D., by James Boswell, with Marginal Comments from Two Copies Annotated by Hester Thrale Lynch Piozzi*, (ed.), E.G. Fletcher, 3 vols (New York, 1963).
7. R.C. Alston, *Books with Manuscript: A Short-Title Catalogue of Books with Manuscript Notes in the British Library . . .* (London, 1994); H.R. Luard, *Catalogue of Adversaria and Printed Books Containing MS. Notes, Preserved in the Library of the University of Cambridge* (Cambridge, 1864); Steven Zwicker, 'Reading the Margins: Politics and the Habits of Appropriation,' in Kevin Sharpe and his (eds.), *Refiguring Revolutions: Aesthetics and Politics from the English Revolution to the Romantic Revolution* (Berkeley, CA, 1998), pp. 101–15; W.E. Slights, 'The Edifying Margins of Renaissance English Books,' *Renaissance Quarterly*, 42 (1989), 682–716; H.J. Jackson, *Marginalia: Readers Writing in Books* (New Haven, CT, and London, 2001).
8. Jackson, *Marginalia*, pp. 18–44; Roger Stoddard, *Marks in Books* (Cambridge, MA, 1985).
9. *Comp. Peer.*, IX, 792; XII, 782–5.
10. RO for Leicestershire, Leicester and Rutland: DG7 Lit. 13, Notes on Burnet's History of His Own Time. For the source, see Gilbert Burnet, *History of His Own Times*, 2 vols (London, 1724–34), I, 538.
11. 'Notes on Burnet's History'; Burnet, *History*, I, 390.
12. Maidstone: Centre for Kentish Studies: U194 F9/2, Commonplace Book of Revd J.E. Gambier, 1789- .
13. BL: C.61.b.6 (1), p. 1.
14. Ibid., p. 11.
15. Ibid., as pp. 122, 141.
16. Ibid., p. 1.
17. BL: 530.g.4, passim.
18. E.H. Butler, *The Story of British Shorthand* (London, 1951), pp. 70–83.
19. John Kerrigan, 'The Editor as Reader: Constructing Renaissance Texts,' in Raven, Small and Tadmor, (eds.), *Practice and Representation*, p. 60.
20. Charles and Mary Anne Lamb, *Letters*, (ed.), E.W. Morris Jr. (Ithaca, NY, 1975), I, 79.
21. Chetham's: W.6.32, p. 459.
22. Chetham's: W.6.28, p. 64.
23. Bodleian: BOD DD35,36 Jur., Vol. I, 2.
24. Ibid., Vol. I, 5.
25. Ibid., Vol. I, 46.
26. Ibid., Vol. I, 47.
27. Ibid., Vol. I, 13–14.
28. BL: 11805.m.6.

29. Ibid., I, 4–5.
30. *ODNB.*
31. BL: 1509/822, pp. 303, 156.
32. BL: 773.1.31, pp. 253, 294.
33. Ibid., p. 265.
34. Exeter: Exeter Cathedral Library: EML/MON 1826586 and EML/HUN 1199832.
35. Ibid., p. 2.
36. Exeter Cathedral Library: EML/SYN 1738873, pp. 88, 347.
37. Exeter Cathedral Library: EML/SYN 1738865, pp. 186–7, 237–8.
38. Michael Worton and Judith Still, (eds.), *Intertextuality: Theories and Practices* (Manchester, 1990).
39. Exeter Cathedral Library: EML/TRA/18/1926254, p. 16.
40. Ibid., p. 22.
41. Sher, *Church and University*, pp. 57–60.
42. Providence, RI: John Hay Library, Brown University: YQE.W77e Lamont, pp. iii, iv, x.
43. Ibid., p. 41.
44. BL: 1078.g.20. Owner's mark on flyleaf.
45. Ibid., pp. 2, 11, 24, 87, 105, 162.
46. BL: G.11387, pp. 4–6, 9, 11.
47. Ibid., p. 77. A nice parallel to Shenstone's perceived need for a glossary to help with the unfamiliar vocabulary often encountered when reading Scots verse is the section 'An Explanation of ye Scotch words' noted down by Melisinda Munbee, a young Suffolk girl around 1750, after she had copied out the poem "The Scotch Wedding." See MS Eng 768 (2), Melisinda Munbee, 'A Collection of various kinds of Poetry,' courtesy of Houghton Library, Harvard College Library, fos. 12v-18v.
48. *CR*, xliii (1777), 472.
49. A later and much less perplexed admirer of early Scots verse, especially that anthologised by Ramsay, was (later Sir) Frederick Morton Eden, who as a young man in the late eighteenth century kept a commonplace book in which poems like James I's "Christ's Kirke of the Greene" and James V's "The Gaberlunzie Man" were copied down: see BL: Add. MSS 43702, 'Commonplace Book of Sir Frederick Morton Eden,' fos. 20r, 20v.
50. Beinecke: Osborn Shelves pc.124; *Letters of David Hume*, (ed.), J.Y.T. Greig, 2 vols (Oxford, 1932), II, 310.
51. Beinecke: Speck Yc M1 760.
52. *Comp. Bar.*, V, 278.
53. Walpole: 53 H882 754b.
54. Steven Zwicker, 'The Constitution of Opinion and the Pacification of Reading,' in Kevin Sharpe and his, (eds.), *Reading, Society and Politics in Early Modern England* (Cambridge, 2003), pp. 295–316 (quotation at p. 301).
55. BL: 4473.e.13(2), p. 22.
56. Ibid., p. 34.
57. *HP(2)*, 308–9.
58. Houghton Library: *fEC75 H8823H, Vol. VI, 458.
59. Ibid., Vol. III, 2.
60. Ibid., Vol. V, 244.
61. Ibid., Vol. V, 244.
62. Ibid., Vol. V, 245.
63. Walpole: 49 3185, Vol. I, 51.
64. Ibid., Vol. I, 307.
65. Kidd, *Subverting Scotland's Past*, pp. 251–3.

66. Jackson, *Marginalia*, p. 215.
67. Beinecke: Osborn Shelves pc.125.
68. Ibid., p. xvii.
69. Ibid., p. xx.
70. Ibid., p. 4.
71. Ibid., p. 111.
72. Ibid., p. 178.
73. Ibid., p. 123.
74. James L. Gifford, *Hester Lynch Piozzi (Mrs Thrale)*, 2nd edition (Oxford, 1968), pp. 91n, 106, 121, 469.
75. Beinecke: IM J637 +Zz 776, p. 29.
76. Ibid., p. 73.
77. Ibid., p. 77.
78. Ibid., p. 231.
79. Gifford, *Piozzi*, p. 284.
80. IM J637 +Zz 776, p. 94.
81. Ibid., p. 191.
82. Ibid., p. 191.
83. Gifford, *Piozzi*, pp. 336, 435.
84. Ibid., p. 121n.
85. BL: 10856.ee.9, p. ii.
86. Ibid., p. 37.
87. Ibid., p. 135.
88. Ibid., p. 173.
89. Chetham's: L.7.44, Vol. I. 351.
90. Ibid., Vol. I, 353.
91. BL: 30.f.14.
92. *Collected Works of Samuel Taylor Coleridge: Marginalia II: Camden to Hutton*, (ed.), George Whalley (Princeton, NJ, and London, 1984), pp. 1203–7.
93. BL: C.126.k.2.
94. *ODNB*.
95. BL: C.60.e.4; *Coleridge: Marginalia II*, pp. 784–91.
96. *Comp. Peer.*, VII, 569n.
97. Edinburgh: Edinburgh University Library, SC F 854–855, Vol. I, 1–27.
98. Ibid., Vol. I, 135, 147.
99. SC F854–855, Vol. I, 156–9.
100. Ibid., Vol. I, 229.
101. Ibid., Vol. I, 156.
102. Ibid., Vol. I, 208.

NOTES TO CHAPTER 7

1. Allan, 'Some Notes and Problems,' pp. 110–18; Stephen Colclough, 'Recovering the Reader: Commonplace Books and Diaries as Sources of Reading Experience,' *Publishing History*, 44 (1998), 5–37.
2. Earle Havens, *Commonplace Books: A History of Manuscripts and Printed Books from Antiquity to the Twentieth Century* (New Haven, CT, 2001); Ann Moss, *Printed Common-place Books and the Structuring of Renaissance Thought* (Oxford, 1996).
3. Ann Moss, 'The *Politica* of Justus Lipsius and the Commonplace Book,' *Journal of the History of Ideas*, 59 (1998), 421–37; Ann Blair, 'Humanist Methods in Natural Philosophy: the Commonplace Book,' *Journal of the History of Ideas*, 53 (1992), 541–51.

4. Richard Yeo, 'Ephraim Chambers' *Cyclopaedia* (1728) and the Tradition of the Commonplaces,' *Journal of the History of Ideas*, 57 (1996), 157–75.
5. P. Beal, 'Notions in Garrison: The Seventeenth-Century Commonplace Book,' in W. Speed Hill, (ed.), *New Ways of Looking at Old Texts* (Binghamton, NY, 1993), pp. 131–47.
6. G.C. Meynell, 'John Locke's Method of Common-Placing. . . . ,' *The Seventeenth Century*, 8 (1993), 245–67; Colclough, 'Recovering the Reader,' 8–9.
7. Havens, *Commonplace Books*, p. 54.
8. Moss, *Printed Common-place Books*, p. 279.
9. Beinecke: Osborn Shelves, c.139, 'A Collection of Poems, Thomas Binns, Liverpool, 1789, Vol. II'; Walpole, 'Commonplace Book of William Chute . . . ' and 'The Effusions of Fancy and Fun Compiled by Joseph Gulston, 1784'; Chetham's: A.4.85, Thomas Wilson, commonplace book; Beinecke: Osborn Shelves d.367, 'Edward Henry Columbine, commonplace book.'
10. Commonplace book of Felicia Dorothea Hemans; MS Eng. 231, Hester Thrale, 'Minced Meat for Pyes,' courtesy of Houghton Library, Harvard College Library; Beinecke: Osborn Shelves d.133, 'Anon. commonplace book,' Osborn Shelves, c.343, 'Anne Milbanke, commonplace book,' and Osborn Shelves c.116, 'Anna Maria Sharpe, commonplace book.'
11. Chichester: West Sussex RO: Add. MSS 20,187, 'Commonplace book compiled by James Dallaway . . . ,' fo. 2r.
12. Shropshire Records and Research Centre: S110/4/3, 'Diary of Edward Williams of Oswestry'; Herefordshire RO: AM79/2, 'Commonplace Book of Mrs Jane Pateshall.'
13. *MR*, v (1751), 137; ibid., xxxiii (1765), 544; ibid., xv (n.s.) (1795), 539; *GM*, xxi (1751), 574; ibid., xlix (1779), 607; ibid., xxvii (1757), 243; ibid., xlix (1779), 508.
14. Beinecke: Osborn Shelves c.94, 'James Moore, commonplace book,' fos. 16v, 17v, 107r-109v.
15. Centre for Buckinghamshire Studies: D114/61, Commonplace book of B. Howlett of Olney, 1808–51, pp. 72, 103–8.
16. Commonplace Book of Revd J.E. Gambier, 1780- , fos. 59v-60r; Kames, *Elements*, p. 12.
17. Commonplace Book of Revd J.E. Gambier, 1780- , fo. 102v; Blair, *Lectures*, p. 431.
18. Beverley: East Riding of Yorkshire RO: DDX/507/2, 'Charts, Tables and Notes on Legal, Philosophical, Theological, Mathematical etc. matters. . . . ,' p. xx.
19. Commonplace book of B. Howlett . . . , p. 159.
20. Osborn Shelves d.133, 'Anon. commonplace book,' pp. 12–13, 31–2, 88–9.
21. Warwickshire RO: CR1998/CD/Drawer 8/12, Commonplace book of Sir Charles Throckmorton, 1780- , passim.
22. 'Commonplace Book of William Chute . . . ,' pp. 64, 153, 214–5, 390. For Chute, see *HP(3)*, III, 443–4.
23. Carlisle: Cumbria RO: In D/SEN/10/Box197, Early nineteenth-century commonplace book.
24. 'A Catalogue of Title Pages of Books Read,' pp. 6–13; Fawcett, 'An Eighteenth-Century Book Club.'
25. Norfolk RO: Yarmouth Library (addnl.) D41/106, 'Commonplace Book of Thomas Sutton of Yarmouth,' no. 107.
26. 'A Catalogue of Title Pages of Books Read,' p. 89.
27. Centre for Kentish Studies: U310 F4, Notebook of G. Norman; *TCM*, iii (1771), 437.

28. Chetham's: A.3.109, William Barton, commonplace book . . . 1780–1810, fos. 1r-1v.
29. Leeds: Brotherton Library, University of Leeds: MS 17, 'Quotation or Commonplace Book, by George Ashby,' pp. 557–9.
30. BL: Stowe 1014, Commonplace Book of Thomas Astle, fos. 7r-9v.
31. BL: Stowe 1013, Commonplace book belonging to Edward Vernon—some entries in the hand of Thomas Astle, fo. 62r.
32. Bedford: Bedfordshire and Luton AS: OR2222/2, Notes on history of Elizabeth I and James I; for Astle's notes on Henry, see Commonplace book belonging to Edward Vernon, fos. 69r-76v.
33. Cambridge: Cambridgeshire RO: R58/8/14/7, Beldam commonplace book, 1778–, passim.
34. Record Office for Leicestershire, Leicester and Rutland: DG21/284.
35. Walpole: 'Walpole's Newspaper Cuttings,' p. 1.
36. Walpole: 'Newspaper Cuttings ca. 1770,' p. 109.
37. Leicester: RO for Leicestershire, Leicester and Rutland: DE718/C/6, R. Martin's commonplace book, c.1800–1820, passim.
38. Beinecke: Osborn Shelves c.35, 'Poetic Trifles, by Charles Burney,' pp. 43–6.
39. Beinecke: Osborn Shelves, c.259, 'Commonplace book of Thomas Stevens,' pp. 39–42.
40. West Sussex RO: Add MSS. 20,189, commonplace book compiled by Joseph Dalloway for Catherine A. Best, pp. 120–1. On Gregory, see Smellie, *Literary and Characteristical Lives*, pp. 1–118.
41. Brewer, *Pleasures*, pp. 107–8, 110. See also Stephen Greenblatt, *Renaissance Self-Fashioning: From More to Shakespeare* (Chicago, IL, 1980).
42. Ibid., p. 9.
43. Beinecke: Osborn Shelves fc.53, 'Anonymous commonplace book, c.1781–3,' pp. 18–19.
44. 'Anon. Commonplace book,' pp. 88–9.
45. BL: Add. MSS 45268, 'Journal and commonplace books of Charles Holte Bracebridge of Warwickshire,' fos. 31v-32r.
46. Carlisle PL: M822, 'Essays on Various Subjects,' p. 27.
47. 'Commonplace Book of William Chute,' p. 521.
48. Patricia Meyer Spacks, *Privacy: Concealing the Eighteenth-Century Self* (Chicago, IL, and London, 2002), p. 47.
49. *Inquiry into the Original of Our Ideas of Beauty and Virtue* (London, 1725), p. 44. Mildmay used the first edition, since the second (1726) substituted 'Dispositions' for 'Positions.'
50. Chelmsford: Essex RO: D/DMy/15M50/1327, Commonplace book, probably belonging to William Mildmay, pp. 69–70.
51. Charles Taylor, *Sources of the Self: The Making of the Modern Identity* (Cambridge, MA, 1989), p. 234.
52. Norfolk RO: MF/RO334/1,3, 'Commonplace book begun in 1750 . . . ,' fo. 48r. Compare *Inquiry*, p. 47.
53. 'Thomas Wilson, Commonplace book,' p. 1. For the source text see Thomas Reid, *An Inquiry into the Human Mind*, 4th edition (London, 1785), p. 53.
54. 'Commonplace Book of William Chute . . . ,' pp. 322–4.
55. 'Commonplace Book of the Reverend James Franks . . . ,' fos. 16r-16v. For another admirer of Reid, this time the *Essays on the Active Powers of Man*, see West Sussex RO: Add. MSS. 13,304, Commonplace book c.1800 of John Cole Tompkins, p. 3.
56. Commonplace book of B. Howlett . . . , pp. 105–6.
57. Ipswich: Suffolk RO: HD79/AF2/4/1, 'MS. Book of Poems, Homilies, etc.,' fos. 9r-9v.

58. Roger Chartier, 'Reading Matter and "Popular" Reading: From the Renaissance to the Seventeenth Century,' in his and Cavallo, (eds.), *History of Reading*, pp. 269–83.
59. I am grateful to Stephen Parks of the Beinecke Library for sharing with me the extensive provenance records for these manuscripts.
60. Beinecke: Osborn Shelves c.541, 'Strutt-Pattison correspondence,' fo. 7r.
61. Ibid., fo. 8r.
62. Ibid., fos. 2r, 3r, 4r.
63. Ibid., fo. 12r.
64. Taylor, *Sources of the Self*, p. 284.
65. 'Strutt-Pattison correspondence,' fo. 15r.
66. Ibid., fos. 18r-21v, 24r-25v.
67. MS Eng 692, Richard Barham, Commonplace Book, 1807- , courtesy of Houghton Library, Harvard College Library, p. 92.
68. Whitehaven: Cumbria RO: DH/565/2, 'Notebook containing miscellaneous information,' fo. 17r.
69. See *The Complete Poetical Works of James Thomson*, ed. J. Logie Robertson (Oxford, 1951), pp. 429, 489.
70. AR, (1781), 199; GM, 66 (1796), 863; Ruth O. Rose, 'Poetic Hero-Worship in the Late Eighteenth Century,' *Proceedings of the Modern Language Association*, 48 (1933), 1182–1202 (at 1186–7).
71. Beinecke: Osborn Shelves c.563, 'M.S. being a choice Farrago of new Poems, lately collected from the papers of that wonder-working Genius, S. Simpson of Coventry Weaver . . . ,' fos. 87r-89r.
72. Ibid., fo. 103r. Compare *The Minstrel* (London, 1827), p. 16, where Beattie's composition reads 'Would Edwin this majestic scene resign/For aught the huntsman's puny craft supplies? Ah! No: he better knows great Nature's charms to prize.'
73. Joseph Cradock, *Literary and Miscellaneous Memoirs*, 4 vols (London, 1828), I, 207. Simpson's chosen metre is actually similar to, though the control of rhythm and rhyme is much less accomplished than, Goldsmith's "The Hermit," first published in 1766, which features another rustic Edwin: see *The Vicar of Wakefield* (London, 1903), pp. 46–50. Simpson's private composition probably draws inspiration from both of these more famous poems.

NOTES TO CHAPTER 8

1. Colclough, 'Recovering the Reader,' 19.
2. CR, xiv (1762), 122.
3. Nottinghamshire Archives: DD/SR/212/12, Gertrude Savile's commonplace book, pp. 3, 7, 9; *Comp. Bar.*, I, 50.
4. *The Letters of Robert Burns*, (ed.), J. De Lancey Ferguson, 2 vols. (Oxford, 1931), II, 136. See also ibid. II, 26.
5. For Horatia Waldegrave, see *Comp. Peer.*, XII: Part II, 309n.
6. Warwickshire RO: CR114A/537/1, Lady Horatia Waldegrave's Verses book, 1775–79, eg., pp. 73, 74; James Thomson, *Tancred and Sigismunda* (London, 1745), pp. 1, 42.
7. Cruse, *Englishman and His Books*, pp. 11–12.
8. Stafford: Staffordshire and Stoke-on-Trent AS: D(W)1082/J/9/1, Weston Yonge, commonplace book, p. 53; *Complete Poetical Works of James Thomson*, p. 249.
9. 'Commonplace book of Thomas Stevens,' pp. 39–42; cf. *Complete Poetical Works of James Thomson*, pp. 139–44.

10. New York: New York Public Library: Pforzheimer Collection: Pforz Ms Bnd (Cornwallis), Mary Cornwallis, commonplace book (1784–1807), p. 228.
11. Pearson, p. 59.
12. CUL: Add. MS. 6664, 'Clayton family commonplace book, c.1750–1850,' pp. 93–6.
13. Godwin, *Enquirer*, p. 27.
14. 'Commonplace book compiled by James Dalloway,' fos. 15v, 16r; cf. *Complete Poetical Works of James Thomson*, p. 177.
15. Commonplace book c.1800 of John Cole Tompkins, p. 48; cf. *Complete Poetical Works of James Thomson*, p. 188.
16. M.J.W. Scott, *James Thomson, Anglo-Scot* (Athens, GA, 1988), pp. 158–62.
17. Commonplace book c.1800 of John Cole Tompkins, p. 60; cf. *Complete Poetical Works of James Thomson*, p. 190.
18. Beinecke: Osborn Shelves c.16, 'John Griffin, commonplace book, 1797,' p. 191; cf. *Complete Poetical Works of James Thomson*, p. 117.
19. Bedfordshire and Luton AS: L30/9/24/20, AL of Elizabeth Carpenter (née Petty) to Marchioness Grey, 9 Aug. 1744.
20. *CR*, xxxi (1771), 144.
21. Taunton: Somerset RO: DD/WO 59/5/11, unbound Second Book of *The Minstrel* (London, 1774); RO for Leicestershire, Leicester and Rutland: DG6/E/40, *The Minstrel* (London, 1801).
22. West Sussex RO: Castle Goring MSS/16, Commonplace Book of Harriett Anne Bisshopp, 1785-, fos., 3v-4r, 4r-4v; *The Minstrel*, p. 20; *Comp. Bar.*, I, 157.
23. BL: Add. MSS 58802, 'Hon. Augusta Leigh née Byron: Literary commonplace book,' fos. 13v-14v; *The Minstrel*, pp. 11, 18.
24. 'A Collection of Poems,' pp. 202–64, 265–7.
25. Bristol: University of Bristol Library: Pinney Miscellaneous Volume 22, 'Commonplace Book of A.E. Smith, The Down House, January 1823,' pp. 9, 38; *The Minstrel*, pp. 10, 41–2.
26. Centre for Kentish Studies: U1776 Z12, Commonplace Book of Edward Hussey, fos. 8v-9r, 9v; UCLA: 170/341, Scrapbook of Matthew G. Lewis, pp. 7–8.
27. MS Eng 630, Commonplace book, 1814–52, courtesy of Houghton Library, Harvard College Library, fos. 3v, 10v.
28. Nottinghamshire Archives: DD1175/1, Commonplace book of Thomas Howitt of Heanor, 1791–1848, fos. 39v-40r, 91v; 'Copy Books of Poetry and Prose,' II, 24–6; *The Canongate Burns*, (eds.), A. Noble and P.S. Hogg, 2 vols (Edinburgh, 2001), I, 105–7.
29. 'Commonplace Book of A.E. Smith,' p. 6; *Canongate Burns*, I, 105–7; I, 5–12; I, 95–6.
30. 'Commonplace Book of A.E. Smith,' p. 7.
31. 'Commonplace Book of William Chute,' p. 540; 'Journal and commonplace book of Charles Holte Bracebridge,' fos. 31v-32r.
32. 'Copy Books of Poetry and Prose,' II, 19–20.
33. *Remains*, p. 82.
34. 12453(1), Commonplace book of Lieut. Hopper, 89th Regt., fo. 26r.
35. Ibid., fos. 26v-27r; *Canongate Burns*, I, 399.
36. Cambridge: Cambridgeshire RO: R57/24/21/6, 'Song sung at Masonic Meeting on 30th November 1815 (St Andrews Day) at Calcutta'; *Canongate Burns*, II, 701–2.
37. BL: C.152.d.1, 'Commonplace Book of Emma Knight of Dodington, c.1830,' fos. 3r, 6v-7r; Sir Walter Scott, *Poetical Works*, (ed.), J. Logie (Oxford, 1909), p. 102.

38. Rose, *Intellectual Life*, p. 119.
39. Scrapbook of Matthew G. Lewis, pp. 156–9, 159–63.
40. BL: Add. MSS 63784, 'Commonplace Book of Jane Nelson,' fo. 36v.
41. BL: Add. MSS 60350, 'Literary Commonplace book of Mrs Elizabeth Scott, 1823–4,' fo. 22v.
42. 'Augusta Leigh née Byron: Literary commonplace book,' fos. 48r, 48v-50r, 51v-52r.
43. Bedfordshire and Luton AS: HG12/4/5, AL of Charlotte Beattie to John Higgins, 19 Mar. 1808, fo. 2r; *Poetical Works*, p. 34.
44. Commonplace book of Edward Hussey, fos. 21r-21v; 'Gustavus Gale,' pp. 216–9; 'Augusta Leigh,' fos. 55v-56r.
45. Ruskin, *Praeterita*, p. 53.
46. Worcester: Worcestershire RO: BA4839/1(iv), 'Commonplace Book of Mrs Anne Rushout,' fos. 105v-106r; *Poetical Works*, p. 136.
47. Ibid., fos. 131v, 182r; *Poetical Works*, pp. 554, 625.
48. Warwickshire County RO: CR611/737/1, Notebook of a young lady c.1810, fos. 10r-10v, 11r; *Poetical Works*, p. 224.
49. Cruse, *Englishman and His Books*, p. 239; Ruskin, *Praeterita*, pp. 5–6. See also Rose, *Intellectual Life*, pp. 40–2, 116–20, and *Collected Works of Samuel Taylor Coleridge: Marginalia IV: Pamphlets to Shakespeare*, (eds.), George Whalley and H.J. Jackson (Princeton, NJ, and London, 1988), pp. 574–614.
50. 'Literary Commonplace book of Mrs Elizabeth Scott,' fo. 33v. See Sir Walter Scott, *The Pirate*, 2 vols. (Edinburgh, 1902), II, 127.
51. Trowbridge: Wiltshire and Swindon RO: 383/940, Extract from The Fortunes of Nigel; Sir Walter Scott, *The Fortunes of Nigel* (Edinburgh, 1902), p. 188; *Comp. Bar.*, V, 256.
52. Scott, *Fortunes of Nigel*, p. 199.
53. 'Commonplace Book of William Chute,' p. 64; *HE*, I, 79.
54. 'Commonplace Book of Sir William Fitzherbert,' p. 295; *HE*, IV, 405; *Comp. Bar.*, V, 245.
55. Stafford: Staffordshire and Stoke-on-Trent AS: D/1548/2, Commonplace book, 1773, pp. 142–4, 147, 148, 149; *Comp. Peer.*, IV, 89–90.
56. Essex RO: D/DBy Z74, Commonplace book of Richard Neville Neville, fo. 11v. See *HE*, III, 300; *HP(2)*, II, 15.
57. Woking: Surrey History Centre: 4458/1, Commonplace book, n.d., fos. 40r-40v; *HE*, I, 166. The direct quotation begins at 'There was . . . '
58. 'John Griffin, commonplace book,' pp. 63–4, 69, 80–4; *HE*, IV, 402; III, 194; II, 428.
59. Northampton: Northamptonshire RO: C(AL) 22, Commonplace book of Robert Pickering, 1800–61, p. 30; *HE*, I, 393. The direct quotation from Hume actually begins at 'he ordered . . . '
60. 12453(6), Commonplace book of Lieut. Hopper, fos. 8v-9v; *HE*, I, 443; I, 453–4; II, 56–7; II, 72; IV, 218; IV, 261–2.
61. 'Eighteenth Century Verse,' fo. 70r; Robert Henry, *History of Great Britain*, 6 vols (London, 1771–93), IV, 473.
62. 'Eighteenth Century Verse,' fos. 111r-112v; William Robertson, *History of the Reign of the Emperor Charles V*, 3 vols (London, 1767), II, 449.
63. 'Memoranda Quaedam,' fos. 119r, 120r; Robertson, *Charles V*, I, 25.
64. 'Memoranda Quaedam,' fos. 120r-121r, 122r-123r, 123r, 123r-124r; Robertson, *Charles V*, I, 47–55; II, 75–6, 315–7; III, 68.
65. Scrapbook of Matthew G. Lewis, pp. 5–6, 6, 6–7, 7, 7, 80, 83–4, 91–2, 97, 98, 99.
66. Huntington: HM 34804, Anonymous commonplace book, c. 1790–1805, p. 91.

67. Sir Charles Throckmorton's commonplace book, fos. 29r-29v, 34r, 55r; Robertson, *Charles V*, I, 13 *et seq.*, 235; *Comp. Bar.*, II, 199.
68. Sir Charles Throckmorton's commonplace book, fos. 46r-54v.
69. For Oakley's service record, I am grateful for the assistance of Edith Philip of the Scottish National War Museum.
70. Dorchester: Dorset RO: D/PLR F48, Commonplace book, fo. 45v; William Robertson, *An Historical Disquisition Concerning the Knowledge Which the Ancients Had of India* (Dublin, 1791), sections I and III; Appendix, pp. 258-9.
71. Commonplace book, fo. 46v; *Historical Disquisition*, Appendix, pp. 315-6.
72. 'Commonplace Book of William Chute,' pp. 89-92; Adam Ferguson, *Essay on the History of Civil Society*, (ed.) Fania Oz-Salzberger (Cambridge, 1995), p. 10.
73. 'Commonplace Book of William Chute,' pp. 295-6; Lord Monboddo, *Of the Origin and Progress of Language*, 6 vols (Edinburgh, 1773-92), IV, 12-19.
74. HM 34804, Anonymous commonplace book, p. 185.
75. Thomas Eagles, Commonplace Book 1781-1802, p. 60.
76. John Brewer, 'Reconstructing the Reader: Prescriptions, Texts and Strategies in Anna Larpent's Reading,' in Raven, Small and Tadmor, (eds.), *Practice and Representation*, pp. 227-8.
77. 'Journal and commonplace book of Charles Holte Bracebridge,' fos. 14r-15r.
78. Winchester: Hampshire RO: 44M69/M2/1/9, 'List of Books and Pamphlets . . . ,' 30 Jun. 1757. The source is indeed p. 174 of the first edition.
79. Warwickshire County RO: CR1998/CD/Drawer 7/5, Miss Frances Throckmorton's commonplace book c.1822-5, fo. 10v.
80. Huntington: Stowe Vol. 111, Commonplace Book of Anna Grenville, Duchess of Buckingham and Chandos, fos. 17r-17v.
81. Bedfordshire and Luton AS: SY48, Commonplace book of Ann Bletchley, 1809-10, fo. 15v.
82. Bedfordshire and Luton AS: SY47, Commonplace book of Miss Ann Bletchley, fo. 3r.
83. 'Eighteenth Century Verse,' fo. 127r.
84. *The Spectator*, 2 September 1712.

NOTES TO CHAPTER 9

1. Greenblatt, *Renaissance Self-Fashioning*; Patricia Meyer Spacks, *Imagining a Self: Autobiography and the Novel in Eighteenth-Century England* (Cambridge, MA, 1976).
2. *Catalogue of Books Belonging to the Gentlemen's Library . . .* (Wigton, 1806).
3. *Characteristicks*, III, 95; I, 201.
4. Spacks, *Imagining a Self*, p. 303.
5. Brewer, 'Reconstructing the Reader,' esp. pp. 244-5.
6. *Letters*, pp. 148, 96. For comparable encouragement from the periodical press, see the article 'On our natural Fondness for History, and its true Use,' *ML*, ii (1774-5), 38-40'; also Pearson, pp. 49-55.
7. Warwick: Warwickshire County RO: CR456/in Box 35, 'Course of History recommended to Lady Philips,' fo. 1r.
8. Ibid., fo. 2r.
9. Ibid., fo. 2r; *Letters*, p. 117.

10. 'Course of History,' fos. 2v-3r; Fielding, *Tom Jones*, p. 254.
11. 'Course of History,' fos. 4r-4v.
12. Ibid., fo. 5v; *Letters*, p. 122.
13. 'Course of History,' fo. 6r.
14. AL of Henrietta Maria Bowdler to Mrs Pares, 5 Sept. 1812, fo. 2r.
15. Mary Cornwallis, commonplace book, p. 259.
16. Ibid., pp. 239–57.
17. Bedford: Bedfordshire and Luton AS: L30/9/56/45, AL of Lady Margaret Heathcote (née Yorke) to Marchioness Grey, 27 Jun. 1759; *Comp. Bar.*, V, 24.
18. *Comp. Peer.*, III, 270.
19. Beinecke: Osborn Shelves d.29, 'Recollections of the late Reverend Thomas Ripley, by his son J.J.J. Ripley,' p. 210.
20. Ibid., pp. 210–11.
21. Ibid., pp. 212–3.
22. Austen, *Mansfield Park*, p. 81; Scott, *Poetical Works*, p. 10.
23. Samuel Bamford, *Passages in the Life of a Radical* (London, n.d.), p. 251.
24. Ibid., p. 248.
25. *HP(3)*, IV, 120.
26. Carlisle: Cumbria RO: In D/SEN/10/Box 197, p. 19.
27. In D/SEN/10/Box 197, p. 18.
28. Ibid., p. 39; cf. Pennant, *Tour*, p. 56.
29. In D/SEN/10/Box 197, p. 27.
30. Whitehaven: Cumbria RO: D/RW/2, 'Notebook Containing Account of Travels in Scotland,' fo. 3r.
31. Ibid., fos. 30v, 31r, 31v-32r.
32. 'Notebook Containing Account of Travels in Scotland,' fos. 28r, 33v; cf. Pennant, *Tour*, p. 68.
33. 'Commonplace Book of Emma Knight . . . ,' fos. 33v-34r.
34. Halifax: West Yorkshire AS: SH:3/MS/2, 'Commonplace Book of Poems, Puzzles, Recipes,' p. 414.
35. Hereford: Herefordshire RO: F76/IV/488, 'Manuscript Journal of a Tour of the Highlands of Scotland, 1807,' p. 3; cf. Pennant, *Tour*, p. 80.
36. 'Manuscript Journal.', p. 2.
37. Notebook belonging to Letitia Napier, 1798- , fo. 48r; cf. Pennant, *Tour*, p. 55.
38. Warwickshire County RO: CR456/in Box 35, 'Tour in Scotland, 1827, ending at Abbotsford,' fo. 3r.
39. Cf. Pennant, *Tour*, p. 51.
40. 'Tour in Scotland, 1827,' fo. 7r; cf. Pennant, *Tour*, p. 60.
41. Preston: Lancashire RO: DDX 274/12, Travel Journal of John Dickenson, fo. 8r.
42. Ibid., fo. 1v.
43. Ibid., fo. 2r; cf. Pennant, *Tour*, pp. 74–5.
44. Whitehaven: Cumbria RO: DH361, 'Copy of Diary of George Gibson of Monk, Northumberland, of a Tour of Scotland in 1777,' p. 9; cf. Pennant, *Tour*, p. 197.
45. Dorchester: Dorset RO: D/PLR FG2, 'Account of a Week in the Western Highlands and Islands of Scotland . . . ,' pp. 8–9.
46. A much fuller account of this reader's experience is provided in my 'A Reader Writes: Negotiating *The Wealth of Nations* In an Eighteenth-Century English Commonplace Book,' *Philological Quarterly*, 83 (2004), 207–33.
47. Beinecke: Osborn Shelves fc.152, 'Anon. Commonplace book' (hereafter 'Westmorland Reader'), fos. 6r, 7r, 8r, 9r, 10r, 49v, 54v, 56v-57v, 61r-61v, 79v-80r, 88v-89v, 94r, 109r-109v, 126r, 127r.

48. Ibid., fos. 37v-38r.
49. Ibid., fo. 121v. See, for possible inspiration for this summary, Smith's observations that 'Both in years of plenty, and in years of scarcity, therefore, the bounty raises the price of Corn above what it naturally would be in the actual state of tillage' (*WN*, I, xi, g, 14), and that 'Both in years of plenty, and in years of scarcity, therefore, the bounty necessarily tends to raise the money price of corn somewhat higher than it otherwise would be in the home market' (*WN*, IV, v, a, 6).
50. 'Westmorland Reader,' fo. 42r.
51. Ibid., fo. 71v; cf. *WN*, I, xi, b, 6.
52. 'Westmorland Reader,' fo. 38r; cf. *WN*, IV, I, 35.
53. 'Westmorland Reader,' fo. 39r; cf. *WN*, IV, ii, 4.
54. 'Westmorland Reader,' fo. 39v; cf. *WN*, IV, ii, 11.
55. 'Westmorland Reader,' fo. 39v; cf. *WN*, IV, ii, 11.
56. 'Westmorland Reader,' fo. 39v; cf. *WN*, IV, ii, 12.
57. Various copies of Gambier's work on tithes survive as Centre for Kentish Studies: U1776 F12/1–4.
58. Commonplace Book of Revd J.E. Gambier, 1789- , fos. 84v, 107r. The references, which use the page numbers of the first edition, are respectively to *WN*, II, ii, 37, where Smith discusses the circulation of capital in a slightly-confusing sentence, and to IV, vii, b, 64, where he dismisses rhetorically the notion that the colonies in America were the product of European governments' deliberate actions rather than of individual endeavour.
59. Commonplace Book, 1789- , fo. 74v.
60. Ibid., fo. 74v.
61. *WN*, I, xi, a, 1.
62. *HP(2)*, 548–50.
63. *On* The Wealth of Nations, (ed.), Ross, pp. 161–4.
64. I am grateful to Stephen Parks for bringing his new acquisition to my attention and for providing a photocopy. Now catalogued as Osborn Shelves d. 413, William Windham Grenville, Baron Grenville, Commonplace Book (1822–3), it provides an interesting counterpart to British Library Add. MSS 69146, Dropmore Papers (Series II), Vol. CIX, Commonplace book of William Wyndham Grenville (1823–c.1826), in which, notably at fos. 14r-17r ('Sinking Fund'), 21r ('Corn Profits'), and 22r ('Paper Money'), similar readings in contemporary political economy are evinced.
65. Beinecke: Osborn Shelves d. 413, William Windham Grenville, Baron Grenville, 'Commonplace Book' (1822–3), pp. 1–2.
66. *WN*, Introduction, 1.
67. 'Commonplace book of William Chute . . . ,' p. 352.
68. Grenville, 'Commonplace Book,' pp. 2–3.
69. Ibid., p. 3.
70. Ibid., p. 4.
71. Ibid., pp. 4–5.
72. Ibid., p. 5.
73. Ibid., p. 7.
74. Ibid., p. 7.
75. Ibid., pp. 7–8.
76. Ibid., p. 9.
77. Ibid., p. 10.
78. *WN*, I, v, 1.
79. Grenville, 'Commonplace Book,' p. 52.
80. Ibid., p. 52.
81. *ODNB*; Clifford, *Piozzi*, pp. 248–9.

82. Warwickshire County RO: CR1707/33, Bertie Greatheed, collections for a commonplace book, c.1783–1797, G26, fos. 1v-1r; cf. *WN*, I, ii, 1 (trucking), I, iii, 3 (land and water transport), I, iv, 10 (Troyes), I, v, 20 (Canton) and I, v, 24 (Rome).

NOTES TO CHAPTER 10

1. I have discussed this case much more extensively in 'Opposing Enlightenment: Revd Charles Peters' Reading of the Natural History of Religion,' *Eighteenth Century Studies*, 38 (2005), 301–21.
2. L.S. Sutherland and L.G. Mitchell, eds, *The History of the University of Oxford: Volume V—The Eighteenth Century* (Oxford, 1986), p. 399; Charles William Boase, ed., *Registrum Collegii Exoniensis* ... (Oxford, 1894), pp. cxxxvi–cxxxvii, cxl.
3. Joseph M. Levine, 'Deists and Anglicans: The Ancient Wisdom and the Idea of Progress,' in Roger D. Lund, ed., *The Margins of Orthodoxy: Heterodox Writing and Cultural Response, 1660–1750* (Cambridge, 1995), pp. 219–39.
4. Shrewsbury: Shropshire Records and Research Centre: D3651/B/24/6/1, 'Meditations of Reverend Charles Peters,' p. 6.
5. Ibid., pp. 6–7.
6. Ibid., p. 7.
7. Ibid., p. 7.
8. Ibid., pp. 19–20.
9. Ibid., pp. 20–1.
10. John Conybeare, *A Defence of Revealed Religion* (London, 1732).
11. Jonathan Lamb, *The Rhetoric of Suffering: Reading the Book of Job in the Eighteenth Century* (Oxford, 1996).
12. *ODNB*.
13. Durham: Durham University Library: Bamburgh MS. R7, Commonplace Book of John Sharp III, e.g. pp. 73, 199, 245.
14. Ibid., p. 9.
15. Ibid., p. 175; Blackwell's *Enquiry*, p. 34.
16. Commonplace Book of John Sharp III, p. 52. The page references to the *Enquiry* are accurate.
17. *ML*, iii (1775), 281; *MR*, xvi (1757), 122.
18. John Thelwall, *Poems Chiefly Written in Retirement* ... (Hereford, 1801), pp. 175–202; David Vincent, ed., *Testaments of Radicalism: Memoirs of Working-Class Politicians 1790–1885* (London, 1997), p. 111.
19. *Burton Constable Hall: The Eighteenth and Nineteenth Centuries* (Hull, 1998), pp. 10–23, 38–53.
20. Ibid., p. 38.
21. Beverley: East Riding of Yorkshire RO: DDCC/150/25, 'Notebook of Extracts from Works of David Hume,' fo. 3r; cf. *HE*, V, 141, 151 (though Shakespeare's death, which Constable gives as 1617, Hume correctly assigns to 1616).
22. 'Notebook of Extracts,' fos. 2r-2v. The passage was one that was later revised and is missing from *HE*. It can be found at *History of Great Britain*, 2 vols (Dublin, 1755), I, 41.
23. 'Notebook of Extracts,' fo. 3v; cf. *HE*, V, 224.
24. 'Notebook of Extracts,' fo. 2v; cf. *HE*, V, 114.
25. 'Notebook of Extracts,' fo. 4r; cf. *HE*, V, 304.
26. Walpole: BOM'59: 'Book of Materials,' p. 47.

27. Colley, *Britons*, pp. 101–45; Sher, pp. 71–2.
28. Bewley and Bewley, *Gentleman Radical*, p. 7.
29. *ODNB*; Spencer, *David Hume*, pp. 140–2.
30. *The Lee Papers 1754–1811*, 4 vols (New York, 1871–4), I, 40–1. I am grateful to Richard Butterwick for originally bringing this source to my attention.
31. Ibid., I, 43.
32. Ibid., I, 101.
33. Ibid., I, 103.
34. Ibid., I, 111.
35. Ibid., I, 114–5.
36. Ibid., IV, 91–2.
37. Ibid., IV, 106.
38. Ibid., IV, 106–7.
39. Commonplace Book of Revd J.E. Gambier, 1789- , fo. 58r.
40. *ODNB*.
41. Commonplace Book, 1789- , fo. 108r.
42. Ibid., fo. 176r; Richard Hurd, *Works*, 8 vols. (London, 1811), IV, 80.
43. Edinburgh: Edinburgh University Library: MS. La.III.496, 'Commonplace Book of Francis Wrangham,' p. 86 (copying Sydney Smith's discussion of 'Glory'); Commonplace Book of Revd J.E. Gambier, eg. fos. 52v (copying on subject of 'Reasoning on Tendencies') and 108r (copying an article on the recent growth of manufacturing). Wrangham's interest in the *Edinburgh* should not be surprising given that he was a friend of its founder: Alan Bell, *Sydney Smith* (Oxford, 1980), pp. 129–32.
44. Commonplace Book, 1789-, fo. 176r. For the source see Wrangham, *The British Plutarch*, 6 vols (London, 1816), I, 492n. Wrangham's critique of Hume was actually very extensive, although confined to intermittent footnotes: see ibid. I, 496n; I, 561; II, 332n; II, 370n; III, 12n; III, 67n.
45. Commonplace Book, 1789-, fo. 168v.
46. *Works of Thomas Jefferson* ed., Paul L. Ford, 12 vols. (New York and London, 1904–5), X, Jefferson to John Norvell, Washington, 14 Jun. 1807; Spencer, *David Hume*, esp. pp. 253–9.
47. Osborn Shelves fc.152, 'Anon. Commonplace book,' fos. 109r-109v.
48. 'A Catalogue of Title Pages of Books Read . . . 1762–1786,' pp. 52–3.
49. Ibid., p. 171; Fawcett, 'An Eighteenth-Century Book Club.'

NOTES TO CHAPTER 11

1. David Allan, '"This Inquisitive Age": Past and Present in the Scottish Enlightenment,' *Scottish Historical Review*, 76 (1997), 69–85.
2. Peter Gay, *The Party of Humanity: Essays in the French Enlightenment* (New York, 1964), p. x; Robert Darnton, 'Social History of Ideas' in his *The Kiss of Lamourette: Reflections in Cultural History* (London, 1990), pp. 219–52.
3. Michel de Certeau, *The Practice of Everyday Life*, (trans.), Steven F. Rendall (Berkeley, CA, 1984), pp. 165–76.
4. Adrian Johns, *The Nature of the Book: Print and Knowledge in the Making* (Chicago, IL, 1998), p. 385.
5. Iser, *Act of Reading*, p. 9.
6. Chartier, 'Reading Matter and "Popular" Reading: From the Renaissance to the Seventeenth Century,' in his and Cavallo, (eds.), *History of Reading*, pp. 275–6.

7. Hans Magnus Enzensberger, *Mediocrity and Delusion: Collected Diversions*, (trans.), Martin Chalmers (London and New York, 1992), p. 11.
8. Quentin Skinner, 'Meaning and Understanding in the History of Ideas,' *History and Theory*, 8 (1969), 3–53. For criticism, see Kenneth Minogue, 'Method in Intellectual History: Quentin Skinner's *Foundations*,' *Philosophy*, 56 (1981), 533–52; J.E. Toews, 'Intellectual History after the Linguistic Turn: The Autonomy of Meaning and the Irreducibility of Experience,' *American Historical Review*, 92 (1987), 879–907; and J.V. Fermia, 'An Historicist Critique of "Revisionist" Methods for Studying the History of Ideas,' in James Tully, (ed.), *Meaning and Context: Quentin Skinner and His Critics* (Oxford, 1988), pp. 156–75.
9. Quentin Skinner, *The Foundations of Modern Political Thought*, 2 vols (Cambridge, 1978), I, xiii.
10. John Dunn, 'The Identity of the History of Ideas,' *Philosophy*, 43 (1968), 85–104.
11. Iser, *Act of Reading*, esp. pp. 54–64; J.G.A. Pocock, *Virtue, Commerce and History* (Cambridge, 1985), p. 18.
12. Stanley Fish, 'Literature in the Reader: Affective Stylistics,' *New Literary History*, 2 (1970), 125.
13. Laurel Brake, Bill Bell and David Finkelstein, eds, *Nineteenth-Century Media and the Construction of Identities* (Basingstoke, 2000), p. 4.
14. Greenblatt, *Renaissance Self-Fashioning*, p. 2.
15. Quoted in Darnton, 'Readers Respond to Rousseau,' p. 227.
16. Clifford Geertz, *The Interpretation of Cultures* (New York, 1973), p. 51.
17. Scott, '"This Cultivated Mind",' p. 30.
18. Spacks, *Privacy*, p. 47.
19. Linda Colley, *Britons: Forging the Nation, 1707–1837* (London, 1992).
20. Benedict Anderson, *Imagined Communities: Reflections on the Origin and Spread of Nationalism* rev. ed. (London, 1983).
21. Ian McBride and Antony Claydon, (eds.), *Protestantism and National Identity: Britain and Ireland, c.1650–c.1850* (Cambridge, 1998).
22. David Allan, 'Protestantism, Presbyterianism and National Identity in Eighteenth-Century Scottish History,' in McBride and Claydon, (eds.), *Protestantism and National Identity*, pp. 182–205.
23. Hannah Barker, *Newspapers, Politics and Public Opinion in Late Eighteenth Century England* (Oxford, 1988).
24. Kathleen Wilson, *The Sense of the People: Politics, Culture and Imperialism in England, 1715–1785* (Cambridge, 1995).
25. Howard Weinbrot, *Britannia's Issue: The Rise of British Literature from Dryden to Ossian* (Cambridge, 1995), p. 571.
26. Davis, *Acts of Union*, p. 168. For Davis on Colley and Weinbrot, see p. 6.
27. 'Essays on Various Subjects,' p. 12.
28. Robert Crawford, *Devolving English Literature* (Oxford, 1992).
29. *St. James's Chronicle* (1767), no. 1035.
30. 'The Last Memorandum Book,' p. 204.
31. *MR*, vi (1791), 11.
32. SUL: MS. 463, John Nourse, commonplace book, loose insert.
33. For more popular Scots balladry absorbed by an English reader, see, for instance, the numerous items in MS Eng 1038.1, Anonymous commonplace book, c. 1774, courtesy of Houghton Library, Harvard College Library, eg. pp. 29–30, 116, 117–8, 121–2 and 125. They also featured heavily in the periodicals: eg. *GM*, liii (1783), 690–1; *TCM*, ii (1770), 662.
34. Davis, *Acts of Union*, p. 178.
35. *St. James's Chronicle* (1767), no. 1012.

36. *Lee Papers*, I, 111.
37. *English Bards and Scotch Reviewers*, 3rd edition (London, 1810), p. 34.
38. Walpole: 'Newspaper cuttings ca. 1770,' p. 30.
39. Ibid., p. 160.
40. Walpole: BOM '59, Book of Materials, p. 48.
41. 'Newspaper cuttings, ca. 1770,' p. 263.
42. *Catalogue of the Entire and Valuable Library of John Ives, jun. Esq.* . . . (London, 1777), pp. 3, 20, 40.
43. Walpole: 'Diary and Letters of John Ives, c.1773–4,' passim.
44. Ipswich: Suffolk RO: HD 321/4, 'Commonplace Book of Samuel Lindsey,' passim.
45. 'Rough list of books and plays, 1807.'
46. Beinecke: Osborn MSS file 18059, Felicia Dorothea Browne Hemans, 1793–1835, AL to Miss Lloyd, 15 Feb. 1820.
47. Scott, '"This Cultivated Mind",' p. 45.
48. Darnton, *Forbidden Best-Sellers*, p. 217.
49. Gay, *The Enlightenment*.
50. H.G. Graham *Scottish Men of Letters in the Eighteenth Century* (London, 1901); Gladys Bryson, *Man and Society: The Scottish Enquiry of the Eighteenth Century* (Princeton, NJ, 1945); Charles Camic, *Experience and Enlightenment: Socialization for Cultural Change in Eighteenth-Century Scotland* (Edinburgh, 1983); Sher, *Church and University*; Broadie, *Scottish Enlightenment*. Lest this observation be thought unkind to others, it should be added that the same approach informs my own *Virtue, Learning and the Scottish Enlightenment*.
51. Immanuel Kant, *Foundations of the Metaphysics of Morals; What is Enlightenment; and a Passage from The Metaphysics of Morals*, (ed.), L.W. Beck (Chicago, IL, 1950), pp. 286–92.
52. Brewer, *Pleasures of the Imagination*, passim.
53. Plumb, *Commercialization of Leisure*; McKendrick, Brewer and Plumb, (eds.), *Consumer Society*.
54. Darnton, 'Social History of Ideas,' p. 252.
55. Ibid., p. 252.
56. *Collected Works of William Hazlitt*, (ed.), P.P. Howe, 21 vols (London and Toronto, 1930–34), XII, 221.
57. *LJ*, p. 782.
58. *A Catalogue of the Sunderland Subscription Library* . . . (Sunderland, 1812), p. iii.

Bibliography

1. PRIMARY SOURCES: MANUSCRIPTS

Aylesbury: Centre for Buckinghamshire Studies
D114/61, Commonplace book of B. Howlett of Olney, 1808–51
D138/16/5/1, Commonplace and letter book of the Russell family, 1715–1751
NQ2/22/2, 'An Account of Books belonging to the Monthly Meeting of Friends of the Upperside in the County of Bucks, 1799'

British Library
Add. MSS 22667: 'Liber memorandorum et referentiarum . . . '
Add. MSS 27617, 'Commonplace book of J.H. Ott, rector of Bexhill'
Add. MSS 43702, 'Commonplace Book of Sir Frederick Morton Eden'
Add. MSS 45268, 'Journal and commonplace books of Charles Holte Bracebridge of Warwickshire'
Add. MSS 58802, 'Hon. Augusta Leigh, née Byron: Literary Commonplace Book'
Add. MSS 60350, 'Literary Commonplace book of Mrs Elizabeth Scott, 1823–4'
Add. MSS 61842, 'Eighteenth Century Verse'
Add. MSS 63784, 'Commonplace Book of Jane Nelson'
Add. MSS 69146, Dropmore Papers (Series II), Vol. CIX, Commonplace book of William Wyndham Grenville (1823–c.1826)
C.152.d.1, 'Commonplace Book of Emma Knight of Dodington, c.1830'
Egerton MSS: 3700B, 'B. Barrett Collection, Vol. XIII, Literary papers etc.'
Stowe 1013, Commonplace book belonging to Edward Vernon
Stowe 1014, Commonplace Book of Thomas Astle

Bath: Bath Central Library
B027.3, 'Marshall's Library, List of Subscribers, 1793–9'

Bedford: Bedfordshire and Luton Archive Service
HG12/4/5, AL of Charlotte Beattie to John Higgins, 19 Mar. 1808
L30/9/24/20, AL of Elizabeth Carpenter (née Petty) to Marchioness Grey, 9 Aug. 1744
L30/9/56/45, AL of Lady Margaret Heathcote (née Yorke) to Marchioness Grey, 27 Jun. 1759

OR2222/2, Notes on history of Elizabeth I and James I
SY47, Commonplace book of Miss Ann Bletchley

Beverley: East Riding of Yorkshire Record Office

DDCC/150/25, 'Notebook of Extracts from Works of David Hume'
DDCC/150/58, 'List of Books lent to Mr de Villedeuil by Mr Constable'
DDX/507/2, 'Charts, Tables and Notes on Legal, Philosophical, Theological, Mathematical etc. matters. . . . '

Bradford: West Yorkshire Archive Service

42D81/1/2/1/3, 'Minutes of Meetings of the Subscribers'
DB17/C37, 'Pontefract Library and News Room Minute Book 1783–1854'

Bristol: Bristol Record Office

12453 (1–6), Commonplace books of Lieut. Hopper, 89th Regt
30251/Bd/51, Broadmead Vestry Library records 1820–7
41213/L/1/1, Thomas Eagles, Commonplace Book 1781–1802

Bristol: University of Bristol Library

Pinney Miscellaneous Volume 22, 'Commonplace Book of A.E. Smith, The Down House, January 1823'

Bury: Bury Archive Service

A.87.4 BUR, Bury Library, Minutes 1825–1848

Bury St Edmunds: Suffolk Record Office

E2/34, 'Memoranda Quaedam, Sir John Cullum F.R.S.-F.S.A.'
P504, 'A Catalogue of the Books belonging to the Revd George Burton. . . . Novr 27th 1753'

Cambridge: Cambridge University Library

Add. MS. 6664, 'Clayton family commonplace book, c.1750–1850'

Cambridge: Cambridgeshire Record Office

R57/24/21/6, 'Song sung at Masonic Meeting on 30th November 1815 (St Andrews Day) at Calcutta'
R58/8/14/7, Beldam commonplace book, 1778-

Cambridge, Massachusetts: The Houghton Library, Harvard University

MS Eng. 231, Hester Thrale, 'Minced Meat for Pyes'
MS Eng 630, Commonplace book, 1814–52
MS Eng 692, Richard Barham, Commonplace Book, 1807-
MS Eng 767, Felicia Dorothea (Browne) Hemans, Commonplace book

MS Eng 768 (2), Melisinda Munbee, 'A Collection of various kinds of Poetry'
MS Eng 1038.1, Anonymous commonplace book, c. 1774

Carlisle: Carlisle Public Library

L33, 'Carlisle Library: Minute Book 1804–1828'
M822, 'Essays on Various Subjects'
M1312, 'Common-Place Book After Locke's Method. By Gustavus Gale'

Carlisle: Cumbria Record Office

D/LONSW20/5/1, Minute Book of the Whitehaven Library, 1823–36
In D/SEN/10/Box 197, Early nineteenth-century commonplace book

Chelmsford: Essex Record Office

D/DBy Z74, Commonplace book of Richard Neville Neville
D/DQs40, 'Catalogue of the Library of Filmer Honywood Esqr . . . '
D/DMy/15M50/1327, Commonplace book, probably belonging to William Mild-may
D/DU 676/1, Journal of William Barnard of Harlow Bury Farm, 1807–1823

Cheltenham: Cheltenham Library

639027.5, 'Subscription Book to Williams's Library for One Lady or Gentleman'

Chester: Cheshire and Chester Archives and Local Studies

DAR/J/10, Commonplace Book of John Arden

Chichester: West Sussex Record Office

Add. MSS. 13,304, Commonplace book c.1800 of John Cole Tompkins
Add. MSS 20,187, 'Commonplace book compiled by James Dallaway . . . '
Add MSS. 20,189, commonplace book compiled by Joseph Dalloway for Catherine A. Best
Cap. I/51/17, Photocopy of Catalogue of Chichester Cathedral Library
Castle Goring MSS/16, Commonplace Book of Harriett Anne Bisshopp, 1785-

Dorchester: Dorset Record Office

D/PLR F48, Commonplace book
D/PLR FG2, 'Account of a Week in the Western Highlands and Islands of Scotland . . . '

Durham: Durham County Record Office

D/HH/10/2/1, Barnard Castle Book Society: Account Book and Subscription Book 1819–1831

Durham: Durham University Library

Bamburgh MS. R7, Commonplace Book of John Sharp III

Edinburgh: Edinburgh University Library

MS. La.III.496, 'Commonplace Book of Francis Wrangham'

Farmington, Connecticut: W.S. Lewis
Walpole Library, Yale University

BOM'59: 'Book of Materials'
'Catalogue of the Library of the Right Honble. Earl of Chesterfield . . . taken in June 1778'
'Commonplace Book of William Chute Esq. of The Vine in Hampshire'
'Diary and Letters of John Ives, c.1773–4'
'The Effusions of Fancy and Fun Compiled by Joseph Gulston, 1784'
'Newspaper Cuttings ca. 1770'
'Walpole's Newspaper Cuttings'

Gloucester: Gloucestershire Record Office

In D45/F39, 'Catalogue of Mr Whitmore's Books, 1st of Jany 1786'

Gosforth: Northumberland Record Office

ZBK/C/1/A12/7, Notebook diary of the Revd James Snowdon

Hackney: Hackney Archives Department

D/S/36/1, Hackney Literary Institution and Subscription Library, 'Minutes of the Proceedings of the Committee, Monthly, & Anniversary Meetings,' 1815–17

Halifax: West Yorkshire Archive Service

MISC 509/10, 'Commonplace Book of the Reverend James Franks . . . '
SH:3/MS/2, 'Commonplace Book of Poems, Puzzles, Recipes'

Hereford: Herefordshire Record Office

AM79/2, 'Commonplace Book of Mrs Jane Pateshall'
F76/IV/488, 'Manuscript Journal of a Tour of the Highlands of Scotland, 1807'

Hertford: Hertfordshire Archives and Local Studies

D/EB650/F3, 'Book Containing daily Occurrences. 12th of Octr 1819'
In D/EGd E9, lists of books
D/EHx/F33, 'Continuation of the Extracts from the *Encyclopaedia Britannica*, vol. xvii part1'

Huntingdon: Cambridgeshire Record Office

1876/28/1, 'Catalogue of Books Belonging to Mr C. Beauchamp. 1793'

Ipswich: Suffolk Record Office

HD79/AF2/4/1, 'MS. Book of Poems, Homilies, etc.'
HD 321/4, 'Commonplace Book of Samuel Lindsey'

Kendal: Cumbria Record Office

WD/K/189, 'Minutebook of the Kendal Coffee Room 1779–1879'
WD/Ry Box 5, 'Catalogue of Books in the Drawing Room'
WDB/63/3a, 'Day Book of Abraham Dent'

Lancaster: Lancaster Public Library

MS. 144, 'Minutes of the Amicable Society, Lancaster, 1769–1785'
MS. 8752–3, Mary Chorley's diaries, 1776–8

Leeds: Brotherton Library, University of Leeds

MS 17, 'Quotation or Commonplace Book, by George Ashby'
MS. 76, 'Diary of Isaac Stockton Clark'
MS. 500, 'A Commonplace Book of Mary Cowgill. . . .'

Leicester: Record Office for Leicestershire, Leicester and Rutland

18D35/1, Minutes of the Leicester Permanent Library 1800-
DE718/C/6, R. Martin's commonplace book, c.1800–1820
DE3077/1, Records of Kibworth and Harborough Book Society, 1772-
DG7 Lit. 13, Notes on Burnet's *History of His Own Time*

Lewes: East Sussex Record Office

AMS 6034/1, 'Northiam Unitarian Chapel Church Book'
NU1 6/1: Westgate Unitarian Chapel, 'Vestry Library, minute book, 1808–1818'
SHR 1349, Notes and memoranda mostly by George Shiffner

Lichfield: Staffordshire and Stoke-on-Trent Archive Service

B/A/22/7, 'Catalogue of the Parochial Library at Stone, Co. Stafford, 21 Oct 1765'

Lincoln, Lincolnshire Archives

FLINDERS 1, 'Diary and Account Book of Mathew Flinders of Donington, 1775–85'
FLINDERS 2, 'Diary and Account Book of Mathew Flinders of Donington, 1785–1802'
MISC DON 315/2, 'Boston Literary Society. Rules'

Liverpool: Sydney Jones Library, University of Liverpool

MS.3.62, Liverpool Literary and Philosophical Society: bound unpublished papers read before the Society [1812–27]

Los Angeles: Charles E. Young Research Library, UCLA

170/341, Scrapbook of Matthew G. Lewis

Lowestoft: Suffolk Record Office

ES 185/3/3, 'Rough list of books and plays, 1807'

Maidstone: Centre for Kentish Studies

U194 F9/1, Commonplace Book of Revd J.E. Gambier, 1780-
U194 F9/2, Commonplace Book of Revd J.E. Gambier, 1789-
U310 F4, Notebook of G. Norman
U1776 Z12, Commonplace Book of Edward Hussey

Manchester: Chetham's Library

A.3.109, William Barton, commonplace book . . . 1780–1810
A.4.85, Thomas Wilson, commonplace book

Matlock: Derbyshire Record Office

D239M/F10224, 'Commonplace Book of Sir William Fitzherbert, c.1770–1790'
D258/14/11/1, Gell of Hopton, 'Extracts No. 1: Jany. 1803'
D307/A11, 'Hartington Union Book Society: Account Book 1787–1805'
D5047/1, 'Journal of the Literary and Philosophical Society of Derby, 1808- '

Newcastle upon Tyne: Robinson Library, University of Newcastle upon Tyne

Hospital Archives 16, 'Medical Society, minutes 1795–1800'

Newcastle upon Tyne: Tyne and Wear Archive Service

1041/6, Brunswick Chapel Library, minute book 1808-

New Haven, Connecticut: Beinecke Rare Book and Manuscript Library, Yale University

Osborn MSS file 433, Dr John Ash to Sir Joseph Banks, n.d.
Osborn MSS file 17834, AL of Henrietta Maria Bowdler to Mrs Pares, 5 Sept. 1812
Osborn MSS file 17945, Charles Burney to J.W. Callcott, 30 Oct. 1799
Osborn MSS file 18059, Felicia Dorothea Browne Hemans, 1793–1835, ALS to Miss Lloyd, 15 Feb. 1820
Osborn Shelves c.16, 'John Griffin, commonplace book, 1797'
Osborn Shelves c.35, 'Poetic Trifles, by Charles Burney'
Osborn Shelves c.83/1, 'Commonplace book compiled by William Warren Porter (1776–1804)'
Osborn Shelves c.94, 'James Moore, commonplace book'
Osborn Shelves c.116, 'Anna Maria Sharpe, commonplace book'
Osborn Shelves c.131, 'Mentor, or the True Guide to Wisdom . . . by the Revd Jas. Ashton . . . '
Osborn Shelves, c.139, 'A Collection of Poems, Thomas Binns, Liverpool, 1789, Vol. II'
Osborn Shelves c.173, 'Botesdale Book Society, list of members, books, borrowings etc. (1778–89)'
Osborn Shelves, c.259, 'Commonplace book of Thomas Stevens'
Osborn Shelves, c.343, 'Anne Milbanke, commonplace book'
Osborn Shelves c.514, 'A Catalogue of Books Left at Norbury'
Osborn Shelves c.541, 'Strutt-Pattison correspondence'

Osborn Shelves c.563, 'M.S. being a choice Farrago of new Poems, lately collected from the papers of that wonder-working Genius, S. Simpson of Coventry Weaver . . . '

Osborn Shelves d.29, 'Recollections of the late Reverend Thomas Ripley, by his son J.J.J. Ripley'

Osborn Shelves d.133, 'Anon. commonplace book'

Osborn Shelves d.367, 'Edward Henry Columbine, commonplace book'

Osborn Shelves d. 413, William Windham Grenville, Baron Grenville, 'Commonplace Book' (1822–3)

Osborn Shelves fc.53, 'Anonymous commonplace book, c.1781–3'

Osborn Shelves fc.152, 'Anon. Commonplace book'

Uncat. MS Vault 757, anonymous (E.D.), 'The Last Memorandum Book' (1754– 55)

New York: New York Public Library

Pforzheimer Collection: Pforz Ms Bnd (Cornwallis), Mary Cornwallis, commonplace book (1784–1807)

New York: Pierpont Morgan Library

MA4960, George Hibbert, commonplace book, 1785–1820

Northampton: Northamptonshire Record Office

C(AL) 22, Commonplace book of Robert Pickering, 1800–61

L(C) 1444, 'Catalogue of Library at Cottesbrooke Hall, 1791'

Norwich: Millenium Library

FAK017.2, 'A Catalogue of the Books given by the Revd. Dr Hooper to the Rectory of Fakenham For Ever'

Norwich: Norfolk Record Office

MF/RO334/1, 3, 'Commonplace book begun in 1750 . . . '

MS4379, T138C, 'A Catalogue of Title Pages of Books Read . . . 1762–1786'

Yarmouth Library (addnl.) D41/106, 'Commonplace Book of Thomas Sutton of Yarmouth'

Nottingham: Nottinghamshire Archives

D463/22, 'Newark Book Society: Rules and Orders, Catalogues of Books, 1779–89'

DD1175/1, Commonplace book of Thomas Howitt of Heanor, 1791–1848

DD/CH/24/22, Will of John Randle of Breaston

DD/SR/212/12, Gertrude Savile's commonplace book

Oxford: The Bodleian Library, University of Oxford

MS.Eng.poet.c.51, Scrapbook of Mary Madan

Oxford: Oxfordshire Record Office

Budd. XIV/2, 'Rules of the Woodstock Book Society'

Parrott II/114, 'An Inventory of . . . Mrs Sarah Long. . . . March 1797'

Palo Alto, California: Stanford University Library

MS. 017, Anonymous commonplace book, 1751–1822
MS. 463, John Nourse, commonplace book

Penzance: Morrab Library

MOR/LIB/1a, Minutes of Penzance Library
MOR/PEN/23, Penzance Ladies' Book Club, rules and minutes, 1770-

Preston: Lancashire Record Office

DDX 274/7, Memorandum Book of John Dickenson
DDX 274/12, Travel Journal of John Dickenson

Reading: Berkshire Record Office

D/Enm2 C5, ALS from Elizabeth Montagu to Matthew Montagu, 20 July 1803
D/EX 1306/1, Diary of Lady East, 1791–2

San Marino, California: The Henry E. Huntington Library

HM 34804, Anonymous commonplace book, c. 1790–1805
Stowe Vol. 111, Commonplace Book of Anna Grenville, Duchess of Buckingham
    and Chandos

Sheffield: Sheffield Archives

MD2221/1, Sheffield Book Society records
Wh.M. 135/3, 'Catalogue of Lady Mary Wortley's Books Packed Up to be Sent
    Abroad, July 1739,' pp. 2–3

Sheffield: Sheffield City Library

Vol. 24, No. 15, *Questions proposed by a Society established in 1810* (Sheffield,
    1820)

Shrewsbury: Shropshire Records and Research Centre

D3651/B/24/6/1, 'Meditations of Reverend Charles Peters'
S110/4/3, 'Diary of Edward Williams of Oswestry'

Stafford: Staffordshire and Stoke-on-Trent Archive Service

D/1548/2, Commonplace book, 1773
D(W)1082/J/9/1, Weston Yonge, commonplace book

Trowbridge: Wiltshire and Swindon Record Office

383/940, Extract from *The Fortunes of Nigel*
1461/1352, Memorandum book of Charles Morgan, 1748–52

Truro: Cornwall Record Office

DD.CY/1712, 'Will of Elizabeth Goodall of Fowey, spinster'

DDX 15/1, 'Minute book, County Library Committee 1792–1849'

Warwick: Warwickshire County Record Office

CR114A/537/1, Lady Horatia Waldegrave's Verses book, 1775–79
CR223/2, Commonplace book of John Smith, Admington, Gloucestershire, 1764-
CR456/in Box 35, 'Course of History recommended to Lady Philips'
CR456/in Box 35, 'Tour in Scotland, 1827, ending at Abbotsford'
CR464/145/2, Notebook belonging to Letitia Napier, 1798-
CR611/737/1, Notebook of a young lady c.1810
CR895/49, 'Inventory of the Furniture and Effects at Grove Park Bequeathed as Heir Looms by The Rt. Hon. Charles Lord Dormer, 1819'
CR1707/33, Bertie Greatheed, collections for a commonplace book, c.1783–1797
CR1998/CD/Drawer 7/5, Miss Frances Throckmorton's commonplace book c.1822–5
CR1998/CD/Drawer 8/12, Commonplace book of Sir Charles Throckmorton, 1780-

Whitehaven: Cumbria Record Office

D/CU/1/18, Charles Curwen, 'Copy Books of Poetry and Prose in French and English'
In D/DA/ 35, 'A List of Books Which I Got From My Wife's Share of Her Mother Palmer's Library . . . '
D/RW/2, 'Notebook Containing Account of Travels in Scotland'
DH361, 'Copy of Diary of George Gibson of Monk, Northumberland, of a Tour of Scotland in 1777'
DH/565/2, 'Notebook containing miscellaneous information'

Winchester: Hampshire Record Office

1/M49/208, Hackwood Library Catalogue, 1828
44M69/M2/1/9, 'List of Books and Pamphlets . . . '
84M95/2, Commonplace book of Robert Bristow of Micheldever, 1793

Woking: Surrey History Centre

1534/6, 'Inventory of the Stock in Trade, Working Tools, &c. of the Late Mr Samuel Russell, taken May 12th 1829'
2346/1, Pulborough Reading Society book, 1807-
4458/1, Commonplace book, n.d.

Worcester: Worcestershire Record Office

BA4839/1(iv), 'Commonplace Book of Mrs Anne Rushout'

2. PRIMARY SOURCES: UNIQUE COPIES OF PRINTED WORKS

Although originally printed in significant numbers, finding details for the following individual copies now seem necessary. Sometimes this is because of their exceptional rarity. In other cases the specific copy identified here is important either because it bears annotations or because of a personal association.

British Library

30.f.14, Dugald Stewart, *Philosophy of the Human Mind*, 3 vols (London and Edinburgh, 1792–1827)

530.g.4, Colin Maclaurin, *Algebra* (London, 1748)

773.l.31, William Cullen, *Synopsis Nosologiae Methodicae* (Edinburgh, 1769)

822.e.19, *Catalogue of a Valuable and Curious Collection of . . . the late Rev. Thomas Clarke, D.D . . .* (York, 1798)

1078.g.20, Allan Ramsay, *Tea-Table Miscellany* (London, 1733)

1164.l.4 (1–2), *Poetical Works* (London, 1793–4)

1509/822, George Fordyce, *Elements of the Practice of Physic* (London, 1771)

1609/3963, David Hume, *Essays and Treatises on Several Subjects* (London and Edinburgh, 1800)

4473.e.13 (2), William Robertson, *The Situation of the World at the Time of Christ's Appearance* (Edinburgh, 1759)

8364.b.24(3), *An Account of the Liverpool Mechanics and Apprentices Library . . .* (Liverpool, 1824)

10856.ee.9, Sir William Forbes, *Life of James Beattie* (Edinburgh, 1807)

11805.m.6, Hugh Blair, *Lectures on Rhetoric and Belles Lettres* (London, 1783)

C.60.e.4, Duncan Forbes, *Whole Works* (Edinburgh, [1755?])

C.61.b.6(1), James Beattie, *Scoticisms Arranged in Alphabetical Order* (Edinburgh, 1811)

C.126.k.2, James Hutton, *Investigation of the Principles of Knowledge* (Edinburgh, 1794)

G.11387, Allan, Ramsay, *The Gentle Shepherd* (Edinburgh, 1755)

Blackburn: Blackburn Central Library

J39/5455, *Rules and Catalogue of the Subscription Library, Established at the Independent Chapel, Blackburn . . .* (Blackburn, 1827)

T31, *Catalogue of Books in the Subscription Library . . .* (Blackburn, 1825)

Bolton: Bolton Archives and Local Studies

BO18/CHU, *Catalogue of Books Belonging to the Church and King Library at Bolton . . .* (Bolton, 1837)

Brighton: Brighton Local Studies Centre

59LEW, *Catalogue of the Books Belonging to the Lewes Library Society . . .* (Lewes, 1827)

Cambridge: Cambridge University Library

Adv.d.100.4, *Laws of the Society for Promoting Useful Knowledge . . .* (Cambridge, 1784)

Munby.c.262, *Arranged Catalogue of the Library of the Literary and Philosophical Society of Newcastle-upon-Tyne . . .* (Newcastle, 1819)

Cambridge, Massachusetts: The Houghton Library, Harvard University

*fEC75 H8823H, David Hume, *History of England*, 2 vols (London, 1761)

Canterbury: Canterbury Public Library

U802.6, *Rules and Orders to be Observed by the Historical Society for the Cultivation of Useful Knowledge* (Canterbury, 1816)

Carlisle: Carlisle Public Library

M1284, *Carlisle Library. Rules for the Regulation of the Carlisle Library* . . . (Carlisle, 1819)
N1/23, *Catalogue of Books Belonging to Edward Banks's Circulating Library* . . . (Cockermouth, n.d.)
1/29N, *Catalogue of Books Belonging to the Gentlemen's Library* . . . (Wigton, n.d.)

Coventry: Coventry Public Library

JN027.2, *A Catalogue of the Books Belonging to the Coventry Library* . . . (Coventry, 1812)

Derby: Derby Public Library

In Vol. 4181, *Rules and Catalogue of the Library Belonging to the Derby Philosophical Society* (Derby, 1835)
In Vol. 4420, *Catalogue of Collinson's Circulating Library* . . . (Wirksworth, 1805)
In Vol. 5348, *A Catalogue of the Ashbourne Moral and Religious Permanent Library* (Derby, 1823)
In Vol. 5348, *Catalogue of* . . . *the late Rev. Francis Gisborne* . . . (Chesterfield, 1822)
In Vol. 5348, *Catalogue of Mr E. Rhodes' Valuable Library* . . . (Sheffield, 1828)
In Vol. 5348, *Catalogue of Standard Books on Sale* . . . *at the Shop of Richardson and Handford* . . . *Market-Place, Derby* (Derby, 1823)
In Vol. 5348, *Moore's Subscription Library and Newsroom* (Buxton, 1826)
In Vol. 5356, *Catalogue of [an] Extensive Sale* . . . *on the Premises of John Longden, Esq., Ashbourne* . . . (Ashbourne, 1827)
In Vol. 5356, *Catalogue of the Valuable* . . . *Property of W.B. Thomas Esq.* . . . . (Chesterfield, 1826)
7510, *Catalogue of the Books in Marriott's Subscription Library* . . . (Stafford, 1795)

Dorchester: Dorchester Library

SHA.D5: 027.52, *The Shaftesbury Subscription Library for Circulation and Reference* . . . (Shaftesbury, 1827)

Edinburgh: Edinburgh University Library

SC F 854–855, William Robertson, *History of Scotland* (London, 1759)

Exeter: Exeter Cathedral Library

EML/HUN 1199832, John Hunter, *Treatise on the Venereal Disease* (1786)
EML/MON 1826586, Alexander Monro, *Anatomy of the Human Bones* (1763)
EML/SYN 1738865, William Cullen, *Synopsis Nosologiae Methodicae* (Edinburgh, 1780)

EML/SYN 1738873, William Cullen, *Synopsis Nosologiae Methodicae* (Edinburgh, 1785)
EML/TRA/18/1926254, *The Art of Puffing; an Inaugural Oration* (Edinburgh,1765)

Farmington, Connecticut: W.S. Lewis Walpole Library, Yale University

49 3185, Sir David Dalrymple, *Annals of Scotland*, 2 vols (London and Edinburgh, 1776)
4to 813 753B, Thomas Blackwell, *Memoirs of the Court of Augustus*, 3 vols (Edinburgh, 1753–63)
53 H882 754b, David Hume, *History of England*, 6 vols (London, 1759–62)
Catalogue of the Entire and Valuable Library of John Ives, jun. Esq. . . . (London, 1777)

Hereford: Hereford Public Library

019.1, *Rules and Regulations of the Hereford Permanent Library . . .* (Hereford, 1815)

Ipswich: Suffolk Record Office

C/5/4/2/1, *An Alphabetical Catalogue of the Books in the Town Library Under the Public Grammar School, Ipswich . . .* ([Ipswich], 1799)

Kettering: Kettering Public Library

KET03, *Catalogue of J. & S. Waters' Circulating Library . . .* (Kettering, 1813)

Leicester: Record Office for Leicestershire, Leicester and Rutland

DG21/284, Bust of David Hume, from *Cooke's Pocket Edition of Hume*
DG6/E/40, *The Minstrel* (London, 1801)
P40, Advertisement for Miss Ward of Ashby-de-la-Zouche

Lichfield: Lichfield Library

Library History Box, *Catalogue of the Books belonging to the Permanent Library, Lichfield . . .* (Lichfield, 1815)
Library History Box, *Laws of the Lichfield Permanent Library* (Lichfield, 1808)

Lincoln, Lincolnshire Archives

DAUB II/2, *Rules and Orders of the Book-Club-Society, at Great Grimsby* (n.p., n.d.)
DAUB II/5, *Rules and Orders of the Book-Club Society, at Market-Rasen* (n.p., n.d.)

Liverpool: Liverpool Record Office and Local Studies

H027.3 LIV, *A Catalogue of the Present Collection of Books in the Liverpool Library . . .* (n.p., n.d.)

H027.31 ATH, *A Catalogue of the Library of The Athenaeum, Liverpool* (Liverpool, 1820)

Liverpool: Sydney Jones Library, University of Liverpool

G35.19(4), *Catalogue of Brunswick Library* . . . (Liverpool, 1805)

Manchester: Chetham's Library

L.7.44, Adam Ferguson, *Principles of Moral and Political Science* (Edinburgh, 1792)
W.6.27–28, David Hume, *History of England*, 2 vols (London, 1762)
W.6.29–30, David Hume, *History of England*, 2 vols (London, 1759)
W.6.31, David Hume, *History of Great Britain*, 1 vol (Edinburgh, 1754)
W.6.32, David Hume, *History of Great Britain*, 1 vol (London, 1757)

Manchester: Manchester Central Library

017.242 M22, *A Catalogue of the Present Collection of Books in the Manchester Circulating Library* . . . (Manchester, [1766?])

Manchester: The Portico Library

A Catalogue of the Books belonging to the Portico-Library . . . (Manchester, 1810)

Newcastle upon Tyne: Newcastle City Library

L018.1, *A Catalogue of the Sunderland Subscription Library* . . . (Sunderland, 1812)
In L042.C46, *A Catalogue of the Books belonging to the Library of the New Jerusalem Temple, Percy Street, Newcastle* . . . (Newcastle, 1836)
In L042.D95, *A Catalogue of the Sunderland Medical Library* . . . (Sunderland, 1820)

Newcastle upon Tyne: Tyne and Wear Archives Service

160/1/209, *A Catalogue of Books in the Library of the Assembly News Rooms in Newcastle* (Newcastle, 1842)

New Haven, Connecticut: Beinecke Rare Book and Manuscript Library, Yale University

A Catalogue of the Entire and Valuable Library of the Late Rev. Michael Lort . . . (London, 1791)
Bibliotheca Beauclerkiana. A Catalogue of the Large and Valuable Library of the Late Honourable Topham Beauclerk . . . (London, [1781])
Catalogue of the Curious and Distinguished Library of the late Reverend and Learned Thomas Crofts . . . (London, 1783)
IM J637 +Zz 776, James Beattie, *Essays* (Edinburgh, 1776)
Osborn Shelves pc.124, James Macpherson, *Poems of Ossian*, 2 vols (London, 1773)
Osborn Shelves pc.125, John Pinkerton, *Dissertation on the Origin and Progress of the Scythians or Goths* (London, 1787)

Speck Yc M1 760, James Macpherson, *Fragments of Ancient Poetry* (Edinburgh, 1760)

Norwich: Millenium Library

N018.2, *A Catalogue of the Books belonging to the Society of the Norwich Public Library* (Norwich, 1792)

N018.2, *A Catalogue of the Library belonging to the Norfolk and Norwich Clerical Society . . .* (Norwich, 1838)

N018.2, *Norwich: Octagon Chapel—Catalogue of Vestry Library* (Norwich, 1825)

Y018.2, *A Catalogue of Books Belonging to the Methodist Subscription Library . . .* (Yarmouth, 1832)

Nottingham: Nottingham Public Library

L02.3 A, *Catalogue of the Books Belonging to the Nottingham Artisans' Library . . .* (Nottingham, 1824)

L02.3 A, *Catalogue of the Standfast Library* (Nottingham, 1817)

L02.3 NOTTINGHAM, *Rules of the Nottingham Medical Book Society* (Nottingham, 1828)

L02.3 WRIGHT, *Catalogue of C.N. Wright's New Circulating Library . . .* (Nottingham, [1821])

Oxford: The Bodleian Library, University of Oxford

BOD DD35,36 Jur., David Hume, *History of Great Britain*, 2 vols (London and Edinburgh, 1754–7)

Portsmouth: Portsmouth Central Library

019.2, *Catalogue of the Congregational Library at the Unitarian Chapel, Portsmouth . . .* ([Portsmouth], 1823)

Providence, Rhode Island: John Hay Library, Brown University

YQE.W77e Lamont, John Witherspoon, *Ecclesiastical Characteristicks* (Edinburgh, 1763)

San Marino, California: The Henry E. Huntington Library

420738, *A Catalogue of Lansdown's Circulating-Library . . .* (Bristol, 1807)

Shrewsbury: Shropshire Records and Research Centre

D87.6, *Catalogue of Books Belonging to the Subscription Library in Shrewsbury . . .* (Shrewsbury, 1812)

Stafford: William Salt Library

bS2072, *Catalogue of Books belonging to the Wolverhampton Library . . .* (Wolverhampton, 1835)

Taunton: Somerset Record Office
DD/WO 59/5/11, unbound Second Book of *The Minstrel* (London, 1774)

Whitby: Whitby Museum
027.242748, *Laws and Regulations of a Subscription Library, at Whitby . . .* (Whitby, 1789)

Whitehaven: Cumbria Record Office
D/LONSW20/2/1, *Catalogue of the Books Belonging to the Whitehaven Library . . .* (Whitehaven, 1808)

Wigan: Wigan Archives Service
WZL 273 B8, *Catalogue of Brown's Circulating Library . . .* (Wigan, 1821)

Worcester: Worcester Public Library
M368/W018.1, *Catalogue of the Worcester Library* (Worcester, 1818)

York: York Reference Library
Y019, *An Alphabetical And a Classed Catalogue of the Subscription Library, York . . .* (York, 1823)
Y252, *Remarks on the Behaviour of Sectaries; occasioned by "The York Select Subscription Library" addressed to the Friends of the Established Church: by a Churchman* (York, 1819)

3. PRIMARY SOURCES: OTHER PRINTED WORKS (TO 1830)

Aikin, John, *Letters from a Father to his Son on Various Topics Relative to Literature and the Conduct of Life*, 2 vols (London, 1806)
The Annual Register (1758–)
Beattie, James, *The Minstrel* (London, 1827)
Blair, Hugh, *Lectures on Rhetoric and Belles Lettres*, 14th edition (London, 1825)
Brown, William, *A Narrative of the Life and Adventures of William Brown . . .* (York, 1829)
Burnet, Gilbert, *History of His Own Times*, 2 vols (London, 1724–34)
Colman, George, *Polly Honeycombe . . .* (London, 1760)
Conybeare, John, *A Defence of Revealed Religion* (London, 1732)
The Critical Review (1756–1817)
Denina, Carlo, *An Essay on the Revolutions of Literature*, ed. and trans. J. Murdoch (London, 1771)
The Edinburgh Review (1802–1929)
Gale, Gustavus, *Miscellanies in Prose and Verse* (London, 1794)
The Gentleman's Magazine (1731–1907)
Godwin, William, *The Enquirer. Reflections on Education, Manners and Literature . . .* (Philadelphia, PA, 1797)
Goodhugh, William, *The English Gentleman's Library Manual . . .* (London, 1827)
Henry, Robert, *History of Great Britain*, 6 vols (London, 1771–93)

Hurd, Richard, *Works*, 8 vols (London, 1811)

Hutcheson, Francis, *Inquiry into the Original of Our Ideas of Beauty and Virtue* (London, 1725)

Knox, Vicesimus, *Essays Moral and Literary*, 12th edition, 2 vols (London, 1788)

Letters on the Improvement of the Mind: Addressed to a Lady. By Mrs Chapone. And a Father's Legacy to His Daughters. By Dr Gregory (London, 1808)

Mangin, Edward, *Essays on the Sources of the Pleasures Received From Literary Compositions* (London and Edinburgh, 1813)

The Monthly Ledger (1773–1776)

The Monthly Magazine (1796–1825)

The Monthly Miscellany (1774–1777)

The Monthly Review (1749–1844)

New Lady's Magazine (1786–1797)

The Oeconomist; or Englishman's Magazine (1798)

Pennant, Thomas, *The Literary Life of the Late Thomas Pennant, Esq., By Himself* (London, 1793)

Pennant, Thomas, *A Tour in Scotland and Voyage to the Hebrides* (Chester, 1774)

Pennant, Thomas, *A Tour of Scotland in 1769*, 3rd edition (Warrington, 1774; repr. Perth, 1979)

Pope, Alexander, *An Essay on Criticism* (London, 1713)

Reid, Thomas, *An Inquiry into the Human Mind*, 4th edition (London, 1785)

Robertson, William, *History of the Reign of the Emperor Charles V*, 3 vols (London, 1767)

Robertson, William, *An Historical Disquisition Concerning the Knowledge Which the Ancients Had of India* (Dublin, 1791)

St. James's Chronicle (1781–1866)

The Spectator (1711–12)

Thelwall, John, *Poems Chiefly Written in Retirement . . .* (Hereford, 1801)

Thomson, James, *Tancred and Sigismunda* (London, 1745)

The Town and Country Magazine (1769–1795)

Wallis's Royal Edition, Patronized by the Queen. Brighton As It Is . . . (Brighton, n.d.)

Warton, Joseph, *An Essay on the Writings and Genius of Pope*, 2 vols (London, 1756–82)

Western County Magazine (1790–1796)

[Whiston, John], *Directions for a Proper Choice of Authors to Form a Library . . .* (London, 1766)

The World (1753)

4. SECONDARY LITERATURE (FROM 1830)

Aitken, William R., *A History of the Public Library Movement in Scotland to 1955* (Glasgow, 1971)

Allan, David, *Adam Ferguson* (Aberdeen, 2007)

Allan, David, 'The Age of Pericles in the Modern Athens: Greek History, Scottish Politics and the Fading of Enlightenment,' *Historical Journal*, 44 (2001), 391–417

Allan, David, 'Eighteenth-Century Private Subscription Libraries and Provincial Urban Culture: the Amicable Society of Lancaster, 1769–c.1820,' *Library History*, 19 (2001), 57–76

Allan, David, *"A Nation of Readers": The Lending Library in Georgian England, c.1720-c.1830* (London, 2008)

Allan, David, 'Opposing Enlightenment: Revd Charles Peters' Reading of the Natural History of Religion,' *Eighteenth Century Studies*, 38 (2005), 301–21

Allan, David, 'Protestantism, Presbyterianism and National Identity in Eighteenth- Century Scottish History,' in Ian McBride and Antony Claydon, eds, *Protestantism and National Identity: Britain and Ireland c.1650-c.1850* (Cambridge, 1998), pp. 182–205

Allan, David, 'Provincial Readers and Book Culture in the Scottish Enlightenment: The Perth Library, 1784-c.1800,' *The Library*, 4 (2002), 367–89

Allan, David, 'A Reader Writes: Negotiating *The Wealth of Nations* In an Eighteenth- Century English Commonplace Book,' *Philological Quarterly*, 83 (2004), 207–33

Allan, David, 'The Scottish Enlightenment and the Politics of Provincial Culture: The Perth Literary and Antiquarian Society, c.1784–1790,' *Eighteenth-Century Life*, 27 (2003), 1–31

Allan, David, 'The Scottish Enlightenment and the Readers of Late Georgian Lancaster: "Light in the North",' *Northern History*, 36 (2000), 267–81

Allan, David, 'Some Notes and Problems in the History of Reading: Georgian England and the Scottish Enlightenment,' *The Journal of the Historical Society*, 3 (2003), 91–124

Allan, David, '"This Inquisitive Age": Past and Present in the Scottish Enlightenment,' *Scottish Historical Review*, 76 (1997), 69–85

Allan, David, *Virtue, Learning and the Scottish Enlightenment: Ideas of Scholarship in Early Modern History* (Edinburgh, 1993)

Alston, Robin C., *Books With Manuscript: A Short-Title Catalogue of Books With Manuscript Notes in the British Library* . . . (London, 1994)

Altick, Richard D., *The English Common Reader: A Social History of the Mass Reading Public, 1800–1900* (Chicago, IL, 1957)

Anderson, Benedict, *Imagined Communities: Reflections on the Origin and Spread of Nationalism*, rev. ed. (London, 1983)

Austen, Jane, *Mansfield Park*, ed., Kathryn Sutherland (Harmondsworth, 2003)

Austen, Jane, *Northanger Abbey*, ed., Anne Ehrenpreis (Harmondsworth, 1985)

Bamford, Samuel, *Passages in the Life of a Radical* (London, n.d.)

Barker, Hannah, *Newspapers, Politics and Public Opinion in Late Eighteenth Century England* (Oxford, 1988)

Barrett, J., 'Spas and Seaside Resorts, 1660–1780,' in J. Stevenson et al, eds, *The Rise of the New Urban Society* (Milton Keynes, 1977), pp. 37–70

Basker, James G., *Tobias Smollett: Critic and Journalist* (Newark, NJ, 1988)

Bator, Paul G., 'Robert Watson,' in Michael G. Moran, ed. *Eighteenth-Century British and American Rhetorics and Rhetoricians* (Westport, CT, 1994), pp. 244–59

Beal, Peter, 'Notions in Garrison: The Seventeenth-Century Commonplace Book,' in W. Speed Hill, ed., *New Ways of Looking at Old Texts* (Binghamton, NY, 1993), pp. 131–47

Beckwith, Frank, 'The Eighteenth-Century Proprietary Library in England,' *Journal of Documentation*, 3 (1947–8), 81–98

Bell, Alan, *Sydney Smith* (Oxford, 1980)

Bermingham, Ann, and Brewer, John, eds, *The Consumption of Culture, 1600–1800. Image, Object, Text* (London and New York, 1995)

Bibliothecae Colfanae Catalogus . . . (Lewisham, 1831)

Bibliothecae Ecclesiae Cirestrensis Librorum . . . (Cicestriae, MDCCCLXXI)

Blair, Ann, 'Humanist Methods in Natural Philosophy: the Commonplace Book,' *Journal of the History of Ideas*, 53 (1992), 541–51

Boase, Charles William, ed., *Registrum Collegii Exoniensis* . . . (Oxford, 1894)

Boddy, Ernest H., 'The Dalton Book Club,' *Library History*, 9 (1991–3), 97–105

Bödeker, Hans Eric, '*Staatswissenschaften* and Political Economy at the University of Göttingen: The Scottish Influence,' *Studies on Voltaire and the Eighteenth Century*, 305 (1992), 1881–4

Bonnell, Thomas F., 'Bookselling and Canon-Making: The Trade Rivalry over the English Poets, 1776–1783,' *Studies in Eighteenth-Century Culture*, 19 (1989), 53–69

Bonnell, Thomas F., 'John Bell's *Poets of Great Britain*: The "Little Trifling Edition" Revisited,' *Modern Philology*, 85 (1987), 128–52

Borsay, Peter, ed., *The Eighteenth-Century Town: A Reader in English Urban History, 1688–1820* (London and New York, 1990)

Borsay, Peter, *The English Urban Renaissance: Culture and Society in the Provincial Town, 1660–1770* (Oxford, 1989)

Boswell, James, *Life of Samuel Johnson* (Ware, 1999)

Brake, Laurel, Bell, Bill, and Finkelstein, David, eds, *Nineteenth-Century Media and the Construction of Identities* (Basingstoke, 2000)

Breski, Duschan, 'Schiller's Debt to Montesquieu and Adam Ferguson,' *Comparative Literature*, 13 (1961), 239–53

Brewer, John, *The Pleasures of the Imagination: English Culture in the Eighteenth Century* (London, 1997)

Brewer, John, 'Reconstructing the Reader: Prescriptions, Texts and Strategies in Anna Larpent's Reading,' in James Raven, Helen Small and her eds, *The Practice and Representation of Reading in England* (Cambridge, 1996), pp. 226–45.

Broadie, Alexander, *The Scottish Enlightenment: An Anthology* (Edinburgh, 1997)

Brookes, Christopher, *English Cricket: The Game and its Players Through the Ages* (Newton Abbot, 1978), pp. 9–66

Brunskill, Elizabeth, *Eighteenth-Century Reading* . . . (York, 1950)

Bryson, Gladys, *Man and Society: The Scottish Enquiry of the Eighteenth Century* (Princeton, NJ, 1945)

Burns, Robert, *The Canongate Burns*, eds A. Noble and P.S. Hogg, 2 vols (Edinburgh, 2001)

Burns, Robert, *Letters*, ed., J. De Lancey Ferguson, 2 vols (Oxford, 1931)

Burton Constable Hall: The Eighteenth and Nineteenth Centuries (Hull, 1998)

Butler, Edward H., *The Story of British Shorthand* (London, 1951)

Butler, Marilyn, 'Culture's Medium: The Role of the Review,' in Stuart Curran, ed., *Cambridge Companion to British Romanticism* (Cambridge, 1993), pp. 120–147

Byron, Lord, *English Bards and Scotch Reviewers*, 3rd edition (London, 1810)

Camic, Charles, *Experience and Enlightenment: Socialization for Cultural Change in Eighteenth-Century Scotland* (Edinburgh, 1983)

Carpenter, Kenneth E., *The Dissemination of* The Wealth of Nations *in French and in France, 1776–1843* (New York, 2002)

Carter, J.J., and Pittock, J.H., eds, *Aberdeen and the Enlightenment* (Aberdeen, 1987)

Catalogue of Books in the Library of the Free Grammar School, Leeds (Leeds, 1840)

Catalogue of Books in the Library of the Parish Church of St Owen, Bromham, Bedfordshire (n.p., 1959)

Catalogue of Books from Parochial Libraries in Shropshire (London, 1971)

A Catalogue of the Books Preserved in the Library of the Free Grammar School of Elizabeth, Queen of England, In Faversham (Faversham, 1865)

Cavallo, Guglielmo, and Roger Chartier, eds, *The History of Reading in the West*, trans. Lydia G. Cochrane (Cambridge, 1999)

Certeau, Michel de, *The Practice of Everyday Life*, trans., Steven F. Rendall (Berkeley, CA, 1984)

Chartier, Roger, *The Order of Books: Readers, Authors, and Libraries in Europe Between the Fourteenth and Eighteenth Centuries*, trans. Lydia G. Cochrane (Cambridge, 1994)

Clark, Peter, *British Clubs and Societies, 1580–1800: The Origins of an Associational World* (Oxford, 2000)

Clark, Peter, ed., *The Early Modern Town* (London, 1976)

Colclough, Stephen, *Consuming Texts: Readers and Reading Communities, 1695– 1870* (Houndmills and New York, 2007)

Colclough, Stephen, 'Procuring Books and Consuming Texts: The Reading Experience of a Sheffield Apprentice, 1798,' *Book History*, 3 (2000), 21–44

Colclough, Stephen, 'Recovering the Reader: Commonplace Books and Diaries as Sources of Reading Experience,' *Publishing History*, 44 (1998), 5–37

Coleman, Donald C., *The Economy of England, 1450–1750* (London, 1977)

Coleridge, Samuel Taylor, *Collected Works: Marginalia I: Abbt to Byfield*, ed., George Whalley (Princeton, NJ, and London, 1980)

Coleridge, Samuel Taylor, *Collected Works: Marginalia II: Camden to Hutton*, ed., George Whalley (Princeton, NJ, and London, 1984)

Coleridge, Samuel Taylor, *Collected Works: Marginalia IV: Pamphlets to Shakespeare*, eds, George Whalley and H.J. Jackson (Princeton, NJ, and London, 1988)

Colley, Linda, *Britons: Forging the Nation, 1707–1837* (London, 1992)

The Commonplace Book of William Byrd II of Westover, ed., Kevin Berland, Jan Kirsten Gilliam and Kenneth A. Lockridge (Chapel Hill, NC, and London, 2001)

The Complete Baronetage, 1603–1800, ed., G.E.C., 5 vols (Exeter, 1900–09)

The Complete Peerage, ed., G.E.C., 12 vols (London, 1910–59)

Cradock, Joseph, *Literary and Miscellaneous Memoirs*, 4 vols (London, 1828)

Crawford, J., 'Reading and Book Use in Eighteenth-Century Scotland,' *The Bibliotheck*, 19 (1994), 23–43

Crawford, Robert, *Devolving English Literature* (Oxford, 1992)

Crawford, Robert, *The Scottish Invention of English Literature* (Cambridge and New York, 1998)

Cruse, Amy, *The Englishman and His Books in the Early Nineteenth Century* (London, 1930)

Daiches, David., 'Style Périodique and Style Coupé: Hugh Blair and the Scottish Rhetoric of American Independence,' in R. Sher and J.R. Smitten, eds, *Scotland and America in the Age of the Enlightenment* (Edinburgh, 1990), pp. 209–26

Darnton, Robert, 'Social History of Ideas' in his *The Kiss of Lamourette: Reflections in Cultural History* (London, 1990), pp. 219–52

Darnton, Robert, 'What is the History of Books?,' *Daedalus*, 111 (1982), 65–83

Davis, Leith, *Acts of Union: Scotland and the Literary Negotiation of the British Nation 1707–1830* (Palo Alto, CA, 1998)

Dawson, Deirdre, and Morere, Pierre, eds, *Scotland and France in the Enlightenment* (Lewisburg, PA, and London, 2004)

Derrida, Jacques, *Of Grammatology*, trans. G. Chakravorty Spivak (Baltimore, MD, 1976)

The Diary of Thomas Turner 1754–1765, ed., David Vaisey (Oxford, 1984)

Dobson, Michael, *The Making of the National Poet: Shakespeare, Adaptation and Authorship, 1660–1769* (Oxford, 1992)

Dodd, William, *The Factory System Illustrated . . .* (London, 1842)

Donaldson, Gordon, 'Stair's Scotland: The Intellectual Heritage,' *Juridical Review* (1981), 128–45

Donoghue, Frank, *The Fame Machine: Book Reviewing and Eighteenth-Century Literary Careers* (Palo Alto, CA, 1996)

Duncan, Ian, 'Adam Smith, Samuel Johnson and the Institution of English,' in R. Crawford, ed., *The Scottish Invention of English Literature* (Cambridge and New York, 1998), pp. 37–54

Dunn, John, 'The Identity of the History of Ideas,' *Philosophy*, 43 (1968), 85–104

Emerson, Roger L., 'Sir Robert Sibbald, Kt., the Royal Society of Scotland and the Origins of the Scottish Enlightenment,' *Annals of Science*, 45 (1988), 41–72

Engell, James, *Forming the Critical Mind: Dryden to Coleridge* (Cambridge, MA, and London, 1989)

Enzensberger, Hans Magnus, *Mediocrity and Delusion: Collected Diversions*, trans., Martin Chalmers (London and New York, 1992)

Evans, Robert C., *Jonson, Lipsius and the Politics of Renaissance Stoicism* (Durango, CO, 1992)

Everitt, Alan., 'Social Mobility in Early Modern England,' *Past and Present*, 33 (1966), 56–73

Fabian, Bernhard, 'English Books and Their Eighteenth-Century German Readers,' in Paul J. Korshin, ed., *The Widening Circle: Essays on the Circulation of Literature in Eighteenth-Century Europe* (Philadelphia, PA, 1976), pp. 119–75

Fawcett, Trevor, 'An Eighteenth-Century Book Club at Norwich,' *The Library*, 23 (1968), 47–50

Feather, John, *The Provincial Book Trade in Eighteenth-Century England* (Cambridge, 1985)

Feiser, James, ed., *Early Responses to Hume*, 10 vols, (Bristol, 1999)

Ferdinand, Christine, 'Constructing the Frameworks of Desire: How Newspapers Sold Books in the Seventeenth and Eighteenth Centuries,' in Joad Raymond, ed., *News, Newspapers, and Society in Early Modern Britain* (London and Portland, OR, 1999), pp. 157–75

Fergus, Jan, 'Eighteenth-Century Readers in Provincial England: The Customers of Samuel Clay's Circulating Library and Bookshop in Warwick, 1770–72,' *Papers of the Bibliographical Society of America*, 78 (1984), 155–213

Fergus, Jan, *Provincial Readers in Eighteenth-Century England* (Oxford, 2006)

Ferguson, Adam, *Essay on the History of Civil Society*, ed., Fania Oz-Salzberger (Cambridge, 1995)

Fermia, Joseph V., 'An Historicist Critique of "Revisionist" Methods for Studying the History of Ideas,' in J. Tully, ed., *Meaning and Context: Quentin Skinner and His Critics* (Oxford, 1988), pp. 156–75

Fielding, Henry, *Tom Jones*, ed., R.P.C. Mutter (Harmondsworth, 1987)

Fielding, Henry, *The Vicar of Wakefield* (London, 1903)

Fish, Stanley., *Is There a Text in This Class? The Authority of Interpretive Communities* (Cambridge, MA, 1980)

Fish, Stanley, 'Literature in the Reader: Affective Stylistics,' *New Literary History*, 2 (1970), 123–62

Fleischacker, Samuel, 'Adam Smith's Reception among the American Founders 1776–1790,' *William and Mary Quarterly*, 3rd series, 19 (2002), 897–924

Forbes, Duncan, *Hume's Philosophical Politics* (Cambridge, 1975)

Fontana, Biancamaria, *Rethinking the Politics of Commercial Society*: The Edinburgh Review, *1802–1832* (Cambridge, 1985)

Gaillet, Lynee Lewis, ed., *Scottish Rhetoric and Its Influences* (Mahwah, NJ, 1998)
Gaskill, Howard, ed., *Ossian Revisited* (Edinburgh, 1991)
Gay, Peter, *The Enlightenment*, 2 vols (New York, 1966–9)
Gay, Peter, *The Party of Humanity: Essays in the French Enlightenment* (New York, 1964)
Geertz, Clifford, *The Interpretation of Cultures* (New York, 1973)
Gerard, Alexander, *An Essay on Taste* (London, 1759)
Gibson, J.S., 'How Did the Enlightenment Seem to the Edinburgh Enlightened?,' *British Journal of Eighteenth-Century Studies*, 1 (1978), 46–50
Gifford, James L., *Hester Lynch Piozzi (Mrs Thrale)*, 2nd edition (Oxford, 1968)
Goldsmith: Selected Essays, ed., J.H. Lobban (Cambridge, 1910)
Gordon, Daniel, 'Sociability and Universal History: Jean-Baptiste Suard and the Scottish Enlightenment in France,' in his *Citizens Without Sovereignty: Equality and Sociability in French Thought, 1670–1789* (Princeton, NJ, 1994), pp. 129–176
Grafton, Anthony, 'Is the History of Reading a Marginal Enterprise?: Guillaume Budé and His Books,' *Papers of the Bibliographical Society of America*, 91 (1997), 139–57
Grafton, Anthony, *Joseph Scaliger: A Study in the History of Classical Scholarship. Vol. I: Textual Criticism and Exegesis* (Oxford, 1983)
Grafton, Anthony, and Jardine, Lisa, '"Studied for Action": How Gabriel Harvey Read His Livy,' *Past and Present*, 129 (1990), 30–78
Graham, H.G., *Scottish Men of Letters in the Eighteenth Century* (London, 1901)
Graham, Walter J., *The Beginnings of English Literary Periodicals: A Study of Periodical Literature, 1665–1715* (New York, 1926)
Greenblatt, Stephen, *Renaissance Self-Fashioning: From More to Shakespeare* (Chicago, IL, 1980)
Grenier, Katherine Haldane, *Tourism and Identity in Scotland, 1770–1914: Creating Caledonia* (Aldershot, 2005)
Haakonssen, Knud, *The Science of a Legislator: The Natural Jurisprudence of David Hume and Adam Smith* (Cambridge, 1981)
Hall, David D., 'The History of the Book: New Questions? New Answers?,' *Journal of Library History*, 21 (1986), 27–38
Halsband, Robert, *The Life of Mary Wortley Montagu* (Oxford, 1956)
Havens, Earle, *Commonplace Books: A History of Manuscripts and Printed Books From Antiquity to the Twentieth Century* (New Haven, CT, 2001)
Hayden, John O., ed., *Scott: the Critical Heritage* (London, 1970)
Hazlitt, William, *Collected Works*, ed., P.P. Howe, 21 vols (London and Toronto, 1930–34)
Heaton, William, *The Old Soldier, The Wandering Lover; and Other Poems . . .* (London, 1857)
Hinnant, C.H., *"Steel for the Mind": Samuel Johnson and Critical Discourse* (Newark, NJ, and London, 1994)
History of Parliament: House of Common, 1715–1754, ed., Romney Sedgwick (London, 1970)
History of Parliament: House of Commons, 1754–1790, ed., Sir Lewis Namier and John Brooke (London, 1964)
History of Parliament: House of Commons, 1790–1820, ed., R.G. Thorne (London, 1986)
Hoare, Peter, 'Nottingham Subscription Library: Its Origins, its Collection and its Management over 175 Years,' in Rosalys T. Coope and Jane Y. Corbett, eds,

Bromley House 1752–1991: Four Essays Celebrating the 175ᵗʰ Anniversary of the Formation of the Nottingham Subscription Library (Nottingham, 1991), pp. 1–48

Hoeveler, J.David, Jr., *James McCosh and the Scottish Intellectual Tradition* (Princeton, NJ, 1981)

Holcomb, Kathleen, 'A Dance in the Mind: the Provincial Scottish Philosophical Societies,' *Studies in Eighteenth-Century Culture*, 21 (1991), 89–100

Holub, Robert C., *Reception Theory: A Critical Introduction* (London and New York, 1984)

Hont, I., and Ignatieff, M., eds, *Wealth and Virtue: The Shaping of Political Economy in the Scottish Enlightenment* (Cambridge, 1983)

Horn, D.B., *A Short History of the University of Edinburgh, 1556–1889* (Edinburgh, 1967)

Houston, R.A., *Literacy in Early Modern Europe: Culture and Education, 1500–1800* (London, 1988)

Howe, Daniel W., 'Why the Scottish Enlightenment Was Useful to the Framers of the American Constitution,' *Comparative Studies in Society and History*, 31 (1989), 572–87

Hume, David, *History of England*, 6 vols (Indianapolis, IN, 1983)

Hume, David, *Letters*, ed., J.Y.T. Greig, 2 vols (Oxford, 1932)

Hume, Robert D., 'Texts Within Contexts: Notes Towards a Historical Method,' *Philological Quarterly*, 71 (1992), 69–100

Hunt, Arnold, 'The Sale of Richard Heber's Library,' in Robin Myers, Michael Harris and Giles Mandelbrote, eds, *Under the Hammer: Book Auctions Since the Seventeenth Century* (New Castle DE, and London, 2001), pp. 143–172

Hunter, J. Paul, *Before Novels: The Cultural Contexts of Eighteenth-Century English Fiction* (New York and London, 1990)

Iser, Wolfgang, *The Implied Reader: Patterns of Communication in Prose Fiction from Bunyan to Beckett* (Baltimore, MD, and London, 1974)

Iser, Wolfgang, *The Act of Reading: A Theory of Aesthetic Response* (Baltimore, MD, and London, 1978)

Jackson, H.J., *Marginalia: Readers Writing in Books* (New Haven, CT, and London, 2001)

Jane Austen's Letters to Her Sister Cassandra and Others, ed., R.W. Chapman, 2nd edition (London, 1969)

Jauss, Hans R., *Aesthetic Experience and Literary Hermeneutics*, trans., M. Shaw (Minneapolis, MN, 1982)

Jauss, Hans R., *Towards an Aesthetic of Reception*, trans., T. Bahti (Minneapolis, MN, 1982)

Jefferson, Thomas, *Works*, ed., Paul L. Ford, 12 vols (New York and London, 1904– 5)

Jervis, Simon, 'The English Country House Library: An Architectural History,' *Library History*, 18 (2002), 175–90

Johnson, Samuel, *The Idler and Adventurer*, eds, W.J. Bate, J.M. Bullitt and L.F. Powell (New Haven, CT, 1963)

Johnson, Samuel, *Life of Savage*, ed., Clarence Tracy (Oxford, 1971)

Johnson, Samuel, and Boswell, James, *A Journey to the Western Islands of Scotland* and *The Journal of a Tour to the Hebrides*, ed., Peter Levi (Harmondsworth, 1984)

Johnson's Lives of the English Poets, ed., G. Birkbeck Hill, 3 vols (Oxford, 1905)

Kames, Lord, *Elements of Criticism* (Honolulu, HI, 2002)

Kant, Immanuel, *Foundations of the Metaphysics of Morals; What is Enlightenment; and a Passage from The Metaphysics of Morals*, ed., L.W. Beck (Chicago, IL, 1950)

Kaufman, Paul, 'Coleridge's Use of Cathedral Libraries,' *Modern Language Notes*, 75 (1960), 395–9

Kaufman, Paul, 'The Community Library: A Chapter in English Social History,' *Transactions of the American Philosophical Society*, 57 (1967), Pt. 7, 3–67

Kaufman, Paul, 'Innerpeffray: Reading for All the People,' in his *Libraries and Their Users* (1969), pp. 153–62

Kaufman, Paul, 'New Light from Parochial Libraries,' in his *Libraries and Their Users* (London, 1969), pp. 93–101

Kaufman, Paul, 'Readers and Their Reading in Eighteenth-Century Lichfield,' *The Library*, 28 (1973), 108–15

Kaufman, Paul, *Reading Vogues at English Cathedral Libraries of the Eighteenth Century* (New York, 1964)

Kerrigan, John, 'The Editor as Reader: Constructing Renaissance Texts,' in James Raven, Helen Small and her eds, *The Practice and Representation of Reading in England* (Cambridge, 1996), pp. 102–24

Ketcham, Michael, *Transparent Designs: Reading, Performance and Form in The Spectator Papers* (Athens, GA, 1985)

Kettler, David, *The Social and Political Thought of Adam Ferguson* (Columbus, OH, 1965)

Klancher, Jon, *The Making of English Reading Audiences, 1790–1832* (Madison, WI, 1987)

Klein, Lawrence, *Shaftesbury and the Culture of Politeness: Moral Discourse and Cultural Politics in Early Eighteenth-Century England* (Cambridge, 1994)

Kontler, László, 'William Robertson and His German Audience on European and Non-European Civilisations,' *Scottish Historical Review*, 80 (2001), 63–89

Kramnick, J.B., *Making the English Canon: Print-Capitalism and the Cultural Past, 1700–1770* (Cambridge, 1998)

Kuehn, M., *Scottish Common Sense in Germany, 1768–1800: A Contribution to the History of Critical Philosophy* (Kingston, Ont., 1987)

Lamb, Charles and Mary Anne, *Letters*, ed., E.W. Morris Jr. (Ithaca, NY, 1975)

Lamb, Jonathan, *The Rhetoric of Suffering: Reading the Book of Job in the Eighteenth Century* (Oxford, 1996)

Landed Gentry of Great Britain, (ed.), Sir Bernard Burke (London, 1914)

Lawrence, C. Frederick, 'Early Cheshire Book Clubs,' *Cheshire Notes and Queries*, no. 24 (1899), 83

Leatherland, John A., *Essays and Poems* (London, 1862)

Lee, Charles, *The Lee Papers 1754–1811*, 4 vols (New York, 1871–4)

Levine, Joseph M., 'Deists and Anglicans: The Ancient Wisdom and the Idea of Progress,' in Roger D. Lund, ed., *The Margins of Orthodoxy: Heterodox Writing and Cultural Response, 1660–1750* (Cambridge, 1995), pp. 219–39

Lindley, Phillip G., *The Town Library of Leicester* (Upton, 1975)

Lodge, David, ed., *Modern Criticism and Theory: A Reader* (London, 1988)

Lough, John, 'Reflections on Enlightenment and *Lumières*,' *British Journal of Eighteenth-Century Studies*, 8 (1985), 1–15

Luard, H.R., *Catalogue of Adversaria and Printed Books Containing MS. Notes, Preserved in the Library of the University of Cambridge* (Cambridge, 1864)

Matheson, Ann, *Theories of Rhetoric in the Eighteenth-Century Scottish Sermon* (Lewiston, NY, and Lampeter, 1995)

Mathias, P., *The First Industrial Nation: An Economic History of Britain, 1700–1914* (London, 1969)

McBride, Ian, and, Claydon, Antony, eds, *Protestantism and National Identity: Britain and Ireland, c.1650–c.1850* (Cambridge, 1998)

McBride, Ian, 'The School of Virtue: Francis Hutcheson, Irish Presbyterians and the Scottish Enlightenment,' in D. George Boyce, Robert Eccleshall and Vincent Geoghan, eds, *Political Thought in Ireland Since the Seventeenth Century* (London, 1993), pp. 73–99

McBride, Ian, and Claydon, Tony, eds, *Protestantism and National Identity: Britain and Ireland c.1650–c.1850* (Cambridge, 1998)

McCosh, James, *The Scottish Philosophy: Biographical, Expository, Critical, From Hutcheson to Hamilton* (London, 1875)

McDougall, Warren, 'Scottish Books for America in the Mid-Eighteenth Century,' in R. Myers and M. Harris, eds, *Spreading the Word: The Distribution Networks of Print, 1550–1800* (Winchester, 1990), pp. 21–46

McKendrick, Neil, Brewer, John and Plumb, J.H., *The Birth of a Consumer Society: The Commercialization of Eighteenth-Century England* (London, 1983)

McKitterick, David, 'Bibliography, Bibliophily, and the Organization of Knowledge,' in David Vaisey and his eds, *The Foundations of Scholarship: Libraries and Collecting, 1650–1750* (Los Angeles, 1992), pp. 29–61

Meynell, G.C., 'John Locke's Method of Common-Placing. . . . ,' *The Seventeenth Century*, 8 (1993), 245–67

Minogue, Kenneth, 'Method in Intellectual History: Quentin Skinner's *Foundations*,' *Philosophy*, 56 (1981), 533–52

Mizuta, Hiroshi, ed., *Adam Smith: Critical Responses*, 6 vols (London, 2000)

Monboddo, Lord, *Of the Origin and Progress of Language*, 6 vols (Edinburgh, 1773– 92)

Morrell, J.B., 'Science in Manchester and the University of Edinburgh, 1760– 1840,' in D.S.L. Carswell, ed., *Artisan to Graduate: Essays to Commemorate the Foundation in 1824 of the Manchester Mechanics' Institution . . .* (Manchester, 1974), pp. 39–54

Morris, R.J., 'Voluntary Societies and British Urban Elites, 1780–1850,' *Historical Journal*, 26 (1983), 95–118

Moss, Ann, 'The *Politica* of Justus Lipsius and the Commonplace Book,' *Journal of the History of Ideas*, 59 (1998), 421–37

Moss, Ann, *Printed Common-place Books and the Structuring of Renaissance Thought* (Oxford, 1996)

Mossner, Ernest C., *The Life of David Hume* (Oxford, 1954)

Mui, Lorna, and Mui, Hoh-cheung, *Shops and Shopping in Eighteenth-Century England* (Montreal, 1989)

Newlyn, Lucy, *Reading, Writing, and Romanticism: The Anxiety of Reception* (Oxford, 2000)

Nokes, David, *Jane Austen: A Life* (London, 1998)

O'Brien, Karen, *Narratives of Enlightenment: Cosmopolitan History from Voltaire to Gibbon (Cambridge, 1997)*

The Old Church and School Libraries of Lancashire, ed., Richard Copley Christie (Manchester, 1885)

On The Wealth of Nations: *Contemporary Responses to Adam Smith*, ed., Ian S. Ross (Bristol, 1998)

Oxford Dictionary of National Biography, ed., Colin Mathew (Oxford, 2004)

Oz-Salzberger, Fania, *Translating the Enlightenment: Scottish Civic Discourse in Eighteenth-Century Germany* (Oxford, 1995)

Palmer, Trevor, *Perilous Planet Earth* (Cambridge, 2003)

The Parochial Libraries of the Church of England . . . [ed. Neil Ker] (London, 1959)

Parrinder, Patrick, *Authors and Authority: English and American Criticism 1750–1990* (Basingstoke, 1991)

Pascal, Roy, 'Herder and the Scottish Historical School,' *Publications of the English Goethe Society*, 14 (1938–9), 23–42

Patten, Robert L., 'Dickens as Serial Author: The Case of Multiple Identities,' in Laurel Brake, Bill Bell and David Finkelstein, eds, *Nineteenth-Century Media and the Construction of Identities* (Basingstoke, 2000), pp. 137–53

Paulson, Ronald, *Breaking and Remaking: Aesthetic Practice in England, 1700–1820* (New Brunswick, NJ, and London, 1989)

Paxman, D.B., 'The Genius of English: Eighteenth-Century Language Study and English Poetry,' *Philological Quarterly*, 70 (1991), 27–46

Pearson, Jacqueline, *Women's Reading in Britain 1750–1835: A Dangerous Recreation* (Cambridge, 1999)

Pennant, Thomas, *Voyage to the Hebrides*, 2 vols, 2nd edition (London, 1776)

Petroski, Henry, *The Book on the Book Shelf* (New York, 1999)

Phillipson, Nicholas, *Hume* (London, 1989)

Phillipson, Nicholas, 'Politics, Politeness and Anglicisation in Early Eighteenth-Century Scottish Culture,' in R.A. Mason, ed., *Scotland and England, 1286–1815* (Edinburgh, 1987), pp. 226–46

Piozzi, Hester, *The Life of Samuel Johnson, LL.D., by James Boswell, with Marginal Comments from Two Copies Annotated by Hester Thrale Lynch Piozzi*, ed., E.G. Fletcher, 3 vols (New York, 1963)

Piozzi Marginalia: Comprising Some Extracts from Manuscripts of Hester Lynch Piozzi and Annotations from Her Books, ed., E.P. Merritt (Cambridge, MA, 1925)

Pittock, J.H., *The Ascendancy of Taste: The Achievement of Joseph and Thomas Warton* (London, 1973)

Plumb, J.H., *The Commercialisation of Leisure in Eighteenth-Century England* (Reading, 1973)

Pocock, J.G.A., *Barbarism and Religion—Volume Two: Narratives of Civil Government* (Cambridge, 1999)

Pocock, J.G.A., *Virtue, Commerce and History* (Cambridge, 1985)

Porter, Roy, *Enlightenment: Britain and the Creation of the Modern World* (London, 2000)

Porter, Roy, 'The Enlightenment in England,' in his and M. Teich, eds, *The Enlightenment in National Context* (Cambridge, 1981), pp. 1–18

Porter, Roy, 'Science, Provincial Culture and Public Opinion in Enlightenment England,' in Peter Borsay ed., *The Eighteenth-Century Town: A Reader in English Urban History, 1688–1820* (London and New York, 1990), pp. 243–67

Raven, James, *Judging New Wealth: Popular Publishing and Responses to Commerce in England 1750–1800 (Oxford, 1992)*

Raven, James, Small, Helen and Tadmor, Naomi, eds, *The Practice and Representation of Reading in England* (Cambridge, 1996)

The Reception of the Scottish Enlightenment in Germany: Six Significant Translations, 1755–1782, ed., Heiner F. Klemme, 7 vols (Bristol, 2000)

Renwick, John, 'The Reception of William Robertson's Historical Writings in Eighteenth-Century France,' in S.J. Brown, ed., *William Robertson and the Expansion of Empire* (Cambridge, 1997), pp. 145–63

Reynolds, Herbert E., 'Our Cathedral Libraries: Their History, Contents and Uses,' *Transactions and Proceedings of the First Annual Meeting of the Library Association . . . 1878* (London, 1879), pp. 32–43

Rivers, Isabel, ed., *Books and their Readers in Eighteenth-Century England* (Leicester, 1982)

Rivers, Isabel, ed., *Books and Their Readers in Eighteenth-Century England: New Essays* (Leicester, 2001)

Rivers, Isabel, 'Responses to Hume on Religion by Anglicans and Dissenters,' *Journal of Ecclesiastical History*, 52 (2001), 675–95

Robertson, John, *The Case for the Enlightenment: Scotland and Naples, 1680–1750* (Cambridge, 2005)

Rose, Jonathan, 'Arriving at a History of Reading,' *Historically Speaking*, (Jan. 2004), 36–9

Rose, Jonathan, *The Intellectual Life of the British Working Classes* (New Haven, CT, 2001)

Rose, Jonathan, 'Rereading the English Common Reader: A Preface to the History of Audiences,' *Journal of the History of Ideas*, 53 (1992), 47–70

Rose, Ruth O., 'Poetic Hero-Worship in the Late Eighteenth Century,' *Proceedings of the Modern Language Association*, 48 (1933), 1182–1202

Rosenfeld, Sybil, *Strolling Players and Drama in the Provinces, 1660–1765* (Cambridge, 1939)

Ross, Trevor, *The Making of the English Literary Canon: From the Middle Ages to the Late Eighteenth Century* (Kingston, Ont. and Montreal, 1998)

Rowland, William G., *Literature and the Marketplace: Romantic Writers and Their Audiences in Great Britain and the United States* (Lincoln, NE, 1996)

Ruskin, John, *Praeterita* (Oxford, 1978)

Scott, Alison M., '"This Cultivated Mind": Reading and Identity in a Nineteenth-Century Reader,' in Barbara Ryan and Amy M. Thomas, eds, *Reading Acts: United States Readers' Interactions with Literature, 1800–1950* (Knoxville, TN, 2002), pp. 29–52

Scott, M.J.W., *James Thomson, Anglo-Scot* (Athens, GA, 1988)

Scott, Sir Walter, *The Fortunes of Nigel* (Edinburgh, 1902)

Scott, Sir Walter, *The Pirate*, 2 vols (Edinburgh, 1902)

Scott, Sir Walter, *Poetical Works*, ed., J. Logie (Oxford, 1909)

Shaftesbury, Lord, *Characteristicks of Men, Manners, Opinions, Times*, 2 vols (Oxford, 1999)

Shaftesbury, Lord, *Characteristicks of Men, Manners, Opinions, Times*, 3 vols (Indianapolis, IN, 2001)

Shapin, Steven, and Barnes, Barry, 'Science, Nature and Control: Interpreting Mechanics' Institutes,' *Social Studies of Science*, 7 (1977), 31–74

Sharpe, Kevin, *Reading Revolutions: The Politics of Reading in Early Modern England* (New Haven, CT, 2000)

Shaver, Chester L. and Alice C., eds, *Wordsworth's Library: A Catalogue* (New York and London, 1979)

Sher, Richard B., *Church and University in the Scottish Enlightenment* (Princeton, NJ, and Edinburgh, 1985)

Sher, Richard B., *The Enlightenment and the Book: Scottish Authors and Their Publishers in Eighteenth-Century Britain, Ireland and America* (Chicago, IL, and London, 2007)

Sher, Richard B., 'Science and Medicine in the Scottish Enlightenment: The Lessons of Book History,' in Paul Wood, ed., *The Scottish Enlightenment: Essays in Reinterpretation* (Rochester, NY, 2000), pp. 99–156

Sher, Richard B., '"Those Scotch Impostors and Their Cabal": Ossian and the Scottish Enlightenment,' in R.L. Emerson, G. Girard and R. Runte, eds, *Man and Nature: Proceedings of the Canadian Society for Eighteenth-Century Studies*, i (London, Ont., 1982), 55–63

Sher, Richard B., and Hook, Andrew, eds, *Glasgow and the Enlightenment* (East Linton, 1995)

Sheridan, Richard, *The Rivals*, ed., Elizabeth Duthie (London, 1979)

Sherman, William H., *John Dee: The Politics of Reading and Writing in the Renaissance* (Amherst, MA, 1995)

Skinner, Quentin, *The Foundations of Modern Political Thought*, 2 vols (Cambridge, 1978)

Skinner, Quentin, 'Meaning and Understanding in the History of Ideas,' *History and Theory*, 8 (1969), 3–53

Slights, W.E., 'The Edifying Margins of Renaissance English Books,' *Renaissance Quarterly*, 42 (1989), 682–716

Sloan, D.S., *The Scottish Enlightenment and the American College Ideal* (New York, 1971)

Smellie, William, *Literary and Characteristical Lives of John Gregory, Lord Kames, David Hume and Adam Smith* (Edinburgh, 1800)

Smollett, Tobias, *The Expedition of Humphry Clinker*, ed., L.M. Knapp (London, 1966)

Smollett, Tobias, *The Expedition of Humphry Clinker*, ed., P. Miles (London, 1993)

Southey, Robert, *Attempts in Verse, By John Jones, An Old Servant* (London, 1831)

Spacks, Patricia Meyer, *Imagining a Self: Autobiography and the Novel in Eighteenth-Century England* (Cambridge, MA, 1976)

Spacks, Patricia Meyer, *Privacy: Concealing the Eighteenth-Century Self* (Chicago, IL, and London, 2002)

Sparrow, Elizabeth and Maurice Smelt, eds, *The Penzance Library: Celebration Essays* . . . (Penzance, 1988)

Spater, George, *William Cobbett: The Poor Man's Friend* (London, 1982)

Spector, R.D., *English Literary Periodicals and the Climate of Opinion During the Seven Years' War* (The Hague, 1966)

Spencer, Mark G., *David Hume in Eighteenth-Century America* (Rochester, NY, and Woodbridge, 2005)

St Clair, William, *The Reading Nation in the Romantic Period* (Cambridge, 2004)

Stafford, Fiona J., *The Sublime Savage: A Study of James Macpherson and the Poems of Ossian* (Edinburgh, 1988)

Sterne, Laurence, *The Life and Opinions of Tristram Shandy, Gentleman*, eds, M. and J. New (Harmondsworth, 2003)

Stewart-Murphy, Charlotte A., *A History of the British Circulating Libraries: The Book Labels and Ephemera of the Papantonio Collection* (Newtown, PA, 1992)

Stoddard, Roger, *Marks in Books* (Cambridge, MA, 1985)

Strickland, John, *The Life of John Strickland* . . . 2nd edition (London, n.d.)

Suderman, Jeffrey M., 'The Context of George Campbell's *Philosophy of Rhetoric*: A New Perspective,' *Eighteenth-Century Scotland*, 9 (1995), 9–11

Suffolk Parochial Libraries: A Catalogue (London, 1977)

Suleiman, Susan R., and Crosman, Inge, eds, *The Reader in the Text: Essays on Audience and Interpretation* (Princeton, NJ, 1980)

Sutherland, Lucy S., and Mitchell, Leslie G., eds, *The History of the University of Oxford: Volume V—The Eighteenth Century* (Oxford, 1986)

Tadmor, Naomi, 'In the Even My Wife Read to Me: Women, Reading and Household Life in the Eighteenth Century,' in James Raven, Helen Small and her, eds, *The Practice and Representation of Reading in England* (Cambridge, 1996), pp. 162–74

Taylor, Charles, *Sources of the Self: The Making of the Modern Identity* (Cambridge, MA, 1989)

Taylor, John T., *Early Opposition to the English Novel: The Popular Reaction from 1780 to 1830* (New York, 1943)

Teichgraeber, Richard F., '"Less Abused Than I Had Reason to Expect": The Reception of *The Wealth of Nations* in Britain,' *Historical Journal*, 30 (1987), 337–366

Terry, Richard, *Poetry and the Making of the English Literary Past* (Oxford, 2001)

Thackeray, William Makepeace, *The Newcomes*, ed., Arthur Pendennis, 2 vols (London, 1911)

Thomson, James, *The Complete Poetical Works*, ed., J. Logie Robertson (Oxford, 1951)

Thompson, Christopher, *The Autobiography of an Artisan* (London, 1847)

Thraliana: The Diary of Mrs Hester Lynch Thrale (Later Mrs Piozzi), 2 vols, ed., K.C. Balderstone (Oxford, 1942)

Tilmouth, M., 'The Beginnings of Provincial Concert Life in England,' in C. Hogwood and R. Luckett, eds, *Music in Eighteenth-Century England* (Cambridge, 1983), pp. 1–17

Toews, John E., 'Intellectual History after the Linguistic Turn: The Autonomy of Meaning and the Irreducibility of Experience,' *American Historical Review*, 92 (1987), 879–907

Trench, Richard, 'The Discovery of Scotland,' in his *Travellers in Britain* (London, 1990), pp. 16590

Trevor-Roper, Hugh, 'The Scottish Enlightenment,' *Studies on Voltaire and the Eighteenth Century*, 58 (1967), 1635–58

Tylecote, Mabel, *The Mechanics Institutes of Lancashire and Yorkshire before 1851* (Manchester, 1957)

Varma, Devendra P., *The Evergreen Tree of Diabolical Knowledge* (Washington, DC, 1972)

Venturi, Franco, 'Scottish Echoes in Eighteenth-Century Italy,' in I. Hont and M. Ignatieff, eds, *Wealth and Virtue: The Shaping of Political Economy in the Scottish Enlightenment* (Cambridge, 1983), pp. 345–62

Vickery, Amanda, *The Gentleman's Daughter: Women's Lives in Georgian England* (New Haven, CT, 2003)

Vincent, David, *Bread, Knowledge and Freedom: A Study of Nineteenth-Century Working Class Autobiography* (London, 1981)

Vincent, David, *Literacy and Popular Culture: England, 1750–1914* (Cambridge, 1989)

Vincent, David, ed., *Testaments of Radicalism: Memoirs of Working-Class Politicians 1790–1885* (London, 1997)

Viviès, Jean, *English Travel Narratives in the Eighteenth Century: Exploring Genres*, trans. Claire Davidson (Aldershot, 2002)

Voltaire, François-Marie Arouet de, *Philosophical Letters*, trans. E. Dilworth (Indianapolis, IN, 1961)

Walpole, Horace, *Correspondence: Volume 33*, ed., W.S. Lewis (London, 1965)

Warner, Malcolm, Marciari, Julia, and McCaughey, Alexander and Patrick, *This Other Eden: Paintings from the Yale Center for British Art* (New Haven, CT, 1998)

Warton, Thomas, *The History of English Poetry*, 3 vols (London, 1840)

Warton, Thomas, *The History of English Poetry* (London, 1870)

Waszek, Norbert, *The Scottish Enlightenment and Hegel's Account of "Civil Society"* (Dordrecht, 1988)

Weinbrot, Howard, *Britannia's Issue: The Rise of British Literature from Dryden to Ossian* (Cambridge, 1995)

Whatmore, Richard, 'Adam Smith's Role in the French Revolution,' *Past and Present*, 75 (2002), 65–89

Willan, Thomas S., *An Eighteenth-Century Shopkeeper: Abraham Dent of Kirkby Stephen* (Manchester, 1969)

Wilson, C., *England's Apprenticeship, 1603–1763* (London, 1967)

Wilson, Kathleen, *The Sense of the People: Politics, Culture and Imperialism in England, 1715–1785* (Cambridge, 1995)

Wollstonecraft, Mary, *The Female Reader* (London, 1789)

Woodward, Gwendolen, and Christophers, R.A., *The Chained Library of the Royal Grammar School, Guildford: Catalogue . . .* (Guildford, 1972)

Wrangham, Francis, *The British Plutarch*, 6 vols (London, 1816)

Wrigley, E.A., 'Urban Growth and Agricultural Change: England and the Continent in the Early Modern Period,' in Peter Borsay, ed., *The Eighteenth-Century Town: A Reader in English Urban History, 1688–1820* (London and New York, 1990), pp. 39–82

Yeo, Richard, 'Ephraim Chambers' *Cyclopaedia* (1728) and the Tradition of the Commonplaces,' *Journal of the History of Ideas*, 57 (1996), 157–75

Zachs, William, *The First John Murray and the Late Eighteenth-Century Book Trade* (Oxford, 1998)

Zwicker, Steven, 'The Constitution of Opinion and the Pacification of Reading,' in Kevin Sharpe and his, eds, *Reading, Society and Politics in Early Modern England* (Cambridge, 2003), pp. 295–316

Zwicker, Steven, 'Reading the Margins: Politics and the Habits of Appropriation,' in Kevin Sharpe and his, eds, *Refiguring Revolutions: Aesthetics and Politics from the English Revolution to the Romantic Revolution* (Berkeley, CA, 1998), pp. 101–15

Index

About the Author

David Allan is Reader in History at the University of St Andrews. His other books include *Virtue, Learning and the Scottish Enlightenment: Ideas of Scholarship in Early Modern History* (1993), *Philosophy and Politics in Later Stuart Scotland: Neo-Stoicism, Culture and Ideology in an Age of Crisis, 1540–1690* (2000), *Scotland in the Eighteenth Century: Union and Enlightenment* (2002), *Adam Ferguson* (2006) and *A Nation of Readers: The Lending Library in Georgian England* (2008).